—TWO VIEWS—
ON
WOMEN
IN
MINISTRY

Books in the Counterpoints Series

Church Life

Exploring Theology

Stanley N. Gundry (S.T.D., Lutheran School of Theology at Chicago) is senior vice president and editor-in-chief of the Book Group at Zondervan. He graduated summa cum laude from both the Los Angeles Baptist College and Talbot Theological Seminary before receiving his Masters of Sacred Theology from Union College, University of British Columbia. With more than thirty-five years of teaching, pastoring, and publishing experience, he is the author or coauthor of numerous books and a contributor to numerous periodicals.

►COUNTERPOINTS◄

—TWO VIEWS—
ON
WOMEN
IN
MINISTRY

Contributors:

Craig S. Keener
Linda L. Belleville
Thomas R. Schreiner
Ann L. Bowman

JAMES R. BECK
CRAIG L. BLOMBERG
General Editors

STANLEY N. GUNDRY
Series Editor

ZondervanPublishingHouse
Grand Rapids, Michigan

A Division of HarperCollinsPublishers

We want to hear from you. Please send your comments about this book to us in care of zreview@zondervan.com. Thank you.

ZONDERVAN™

Two Views on Women in Ministry
Copyright © 2001 by James R. Beck and Craig L. Blomberg

Requests for information should be addressed to:

Zondervan, *Grand Rapids, Michigan 49530*

Library of Congress Cataloging-in-Publication Data

Two views on women in ministry / James R. Beck and Craig L. Blomberg, general editors.
     p. cm.—(Counterpoints)
   Includes bibliographical references and index.
   ISBN 0-310-23195-7
   1. Women clergy. I. Beck, James R. II. Blomberg, Craig L. III. Counterpoints
(Grand Rapids, Mich.)
   BV676 .T96 2001
   262'.14'082—dc21   2001017807

Printed in the United States of America

04 05 06 07 08 09 10 /❖ DC/ 10 9 8 7 6 5

To Vernon C. Grounds,
whose fifty years of ministry have demonstrated
the very irenic spirit this book seeks to inspire

ABBREVIATIONS

ASV	American Standard Version
CEV	Contemporary English Version
JB	Jerusalem Bible
KJV	King James Version
NAB	New American Bible
NASB	New American Standard Bible
NEB	New English Bible
NIV	New International Version
NIVI	New International Version, Inclusive Language Edition
NJB	New Jerusalem Bible
NKJV	New King James Version
NLT	New Living Translation
NRSV	New Revised Standard Version
PHILLIPS	*The New Testament in Modern English*, J.B. Phillips
REB	Revised English Bible
RSV	Revised Standard Version
TEV	Today's English Version (= Good News Bible)

CONTENTS

INTRODUCTION

James R. Beck and Craig L. Blomberg

In light of the massive literature already available on the topic, why are we publishing another book on gender roles in ministry? Our introduction to this volume is arranged according to three broad answers to this question.

First, the evangelical church has not yet arrived at a clear-cut consensus in the debate. The relevant theological, biblical, and exegetical issues are all very much still open for examination. This should not cause surprise; throughout its history the church has repeatedly faced challenging issues that required rigorous and extensive debate. Already within the pages of the New Testament, the first apostolic council was convened (see Acts 15:1–29) to determine if circumcision, and thus the keeping of the entire Mosaic Law, was a prerequisite for salvation. Although a preliminary agreement was reached, steering a balanced course between Judaizers on the one hand and antinomians on the other continues to be a difficult problem throughout the subsequent New Testament epistles (for example, Galatians, 2 Corinthians 10–13, Philippians 3, 1 Timothy 1, and 2 Peter 2) and remains with us in many forms today.

Other theological debates have punctuated church history. Christians in the first several centuries wrestled with issues surrounding the Trinity and the full humanity and full deity of Christ.[1] Often the debates have involved synthesizing seemingly discrepant aspects of biblical revelation, as in the lengthy disputes between Calvinists and Arminians or between covenant

---

[1]See Harold O. J. Brown, *Heresies* (Garden City, N.J.: Doubleday, 1984), 6–195.

theologians and dispensationalists. Sometimes the issues have been raised by the broader culture or society, including by developments in science and history.[2] One thinks especially of all of the issues stemming from the Enlightenment of the 1700s and beyond—from questions about evolution and creation, to the credibility of miracles, to responses to the development of modern literary criticism.[3] At times these debates have spanned centuries, as with the major theological divisions within Protestantism, now having gone on for five hundred years, or have overturned the consensus of a majority of previous church history, as most notably with the Reformation's rejection of a millennium of very different Roman Catholic understandings of justification by faith.

The major theological debates of the ages have led to very differing outcomes. Sometimes the church has come to a relatively unified voice and dissenting opinions are declared heterodox. The approaches of ancient councils and creeds to the nature of God and the two natures of Christ form obvious examples. In our own day, high-level Roman Catholic and Protestant dialogues have increasingly led Catholics to embrace an understanding of justification that more closely resembles Lutheran views than medieval Catholic Counter-Reformation perspectives.[4] Sometimes the church has built strong biblical cases for two sides of an issue, never declaring one as heretical, but a clear majority opting for one of the two approaches nevertheless. One thinks especially of the nearly universal rejection of slavery as a legitimate Christian alternative, despite mid-nineteenth-century admissions that the biblical evidence was finely balanced and could be interpreted consistently in two quite different ways. Or take the issue of war. While not a few full-fledged pacifists may be found in Christian circles worldwide, the majority of believers in most cultures have been convinced that there are at least certain circumstances in which the state justly "bears the sword." Yet the exegetical evidence in support of this approach is by no

[2]The classic treatment of this issue is the nineteenth-century work by Andrew Dickson White, *A History of the Warfare of Science with Theology in Christendom* (New York: D. Appleton & Co., 1896).

[3]See Mark A. Noll, *Between Faith and Criticism: Evangelicals, Scholarship and the Bible*, 2d ed. (Grand Rapids: Baker, 1991).

[4]Compare *Evangelicals and Catholics Together: The Christian Mission in the Third Millennium* (1994) with the Lutheran World Federation and the Roman Catholic Church, *Joint Declaration on the Doctrine of Justification* (1999).

means as one-sided as one might suspect from the sizable majority that endorses it.[5]

Sometimes theological debates boil down to two or three options that continue to be defended vigorously.[6] Here one thinks about ongoing divisions between advocates of believers' baptism and advocates of paedobaptism, or about how church polity typically boils down to episcopal, presbyterian, or congregational models, with variations on each of these. In situations where fundamental core beliefs of Christianity are not deemed to be at stake, evangelical, Bible-believing Christians have increasingly agreed to disagree in love and to move ahead with the work of the church despite their disagreements. The last half of the twentieth century produced an explosion of parachurch organizations whose doctrinal statements more often than not closely resembled each other and reflected widespread agreement on the fundamentals of the faith, yet agreed not to include specific stances on still-divisive issues such as baptism, election, ecclesiology, and certain eschatological questions.

How do current debates about gender roles in home and church fit into these broader trends? We do not pretend to be able to predict the future and foresee if the evangelical church will reach a consensus or if one view will de facto fall by the wayside. The intense current interest in the debate may not be accounted for merely by citing ways in which secular culture has brought the issue to the fore, nor merely by citing proactive Christian liberation movements throughout history. Both factors clearly intermingle in complex fashion.[7] But we are strongly convinced of the following five affirmations:

---

[5]For both of these examples, see Willard M. Swartley, *Slavery, Sabbath, War and Women* (Scottdale, Pa.: Herald, 1983).

[6]Many of these are enshrined in books with formats similar to this one. Three-, four-, and even five-view books have been published, especially by Zondervan and InterVarsity Press, on such topics as spiritual gifts, predestination and free will, the millennium, the tribulation, the fate of the unevangelized, and so forth. But often what are listed as two separate views are basically variations on one major view; one thinks, for example, of dispensational versus classic premillennialism in the eschatology debate. In other cases, one view really has not often been accepted as an orthodox Christian option, for example, the view that posits a second chance for salvation after death for those who have never heard the gospel.

[7]See Rebecca Merrill Groothuis, *Women Caught in the Conflict: The Culture War Between Traditionalism and Feminism* (Grand Rapids: Baker, 1994).

1. The exegetical issues are sufficiently complex that one cannot legitimately maintain that a true believer in biblical inerrancy must land in one particular camp. Equally committed, godly, scholarly evangelical Christians have come to well-supported but diametrically opposing perspectives on the meaning and significance of numerous key biblical texts and themes related to the debate. Clearly, there are forms of both feminism and traditionalism that do not begin from an acceptance of the complete trustworthiness and authority of the Scriptures, but engaging these perspectives lies largely outside the scope of this volume.[8] Here we are focusing on the *intra*-evangelical debate.

2. The current debate, when conducted with integrity, is healthy for the church and necessary for her witness in the twenty-first century. Too many Christians nurtured only in traditions that do not permit women's full participation in all the offices of the church are unaware both of the long history of exceptions to the traditional restrictions and of the serious biblical case that can be mounted for doing away with such restrictions in the modern church altogether. By the same token, too many Christians nurtured only in traditions that decided, at times more than a generation ago, to ordain women are unaware of the extent and nature of biblically based arguments against this practice throughout church history. Decisions informed by the full-orbed debate stand the best chance of proving valid.[9]

---

[8]For a brief overview and taxonomy of the larger world of feminist exegesis, with reference to additional secondary literature, see William W. Klein, Craig L. Blomberg, and Robert L. Hubbard Jr., *Introduction to Biblical Interpretation* (Dallas: Word, 1993), 453–57.

[9]One of the best histories of the discussion is Ruth A. Tucker and Walter L. Liefeld, *Daughters of the Church: Women and Ministry from New Testament Times to the Present* (Grand Rapids: Zondervan, 1987). See also Janette Hassey, *No Time for Silence: Evangelical Women in Public Ministry Around the Turn of the Century* (Grand Rapids: Zondervan, 1986). It comes as a surprise to many, for example, to learn that, earlier in their history, organizations such as the Moody Bible Institute and the Evangelical Free Church of America supported the ordination of women, even though they no longer do so. On the other side, Tucker and Liefeld, despite their egalitarian stance, admirably demonstrate the strength of traditional exegesis of numerous passages.

3. The importance of the issue requires that we apply our best scholarship to the task.[10] In an increasingly biblically illiterate society, fewer and fewer people, even in evangelical churches, seem to be interested in the meaty study of doctrine. People often join a church *in spite of* rather than *because of* certain tenets in that church's statement of faith. People make decisions as to what they will believe on the basis of numerous factors other than the careful, serious study of Scripture. Those of us called to serve the church through scholarship must help people swim against this tide.

4. It is possible that we will never reach a unified consensus on the debate. If this turns out to be an issue that boils down to two or three options that continue to compete for adherents, then it will be important for the church to agree that gender-role debates do not touch on the fundamentals of the faith—matters on which one's salvation depends—and to agree to disagree in love. We can imagine the situation playing out very much like the current debates on baptism, ecclesiology, or spiritual gifts: There would undoubtedly continue to be believers who passionately felt they could in good conscience support only one model but who would agree to support rather than attack fellow Christians who in equally good conscience practiced a different model. Different churches could then adopt different policies but not engage in polemics against others.[11]

5. At the present time the issue is far from settled and the discussion still incomplete. Those on either side who think otherwise and declare "victory" are premature. Even after so much analysis, new exegetical insights are emerging and finding acceptance across party lines.[12]

---

[10]See Wayne Grudem, "Do We Act As If We Really Believe That 'the Bible Alone, and the Bible in Its Entirety, Is the Word of God Written'?" *Journal of the Evangelical Theological Society* 43 (2000), 5–26.

[11]See the exemplary books by Donald Bridge and David Phypers, *The Water That Divides: A Survey of the Doctrine of Baptism* (Leicester: InterVarsity Press, 1977); *The Meal That Unites?* (London: Hodder & Stoughton, 1981); and *Spiritual Gifts and the Church* (London: InterVarsity Press, 1973).

[12]To take just two examples, in our society very few people anymore seriously defend the argument that 1 Corinthians 14:33–38 is intended to silence all women in all parts of the worship service or that women must wear head coverings in church in obedience to 1 Corinthians 11:2–16. Yet major segments of the church throughout the world still believe in and insist on both of these restrictions.

Intermediate, moderate (and moderating) models are increasingly coming to the fore. Closing the debate now would preclude further progress that could be made and prove ultimately to be unhealthy and harmful.

Second, there is an acute need for a new (or renewed) commitment to an irenic spirit in this debate. Emotions understandably run high when one discusses whether or not (normally) unchangeable characteristics bequeathed to a person at birth dictate what roles this person can play in ministry. A generation ago it was more common than today for conservative evangelicals to stress the belief that theological decision making must be founded on the Bible alone, apart from human experience. But some of the early scholarly publications on gender roles in home and church developed a pattern of appealing to personal experience as an unavoidable factor in the positions and attitudes one adopts in this debate.[13] At the popular level, countless Christians have admitted that it was largely their upbringing, their tradition, and their positive or negative experiences with women in ministry, including at the highest levels of leadership, that shaped their views. At the scholarly level, it is far less unusual today to see evangelicals arguing for existential viability as a key criterion for theological decision making, even as scriptural exegesis remains primary.[14]

Sensitive psychological analysis further demonstrates how much is at stake and how deeply individual psyches and personalities are involved in the discussion.[15] The task of forming a biblically based position regarding women in ministry is complicated by layers of psychological factors. While this dimension of the task lies beyond the scope of this book, it is important to note that the process of deciding what women can and cannot do in ministry is not just influenced by one's theological commitments and exegetical discoveries. A man's attitudes toward women in general, a woman's attitudes toward men in general,

---

[13]See, for example, Patricia Gundry, *Woman Be Free: Biblical Equality for Women* (Grand Rapids: Zondervan, 1977), 9–13; Alvera Mickelsen, ed., *Women, Authority and the Bible* (Downers Grove, Ill.: InterVarsity Press, 1986), 10–27.

[14]See, for example, Gordon R. Lewis and Bruce A. Demarest, *Integrative Theology* (Grand Rapids: Zondervan, 1987), 1:25–40.

[15]See Mary Stewart Van Leeuwen, *Gender and Grace: Love, Work and Parenting in a Changing World* (Downers Grove, Ill.: InterVarsity Press, 1990).

and our attitude toward our own gender can all influence the process. We know that attitudes toward women have liberalized in the last thirty years nationwide, with women displaying more liberalized attitudes toward roles for women than men display.[16] Persons of strong religious convictions, however, tend to value the traditional female role.[17] Sociologists who study conservative Protestants, a category that includes evangelicals, find that this group is more patriarchal than the general population, although generalizations are difficult to make, given the many nuanced attitudes toward gender within the group.[18] Some evidence also exists that women in egalitarian churches feel more able to gain or regain their voice than do women in other types of conservative congregations.[19] In sum, one's own psychological configuration, as well as the attitudes of one's group, when viewed from social, psychological, and sociological perspectives, can strongly influence the task that concerns us most in this book: How do we determine what the Bible prescribes, describes, and/or proscribes for women in ministry?

All of this strongly suggests that we should declare a moratorium on unnecessarily inflammatory language in the debate.[20] It is neither accurate nor edifying for one side to declare that its

---

[16]Noted in Jean M. Twenge, "Attitudes toward Women, 1970–1995: A Meta-Analysis," *Psychology of Women Quarterly* 21 (1997), 35–51. Southern United States men and women are generally more conservative in attitudes toward women, although these regional differences are fairly small.

[17]Noted in Larry Jensen and Janet Jensen, "Family Values, Religiosity, and Gender," *Psychological Reports* 73 (1993), 429–30.

[18]Robert Loo and Karran Thorpe, "Attitudes Toward Women's Roles in Society: A Replication after 20 Years," *Sex Roles* 39 (1998), 903–12.

[19]Noted in Jennette Lybeck and Cynthia J. Neal, "Do Religious Institutions Resist or Support Women's 'Lost Voice'?" *Youth and Society* 27 (1995), 4–28.

[20]By far the most extreme and offensive example of recent vintage we have encountered on either side of the debate is John W. Robbins, *Scripture Twisting in the Seminaries, Part I: Feminism* (Jefferson, Md.: Trinity Foundation, 1985). But the running polemic, especially in the endnotes, of Gilbert Bilezikian (*Beyond Sex Roles: What the Bible Says About a Woman's Place in Church and Family,* rev. ed. [Grand Rapids: Baker, 1985]) demonstrates that both sides can display a singular lack of charity. In a quite recent work, Alexander Strauch (*Men and Women, Equal Yet Different: A Brief Study of the Biblical Passages on Gender* [Littleton, Colo.: Lewis & Roth, 1999], 116) wrongly and divisively describes the debate as "spiritual warfare over the Creator's sovereign design for marriage, the family, the church family, and godly manhood and womanhood."

view is the only legitimate position for adherents of biblical inerrancy to hold. It is simply false to say that the church historically has accepted only one position as orthodox and labeled everything else heretical. It is inappropriately emotive and manipulative to call evangelical feminists liberal, lump them together with nonevangelical or secular feminists, and dismiss them without carefully hearing and engaging their arguments. It is equally irresponsible to label views that see biblical justification for certain timeless restrictions on women's roles as merely traditional or as inherently sexist, chauvinistic, or abusive. It is important to recognize that there is a large spectrum of views and numerous styles of implementation within the two main camps. Equally loving, godly, and thoughtful Christians can work together in either model and testify that the centrality of Scripture has been upheld in the context of humble service carried out for our Lord.

To this end, we have wrestled with what labels to apply to the two main positions we are presenting. Those who believe there are no biblically mandated timeless distinctions between men and women in the church have often referred to themselves as *evangelical feminists* or *biblical feminists,* with the emphasis on the adjective in each case. These seem to be very appropriate labels, but the pejorative sense of the term "feminism," however it has been qualified, may wave red flags in the minds of many who would not use this label. The real heart of this position seems to be the stress on *equality* of men and women, not merely for salvation or in essential personhood, but in opportunities to hold every office and play every role that exists in church life. Thus, we have chosen to use the term *egalitarian* for this position, while heartily recognizing that those who are not in this camp also affirm the fundamental equality of all humans in God's sight. Our contributors, of course, are free to use any labels they prefer.

On the other side of the debate, those who favor certain timeless restrictions on women's roles in the church have in recent years increasingly opted for the term *complementarian.* To their credit they are trying to avoid the unnecessarily pejorative implications that such labels as "traditionalist" or "hierarchicalist" engender in the minds of many. After all, these are Christians who are basing their beliefs, they insist, not primarily on church tradition, but on their understanding of Scripture itself. And to the extent that *hierarchicalist* can sound authoritarian rather than merely authoritative, they want to stress that persons in positions of authority can function in loving, supportive ways that do not lead to the abuse of those in subordinate positions. On the other hand, it is not clear that the idea of men and women playing complementary roles inherently suggests that certain roles are altogether prohibited for one gender. Some egalitarians have complained, rightly it seems to us, that their view can equally be described as complementarian. For one of the major ways evangelical feminists can be distinguished from liberal or secular counterparts is by their general rejection of unisex theories that attribute no God-given gender-related differences to human personality or psychology. They emphasize merely that none of these differences should automatically and for all time hinder women from holding certain church offices or performing certain ministries. Conversely, it seems to us that *hierarchicalist* is the more natural opposite of *egalitarian* and more clearly describes the essence of the position—that in certain contexts there *are* relationships of authority and submission in which gender roles may not be reversed. Again, our contributors are free to use whatever language they wish. We stress that we are not trying to offend anyone with our choice of terminology, but we do recognize that, no matter what terms we choose, someone will wish that we had used something else.

Third, an enormous amount of scholarship has appeared in the last decade on our topic. Much of this material is accessible only to specialists; this volume hopes to make it available to a wider audience.[21] In the 1980s, two books following formats similar to ours provided precisely such comparative studies on gender roles,[22] but in rereading them we are struck by how much has occurred in recent years and how the debates have taken significantly different turns at key points.

In the United States, perhaps the most prominent development has been the growth and increasing influence of two nationwide

---

[21]For the Old Testament, one may consult the detailed bibliography by Mayer I. Gruber, *A Study Guide: Women in the World of Hebrew Scripture*, Volume 1 of *Women in the Biblical World*, ATLA bibliography series no. 38 (Lanham, Md.: Scarecrow, 1995). It would seem that a second volume related to the New Testament was conceived but has not yet appeared.

[22]Shirley Lees, ed., *The Role of Women* (Leicester: InterVarsity Press, 1984); Bonnidell Clouse and Robert G. Clouse, eds., *Women in Ministry: Four Views* (Downers Grove, Ill.: InterVarsity Press, 1989).

organizations on each side of the debate—Christians for Biblical Equality (promoting egalitarianism) and the Council on Biblical Manhood and Womanhood (promoting hierarchicalism, or, to use their preferred term, complementarianism). Scholars officially associated with one of these groups or unofficially sympathetic to their aims have poured forth a flood of literature. The highly touted anthology *Recovering Biblical Manhood and Womanhood* (Wheaton, Ill.: Crossway), edited by John Piper and Wayne Grudem, appeared in 1991 as a comprehensive response to what it called evangelical feminism. Twenty-six chapters addressed all the major exegetical and theological issues, incorporated input from related disciplines, such as church history, biology, psychology, sociology, and law, and discussed contemporary applications and implications on numerous fronts. No equally comprehensive response from egalitarians has yet appeared, but the volume by Richard Clark Kroeger and Catherine Clark Kroeger, *I Suffer Not a Woman: Rethinking 1 Timothy 2:11–15 in Light of Ancient Evidence* (Grand Rapids: Baker, 1992), generated at least as much interest and attention, convincing a number of people that there really was compelling exegetical evidence for understanding Paul's original intent in this passage as more limited than prohibiting all women from certain church offices or roles.

Arguably even more significant was Craig S. Keener's 1992 offering, *Paul, Women and Wives* (Peabody, Mass.: Hendrickson), which expanded the focus to all of the disputed Pauline texts. A scholar distinguished for his voluminous mastery of New Testament background literature, Keener excelled at addressing the historical settings of the relevant texts. In 1995 hierarchicalists Andreas J. Köstenberger, Thomas R. Schreiner, and H. Scott Baldwin edited and contributed to *Women in the Church: A Fresh Analysis of 1 Timothy 2:9–15* (Grand Rapids: Baker, 1995), rebutting, among other things, a number of the claims of the Kroegers. All this just scratches the surface of the last decade of publications, which include denomination-wide studies,[23] testimonies of scholars who have changed their minds on the issue,[24]

---

[23]See, for example, Carroll D. Osburn, ed., *Essays on Women in Earliest Christianity*, 2 vols. (Joplin, Mo.: College Press, 1993–95); Clarence Boomsma, *Male and Female, One in Christ* (Grand Rapids: Baker, 1993).

[24]See especially R. T. France, *Women in the Church's Ministry: A Test Case for Biblical Interpretation* (Grand Rapids: Eerdmans, 1995).

analyses of broader ideological and philosophical factors in the debate,[25] considerably improved sophistication in our understanding of the Jewish, Greek, and Roman views of men and women in the first century,[26] and detailed exegetical analysis of virtually every conceivably relevant passage from Scripture.

We spoke above of two previous books somewhat similar to our own. One was published only in Great Britain in 1984 and did not become well-known in North America. Titled *The Role of Women: 8 Prominent Christians Debate Today's Issues* (edited by Shirley Lees), it tackled debates concerning gender roles in both home and church, and it paired male and female authors for both hierarchicalist and egalitarian perspectives in each arena. Each pair of essays was followed by brief responses from two of the book's other contributors. In the United States a volume titled *Women in Ministry: Four Views* (edited by Bonnidell Clouse and Robert Clouse) was published by InterVarsity Press in 1989. It contained four contributions, two by hierarchicalists and two by egalitarians, one man and one woman on each side, but there were intentionally distinguishable differences between the two who wrote for each side. In the hierarchicalist camp was a contribution defending very traditional role relationships that forbade women numerous positions of authority alongside one that judged only the ecclesiastical office of elder to be forbidden. On the egalitarian side, one writer defended equal opportunity for women largely on the basis of his rejection of any biblical support for the notions of ordination or office, while recognizing that various exegetical arguments did lend credence to certain role restrictions in certain contexts. The other writer much more unambiguously defended egalitarianism on all fronts. After each chapter, all three other contributors responded briefly.

Our book shares elements of the formats of both of these books. Like Clouse and Clouse, we are not focusing on the debate about domestic roles, only about ministry roles. Like Lees, we are deliberately pairing a male and a female author who articulate relatively the same perspective on the issues they address, but who defend these perspectives from different

---

[25]See especially Rebecca Merrill Groothuis, *Good News for Women: A Biblical Picture of Gender Equality* (Grand Rapids: Baker, 1997).

[26]Of numerous treatments, the broadest in coverage is Deborah F. Sawyer, *Women and Religion in the First Christian Centuries* (London: Routledge, 1996).

angles. Unlike both volumes, we have chosen not to have contributors interact with each other by responding to the various chapters, but to provide some of our own editorial commentary, which will help to locate each chapter in the broader scholarly spectrum of views. We also have framed three questions for each contributor that he or she will briefly address immediately following the essay at hand. By doing so we hope to avoid some of the inevitable redundancy, and equally inevitable omissions, in the critiques that appear when books follow the format of inviting every writer to respond to every other position. We have tried to comment, however, with both egalitarian and hierarchicalist positions in mind, responding as we believe various scholars in each camp would and trying to keep our affirmation and critique in some balance.

We have also aimed for parity in several other respects. This is a coedited volume, with one author viewing himself as a hierarchicalist (Blomberg) and one as an egalitarian (Beck), though each of us would generally find more in common with relatively centrist perspectives on the other side than with extremists in his own camp. One of us is a biblical scholar by training (Blomberg), the other a counselor and psychologist (Beck). But both of us have been active in writing and speaking on the topic at every level—from detailed scholarship to grassroots church-related settings.[27] We have team-taught an elective course together at Denver Seminary on "Women—Then and Now: Biblical and Psychological Perspectives." We are both employed by an evangelical seminary that affirms biblical inerrancy but has intentionally not included a section on gender roles in its doctrinal statement, believing that such positions are to be the choice of local churches and individual denominations. We do not believe that Scripture unambiguously promotes one perspective to the exclusion of all others. Thus our faculty reflects what we believe to be commendable diversity on these issues.

---

[27]See especially James R. Beck, "Gender Role Attitudes in Christian Marital Therapy," *Marriage and Family: A Christian Journal* 3 (2000): 349–61; Catherine C. Kroeger and James R. Beck, eds., *Healing the Hurting: Giving Hope to Abused Women* (Grand Rapids: Baker, 1998); Craig L. Blomberg, "Not Beyond What Is Written: A Review of Aída Spencer's *Beyond the Curse: Women Called to Ministry*," *Criswell Theological Review* 2 (1988), 403–21; Blomberg, "woman," in *Evangelical Dictionary of Biblical Theology*, ed. Walter A. Elwell (Grand Rapids: Baker, 1996), 824–28.

Unlike its predecessors, our volume has four contributors who are all New Testament professors at evangelical Christian seminaries in the United States. All have previously distinguished themselves by writing on this topic and are familiar with the current status of the debate.[28] Credentials, experience, and job descriptions, of course, do not by themselves guarantee uniform quality, but we hope we have improved on the rather disparate levels of scholarship and areas of expertise that informed certain other works on this topic. We have also solicited contributions that will model the appropriately irenic spirit to which we are committed and that will relate each author's position to his or her personal experience with the issue.

By titling our work *Two Views on Women in Ministry*, we reflect our conviction that evangelicals have made progress in the debate and that, with variants on each perspective, basically two views are emerging as the major, viable, biblically based options. On the hierarchicalist side, more and more scholars are limiting the timeless restrictions on women to a single role—that of the authoritative teacher in the church, often associated with a single office, that of elder (presbyter) or overseer (bishop). On the egalitarian side, idiosyncratic exegesis of various texts is increasingly being abandoned, with the recognition that biblical authors did in their day forbid women from holding certain leadership positions, but that the rationales for these restrictions do not necessarily transcend time and culture.

After submitting the manuscript for this book to the publisher, Dr. Blomberg wrote an essay on gender roles in Paul that he had agreed to produce for a collection of chapters in a book on Pauline theology, edited by Stanley E. Porter and Brook W. A. Pearson, to be published by Brill no earlier than late 2002. Dr. Beck recommended (and the Zondervan editorial team enthusiastically agreed) that it should be added to this volume

[28]See especially Craig S. Keener, *Paul, Women and Wives: Marriage and Women's Ministry in the Letters of Paul* (Peabody, Mass.: Hendrickson, 1992); Linda L. Belleville, *Women Leaders and the Church: Three Crucial Questions* (Grand Rapids: Baker, 2000); Thomas R. Schreiner, "An Interpretation of 1 Timothy 2:9–15: A Dialogue with Scholarship," in *Women in the Church: A Fresh Analysis of 1 Timothy 2:9–15*, eds. Andreas J. Köstenberger, Thomas R. Schreiner, and H. Scott Baldwin (Grand Rapids: Baker, 1995), 105–54; Ann L. Bowman, "Women in Ministry: An Exegetical Study of 1 Timothy 2:11–15," *Bibliotheca Sacra* 149 (1992): 193–213. This article is also available on the Internet at http://www.leaderu.com/isot/docs/womenmin.htm.

as well, as a kind of large appendix. Precisely because Ann Bowman uses a significant portion of her essay to discuss broader ministry concerns that impact men and women alike, yet comes to nearly identical conclusions as Blomberg, his essay could be viewed as supplying much of the exegetical support that Bowman presupposes but does not actually spell out. In this way we preserve the balance and parity between the two positions in the debate that this book is designed to present.

There is not the slightest indication that this debate is going to go away in the near future, as some idealistically hope, or that it can be avoided forever by churches and parachurch groups that have not yet addressed it in detail. The importance of the issue requires that both the leaders and the laity of the church be fully informed about the biblical issues attendant to both sides of the debate. Christians can make good decisions only if all parties are aware of the debate in its entirety. We hope the following essays will contribute to this goal. We will rejoin you after each half of the volume with further commentary, and then make concluding observations at the end. For the curious, the division of labor between Craig Blomberg and James Beck was as follows: Blomberg was the primary author of this introduction and the commentary on the hierarchicalist views, while Beck was the primary author of the commentary on the egalitarian views and the conclusion. Both of us, however, gave considerable input to every section, and successive drafts of each section underwent significant revisions in light of the input. We also allowed our contributors to see a penultimate draft of our remarks on their respective material, and at times we made revisions in light of their response to our commentary.

Part One

WOMEN IN MINISTRY THE EGALITARIAN VIEW: TWO PERSPECTIVES

Chapter One

WOMEN IN MINISTRY

Craig S. Keener,
Eastern Baptist Theological Seminary

WOMEN IN MINISTRY

Craig S. Keener

Most Christians do not realize how much our backgrounds and traditions affect the ways we read the Bible. Having held both egalitarian and complementarian (or hierarchicalist) views on women's ministry with sincerity at different times in my life, in both cases dependent on my desire to be faithful to God's Word, I recognize the sincere reasons for which many believers stand on either side of the issue. I am firmly convinced that the Bible supports women's ministry, but I have good friends (some of whom are women) who disagree.

A major reason believers have come to hold different views on the matter, however, is that different passages, taken by themselves, seem to point in different directions. Christians with equally high views of Scripture thus often end up with different ways to understand how God intends us to fit these varied texts together.[1]

THE PROBLEM

Some passages in the Bible support a wide variety of women's ministry, especially those passages that give explicit

---

[1] Because this essay is intended for a more general audience and because I have provided detailed documentation for most of my points elsewhere (see my *Paul, Women and Wives: Marriage and Women's Ministry in the Letters of Paul* [Peabody, Mass.: Hendrickson, 1992]; articles on gender roles in InterVarsity's *Dictionary of Paul and His Letters*; *Dictionary of the Later New Testament and Its Developments*; and *Dictionary of New Testament Background*), I document relatively lightly in this essay.

examples of women prophetesses, a judge with authority over all of God's people, a probable apostle, and women who shared in Paul's ministry of the gospel. Another passage (1 Tim. 2:11–14) appears to forbid women from teaching Scripture in the presence of men, and it is one of two passages that actually can be understood to prohibit women's public speech in church altogether. Unfortunately, some Christians who start with one group of texts view with suspicion Christians who start with the other group of texts, sometimes even questioning their evangelical commitments. I am thus grateful to my colleagues in this volume for the opportunity to engage in dialogue with them as fellow evangelicals working together to understand God's Word better.

If some texts seem to point in one direction and others in a different direction, this leaves us several options:

1. One group of texts is mistaken. (This is not an option, however, for conservative evangelicals, including the contributors to this book.)
2. The Bible permits to women some kinds of ministries but prohibits others.
3. The Bible prohibits women's ministry under most circumstances but allows exceptions in specific cases, in which case we should allow such ministry today in exceptional cases.[2]
4. The Bible permits women's ministry under normal circumstances but prohibits it in exceptional cases, in which case we should allow it under most circumstances today.

The second position appeals to many Christian interpreters today, but those who hold this position must make many of the same interpretive judgments made by those who affirm women's ministries more generally. The texts to which this position appeals do not specify one kind of verbal ministry but actually enjoin complete silence on the part of women in church, and one text explicitly speaks against any teaching in the presence

---

[2]Combining positions 2 and 3 as we have summarized them, Robert W. Yarbrough ("The Hermeneutics of 1 Timothy 2:9–15," in *Women in the Church: A Fresh Analysis of 1 Timothy 2:9–15*, eds. Andreas J. Köstenberger, Thomas R. Schreiner, and H. Scott Baldwin [Grand Rapids: Baker, 1995], 195, note 181) recognizes that Scripture shows that God could use women as prophets or judges, though not explicitly as pastors.

of men. If these texts mean all that they sound as though they mean, then they prohibit women's public ministry altogether (indeed, their apparent demand for absolute silence would prohibit even singing in the choir or reading publicly a list of announcements). If, by contrast, they do not mean all that they sound as though they mean, views 3 and 4 are as legitimate an option as view 2. What's more, as I argue below, some of the roles by which women carried out ministry in the Bible were more authoritative than the offices from which they are often now restricted.

I argue in this essay for the fourth view, namely, that the Bible permits women's ministry under normal circumstances and prohibited it only under exceptional circumstances. Because Paul's letters to Timothy address a specific situation (women were, in fact, vehicles for propagating false teaching, as we can demonstrate from the letters themselves), the nature of the exceptional circumstances seems fairly clear. The one Bible passage that explicitly prohibits women from teaching the Bible—in contrast with numerous passages that endorse various women communicating God's message—is addressed to the one church where we specifically know that false teachers were effectively targeting women. Is this a coincidence?

SCRIPTURE PASSAGES THAT APPEAR TO AFFIRM WOMEN'S MINISTRY

Prophetesses

One ministry in which we most frequently see women's direct involvement described in Scripture is that of *prophecy*. Today most people think first of pastors when they hear the word *ministers*, but in the Old Testament the most common form of ministry with respect to declaring God's word was the prophetic ministry.[3]

---

[3]Some distinguish *gifts* from *offices*, but in Ephesians 4:11, the role of prophet stands alongside apostles, evangelists, and pastors/teachers as one of the ministries of the word that equips God's people for ministry. We should avoid distinguishing offices from gifts too arbitrarily, especially when someone receives a title (as in Ex. 15:20; Judg. 4:4; 2 Kings 22:14; Isa. 8:3; Luke 2:36) and our term for "office" does not exist in Scripture (Eph. 4:8–11 calls ministers "gifts"; "prophets" in 1 Cor. 14:29, 32 seems to refer to those who prophesy).

In the Old Testament, true prophetesses included Miriam (Ex. 15:20), Deborah (Judg. 4:4), Huldah (2 Kings 22:14; 2 Chron. 34:22), and apparently Isaiah's wife (Isa. 8:3). In the New Testament they included Anna (Luke 2:36) and Philip's four virgin daughters (Acts 21:9; in that culture, their virginity probably also suggested their youth). Paul seems to assume that prophetesses were a regular phenomenon in the early Christian churches; he in fact affirms women both praying and prophesying publicly, provided their heads are covered (1 Cor. 11:4–5).[4] Luke, who throughout both his Gospel and the book of Acts shows particular gender sensitivity in reporting about women almost as often as about men, reports Peter's inspired interpretation of Joel 2:28–29: When God pours out his Spirit once the Messiah has come, women as well as men will prophesy (Acts 2:17–18). This passage is as paradigmatic for Acts as Isaiah 61:1–2 was for Luke (Luke 4:18–19). The New Testament church's witness (cf. Acts 1:8) is characterized by the Old Testament prophetic mantle (in a general sense), irrespective of class, gender, age, or (most surprisingly to the Jerusalem church) race.[5]

To be sure, most prophetic voices (especially in the Old Testament) were male, but this was to be expected in a culture where most public voices were male. Even in the Old Testament, however, the prophetic office was not exclusively male, like the priestly office was. The priestly office provides some lessons for ministry, but not necessarily the conclusion that ministers must be male; Protestants apply the priestly analogy to all believers (cf. 1 Peter 2:5, 9; Rev. 1:6; 5:10; 20:6). Further, if we restrict ministry to men because priests were male, why should we not restrict it also to a particular tribe, as the law clearly did? Many of the regulations God gave the priesthood would have communicated well to his people in an ancient Near Eastern setting—Hittite ritual purity customs, Egyptian architectural features in the tabernacle,

---

[4]Rather than devote space here to what head coverings mean, see my article on "head coverings" in *Dictionary of New Testament Background* (Downers Grove, Ill.: InterVarsity Press, 2000, 442–47); in less detail, my *Paul, Women and Wives*, 19–69. Gender segregation was impossible in house churches (see, for example, Bernadette J. Brooten, *Women Leaders in the Ancient Synagogue: Inscriptional Evidence and Background Issues* [Chico, Calif.: Scholars Press, 1982], 103–38), so men would invariably hear women's prophecies.

[5]See my earlier work in *The Spirit in the Gospels and Acts* (Peabody, Mass.: Hendrickson, 1997), 190–213.

and so forth. An exclusively male priesthood made sense in view of some of the ancient Near Eastern cults surrounding Israel.

The prophetic office, however, depended on personal calling and on gifts. I address in greater detail below the issue of more men prophets than women prophetesses in Bible times, but suffice it to point out here that fewer women would have had the mobility and social respect to be effective prophetic voices; further, prophetic leaders like Samuel and Elisha would probably not mix genders in the bands of prophets they were mentoring. These factors make the activity of some prophetesses all the more noteworthy.

Some might argue that the prophetic office is irrelevant today because, in their perspective, prophecy has ceased. In my opinion, various texts suggest that prophecy, like other gifts, will continue until Christ's return, even in the narrowest sense of the term (1 Cor. 13:8–12; Eph. 4:11–13; Rev. 11:3–7). Moreover, Acts 2:17–18 must remain decisive, for it describes the Spirit-filled church from Pentecost forward, all whom God would call (2:38–39) in the era of salvation (2:21). But even if this gift of prophecy were to continue today in a more restrictive sense, the text at the least indicates that women as well as men must speak God's message with the Spirit's power. But let us grant for a moment the claim some make that prophecy has ceased. Even if this claim were correct, it would not erase the record that in the biblical period some women held an office more directly influential than offices now frequently denied them.

Wishing to allow women to prophesy but not to teach, some claim that from the time of Ezra onward the prophets were on a level less authoritative than the scribes, because scribes handled the Scriptures. This distinction, however, is not quite accurate. Although prophecy is not the same gift as teaching, hearers can learn from it (1 Cor. 14:31). Most of the prophets whose messages are contained in the Bible do interpret and apply earlier biblical messages, especially the law but also images from earlier prophets. (In keeping with this genre, the book of Revelation contains more Old Testament allusions than any other New Testament book, though it lacks specific quotations.)[6] Indeed,

---

[6]For my comments on biblical allusions in Revelation, see my commentary *Revelation* in The NIV Application Commentary Series (Grand Rapids: Zondervan, 2000), various pages; Gregory K. Beale provides fuller detail in *The Book of Revelation: A Commentary on the Greek Text* (Grand Rapids: Eerdmans, 1999), various pages.

most of the Old Testament was *written* by prophets. In any case, prophets delivered God's message; to voice the objection that women are allowed to deliver God's message in prophecy but not by teaching Scripture is essentially to claim that they can minister as long as they do it *without* using Scripture!

A prophetic commission connotes some sort of authority or authorization (Rev. 11:3).[7] Of course, not all prophets exercised the same measure of authority. Samuel, Elijah, and Elisha supervised prophetic movements that recognized their authority. But at least some women, such as Deborah (see comment below), exercised authority in this prophetic office. In any case, prophets of either gender had no authority outside of their message. Nathan, for example, had to retract his counsel to David when he discovered that it contradicted what the Lord was actually saying (2 Sam. 7:3–5). If the authority inheres in the message proclaimed, Huldah exercises great authority to apply the Book of the Law to her generation (2 Kings 22:14–20). There was also undoubtedly a reason that Josiah sent messengers to her (22:13) rather than to other prophetic figures; perhaps hearing the law forced him to recognize truths she had already been proclaiming.[8] The most obvious example of an authoritative prophetess, however, is Deborah, to whom I now turn.

Deborah the Judge

Along with her brother Aaron, Miriam overstepped her authority when she challenged the greater prophetic office of Moses (Num. 12:1–14), who functioned as the closest Old Testament model for New Testament apostolic ministry (2 Cor. 3:6–18; cf. John 1:14–18).[9] Moses was not only a prophet but also a chief

---

[7]Against the distinctions some make between prophets and those who prophesy, Paul seems to apply the former title to those who fulfill the latter function, at least on a frequent basis (1 Cor. 14:29, 32).

[8]Jeremiah was still very young (2 Kings 22:3; Jer. 1:2, 6). In any event, 2 Kings draws numerous parallels between the revivals under Josiah and, a century earlier, under Hezekiah—and Huldah's role in this narrative precisely parallels that of Isaiah in Hezekiah's day in 2 Kings 19:2–7.

[9]For the Moses allusion in John 1:14–18, see Marie-Emile Boismard, *St. John's Prologue* (London: Blackfriars, 1957), 136–39; Anthony Hanson, "John I.14–18 and Exodus XXXIV," *New Testament Studies* 23 (1976): 90–101; Henry Mowvley, "John 1.14–18 in the Light of Exodus 33.7–34.35," *Expository Times* 95 (1984): 135–37.

leader, and occasionally he was even compared with a king (Deut. 33:5). The closest equivalents after Moses and before the apostles would be prophets who also led Israel (Deborah, Samuel, and David—see Acts 2:30) and perhaps those who led the remnant in times of great wickedness (like Elijah and Elisha). Of the two explicit prophetic judges (Samuel and Deborah), one was a woman.

In the entire era of the judges only one woman was a judge, and the book of Judges makes a point of showing that this was noteworthy. The Hebrew is emphatic: "a *woman* prophet [prophetess], the wife of Lappidoth" (Judg. 4:4). But while its rareness made it remarkable, the text offers no note of condemnation. One of the main features of the book of Judges is its insistence that Israel regularly turned from God's commandments, and that God, rather than the judges he raised up, was the real hero. Most of the judges whose stories are narrated in detail exhibit significant problems in their personal lives (8:27; 11:30–39); the book even skips over twenty years of Samson's ministry to reveal his sexual entanglements (15:20–16:31), rooted in what we might today call his earlier dysfunctional relationships (14:2–3)! Even Samuel may have had some problems (1 Sam. 8:3; cf. 1 Sam. 2:12–17, 29), although they were not serious enough to sidetrack his ministry.

But Deborah, who does not grasp for power but shares it willingly with Barak, comes off pretty much squeaky-clean—as in fact a woman would have had to have been in order to have maintained leadership in her era.[10] In any case, she clearly exercised authority over Israel. She apparently even shared Barak's military leadership, though this was because Barak refused to accept his commission alone (Judg. 4:6–10). Some object that God appoints women only when men are not getting the job done. Even if one were to grant this premise, it would hardly provide an argument against women's ministry today, given the fact that perhaps over half the world's population has yet to hear the gospel of Jesus Christ in a culturally intelligible way and that most of Christ's church and presumably many of its teachers remain too asleep to rise to his call.

---

[10]Deborah perhaps once took the opportunity to affirm members of her gender in a distinctive way when she warned Barak—perhaps to shame him—that God would give Sisera into the hands of a woman; in any case, however, God fulfilled this prophecy when Jael put a spike into Sisera's head (Judg. 4:9, 21).

An Apostle

If Moses and the prophetic leaders were the closest Old Testament equivalent to the New Testament apostles, Deborah merits a place among them. Clearly a number of New Testament women also continued the prophetic office, as noted above. But were there any explicit women apostles in the New Testament? Because of apostles' special rank and their role in breaking new ground for God's kingdom, women would have faced special obstacles in that culture, as they would in many cultures even today. Thus, we should not expect great numbers of women apostles in Scripture, but if we have even one woman apostle, that occurrence would confirm our suspicion (based on Deborah and what I have noted from the prophetesses) that a woman could hold this office.[11]

Paul does not hand out the title lightly; he applies the title explicitly only to a handful of leaders in his day besides the Twelve and (often) himself (1 Cor. 9:5–6; Gal. 1:19; cf. 1 Thess. 2:6 with 1:1). But neither does he restrict the title to the Twelve; in fact, he clearly distinguishes it from them (1 Cor. 15:5–7). Even Luke, who usually restricts the term to the Twelve, allows it for Paul and Barnabas in at least one passage (Acts 14:4, 14). By "apostles" I do not mean those who write Scripture or speak with canonical authority; most apostles did not contribute to the Bible, nor were all New Testament writers apostles. But a survey of every use of "apostle" in the New Testament (a survey I've done but can only summarize here) includes in most cases special authority that stemmed from a special commission and message (rather than purely administrative authority), a ministry that typically included signs and wonders and broke new ground for God's kingdom (whether in founding the Jerusalem church or other churches)./

In Romans 16:7 Paul speaks of Andronicus and Junia, who are "of note among the apostles" (KJV). Some think that "of note among the apostles" means simply that the apostles thought well of them. While this position is grammatically possible, Paul nowhere refers to "the apostles" as a group to whose opinion he

---

[11]For comments about those who wish to distinguish official ministry roles from gifts, see note 3 above. When the title is applied, as in Romans 16:7, we have good reason to see there a ministry role.

appeals. Indeed, the most natural and common sense of "among" a group means that they are members of that group (see, for example, Rom. 1:13; 8:29), hence here "well-known apostles," which was how the Greek fathers (and most modern scholars) take the phrase. Less persuasively, some try to circumvent the implications of this phrase by arguing that they are a special kind of nonauthoritative apostle like the "messengers of the churches" in 2 Corinthians 8:23 (cf. also Phil. 2:25). This attempt also has little to commend it; for one thing, we do not know that the "messengers of the churches" lacked authority (they were probably often Paul's ministry companions—cf. Acts 20:4). More important, it is unsound interpretive methodology to read a more specific meaning into a phrase than its use in that context and situation warrants. Paul does not qualify *apostles* in Romans 16:7 as "apostles of the churches" or "your apostles," and everywhere else in the New Testament where the phrase remains unqualified it refers to apostles with rank. Would Paul commend them for being something less than what an unqualified *apostle* means in every other New Testament instance and yet expect Roman Christians to understand what he means?

An even less plausible way to get around Junia being an apostle is to claim that Junian (the direct object form of the common female Junia, not of the male Junius) is really a contraction for the male name Junianus. But this contraction never appears in Greek literature (including in Rome's inscriptions). Indeed, because of the way Latin names are transcribed into Greek, *Junia* grammatically *can* be nothing other than a woman's name here, though many earlier scholars failed to notice this.[12]

The only reason why someone would deny that Junia is a woman here, against the otherwise plain reading of the text, is the assumption that Paul cannot describe a woman as an apostle. If we know that Paul would never allow a woman to be an apostle, one might be forced to make the inference that Junia is

---

[12]See Richard S. Cervin, "A Note Regarding the Name 'Junia(s)' in Romans 16.7," *New Testament Studies* 40 (1994): 464–70 (this article was brought to my attention by Michael Holmes). For a woman apostle here, see, for example, Wayne Meeks, *The First Urban Christians: The Social World of the Apostle Paul* (New Haven, Conn.: Yale Univ. Press, 1983), 57. J. B. Lightfoot (*Saint Paul's Epistle to the Galatians* [London: Macmillan, 1910], 96, note 1), who thought Junia to be male, doubts that any would have taken the phrase as "esteemed *by* the Apostles" were it not to circumvent the extension of the apostolate beyond the Twelve.

not what Paul normally means by an *apostle* and that perhaps the Roman believers could be expected to know what he might mean based on their own knowledge of Junia. But such an argument merely assumes what one hopes to prove, for nothing in the text itself points to Junia being anything other than a woman apostle, as even church father John Chrysostom recognized. At the least, those who deny women's public ministry roles should admit that the simplest reading of Romans 16:7 is a "hard" case for their position, as many egalitarians would admit the simplest reading of 1 Timothy 2:11–12 is for theirs.

Because an unmarried man and woman working together (as this couple apparently does) would generate scandal, Andronicus is probably either Junia's brother or, far more likely in that culture, her husband. We know that some married male apostles took their wives with them when they traveled (1 Cor. 9:5), but this text claims more than that she simply traveled with him. The shared title indicates that she actually shared in his ministry in a special way, the way many couples in other professions also worked together.[13]

Laborers in the Word

Although today we often think of ministry especially in terms of senior pastors, apostles and prophets were in some sense the highest-ranking ministers of the New Testament church; whenever Paul lists them among gifts or ministries he lists them first, including on the one occasion where he enumerates some ministries (1 Cor. 12:28). As I will observe later, they were more prominent than local pastors, and, in at least some churches, "prophets and teachers" apparently *were* the pastors (Acts 13:1). I'll return to the issue in a special section below, but for now let me note that women are mentioned in some of the highest offices of early Christianity and are abundant at least as prophetesses. Although less dramatic than testimony to prophetic and apostolic roles, two passages provide further evi-

---

[13]On husband-wife teams in other professions, see Jane F. Gardner, *Women in Roman Law and Society* (Bloomington, Ind.: Indiana Univ. Press, 1986), 240. To say that Andronicus and Junia are both simply called by the husband's proper title is to deny that Paul stated correctly what he meant, for he specifically employs a plural pronoun and verb in making the point.

dence for their ministry in God's word: Romans 16:1–12 and Philippians 4:3. Especially in the former passage Paul employs the same terms to describe the ministry of women that he commonly uses to describe that of men.

Paul conveys personal greetings to more men than women in Romans 16. Some insist that the greater number of male ministers in the New Testament suggests that ministry is an exclusively male vocation, so when we come to a discussion of Romans 16, I sometimes joke with my students that we should greet only men in public. But while Paul greets more men than women here, he commends the ministries of women much more often than the ministries of men.[14] He commends for ministry most of the women he cites but fewer than one-quarter of the men. (I sometimes tell my students that on the basis of this commendation we should institute a quota in which most ministers should be women! I am, of course, only joking in order to provoke some interpretive observations.) Paul may very well be going out of his way to commend the women because in a culture biased against their ministry they needed special encouragement. But I use the fact of the larger percentage of women commended to illustrate how our conclusions about women's ministry often stem from the particular texts we read most closely.

The nature of some of the ministries commended in Romans 16 is ambiguous: Mary, Tryphaena, Tryphosa, and Persis "worked hard in the Lord" (16:6, 12). This phrase implies ministry, probably especially in evangelism and discipling (1 Cor. 15:10; Gal. 4:11; Phil. 2:16; Col. 1:29). It does not need to connote administrative authority (the most frequent matter of debate today), although the language does not at all rule out this possibility (1 Cor. 16:16; 1 Thess. 5:12; 1 Tim. 5:17; 2 Tim. 2:6). I state these conclusions cautiously, but it should be noted that the same language is used for many male ministers in the New Testament and that our conclusions about the ministries of both genders should be equally cautious. That Euodia and Syntyche shared Paul's struggle for the cause of the gospel in Philippi (Phil. 4:2–3) likewise implies their involvement in ministry,

---

[14]This is still true even if, as is probable, Paul's greetings to men along with their households imply that these men held some positions in the churches that met in their homes.

probably evangelism, though this is a call for which all believers are responsible (Phil. 1:27).

Priscilla, with her husband, Aquila, is Paul's fellow worker (Rom. 16:3), a frequent term in Paul's letters. He especially applies it to those who shared his ministry labors (Rom. 16:9; 1 Cor. 3:9; Phil. 4:3; Col. 4:11)—including fellow itinerants like Timothy (Rom. 16:21; 1 Thess. 3:2), Titus (2 Cor. 8:23), Epaphroditus (Phil. 2:25), and others (Philem. 24), as well as house-church leaders like Philemon (Philem. 1). The possible more general sense of the term (2 Cor. 1:24) does not fit the particular commendation of this passage. Other passages may fill in a few more particulars of this married team's ministry, which included instructing ministers and leading a house church (Acts 18:26; 1 Cor. 16:19; cf. Philem. 1–2).

The nature of certain other women's ministries in Romans 16 is clearer. Junia was, as I noted above, an apostle (16:7), most likely as part of a husband-wife apostolic team. The chapter opens with mention of Phoebe, who carried Paul's letter to Rome, hence plainly functioning as Paul's agent. Given his commendation, it is possible that Paul expects her to be able to explain to the Roman Christians details of his letter if she is questioned (16:1–2), as letter bearers sometimes were.[15] Would she have been qualified to answer questions about the content of Paul's teaching in that letter? In any case, Paul provides her qualifications. She will depend on the hospitality of the Roman Christians but has provided such hospitality to many others (16:2); the term used for her providing help here customarily referred to patrons, including sponsors of religious groups that met in wealthy homes. In ancient inscriptions as many as 10 percent of these sponsors were women, and Paul has no objections to the church continuing this practice. Phoebe is a well-to-do woman, probably a businesswoman, perhaps a widow or freedwoman, in whose home the church could meet (similarly Nympha in Col. 4:15). The person in charge of synagogue buildings held an important role in the synagogue, and most hosts of house churches held prominent roles in the churches.

A position of prominence and responsibility might not necessarily require Phoebe to explain Scripture, so let's turn to Romans 16:1, where Paul calls her a "servant of the church" in Cenchrea, Corinth's port town on the Aegean Sea. The term

---

[15]See, for example, Xenophon, *Cyropaedia* 4.5.34.

translated "servant" here is a term Paul sometimes used for Jesus (Rom. 15:8) but most often for Paul himself (2 Cor. 11:23; Eph. 3:7; Col. 1:23, 25), his other fellow ministers of the word (Eph. 6:21; Col. 1:7; 4:7), or Paul and other ministers of the word together (1 Cor. 3:5; 2 Cor. 3:6; 6:4). The term can mean "deacon" (Phil. 1:1; 1 Tim. 3:8, 12)—but the New Testament nowhere specifically defines what this title means. It may relate to the more common usage of *diakonos*. Deacons must be committed to sound doctrine (1 Tim. 3:9), so we cannot even rule out that they may have taught others, even if they possessed an office distinct from Paul's normal usage. But there is no reason to make the term here mean something different from its most common sense in Paul (and its almost exclusive sense in Paul in this period of his writings).

Some churches today have redefined Phoebe's role as a deaconess on a level of authority lower than deacons, but Paul does not even employ any special feminine form of *diakonos* here. There is no reason to assume that Paul means by Phoebe's title something other than what he normally means by the term (that is, a minister of God's message, such as Paul himself)—unless we presuppose that he does not allow women's ministry (by reading an interpretation of another passage into this one).[16] But as I've noted, he clearly allows women some speaking ministry as prophets and, very likely, at least sometimes, as apostles. It is natural that most of Paul's fellow ministers, especially his traveling companions such as Timothy and Titus, would be male; but that Paul can employ the same title for a woman challenges the prejudice that women cannot fill the same sort of ministry roles.

One could argue that because Paul instructs women to teach women (Titus 2:3–4), his other counsel about women's ministry applies only to ministering to women. Given first-century social conditions, I suspect that in evangelism and teaching, Paul's female colaborers probably *did* regularly minister, both privately and corporately, to other women—though there are some explicit exceptions (Acts 18:26, which at least allows a married couple to privately tutor a prominent minister!).[17] But

---

[16]For more detailed documentation, see my *Paul, Women and Wives*, 238–40.

[17]On a somewhat entertaining note, Rebecca Merrill Groothuis (*Good News for Women: A Biblical Picture of Gender Equality* [Grand Rapids: Baker, 1997], 222–23) points out that those who prohibit women from teaching men because "women are more easily deceived" often allow women to teach other women—the very people they would most easily lead into further deception!

given what we know about the house churches, it is also impossible to completely restrict women's ministry of God's message in this manner even in the first century. Women and men met together in the largest room in the house churches, and even if they were seated separately (a situation for which we lack early evidence), it would hardly be possible for women to pray and prophesy without men hearing them![18]

If we do not read 1 Timothy 2 into the earlier texts, whose original readers had no access to Paul's first letter to Timothy, we have no reason to doubt that Paul accepts women in ministry. Paul describes the ministries of women in the same language he employs to describe those of men.

Does Paul Permit Only Some Ministry Roles?

Some argue that 1 Timothy 2 (treated below) prohibits, not every kind of Bible teaching role, but only those kinds of teaching exercised "with authority," namely, that of a senior pastor. Thus, women can teach Sunday school, direct the Christian education department, and do youth ministry, worship ministry, evangelism work, community ministry, counseling ministry— virtually anything except be "in charge." Because in many circles women in ministry are not senior pastors, this perspective may be closer in practice to the one that accepts all women's ministries than to the one that restricts all women's ministries. (In fact, when a male senior pastor propounds this view, he is usually not restricting women's ministries in his particular congregation at all, because in his congregation he holds the senior-pastor position himself.)

But this view actually represents something of an accommodation between the traditional restrictive position and the customary egalitarian position. The problem with this accommodation, of course, is that the words in 1 Timothy restrict women from speaking altogether; whether or not we read this text as a universal prohibition, the text itself says nothing about senior pastors. The most probable way to take the grammar of

---

[18]On the lack of early evidence for gender segregation even in the synagogues, see Brooten, *Women Leaders in the Ancient Synagogue*, 103–38; Shmuel Safrai, "The Synagogue," in *The Jewish People in the First Century* (Philadelphia: Fortress, 1974), 908–44.

1 Timothy 2:12 is not that women may not teach in an authoritative way (as I once took it), but that they may not teach *or* hold (or usurp) authority, as some complementarian scholars have argued.[19] Once you protest that Paul did not *mean* to prohibit *all* speaking, you have already raised the interpretive question of what he actually did mean in his historical context and how it might be applied in our context today.

Consider some of the problems with this mediating position, close as it is in many respects to a fully egalitarian position. First, it is not, as I have noted, a description of what this text *says*, taken at face value and without appeal to the local situation, any more than the full egalitarian position is. The text does not specifically mention senior pastors—rather it seems to suggest all kinds of (Bible) teaching and all kinds of authority. No more Sunday school teachers in gender-mixed classes either! But if the text's words should be qualified, what prevents one from qualifying them toward a full egalitarian position, which makes the other texts (below) easier to explain?

Second, reducing this text to the issue of rank or authority does not answer the question of other texts that appear to support women's ministry. Paul seems to think that apostles and prophets are the highest-ranking leaders in the body of Christ (1 Cor. 12:28; Eph. 4:11; cf. Rom. 12:6), yet he apparently endorses a woman apostle (Rom. 16:7) and certainly endorses prophetesses (1 Cor. 11:5; cf. Acts 2:17–18; 21:9). At least in exceptional circumstances, some prophetesses held supreme administrative authority (Judg. 4:4). Once you admit that at least in exceptional circumstances women can exercise authority, you are moving toward the third and fourth views articulated at the beginning of this chapter.

---

[19]See especially the argument in Andreas J. Köstenberger, "A Complex Sentence Structure in 1 Timothy 2:12," in *Women in the Church: A Fresh Analysis*, 81–103, which, though not foolproof, is on the whole persuasive (see my review in *Journal of the Evangelical Theological Society* 41 [1998]: 513–16, against my earlier position in *Paul, Women and Wives*, 109). One could take both expressions as negative (false teaching and domineering), but I believe I can make my case, even granting the complementarian reading of much of the evidence. One could link "teaching" with elders (1 Tim. 3:2; 5:17), but that association is not always explicit (1 Tim. 1:3; 4:11, 13, 16; 6:2; 2 Tim. 2:2, 24; 3:10, 16; cf. especially Titus 2:3), and even if this passage prohibits women elders, we would still have to address whether the prohibition is local or universal.

Finally, this view risks imposing a modern understanding of church leadership on the New Testament setting. Only a small portion of what the Bible teaches about ministry actually focuses on pastors. What's more, "senior pastors" did not exercise the same kind of authority in Paul's day that most do today. Typically, local churches in Paul's day held at most around fifty members, since they met in homes. Fifty members on average probably represented several families and a number of individuals who attended without families, meeting in the spacious home of a well-endowed family. Church leaders were chosen from among the members, and following the model of the synagogues, churches probably often had a plurality of elders (Acts 13:1; 14:23; 1 Tim. 4:14; 5:17; Titus 1:5) who were also called "overseers" (Acts 20:17, 28; Titus 1:5, 7; probably 1 Peter 5:1–2). Thus it is possible that a significant percentage of family leaders were also in church leadership of some sort! Our modern emphasis on pastoral authority may read our modern situation into early Christian house churches. Many women Sunday school teachers may in fact be exercising more teaching authority today than many first-century elders did!

Paul's ideal for the church was that everyone would exercise their spiritual gifts in these house churches (1 Cor. 14:26). Among these gifts Paul emphasizes prophecy no less than teaching (1 Cor. 14:1). (To be sure, prophecy can be abused, for we "prophesy in part," but so also can teaching, for we also "know in part," 1 Cor. 13:9, 12.) Pastors had very important roles as supervisors in local congregations, but it seems doubtful that they exercised the sort of authority pastors do in many modern evangelical churches. This is not to say that all churches must reinstitute the specific forms of church leadership practiced in the first century. The early church often adapted forms of leadership from the synagogue and used structures that best fit their culture; our situation differs from theirs, as does what is practical to apply in our setting. But many aspects of gender roles have also changed in our culture, and we ought to take this into account at the same time that we consider appropriate leadership forms.

In Greco-Roman culture and in the house-church setting, it is hardly surprising that most leaders in the church were men, probably most often older men who were respected heads of stable families (1 Tim. 3:2–5; 5:17–19).[20] At the same time, we know that not all church leaders were older heads of families—Paul himself was not, and Timothy was young (1 Tim. 4:12; from Acts we may deduce that he may have been in his thirties).

Furthermore, although we have no women pastors named in the New Testament, in the most specific sense we have no male pastors named either. To be sure, we do know that most elders were male (1 Tim. 3:2), but this appears to be the text's assumption (reflecting a given cultural situation) rather than its exhortation: Paul may have been specifying marital fidelity in language applicable to the majority of elders in his day. Again, it is doubtful that ancient readers would have considered Paul himself literally the husband of one wife (or a "one-woman man"), but as a church leader he fit the basic sense of the requirement because he was not unfaithful to a wife.[21]

In addition to this text, we have the names of some of Paul's male traveling companions whom he had appointed to oversee local churches and church leaders in certain areas—men such as Timothy and Titus. But Paul lived in a culture where female traveling companions would have proved scandalous, hence counterproductive for spreading the gospel.[22]

Nevertheless, the most common terms Paul uses to describe himself and his male fellow laborers—*diakonos* (1 Cor. 3:5; 2 Cor.

---

[20]Despite the use of the word *man* in many translations of this verse, 1 Timothy 3:1 uses a gender-neutral term, not the gender-specific *anēr*, to designate one seeking the office of elder.

[21]Besides the smaller pool of educated women, the majority of "respectable" leaders in that culture (1 Tim. 3:2; contrast 2:9) would be men; part of the culture also mistrusted religions that had liberated women from traditional roles (see my *Paul, Women and Wives*, 139–56). On the meaning of "one-woman man" in its first-century context, see my *And Marries Another: Divorce and Remarriage in the Teaching of the New Testament* (Peabody, Mass.: Hendrickson, 1991), 83–103; even if Paul had been married before, it is unlikely that anyone in the first century would have applied the phrase to him at this point. On the widespread understanding that general principles might sometimes be qualified, see my *And Marries Another*, 21–28.

[22]Jesus' disciples did have female traveling companions (Mark 15:40–41; Luke 8:1–3), despite probable scandal (see Lucian, *The Runaways* 18; Ben Witherington III, *Women in the Ministry of Jesus*, Society for New Testament Studies Monograph Series 51 [Cambridge: Cambridge University, 1984], 117), but Paul had to exhibit greater concern for the scandal factor because he was trying to establish a church within Greco-Roman society. Jesus, by contrast, was moving toward confrontation with the authorities.

3:6; 6:4; 11:23; Eph. 3:7; 6:21; Col. 1:7, 23–25; 4:7) and *synergos* ("fellow worker," cf. Rom. 16:9, 21; 1 Cor. 3:9; 2 Cor. 1:24; 8:23)— he also uses to describe women colleagues, though they proba- bly did not travel with him (Rom. 16:1, 3; perhaps Phil. 4:3). Other phrases he uses to describe his male colleagues he also applies to some women in Romans 16, as we have seen ("work hard" in 16:6, 12; cf. 1 Cor. 16:16; 1 Thess. 5:12). We can frame our questions so narrowly that we exclude the value of the evi- dence we do have (as scholars frequently do to prove a variety of positions), but the evidence we do have is certainly abundant when we consider that it comes from occasional documents. Women filled these ministry roles less frequently than men, but they did fill them. If Paul acknowledges women apostles and prophets, who communicate God's word with authority,[23] need we suppose that he rejected all women *pastors*—especially since this is not what he actually says?

Why More Men Than Women?

Some allow that women may minister under exceptional circumstances but argue that male church leadership is the norm. Those who hold this view often allow all the successful women ministers they know to be "exceptions" and thus do not restrict women's ministry. In practice, then, those who hold this technically nonegalitarian position may *function* as egalitarians. It is nevertheless important to consider the question they raise: If God supports women's ministry, why are most of the minis- ters in the Bible men?

The question is legitimate, but some knowledge of the bib- lical world is helpful in answering it. Social conditions do affect both people's response to God's call and the areas to which God will call people for the most effective ministry. Thus, for exam- ple, most of the women Paul mentions as sharing with him in the gospel in some way (apart from prophecy, which seems more widespread) are in Rome or Philippi (Rom. 16:1–12; Phil.

---

[23]I follow my own research on the nature of apostles and prophets here (*The Spirit in the Gospels and Acts*, as well as "The Function of Johannine Pneumatology in the Context of Late First-Century Judaism" [Ph.D. diss., Duke University, 1991]) rather than that of Wayne Grudem (*The Gift of Prophecy in 1 Corinthians* [Lanham, Md.: University Press of America, 1982]), though I respect all and affirm most of Gru- dem's work on the subject.

4:3)—locations in which women appear to have exercised greater social mobility than in Greece or in much of the parts of urban Asia Minor influenced by Hellenistic culture.[24]

Some people question why Jesus, who often showed himself to be countercultural, chose only men for his twelve most prominent disciples. Jesus was indeed countercultural in advancing the status of women (Luke 8:1–3; 10:38–42), but even Jesus did not directly challenge every detail of his culture, choosing his closest workers most strategically for the culture he intended to reach. None of the Twelve was a Gentile, a slave, or, as far as we know, a peasant or even a Judean. Most were Galileans, and the five whose occupations we know apparently come from the top 10 percent of wage-earning occupations in Galilee.[25] Does this mean that Jesus would never choose Gentiles to follow him later? Shall we restrict the ministries of Gentiles today or impose a quota system to make sure the majority of ministers are Jewish? One suspects we would quickly experience a leadership shortage in our churches!

CONCLUSIONS SUPPORTING WOMEN'S MINISTRY

Women appear at least occasionally in most ministry positions in which men are attested frequently in the New Testament. Paul normally traveled with men, but while he often sent his male traveling companions, he could also send a woman like Phoebe (Rom. 16:1–2). Most apostles and prophets were men, but at least one apostle and many prophetic figures were women. We have few specific leaders of house churches named, whether male or female; we do have the names of some in whose homes church members met, as well as those with other titles like *diakonos* ("servant") or *synergos* ("fellow worker"), but these homeowners and titles apply to women as well as to men.

We cannot list many specifically titled senior pastors of either gender in the first century, but if we can accept women as prophets and other ministers, there is no reason to exclude women from the pastoral office. Men clearly predominated—

---

[24]See, for example, Valerie Abrahamsen, "The Rock Reliefs and the Cult of Diana at Philippi" (Th.D. diss., Harvard Divinity School, 1986).

[25]I summarize the data more fully in *A Commentary on the Gospel According to Matthew* (Grand Rapids: Eerdmans, 1999), 151, 311.

but so did free persons and, in the earliest period, Jews. Today we recognize a different social setting—one that allows more Gentiles to minister; our different setting also invites more women to embrace the roles that some had begun to embrace already in the New Testament.

PASSAGES THAT APPEAR TO PROHIBIT WOMEN'S MINISTRY

If one could win the debate concerning women's ministry simply by the number of Bible passages one could cite, the clear weight of the debate would favor women's ministry. But for those who hold the entire Bible to be God's inspired word, we cannot dismiss any passage. Our goal must be to understand what each one says in its historical context, not simply to count texts. Two texts can be used to prohibit women's ministry, of which one (and only one) explicitly addresses women's ministry in particular. While that one is indeed rather explicit, if it means all that it could possibly mean, it would represent a radical departure from everything else Paul taught on the subject—and it would restrict women even more than today's most conservative voices on the subject do.

Might These Passages Be Addressing Specific Situations?

Some people conclude that we must accept as transcultural everything Paul says, regardless of the situations that prompted it. They are partly right: Everything the Bible says is for all time. But not everything the Bible says is for all circumstances, and there is not a single Christian in the world today, regardless of their views on the issue of women in ministry, who applies every text to all circumstances—not even all the straightforward commands.

Our theological backgrounds often shape what we characterize as cultural. Thus, a nonegalitarian scholar (an esteemed friend of mine) cited approvingly my treatment of head coverings in 1 Corinthians 11:2–16 (for which I am grateful), acknowledging that head coverings are not a transcultural requirement. He then curiously proceeded, however, to deny without debate that one could approach 1 Timothy 2 similarly (which makes an identical argument from the creation order)!

Others more consistently not only prohibit women from teaching but require them to wear head coverings to church in *all* cultures. Close to half my students in northern Nigeria, where head coverings are part of the culture, held this view, so after they had finished debating with the other half of the students, I asked why none of them had greeted me with a holy kiss—and they laughed! The holy kiss is an explicit command repeated in Scripture five times as often as head coverings (Rom. 16:16; 1 Cor. 16:20; 2 Cor. 13:12; 1 Thess. 5:26; 1 Peter 5:14), but the usual response is, "That was merely a cultural form of greeting." Indeed it was, but head coverings were also merely a cultural expression of sexual modesty, as can be demonstrated from a massive number of ancient sources.[26] Yet a few of my students bordered on calling other students "liberal" because they did not insist on head coverings as a transcultural requirement! Who determines where to draw the line? Is everyone liberal who holds as cultural something we hold as transcultural?

But some demand to know whether Paul could have addressed a specific situation in such broad, sweeping terms? When one reads the rest of Paul's letters, one can only answer: Definitely! Paul regularly writes in the language and figures of speech of his day; he also uses cultural images presupposed in his day.[27] More to the point, Paul's letters are full of statements that are locale-specific and cannot possibly have meaning apart from the local situation.[28] Sometimes Paul even alludes to matters known only to local congregations (see, for example, 2 Thess. 2:5; 1 Cor. 1:16; 3:4–6; perhaps 15:29).

To be sure, Paul's letters are full of principles that are directly applicable to today's situations; the practices of complaining and arguing, for instance, are probably not much different today than they were when Paul wrote Philippians. At the

---

[26]See my articles on "kissing" and "head coverings" in *Dictionary of New Testament Background*, 628–29; 442–47; or, less thoroughly, my *Paul, Women and Wives*, 19–69.

[27]I sought to provide (albeit on a relatively popular level) much of the background that illustrates this point in *The IVP Bible Background Commentary: New Testament* (Downers Grove, Ill.: InterVarsity Press, 1993), 407–646.

[28]See Romans 1:7, 10, 13; 15:22–24; 16:1–27; 1 Corinthians 1:2, 11–12; 4:17; 5:1–6; 6:6–8; 7:5; 8:9; 11:17–22; 16:5–12; 2 Corinthians 1:1, 15–17; 1:23–2:13; 6:11–13; 7:5–16; 9:2–5; 10:6–16; 11:1–21; 12:11–13:10; Galatians 1:2; 4:12–20; Philippians 1:1, 4–8, 19; 4:2–3, 10–19; Colossians 1:2; 2:1; 1 Thessalonians 1:1; 2:1, 17–18; 2 Thessalonians 2:1.

same time, other passages require some sensitivity to the original situation in order to be able to translate the principles into our contemporary situation—matters like head coverings or food offered to idols, for instance. Even in these cases Paul works with transcultural principles, but he articulates them in specific ways that address specific situations, and if we choose to ignore these situations when we interpret his writings, it follows that we must greet each other with holy kisses in church (in keeping with ancient family customs, they may have often been light kisses on the lips) or risk disobeying the apostle!

Some people conclude that whereas some texts are culture-specific, texts that give specific commands are universally applicable.[29] I would respond that *all* Scripture is universally applicable (2 Tim. 3:16). But all Scripture is also articulated in culture-specific and language-specific ways (for example, in Hebrew or Greek). Often biblical writers addressed specific situations in specific churches, inviting us to read their letters as case studies applying to specific situations so we can identify their principles, which we will then reapply in other situations. Inspiration does not change a writing's *genre*, or type of literature. Psalms are still psalms, narrative is still narrative, and epistles are still epistles. Pastoral letters, like sermons addressed to local congregations, can contain both universal and culture-specific exhortations side by side; this should be true, whether they are inspired or not.

This character of the genre of pastoral letters seems evident. Consider this: I sometimes write people letters of exhortation containing mainly universal principles that are also relevant to the particular situation I am addressing. Yet in those same letters I may include some exhortations relevant only to the situation I am specifically addressing. Unless I consciously write with the expectation that there will be other future readers who are *outside* the particular situation, I may never stop to differentiate my universal and situation-specific exhortations. Because I intend all my exhortations to be relevant to my immediate audience, I do not write these two kinds of exhortations in different ways or express them in different literary forms. A later reader

---

[29]See T. David Gordon, "A Certain Kind of Letter: The Genre of 1 Timothy," in *Women in the Church: A Fresh Analysis*, 53–63, who argues from some universal instructions in the Pastoral Epistles.

might therefore distinguish whichever I thought was which only by reconstructing the situation and comparing my other writings that addressed specific situations. Thus it is significant that the Bible always portrays complaining attitudes and homosexual behavior as wrong; eating food sacrificed to idols is often wrong; women's authority as ministers of the word was sometimes limited but sometimes commended, as noted above.[30]

Paul provides many direct commands we do not observe today, and some we cannot observe. How many Christians today put money into savings the first day of every week for a collection for the saints in Jerusalem (1 Cor. 16:1–3)? Paul commands his readers to receive Epaphroditus (Phil. 2:29), but because Epaphroditus is no longer living, we cannot fulfill this command literally. Paul exhorts his readers to pray for him and his companions (2 Thess. 3:1–2), but we who reject prayer for the dead cannot fulfill this command today. Instead, we learn from these passages general principles about hospitably receiving and praying for God's servants.

Must a transcultural application be absurd before we will limit it? Or do these "absurd" examples point out the way we ought to read Paul's letters consistently? To claim that only the *obviously* culturally limited passages are in fact culturally limited is simply to beg the question of interpretation methods. When slaveholders read Paul's command to slaves to obey their masters (Eph. 6:5), they did not think this command absurd for other settings, so they took it as a transcultural endorsement of slavery.[31] Because Paul always sought to be sensitive to his readers' situations (1 Cor. 9:19–23; 10:31–33), we dare not presuppose that every command applies to all circumstances.[32]

---

[30]On passages commending women's ministry, see my *Paul, Women and Wives*, 237–57 (citing other sources); for the hermeneutical principle, see Gordon D. Fee and Douglas Stuart, *How to Read the Bible for All Its Worth*, 2d ed. (Grand Rapids: Zondervan, 1993), 72–73.

[31]On the different interpretations undergirding and opposing slavery, see Glenn Usry and Craig S. Keener, *Black Man's Religion: Can Christianity Be Afrocentric?* (Downers Grove, Ill.: InterVarsity Press, 1996), 98–109; my *Paul, Women and Wives*, 184–224; and especially Willard M. Swartley, *Slavery, Sabbath, War and Women* (Scottdale, Pa.: Herald, 1983), 31–64, 198–204 (my *Paul, Women and Wives* would have profited had I read Swartley first).

[32]Even some general principles in Paul's letters, like many general exhortations in antiquity, could admit exceptions. To his call to submit to governing authorities

1 Corinthians 14:34–35

This passage enjoins "silence" without explicitly specifying what silence is being addressed. If it means silence in every situation, then women cannot sing in the choir, sing in the congregation, or pray aloud or prophesy. Whatever else Paul may mean, however, he cannot mean *complete* silence, because earlier in the same letter he allowed women to pray and prophesy (1 Cor. 11:5); most likely he would also allow them to sing (1 Cor. 14:15, 26; cf. Eph. 5:19; Col. 3:16). So what particular kind of speech is he restricting?

Interpreters have approached this passage from a variety of angles, which I have surveyed and addressed in detail elsewhere.[33] The context might suggest spiritual gifts, but as I've noted, Paul permitted women to prophesy (1 Cor. 11:5). Some have suggested that Paul opposes women evaluating other prophecies, but this proposal makes little sense of the text itself (which speaks of asking questions) as well as of Paul's suggestion that all those who prophesy are to participate in evaluating prophecies (1 Cor. 14:29). Some have suggested that the passage means that women cannot teach, but nothing in the context or elsewhere in Paul's Corinthian correspondence indicates that this is the issue he is addressing here.

The problem seems not to be *teaching*, but rather that the women are *learning*—too loudly. Unless Paul changes the subject from women's general silence in church (1 Cor. 14:34) to them asking questions to learn (14:35, first part) and then back to women's general silence in church (14:35, last part), Paul is addressing their asking questions in church in an effort to learn. That the two ideas are connected is clear from the grammar of 14:35; he bases women's silence regarding questions on the statement (*gar*, "for") that it is "shameful" (a term that can mean culturally inappropriate) for women to speak in church.

(Rom. 13:1–7) Paul nowhere adds an explicit exception for disobeying immoral commands (see Acts 5:29), but his emphasis and priorities throughout his letters make it clear that he would expect us to recognize such exceptions. For the same reason, even those who hold that husbands have a transcultural right to rule their families cannot ignore the general rules summoning all Christians to serve one another, submit to one another, and seek one another's good—exhortations that at the very least qualify any Christian's use of authority!

[33]See my survey of views in *Paul, Women and Wives*, 74–80, where I also offer more detailed responses to the views cited in the next paragraphs.

Throughout the first-century Mediterranean world, novices were expected to learn quietly, but more advanced students were expected to interrupt all kinds of public lectures with questions.[34] What was wrong with the women interrupting with questions? Perhaps the issue was the church's witness in terms of cultural propriety; it was culturally shameful for the women to ask questions.[35] (Their prophesying would probably prove no more culturally unusual than that of the men.)

But why was it shameful for the women to be asking questions? Perhaps it was because of the culturally expected submissive role of their gender;[36] if we conclude that this was Paul's reasoning, it would not require us to prevent women from asking questions today. Another possibility, however, is that they were asking unlearned questions. Whereas questions at public lectures were expected, ancient literature testifies that unlearned questions were considered foolish and rude—and women generally possessed inadequate education and were most often unlearned. (Although there were always exceptions, anyone who has read through numerous pages of ancient literature without reading simply the collected exceptions will recognize that in the vast majority of cases, men were more educated than women of the same social class.[37]) Jewish women could learn the law by listening in synagogue, but in the overwhelming majority of cases they were not trained in it. Unlike boys, girls were not normally taught to recite Torah. In the first-generation church in Corinth, most women were novices and therefore should learn quietly.

Paul's short-range solution, then, is to call for an end to the women's public questions. (This would not be the only place where Paul would address a group—even a gender—with a general rule even though it might not apply to every member; see 1 Tim. 4:7; 5:11, 14; Titus 1:12.) At the same time, however,

---

[34]Plutarch, *On Listening to Lectures,* various passages; Aulus Gellius 18.13.7–8; 20.10.1–6; *Tosefta Sanhedrin* 7:10.

[35]For documentation of Roman concern with Eastern cults subverting Roman traditional values, see my *Paul, Women and Wives,* 139–56.

[36]See Heliodorus, *Aethiopica* 1.21.

[37]On rude questions, see Plutarch, *On Listening to Lectures* 4, 11, 13, 18; *Moralia* 39CD, 43BC, 45D, 48AB; on women's lesser education (as a general rule), see documentation in my *Paul, Women and Wives,* 83–84, 126–27; also my article on "marriage," *Dictionary of New Testament Background,* 680–93.

of Webb

52 | Two Views on Women in Ministry

he provides a long-range solution: These women should ask their husbands at home to explain matters. In today's culture this may sound repressive, but in Paul's day it expressed the opposite attitude. Ancient writers testified that most husbands thought their wives to be incapable of learning academic disciplines. Those who thought husbands should provide private tutoring for their wives who had less education opportunities were a more progressive minority, and Paul's language here is more progressive even than most of their own.[38] His long-range solution to their being uneducated novices is that they should be allowed to learn, and their marriage partners should be committed to furthering their learning.

1 Timothy 2:11–14

This passage is part of a broader set of instructions about decorum in public worship in the Ephesian church. After briefly addressing a problem with the men (1 Tim. 2:8), Paul focuses on what seems to be a more pervasive problem with the women, who are given to outward adornment (2:9–10) and apparently are seeking to teach rather than to learn (2:11–12).

Paul's instructions are firm: The women must remain silent. Again, if pressed to mean all that it could mean, this would prohibit even singing in public worship, but the specific issue at hand is probably simply the explicit prohibition of teaching. Pressing even this more specific prohibition to mean all that it could mean, however, women should not even teach Sunday school classes in which men are in attendance. (Though most churches today do not meet in homes, saints presumably remain the church whenever they gather.) Whether Paul prohibits women from having authority altogether or simply from usurping authority (which would be prohibited for men as well) remains a matter of debate.[39] In contrast to my former position

---

[38]Plutarch urges taking an interest in one's wife's learning, against what he regards as the common view (*Advice to the Bride and Groom* 48; *Moralia* 145BC), though he (unlike Paul) explicitly regards women as intellectually inferior (*Moralia* 145DE).

[39]For usurping authority, which neither men nor women should do, see David M. Scholer, "1 Timothy 2:9–15 and the Place of Women in the Church's Ministry," in *Women, Authority and the Bible*, ed. Alvera Mickelsen (Downers Grove, Ill.: Inter-Varsity Press, 1986), 205; Carroll D. Osburn, "*Authenteō* (1 Timothy 2:12)," *Restora-*

on this issue, however, I believe that Paul probably prohibits not simply "teaching authoritatively," but both teaching Scripture at all and having (or usurping) authority at all. In other words, women are forbidden to teach men—period.

Is this a universal rule? If so, it is a rule with some exceptions, such as for a husband-wife team teaching a ministerial student (Acts 18:26) and for Spirit-directed utterance, like prophecy (1 Cor. 11:4–5), from which people could also learn (1 Cor. 14:31). But it is also possible that this text is the exceptional one, which can be argued if it can be shown to address a particular situation. After all, if it were to be a universal rule, one might have expected Paul to have paused when praising women's ministry earlier to note that these were exceptional cases. One might also have expected Timothy, who had worked with Paul for many years, to be aware of this rule already, perhaps contrary to the way Paul now frames its wording ("I am permitting"—present tense).[40]

Ultimately, the question of universality must be tested by two issues: First, are there in fact exceptions to the general prohibition here, despite the fact that such exceptions would contradict the tendency of the broader culture? As noted above, there *are* exceptions, in contrast to genuinely universal biblical rules like those prohibiting homosexual behavior. Second, do Paul's letters to Timothy, who is caring for the church at Ephesus, reveal a situation that would elicit such instructions as these?

The latter question is relatively easy to answer. The one passage in the Bible that specifically prohibits women from

---

tion Quarterly 25 (1982): 2–4 (this interpretation was argued as early as the 1800s; "usurp authority over" appears earlier in the KJV). "Have authority over" seems supported by the thorough and careful survey of H. Scott Baldwin ("A Difficult Word: *Authenteō* in 1 Timothy 2:12," in *Women in the Church: A Fresh Analysis*, 65–80), but this makes the somewhat controversial move of omitting the noun cognates and leaves only *two* pre-Christian references. It seems precarious to hinge the prohibition of half of Christians from acknowledging a call on such a disputed term. But in any event, the passage also prohibits teaching.

[40]These arguments merely establish the possibility; one could conversely argue that Paul *does* draw on a more common rule from the stricter wording in 1 Corinthians 14:34 (the only other Pauline passage using this word for "permitting")—except that another Corinthian passage reveals that this passage must allow public prayer and prophecy (1 Cor. 11:4–5). In the same way, other statements within the Pastoral Epistles must qualify our understanding of this one.

teaching is addressed to the one church where we know that false teachers were effectively targeting women. A primary problem in Ephesus was false teaching (1 Tim. 1:3–20; 4:1–7; 6:6–10, 20–21; 2 Tim. 2:16–26; 3:5–13; 4:3–4), and the primary false teachers (who were men—1 Tim. 1:20; 2 Tim. 2:17) were exploiting the women in order to spread their false teaching. How do we know this? If women as a rule were less educated than men, they would become a natural target as those particularly susceptible to such false teaching. Thus, it isn't surprising to learn that these false teachers targeted women in the households (2 Tim. 3:6), who were proving to be incapable of learning correctly (2 Tim. 3:7; cf. 1 Tim. 4:7). Churches met in homes, so false teachers needed large homes that would welcome them; the homes headed by women were usually those of widows. Thus, it would not be at all unexpected for some widows to go from house to house spreading "nonsense" (1 Tim. 5:13). As Gordon Fee has shown me, a survey of every use in extant Greek literature of the word often translated "busybodies" in 1 Timothy 5:13 reveals that the word was used for those speaking nonsense, and in moral and philosophical contexts it typically refers to those spreading false or improper teaching.[41] In this case, as in some of Paul's other social instructions in the Pastoral Epistles (1 Tim. 6:1; Titus 2:8, 10), Paul is concerned that social improprieties may turn people away from the gospel's eternal truth (1 Tim. 5:14–15). The church was being persecuted and slandered, and its reputation was important for the gospel's sake.[42]

Two objections are typically raised at this point. The first (raised especially on a popular level) is that even when provoked by specific situations, Paul's situation-specific instructions must retain permanent force; yet no one holds this position consistently. The second (maintained by scholars and popular readers alike) is more compelling on the surface, namely, that Paul grounds his case in Scripture (1 Tim. 2:13–14); I address each objection in turn in more detail below.

---

[41]Gordon Fee provided me not only a list of all the occurrences in extant Greek literature, but also copies of the fuller context of most of these texts, and the evidence is, as he points out, overwhelming.

[42]On slander against the church for social roles, see full documentation in my *Paul, Women and Wives*, 139–56.

Dare We Appeal to Local Situations to Interpret 1 Timothy?

Let's grant that Paul addresses a concrete local situation. Dare we argue that he might have given different instructions to address a different local situation or culture elsewhere? His letters to Timothy do invite us to take account of the specific situations addressed. When in the context of 1 Timothy 2:11–12 Paul exhorts men to pray properly (1 Tim. 2:8), shall we assume that Paul does not care whether women pray properly? Or should we assume instead that, just as Paul had a specific situation to address with the women (2:9–15), he also had a specific problem in mind and therefore was addressing the behavior of the Ephesian men (2:8)?

If the problem with the Ephesian women was their lack of education and consequent susceptibility to false teaching, the text provides us a concrete local example of a more general principle: Those most susceptible to false teaching should not teach. But are women always the ones most susceptible to false teaching today? And can interpreters who insist on maintaining the "straightforward sense" without taking into account dramatic cultural differences be consistent in how they apply different biblical texts? This is a crux in the debate; whereas egalitarian interpreters like Gordon Fee and Catherine Clark Kroeger may approach 1 Timothy 2 with radically different understandings of the background, they share a common approach of recognizing that a passage's background can actually affect the meaning we find there.[43]

Some object to this way of approaching 1 Timothy, but the Pastoral Epistles, like Paul's other letters, summon us to read them this way. Paul specifically writes to Timothy (1 Tim. 1:2; 2 Tim. 1:2) and Titus (Titus 1:4) in these letters. Paul specifically left Timothy in Ephesus to oppose those who were teaching false doctrines (1 Tim. 1:3), and he exhorts Timothy to do so in keeping with the prophecies given him (1 Tim. 1:18; 4:14; cf. 2 Tim.

---

[43]See the different interpretations in Gordon D. Fee, *1 and 2 Timothy, Titus,* New International Biblical Commentary (Peabody, Mass.: Hendrickson, 1988); Richard Clark Kroeger and Catherine Clark Kroeger, *I Suffer Not a Woman: Rethinking 1 Timothy 2:11–15 in Light of Ancient Evidence* (Grand Rapids: Baker, 1992). Much of what I say in this section is borrowed from my article "Interpreting 1 Timothy 2:8–15," *Priscilla Papers* 12.3 (1998): 11–13.

1:6); he also addresses specific false teachers (1 Tim. 1:20) who are no longer living. Although Paul did not leave *us* in Ephesus, as he did Timothy, nor did *we* receive Timothy's prophecies, there are plenty of transcultural principles here to embrace, such as the need to oppose dangerous doctrines and to heed words of wisdom or properly tested prophecy. But again, noting that specific exhortations can have more general relevance does not allow us to simply assume that we know what the transcultural relevance is before we have studied the situation carefully.

How many would regard as transcultural the warning that widows younger than sixty will speak nonsense (1 Tim. 5:11–13) or that fables circulate especially among older women (4:7)? If we must follow all commands in 1 Timothy as transcultural, even the most conservative churches are falling woefully short. Most do not prohibit the drinking of only water for those with stomach ailments and compel them to use wine as well (5:23). Similarly, if we are to obey 2 Timothy, each of us should come to Paul quickly, making sure we pick up his cloak and books from Troas before coming to him (2 Tim. 4:9–13)—a command that may prove difficult to fulfill for anyone after Paul's death, especially if Timothy *already* collected Paul's belongings in Troas. (That Paul also calls Titus to come to him in Titus 3:12 surely attests this as a transcultural requirement many times over: We all should try to visit Paul in Rome. We should also beware of Alexander the coppersmith [2 Tim. 4:14–15], despite the fact that he is most assuredly dead—the mortality rate for people over 1,500 years old being what it is.)[44]

Perhaps more significant are passages providing instructions not merely to Timothy but to the church as a whole. Here, for example, widows must not be put on the list for church support unless they are at least sixty years old, have been married only once (1 Tim. 5:9), and have brought up children and washed saints' feet (5:10). Apart from our general neglect of caring for widows to begin with (to some degree influenced by differences between today's welfare system and that of ancient Judaism), so few widows today have washed saints' feet that our churches can claim to be obeying Paul's teaching even when they don't include them on their list and withhold money for

---

[44]For other unquestionably situation-specific allusions, see 2 Timothy 1:2–6; 3:14–15; 4:20; Titus 1:4–5.

their support! Younger widows are encouraged to remarry, not taking the pledge of membership in the order of older widows supported by the church (5:11, 14). How widows today can obey this precept if they fail to find another husband is not quite clear, but in Paul's day men outnumbered women by a considerable margin; remarriage for women was much easier than it is today.[45]

Paul is clear that some of his commands in the Pastoral Epistles relate to avoiding apostasy (1 Tim. 5:15) and—a matter related to the views of the broader culture—public reproach (1 Tim. 3:2, 6–7, 10; 6:1; Titus 1:6–7; 2:8, 10). This explicitly includes not only some of his exhortations concerning gender roles (Titus 2:5) but also his exhortations concerning the obedience of slaves (1 Tim. 6:1–2; cf. Titus 2:9–10), which most evangelicals today would admit addressed a specific cultural situation. If the principles are more binding than the situation-specific exhortations that illustrate them, we may wish to consider how today's situation differs from that of the first century and how the act of diminishing women's opportunities rather than strengthening them challenges the church's witness.[46]

In short, as Rebecca Merrill Groothuis points out:

> If 1 Timothy 2:11–15 can legitimately be understood as a prohibition relevant only for women in a historically specific circumstance (which it can), and if there is no other biblical text that explicitly forbids women to teach or have authority over men (which there is not), and if there *are* texts that assert the fundamental spiritual equality of women with men (which there are), then women who are not in the circumstance for which the 1 Timothy 2:12

---

[45]Even in Paul's day this was probably one of his general principles to which he might permit exceptions; thus, church leaders should be husband of one wife (1 Tim. 3:2; Titus 1:6), possibly directed against teachers who advocated mandatory celibacy (1 Tim. 4:3; see my *And Marries Another*, 83–103, though also noting the emphasis may be marital fidelity). But Paul himself was unmarried and probably had never married (he was too young to have been a member of the Sanhedrin, even if the marriage rules were in force in his day). Paul warned Timothy not to rebuke others harshly (1 Tim. 5:1–2), but under different circumstances Paul rebuked Peter publicly (Gal. 2:14), which was normally considered inappropriate behavior (even by Paul himself—see 1 Tim. 5:19–20).

[46]See Alan Padgett, "The Pauline Rationale for Submission: Biblical Feminism and the *hina* Clauses of Titus 2:1–10," *Evangelical Quarterly* 59 (1987): 39–52.

prohibition was intended may safely follow whatever call they may have to ministry. In other words, it ought at least be acknowledged that the traditionalist interpretation is debatable on biblical grounds. This being the case, we should give the benefit of the doubt to any woman who is called to and qualified for pastoral leadership.[47]

But Paul Cites the Old Testament

If we could stop here, there might be little debate about 1 Timothy 2:11–12, hence about any level of women's ministry in the church. The evidence for a specific situation behind 1 Timothy 2 is clear enough in Paul's letters to Timothy, and the evidence that Paul elsewhere affirmed ministries of women is compelling enough that evangelical scholars as a whole might well agree but for one problem—the fact that Paul goes on to base his argument on the Old Testament, citing biblical authority for what he says. Surely this means that he intends it for transcultural situations!

Or does it? Does Paul apply all Old Testament texts universally, or does he sometimes apply them to local situations? Before we can determine how Paul uses Scripture in 1 Timothy 2, we must first ask how he uses Scripture in general. (I'll return to a specific discussion of Genesis 1–2 later.) If he always uses it in a straightforward manner, then presumably 1 Timothy 2 *must* silence all women after all. His arguments here are that God created men first, women are more easily deceived than men, and therefore women should not teach men. We should make sure that if we universally prohibit women from teaching, we should do so for the reason the text on which we base our practice cites; that is to say, for Eve's deception to constitute a universal argument, we must assume that all women are easily deceived (presumably always more deceived than most believing men are)— the usual historic interpretation of the verse. Thus this analogy between Eve and women would tell us something about their *nature* rather than about first-century women's educational status. If we say that only most women are easily deceived, then we can prohibit only most women from teaching by this argument. If we say that the women in Ephesus were deceived like

---

[47]Groothuis, *Good News for Women*, 211.

Eve because they were uneducated, the principle is that the untrained are more susceptible to deception. But if it is a universal prohibition based on gender, it is a statement, not about first-century women's education, but about all women's ontological inferiority in discerning truth. This is a claim we ought to be able to verify or refute empirically, yet most empirical research suggests that, when educational opportunities are the same, women are as adept in discerning deception as men are.

But what if Paul is simply drawing a local analogy between Eve and the easily deceived women in Ephesus (or the majority of women in his day who were uneducated, hence easily deceived)? What if Paul is simply making a local analogy, as he did elsewhere when he drew an analogy between Eve and all the Corinthian Christians (male and female alike, 2 Cor. 11:3)? Is this possible? If Paul often argues by analogy and sometimes uses Scripture in an ad hoc manner, there is no reason to doubt that Paul may be doing so in 1 Timothy 2—which would undercut the main pillar for applying this text to women transculturally.[48]

Often, perhaps even usually, Paul reads the Old Testament in a straightforward manner, just as we typically do. For instance, he often applies commands given to Israel to all believers who have accepted Israel's Bible (see, for example, Rom. 13:9); principles from Israelite law can help guide the church (see, for example, 2 Cor. 13:1). But what happens when we must address an issue that no specific biblical text addresses? In these cases we customarily look for texts that address similar principles and draw analogies between those texts and the situation we must address; Paul did the same thing.

Arguments by Analogy

Paul often universalizes biblical texts by analogy. Because his contemporaries, both Jewish and Gentile, customarily drew on both positive and negative models in history to make their points, Paul's audience would have followed his approach easily. Thus, for example, an ox that treads out the grain provides an analogy for a minister of the gospel (1 Cor. 9:9–10; 1 Tim. 5:18). In many cases Paul could have applied his analogies to

---

[48]Here I have used parts of my article "How Does Paul Interpret Eve in 1 Timothy 2?" *Priscilla Papers* 11.3 (1997): 11–13.

situations other than those to which he specifically applied them.[49] Thus, as God gave to the poor (Ps. 112:9), so he would also provide for the Corinthians if they gave sacrificially (2 Cor. 9:9).[50] Paul's specific applications are often christological, because Christ is rightly his focus.[51]

Sound arguments by analogy depend on correct exegesis but are not themselves intended as exegesis. Some of Paul's analogies are closer to the original sense of the texts he cites than others. Those that are more distant from the original sense of the text should not be pressed beyond their immediate application, and sometimes we can recognize that Paul himself would not wish us to press his analogies beyond the immediate service to which he puts them. For example, creation's proclamation in Psalm 19:4 parallels the gospel proclamation in Romans 10:18. The incomprehensible language of the Assyrian invaders was a divine message of judgment toward Israel after they had rejected God's other attempts to get their attention (Isa. 28:11; cf. 33:19; Deut. 28:49); Paul applies the incomprehensible nature of this language to speaking in tongues (1 Cor. 14:21), perhaps because it also functions as a warning to unbelievers (14:22). Hosea tells

---

[49]For example, in Galatians 4:22–31 Paul specifically applies Hagar and Sarah to spiritual Ishmaelites (who want to circumcise Gentiles) and spiritual descendants of Abraham, but these are hardly the only analogies one might draw from these biblical characters. Other inspired interpreters use Sarah as a model for Christian wives (1 Peter 3:6) or for all believers (Heb. 11:11).

[50]Given Paul's mission, it is not surprising that many of his analogies concern the era of salvation he proclaims. Paul draws a natural analogy between the law of Moses and the gospel he preaches (Rom. 10:6–8); both, after all, are God's word. Likewise the proclamation of Israel's restoration is an analogy for the gospel message (Rom. 10:15). He draws an analogy between the preservation of a remnant from the Assyrian judgment (Isa. 10:5, 21–24) and the ultimate future restoration of the survivors of his people (Rom. 9:27–29). Likewise, by faith the righteous would live through the impending Chaldean invasion (Hab. 2:4 in context); Paul applies the principle to the day of judgment (Rom. 1:17; Gal. 3:11). Perhaps for similar reasons, he applies imagery for Israel's future salvation (Isa. 49:8) to the present offer of salvation through his gospel (2 Cor. 6:2). Paul can draw a large-scale analogy between Moses and the apostolic ministry of the new covenant (2 Cor. 3:6–16), in which Moses' transforming revelation of the Lord in the Exodus narrative corresponds to believers' transforming experience of the Spirit (2 Cor. 3:17–18).

[51]Thus Paul can draw analogies between Israel's provision in the rock and provision in Christ, between God's provision of food in the wilderness and his provision in the Lord's Supper, and between Israel's crossing the sea and the experience of Christian baptism (1 Cor. 10:1–4).

of Israel's rejection and their restoration (Hos. 1:10); perhaps because Paul believes the conversion of the Gentiles will provoke Israel to repentance (Rom. 11:13–14), he applies this text to the salvation of the Gentiles (Rom. 9:25–26). The primary analogy between Psalm 116:10 and 2 Corinthians 4:13 is the need to speak in accordance with what one believes. Paul even quotes one of Job's comforters to make a point (1 Cor. 3:19), in spite of the fact that, on the whole, these comforters' specific application of their wisdom was wrongheaded (Job 42:8).

Like other Jewish teachers, Paul will on occasion even rephrase a text. For instance, Psalm 68:18 speaks of a divine conqueror *receiving* gifts. Because conquerors would normally distribute such plunder among their troops, Paul and some other Jewish traditions on this passage can apply it to *giving* gifts, and Paul applies it to the ascended Jesus giving ministers to his church (Eph. 4:8). When Paul wants to, he can argue that "seed" is singular and must refer to Christ (Gal. 3:16), even though he knows very well (contrary to his modern detractors) that it can refer to "descendants" in the plural; indeed he uses it in that manner elsewhere (Rom. 4:13, 16, 18; 9:7–8; 11:1), even in the same chapter (Gal. 3:29)! In the polemical context of Galatians 3:16, where Paul may be responding to his opponents by using their own methods, he employs a standard interpretive technique of his contemporaries: Apply the text the way you need to in order to make your point.

While some of us may not want to accept that Paul uses Scripture in an ad hoc way at times (it makes it more difficult for us to teach sound hermeneutics to our students), respect for Scripture requires us to revise our preconceptions in light of what we find in the text, rather than forcing the text to fit philosophical assumptions about what we think it *should* say. Those who wish to maintain, on the basis of Paul's allusion in 1 Timothy 2:13–15 to a passage from Genesis, that verses 11 and 12 *necessarily* contain a transcultural principle should reread Paul's other letters carefully with respect to his use of the Old Testament. To be sure, Paul often uses Scripture with a universal import; often, however, he makes analogies to argue points he intends only for a specific situation. Given Paul's support of women's ministry in other passages, as well as the presence of occasional authoritative models like Deborah in Scripture, I believe the burden of proof should rest on those who argue that he means his biblical allusion to be understood more universally here.

Creation Order and the Fall in 1 Timothy 2:13–14

Some of Paul's analogies may be more relevant than others for his comparison of women with Eve in 1 Timothy 2. Although he can make general comparisons with Eve (see, for example, 1 Cor. 6:16; Eph. 5:31–32), the two most relevant comparisons are in 1 Corinthians 11:8–9 and 2 Corinthians 11:3. In these texts Paul can use the Eve analogy in an ad hoc manner. Eve was created for Adam's sake; therefore women should wear head coverings. Having offered this argument, however, Paul reminds us that, in the end, neither men nor women are independent of the other (1 Cor. 11:7–12). The "creation order" argument applied to women's silence in 1 Timothy 2 is precisely one of the arguments he employs in 1 Corinthians 11:8–9 to admonish wives to cover their heads in church. We cannot consistently require a transcultural application prohibiting women's teaching or holding authority based on 1 Timothy 2:11–12 without also requiring all married women to cover their heads in keeping with 1 Corinthians 11:2–16 (a point Paul in fact argues at much greater length).

Another text, however, is more relevant, referring specifically to Eve's deception, as in 1 Timothy 2:14. Paul draws an analogy between Eve and the Corinthian Christians in 2 Corinthians 11:3; the basis for the comparison is that both were easily deceived. This example indicates that he could apply the image to anyone easily deceived, including most of the women in the Ephesian church, but that Paul does not always make this analogy on the basis of gender. As we have seen, some of his other analogies are also situation-specific.

Some interpreters today appeal to the creation order argument by noting that Adam, not Eve, names the animals (Gen. 2:20)—but of course Eve hadn't yet been created at this point (2:22). Some claim that Adam names Eve the way he names the animals he rules, but Genesis distinguishes his recognition of Eve (2:23) from the naming formula used for the animals (2:20)—until after the Fall (3:20). Others apply to Adam's prior creation the ancient principle of primogeniture (the state of being the firstborn), but this would work only if the passage implied that Adam and Eve were both children expecting an inheritance (in which case Adam gets twice as much; but see 1 Peter 3:7) and only if inheritance rights controlled all rank; it would also work better if Genesis did not elsewhere specifically challenge the custom of primogeniture (Gen. 25:23; 48:19; 49:4).

The Fall introduced marital tension into the world (Gen. 3:16), but it is surely not wrong for us to work to reduce marital conflict, as with most other aspects of the Fall (pain in childbirth, the hardship of toil, and ultimately the reality of coping with sin and death in the world).[52] In the creation order, man and woman together comprised "man" in God's image and together ruled the earth (Gen. 1:26–28; 5:1–2). Likewise, given the use of the Hebrew terms elsewhere (which anyone may check with the help of a concordance), "suitable helper" (2:18, 20) points to male and female correspondence, not to one partner's subordination.

Some interpreters today will ultimately object that we must find Eve's subordination in the creation order because Paul does, but that brings us back to our original point: Does Paul in fact subordinate all women (more specifically, demanding their silence in church) because Eve was created second? Would he use chronology as a transcultural argument? Elsewhere in his writings the first can be inferior to the second, a mere prototype of God's plan (1 Cor. 15:45–47). Adam is not a mere prototype of Eve, but neither does Paul use chronological priority as a universally self-evident argument; his argument here is constructed for a specific situation.

OTHER CONSIDERATIONS

What about the Biblical Pattern of Male Headship in the Home?

Because the question of gender relations in the home is a separate issue (and space is limited here), I mention this objection only in passing and offer two brief responses. First, I have argued

---

[52]Genesis 3:16 and 4:7 are the only two Old Testament texts that use these terms for "desire" and "rule" together (and two of only three using this term for "desire"); their proximity and identical construction invite us to interpret their construction together and to view 3:16 as a statement of marital contention in which the husband, being stronger, will prevail. An inspired, accurate description of the Fall is not necessarily prescriptive, in contrast to inspired apostolic *affirmations* of women's ministry (see Rom. 16:1–2, a letter of recommendation, as is widely recognized—see Meeks, *The First Urban Christians*, 109).

elsewhere at considerable length that in his most detailed exposition of the matter, Paul's ideal is *mutual submission* and *servanthood*. Various interpretive assumptions lead interpreters to express different beliefs as to whether the husband should always lead the home in all respects. But I believe it is biblically impossible to doubt that Christian husbands and wives should practice mutual submission and servanthood (Eph. 5:21), even if it is specified more explicitly for the wives (5:22), just as all Christians should practice mutual love (5:2), even if it is specified here more explicitly for the husbands (5:25). Moreover, Paul believes in submitting to authority structures within the culture, yet he no more mandates as permanent the ancient patriarchal marriage patterns (5:21–33) than he mandates as permanent the practice of urban household slavery (6:5–9), both of which are part of the same section of household codes (5:21–6:9).[53] Paul addresses the roles as they existed in his day, but the principle is *submission to those in authority, and becoming servants even when we hold authority.*[54] "Helper" (Gen. 2:18) is usually a term of strength, often used even of God as our helper; wives' subordination probably stems from the Fall (Gen. 3:16; see above).

Second, the issues of women's ministry (affirmed by many passages, apparently limited in, at most, two) and gender roles in the home *are* distinguishable. A person may have different roles in different situations; thus, for example, I have taught students in an academic setting who, in a church setting, were my pastors. Further, the question of how these two issues relate would prove less relevant for a single woman. Likewise, I know evangelical couples whose bishops assigned the husband and wife each to serve as pastors of separate (though nearby) churches. Some nineteenth-century evangelical missionary couples similarly divided their ministry outreach in order to reach more people. In other words, even a person who does not accept the egalitarian or mutual-submission arguments for the home need not prohibit women's ministry.

---

[53] As I noted in *Paul, Women and Wives* (208), the point of this comparison is not whether marriage is God-ordained (of course it is), but whether the patriarchal structures of marriage that undergird Greco-Roman household codes are God-ordained.

[54] I have argued this at length, with fuller documentation than possible here, in *Paul, Women and Wives*, 139–224; for cultural comments regarding other passages, see the relevant texts in *The IVP Bible Background Commentary*.

What about the History
of Interpretation of These Passages?

As biblically faithful Christians, we accept the views of the Bible over tradition because we view the Bible as God's most direct revelation of his will (cf. Mark 7:7–13). We are, therefore, less concerned with how others have interpreted the Bible—often in light of their own cultures and church traditions—than in the biblical message itself. But because we ourselves are part of specific cultures and church traditions, the history of interpretation does help us to gain perspective.

The most common view on women's ministry in the history of the church has been that women could not minister God's word to men. This was, of course, no mere restriction of women in the pastorate! But this view rested on a premise that was almost equally widespread, namely, that women cannot teach the Bible to men because women are more easily deceived than men and ontologically inferior to men, at least in those gifts most necessary for the practice of church leadership and doctrinal scrutiny.[55] Is it fair to appeal to the conclusion (on the basis of historic precedent) without accepting the logic behind that conclusion (on the basis of the same precedent)? This view of women's nature reflects Aristotelian premises and a consensus from the larger culture, a culture that I believe reflects male-female relations that are a result of the Fall (Gen. 3:16).

To be sure, the burden of proof rests on any person who advocates a view that no one ever thought of before, because if it was obvious in Scripture, it should surprise us that we would be the first to discover it! Often, however, the church has on enough occasions missed or suppressed truths that are clear enough in Scripture to allow us to accept the burden of proof and advocate a position previously not widely accepted, such as justification by faith. At many points Martin Luther, for instance, challenged the status quo of traditions in his day. For strategic purposes, however, he felt it necessary to maintain many traditional practices, so that most of his people would find familiarity in many aspects of church

---

[55]See the data in Daniel Doriani, "A History of the Interpretation of 1 Timothy 2," in *Women in the Church: A Fresh Analysis*, 213–67.

worship.[56] Some other Reformers sought to "reform" tradi-tions further, and this often led to conflict among early Protes-tant leaders.[57] Most Protestants today recognize that the Reformation did not settle all questions of which particular church traditions may still require revision. I believe we have sufficient biblical evidence in favor of women's ministry to accept the burden of proof. I would argue that the majority view in the church throughout history—the view that came down to most of us through tradition—reflects the restrictive cultures of human history in which the tradition was formed rather than the clearest reading of the biblical evidence.

Having acknowledged the dominant historical testimony of the older churches, however, it should be noted that some reform movements have always affirmed the ministry of women. One group that sought reform during the Middle Ages was the Waldensians; they ultimately incurred persecution from the medieval Roman church. But alongside justification by faith and an appeal to Scripture's authority, the earliest Waldensians were accused of letting women preach.[58] Women's ministry also became increasingly accepted in many times of revival, includ-ing the Wesleyan revival, which changed the course of spiritual life in Britain, and the Second Great Awakening in the United States. Pentecostal and Holiness groups were ordaining women long before modern secular feminism and unbiblical arguments for women's ordination made it a divisive issue in some other circles. Many Baptist and other evangelical churches permitted more freedom for women's ministries until the fundamentalist-modernist controversy of the 1920s; Freewill Baptists and (in its earlier years) the Christian and Missionary Alliance also affirmed women's ministry. The oft-repeated charge in some cir-cles that even among evangelicals women's ministry is a thinly veiled secular agenda may be well-meaning, but it is certainly misinformed historically. Revivals brought to the fore women's

---

[56]See Luther's conservative but critical use of the Roman liturgy (Paul J. Grime, "Changing the Tempo of Worship," *Christian History* 39 [1993]: 16–18); bear in mind, though, that Luther's views on gender roles were progressive in his historical setting (see Steven Ozment, "Re-inventing Family Life," *Christian History* 39 [1993]: 22–26).

[57]See Robert D. Linder, "Allies or Enemies?" *Christian History* 39 (1993): 40–44.

[58]See "Did You Know?" *Christian History* 30 (1991): 3; also the more radical Hussites in Elesha Coffman, "Rebels to Be Reckoned With," *Christian History* 68 (2000): 39–41.

spiritual gifts and a fresh reading of Scripture in settings where no one had thought of modern secular feminism![59]

STILL MORE CONSIDERATIONS

Few evangelicals on either side of the women's ministry debate would dispute that Jesus' acceptance of women in many respects proved unusual in his day (e.g., Luke 8:1–3). What is more striking is his acceptance of women as actual disciples—something few if any other rabbis did.[60] People of any means usually sat on chairs, or at banquets reclined on couches. To sit at a teacher's feet, however, was to adopt the posture of a disciple.[61] This is the posture that Mary adopts, and Jesus defends her adoption of this role against Martha's preference for traditional matronly roles (Luke 10:38–42). All disciples—male and female—best learn discipleship by following Jesus. But it is easy for modern readers to forget that rabbis restricted women from being disciples (albeit not from listening in the synagogues) largely because, after the elementary levels, disciples became rabbis-in-training. Mary might have been learning simply for herself—but she also might have been learning in order to share Jesus' message with others who would listen.

What do such acts of Jesus indicate in the broader context of his ministry? Jesus regularly crossed the boundaries of clean and unclean (Mark 1:41–42; 2:16; 5:30–34, 41–42; 7:2, 19), even though many of these boundaries were grounded in the Old Testament (Lev. 11:2–47; 13:45–46; 15:25–27; Num. 19:11–13; Ps. 1:1).

---

[59]For some surveys, see Stanley J. Grenz with Denise Muir Kjesbo, *Women in the Church: A Biblical Theology of Women in Ministry* (Downers Grove, Ill.: InterVarsity Press, 1995), 36–62; Nancy Hardesty, *Women Called to Witness: Evangelical Feminism in the Nineteenth Century* (Nashville: Abingdon, 1984); Catherine Booth, *Female Ministry: Woman's Right to Preach the Gospel* (New York: Salvation Army, 1975; first published 1859). See especially the lengthy treatment in Ruth A. Tucker and Walter L. Liefeld, *Daughters of the Church: Women and Ministry from New Testament Times to the Present* (Grand Rapids: Zondervan, 1987). Note the expectation suggested by Acts 2:17–18.

[60]See Leonard Swidler, *Women in Judaism: The Status of Women in Formative Judaism* (Metuchen, N.J.: Scarecrow, 1976), 97–111; my *A Commentary on the Gospel of Matthew* (Grand Rapids: Eerdmans, 1999), 689–90.

[61]See Acts 22:3; *Mishnah Avot* 1:4; *Avot of Rabbi Nathan* 6; 38a; 11, §28B; *Babylonian Talmud Pesahim* 3b; *Palestinian Talmud Sanhedrin* 10:1, §8. For sitting on chairs normally, see Safrai, "Home and Family," in *The Jewish People in the First Century*, 737.

He did not oppose the Old Testament teachings (Matt. 5:17–20; Luke 16:17), but he interpreted them in such a way as to reflect on and reapply their purpose in fresh situations (Matt. 5:21–48). He also demanded that we keep first things first, not missing the forest for the trees; broader principles like justice, mercy, and faith took precedence over biblical details adapted for specific situations (Matt. 23:23–24; Mark 10:5–9). In our commendable attention to grammatical details in some passages addressing specific situations, we must still be vigilant against the temptation to ignore broad principles about what matters most to God.

To issue a warning about such a temptation is not to answer to everyone's satisfaction which positions in fact reflect such principles, but to fail to ask the question is to ignore a dynamic principle of interpretation to which Jesus' ministry summons us. Given even a few clear examples of women's ministry in the Bible, is one text (or at most two texts), which may be situationally conditioned, enough to deny or substantially restrict a group of laborers for the kingdom? Some say they do not have enough certainty in order to permit women's ministry, but should those who are less than absolutely certain deny the calling of others, or should they perhaps keep silent on the issue? If these women claim to be called and bear the same sort of fruit on average as men (criteria we typically use to evaluate a man's calling), how objectively can we evaluate men's calls to ministry? A number of people tell me they reject women's callings because they have seen women fail at ministry, but have they never seen men fail at ministry? Some have never witnessed an effective public ministry by a woman. On the other hand, I have seen more male ministers fall into sexual sin than women ministers; a few years ago I worked under a woman pastor who led more people to Christ in one year than I've seen any male pastor of a comparably sized congregation achieve. Our personal experiences may differ, but in the end is it not as dangerous to risk forbidding what God endorses as to risk promoting what he forbids?

A PERSONAL NOTE

I mentioned earlier that I have been on both sides of the issue at different times in my life. After my conversion to Christianity I spent my earliest years in conservative evangelical circles that had affirmed women's ministry since the early twentieth century (when women in ministry was even more accepted in some evangelical circles than it is today). In such circles the "conservative" position supported women's ordination, and some of my most effective Bible teachers were women. At the time, however, I believed that 1 Timothy 2 prohibited women's ministry, and I found myself in the uncomfortable situation of appreciating the divinely blessed ministry of people whom I did not think should be involved in such ministry! When I gently engaged in dialogue with female friends who were preparing for ministry, I struggled to square my view of 1 Timothy 2 with their apparent strong sense of calling—and everything else I knew about God in the Bible.

Such a setting sparked my interest in the question, but it took several years before I could resolve it. I continued to believe that 1 Timothy 2 excluded women from Bible teaching, as gently and humbly as I desired to express it. Yet as I read forty chapters of the Bible each day, I increasingly began to recognize the way the Bible was inviting me to read it. I made it a goal to develop a fresh, consistent interpretive method from studying Scripture itself. The Bible summoned me to understand the world it first addressed, and as I studied the background of the Bible, I grew increasingly convinced that the Bible did in fact affirm women's ministries.

By this time, however, I was starting to spend time in different evangelical circles, where the "conservative" view was that women could *not* be ministers! Thus—being the "brave" young scholar I was—I planned to keep my convictions to myself. In time, however, several factors combined to convince me that I needed to speak out. First, by this point I was seeing the way many godly evangelical friends of mine—women who were in ministry—were being regularly mistreated, and wanting to support them came to matter more than my reputation. (I should hasten to add, however, that many complementarians do not mistreat women in ministry and that, like myself in my complementarian days, they wish to be *personally* supportive.)[62] Second, the church's treatment of women in general had become a major apologetics issue on many university campuses, and I was heavily involved in campus ministry and apologetics. Certainly the credibility of the

---

[62]For one commendable example, see Thomas R. Schreiner, "An Interpretation of 1 Timothy 2:9–15: A Dialogue with Scholarship," in *Women in the Church: A Fresh Analysis*, 105.

gospel mattered more than my reputation! Third, I saw this as an opportunity to demonstrate the importance of cultural background in Bible interpretation, hence a useful test case for promoting the importance of sound interpretation. Fourth, as I communed with God in prayer I began sensing that he wanted me to articulate the evidence I had found. Finally, being a young scholar, I did not yet have much of a reputation to lose!

It was only after I published on the issue, however, that I realized how vitriolic the debate was becoming. Some evangelicals were denying the genuine evangelical commitment of those who did not share their views on the subject, and some trivialized rather than responded to our scholarship. They had every right to disagree charitably, as many of my friends do even today, but when some people misrepresented us and resorted to political power ploys, they stooped to non-Christian methods of engaging in the debate. Disagreement on matters secondary to the gospel invites dialogue; slander, however, is a sin that must be addressed by means of repentance. This is true for whichever side is guilty of the slander, no matter how deeply our personal passions run on this or other issues.

CONCLUSION

A number of passages clearly support women sharing God's word—and sometimes sharing it in more authoritative ways than the passages most often in dispute. Paul applies the same titles to ministries of women as to those of men, and he explicitly affirms women in the most prominent ministry roles of the early church. Context and background demonstrate that the two passages used to argue against women's ministry apply to particular situations within the two particular congregations; these texts, therefore, do not contradict those that support women's ministry. The passage specifically prohibiting women from teaching the Bible (1 Timothy 2) is also addressed to the one congregation where false teachers were specifically targeting women with their views. We should, therefore, not allow our traditions or an (at best) uncertain (and most likely mistaken) interpretation of a single passage to deny the calling of women who otherwise prove themselves fit for ministry.

QUESTIONS FROM THE EDITORS

Many egalitarian authors begin their discussion of biblical support for their position with an analysis of Genesis 1 and 2. Here you have chosen to begin with the role of prophets in both the Old and New Testaments. Why have you taken this approach?

The question is whether one begins with a more deductive theological method or a more inductive exegetical one. The broader theological method has its place; for example, the abolitionists typically argued their case more by identifying principles, and the slaveholders more by pointing to concrete texts they thought at least allowed slavery (though they ignored the cultural setting). Broad models like Creation (Gen. 1–2) and Christ's redemptive work (for example, Gal. 3:28) are excellent places for biblical theology to start.

Some of my complementarian friends, however, have argued that egalitarians' broad principles address only status in Christ but not roles. Although I may not agree with their conclusion, they offer a legitimate hermeneutical caution. Some people do make excessive theological extrapolations that actually contradict examples in specific biblical texts. In the same way, some complementarians treat Paul's prohibition in 1 Timothy 2 as a principle, and I challenge that interpretation based on specific examples (in Rom. 16 and elsewhere). To be methodologically consistent, I look first at the concrete data that often show us how general principles are fleshed out in various situations. I do, of course, address the creation texts later in my argument, so I do not mean my own approach to be a condemnation of a different approach.

Hierarchicalist interpreters often distinguish between the gifts of the Spirit, which are given without gender considerations, and the offices of the New Testament, such as pastor/elder/overseer, which, they argue, do have gender considerations attached to them. How do you distinguish between gift and office?

Although I touched on this issue briefly in certain footnotes, I must respond with another question: What is an office in the New Testament? Since the term does not appear (where some translations do use the word *office*, it does not reflect a Greek equivalent), one can define it in such a way as to exclude any ministries in which women ever appear, which is most ministries in the New Testament. But on what objective basis do we limit our definition this way? Certainly 1 Timothy 2 and 1 Corinthians 14 say nothing about office; they simply tell women to be silent in church. If we consider *pastoring* to be an office, why not do the same for apostles and prophets, who appear in the same list (Eph. 4:11)—roles that, we have argued, women sometimes did fill? Was *judge* not an office, or did Deborah not fill it (and that of prophetess as well)?

We could define as office any role that required the laying on of hands for commissioning to ministry; our few specific examples here are men (Acts 6:6; 1 Tim. 4:14; 2 Tim. 1:6; perhaps Acts 13:3). But no one denies that men made up the majority of leadership in the early church; consequently, the fact that the few specific examples are men is not surprising. Yet there is no evidence that hands were regularly laid on apostles or prophets or other possibly translocal ministries, and as we have argued, these were not lesser callings. Further, it is arbitrary to limit one's sample for office only to the few examples of the laying on of hands, while ignoring language suggesting that women may have filled some of the same kinds of offices (as argued in my essay). By narrowing the pool sufficiently, one can make almost any case. But the act of so narrowing the pool here looks suspiciously like limiting the examples to those that support one's case. Those who believe that 1 Timothy 2 excludes women from office may have reason to try to make such a case, but again, 1 Timothy 2's prohibition is much broader than any such narrow definition of office would cover.

In your writings you have often shown yourself to be an advocate of an irenic spirit with regard to gender questions. What advice would you give to those egalitarians who disagree with you as to how they should conduct their interactions with hierarchicalists?

I do empathize with the passion many of my fellow egalitarians bring to this subject. It can certainly be frustrating to feel called to ministry, yet to have to confront others who deny the possible validity of that call for reasons not based on one's Christian character or quality of preparation. (This is an experience that some of us men have also shared for different reasons, and all of us who have experienced it recognize the fact that much pain can be involved.) Some of us have also been stung by criticisms from some extreme complementarians who, instead of arguing the case on an exegetical level, have resorted to challenging our motives or to stereotyping us by lumping us with radical feminists who support agendas we emphatically reject.

But the passion many complementarians bring to the subject is often accompanied by a fear that to support women's ministry connects them to a larger and increasing pattern of the ignoring by Western Christians of biblical claims. Some extreme egalitarians appear to confirm this fear by resorting to accusations and stereotyping instead of making a biblical case. Rather than desiring to repress women, many complementarians are in fact trying to grapple sincerely with what they find in the text, expressing an exegetical opinion and not any sort of personal malice. We may disagree with their conclusions and yet appreciate their concern for fidelity to Scripture, a concern that biblical egalitarians surely share. The exegetical and cultural background issues here are some of the most complex in the New Testament, and Bible-believing Christians on both sides of the issue dare not conclude that hidden agendas dictate all the exegetical findings on the other side.

This is not a call for less passion or for less fidelity to what we believe is the biblical position; it is a plea for more understanding and a greater expression of Christian charity. Whatever else we debate in Scripture, we cannot deny that our Lord summons us to love one another, to lay down our lives for one another, and to forgive one another when we and others fall short of that ethic (John 13:34–35; 15:12–13; Eph. 4:29–5:2). Polarizing the church does not persuade anyone, nor is it healthy for the church; although some issues affect us personally more deeply than others, there are countless other issues over which the church is tempted to divide. The only result of such divisions is a progressive fragmentation of biblical Christians into smaller sects, a division that severely diminishes our collective voice for Christ within our society. If we trust that our call comes from Christ himself, we can be secure enough in it, as I have witnessed in the lives of many of my brothers and sisters, to love each other and to maintain fellowship even where we disagree. Complementarians are our brothers and sisters in Christ for whom we must be ready to lay down our lives.

Chapter Two

WOMEN IN MINISTRY

Linda L. Belleville,
North Park Theological Seminary

WOMEN IN MINISTRY

Linda L. Belleville

One of the continuing hotbeds of debate in evangelical circles today is the nature and scope of leadership roles open to women in the church. Can a woman preach God's word? Can she serve communion, baptize, or lead in worship? Can she marry and bury? Can she serve as the senior or solo pastor? Can she teach an adult Bible class? Can she serve as a bishop, elder, or deacon? Can she put "Reverend" or "Pastor" before her name?

These are the questions with which numerous churches in the last forty years have struggled and over which some have divided. In large part this has been due to the absence of any middle ground. The issues and terms have generally been defined so as to force a choice either wholly for or wholly against women in leadership. The focus typically has been on one or two highly debated passages, with little acknowledgment of the roles of women in Scripture as a whole.

What about today? Has any middle ground been reached? What currently separates traditionalists and egalitarians? As recently as two decades ago the polarity was vast. It was not uncommon to hear evangelicals talking about a woman's flawed nature and intrinsic self-deception, which ruled out any leadership role for her in the church.[1] Now there are very few who

---

[1] See, for example, Douglas Moo, "1 Timothy 2:11–15: Meaning and Significance," *Trinity Journal* 2 NS (1981): 175.

would go this far,[2] and most who thought this way in the past have changed their minds.[3]

What accounts for the change? It is not that a biblical consensus has emerged—for many traditionalists still claim that theirs is the "Christ-honoring, Bible-believing perspective" and that the egalitarian perspective is the "liberal, culturally acceptable view."[4] The primary impetus is actually social in nature. The feminist movement and the force of economic pressures have catapulted women into the workplace, where they have shown themselves to be equally talented, equally wise, and equally levelheaded—so that whereas twenty-five years ago only young adult males were challenged with the slogan *Uncle Sam Wants You*, more recently women and men were equally encouraged to *Be All That You Can Be.*

To a great extent evangelicals have followed suit. There is now general agreement that women possess exactly the same spiritual gifts men do and are to be encouraged to develop and exercise these gifts to their fullest potential. In effect, women are urged to *be all that you can be spiritually.* A case in point is the catalog statement of one of the largest and most conservative evangelical seminaries. To quote: "As members of the faculty of Trinity Evangelical Divinity School ... we recognize that God has given His gifts to both men and women in the body of Christ," and "It is our goal that each woman be encouraged and receive the training she needs to be fully prepared for future ministry."[5]

---

[2]See, however, Robert Culver, "A Traditional View: Let Your Women Keep Silence," in *Women in Ministry: Four Views*, eds. Bonnidell Clouse and Robert G. Clouse (Downers Grove, Ill.: InterVarsity Press, 1989), 36. Evangelical scholars have come to see that a belief in female self-deception conflicts with scriptural teaching elsewhere. If women were, by nature, thus inclined, Paul would not have instructed older women to teach and train the younger women (Titus 2:3–4). Also, while Paul does assert that all human beings without exception sin, at no time does he suggest that women are more susceptible to sin's deceiving activity than men (Rom. 3:9–20). In fact, it was two *men* (not women) whom Paul expelled from the Ephesian church on account of false teaching that stemmed from personal deception (1 Tim. 1:20).

[3]Compare Moo's view in "1 Timothy 2:11–15" (175) with his view in "What Does It Mean Not to Teach or Have Authority over Men? 1 Timothy 2," in *Recovering Biblical Manhood and Womanhood: A Response to Evangelical Feminism*, eds. John Piper and Wayne Grudem (Wheaton, Ill.: Crossway, 1991), 189–90.

[4]"Baptists Take Stand on Role of Women," in *The Dallas Morning News*, November 10, 1999, 1. See the archives at http://www.dallasnews.com.

[5]Trinity Evangelical Divinity School Catalog General Information, Community Life, "Statement on Gender References in Speech and Writing"; and "Women's Programs (Dean of Women)." Visit the Web site at http://www.tiu.edu.

So the issue that divides the traditionalist (now self-identified as "complementarian") and the egalitarian today is not that of *women in ministry* per se, that is, women exercising their spiritual gifts, but rather *women in leadership,* for while a consensus has developed regarding women and spiritual gifting, a great divide has emerged on the issue of women in leadership—especially women leading men.

What accounts for the great divide? The patriarchal structures that were in place in the American workplace twenty-five years ago have been replaced by an ethic of gender equality—in theory, if not always in practice. Here, however, evangelicals have not generally followed suit. It is the rare evangelical church that has a woman in its pulpit on Sunday morning, a female pastor in its senior position, a female chairperson or presiding elder of its council, or a female teacher of its adult Bible class. It is also the uncommon evangelical denomination that ordains women, installs women in key administrative positions, or appoints women to governing boards.

The reason for this state of affairs is not hard to pinpoint: The relationship of male and female continues to be perceived in hierarchical ways. God created men to lead; God created women to follow.[6] It is this perception that fundamentally differentiates a traditionalist from an egalitarian today.

It is a distinction that has become highly politicized. Councils are formed, supporters are sought, newsletters are generated, speaker bureaus are created, business meetings are held, and funds are solicited. For example, the Council on Biblical Manhood and Womanhood was formed and the Danvers Statement formulated in 1987 in reaction to the egalitarian view espoused by participants at the "Evangelical Colloquium on Women and the Bible," held October 9–11, 1984, in Oak Brook, Illinois.[7] Furthermore, there seems to be little room for dialogue on this issue. Only the publications that fully follow the party line are referenced.[8] Bible translations are judged on the basis of

[6]See John Piper, "A Vision of Biblical Complementarity: Manhood and Womanhood Defined According to the Bible," in *Recovering Biblical Manhood and Womanhood,* 35–36.

[7]Preface to *Women, Authority and the Bible,* ed. Alvera Mickelsen (Downers Grove, Ill.: InterVarsity Press, 1986), 4.

[8]"Books and Resources," *CBMW News* 1995–.

the presence or absence of gender-inclusive language.[9] Books are either wholly in or wholly out.[10] And organizations (Inter-Varsity and Fuller Theological Seminary, for example) and denominations (Presbyterian Church-U.S.A. and United Methodist Church, for example) are either entirely affirmed or not affirmed.[11]

Invariably the debate between egalitarians and traditionalists comes down to four basic questions:

1. Do we find women in leadership positions in the Bible?
2. Do women in the Bible assume the same leadership roles as men?
3. Does the Bible limit women from taking on certain leadership roles?
4. Does the Bible teach a hierarchical structuring of male and female relationships?

WOMEN IN LEADERSHIP

Gifting for Ministry

If to be egalitarian is to believe in the mutual gifting of women and men, the biblical support is easy to come by. One can hardly move from one chapter of the New Testament to the next without the matter-of-fact mention of a woman prophet, teacher, evangelist, or the like.

The stage is already set in Judaism for a wide range of female ministry roles. Israel from the start had its female prophets, judges, counselors, and worship leaders. Some, in fact, were multigifted women. Moses' sister, Miriam, possessed instrumental, hymnic, and prophetic gifts that served Israel well during the wilderness years (Ex. 15:20; Mic. 6:4). Deborah was named a "prophetess" (Judg. 4:4, 6–7), "judge" (4:5), and "mother in Israel" (5:7).[12]

---

[9]*CBMW News*, 1997–.

[10]For example, *Women in Ministry: Four Views* is labeled as "feminist" on account of the "clear editorial sympathies of the editors" (*CBMW News* 1 [11/1995]: 12).

[11]See *CBMW News* 1 (8/1995): 6.

[12]"Mother" and "father" were titles given to benefactors and synagogue officers of some stature in the Jewish community. See, for example, *Corpus Inscriptionum Iudaicarum* 694 (third century): "I Claudius Tiberius Polycharmos . . . father of the synagogue at Stobi . . . erected the buildings for the holy place . . . and with my own

The foremost female ministry role was that of *prophet*. Women functioned as prophets during every epoch of Israel's history. Besides Miriam and Deborah, there was the prophetess whom God instructed Isaiah to marry (Isa. 8:3); the prophetess Huldah, active during the time of Jeremiah and Zephaniah (2 Kings 22:14; 2 Chron. 34:14–33); the prophetesses of Judah during Ezekiel's day (Ezek. 13:17–24); and the postexilic prophetess Noadiah during the time of Nehemiah (Neh. 6:14)—to name a few.

Another female ministry role was that of *counselor*. Joab (David's military commander) sent a female counselor from Tekoa to persuade David to forgive Absalom's act of violence against his stepbrother and so pave the way for reconciliation (2 Sam. 14). It was also the expert counsel of a woman who saved her city, Abel Beth Maacah, from destruction at the hands of David's troops (2 Sam. 20). Then too, wisdom in the book of Proverbs is pictured as a woman, and the ideal woman of Proverbs 31 is she whose husband praises her because of her wisdom. Such affirmations rule out any sort of mainstream Jewish theology that viewed the female as a self-deceived and deceiving creature.

A ministry that was almost exclusively female was that of *mourning*. David in his lament for Saul calls on the daughters of Israel to weep for the king (2 Sam. 1:24). The prophet Jeremiah refers to professional female lamenters, who were paid to mourn at funerals and other sorrowful occasions (Jer. 9:17–18). The prophet Ezekiel speaks of the lament that the daughters of the nations will chant for Egypt (Ezek. 32:16).

Women also actively used their gifts in and for worship. They helped build and furnish the tabernacle (Ex. 35:22–26). They played musical instruments in public processions (Ps. 68:25–26). They danced and sang at communal and national festivals (Judg. 21:19–23). They chanted at victory celebrations (1 Sam. 18:6–7). They sang alongside the men in the temple choir (2 Chron. 35:25; Ezra 2:65; Neh. 7:67).

---

means without in the least touching the sacred [funds]." An early second-century inscription from Italy ranks "father of the synagogue" before *gerousiarch* (a high-ranking official of the local Jewish ruling council). For further inscriptions and discussion, see Bernadette J. Brooten, *Women Leaders in the Ancient Synagogue: Inscriptional Evidence and Background Issues* (Chico, Calif.: Scholars Press, 1982), 83–90.

One of the more intriguing Old Testament ministry references is to the women who served at the entrance to the tabernacle (Ex. 38:8; 1 Sam. 2:22), for the Hebrew word translated "served" (*ṣābā'*) is used elsewhere in the Old Testament of the work of the Levites in the tabernacle (Num. 4:23; 8:24) and of Israel's warriors (Num. 31:7, 42). While certainty is impossible, it is plausible to suppose that these women guarded the entrance to the tabernacle. Indeed, when Jesus was brought for questioning before Annas (the patriarch of the high priestly family), the guard on duty was a woman (John 18:16, *thyrōros*.)[13]

The number and range of female ministry roles take a leap forward in the early church. Paul's greetings to the Roman church reflect this. No less than nine of the twenty-eight individuals greeted are women. It is the same with the rest of the New Testament record. Women are singled out in the early church as apostles (Rom. 16:7), prophets (Acts 21:9; 1 Cor. 11:5), evangelists (Phil. 4:2–3), patrons (Rom. 16:2), teachers (Acts 18:24–26; Titus 2:3–5), deacons (Rom. 16:1; 1 Tim. 3:11), prayer leaders (1 Cor. 11:5), overseers of house churches (Acts 12:12; 16:14–15; Col. 4:15), prayer warriors (1 Tim. 5:5), and those who were known for their mercy and their hospitality (5:10).

What accounts for this leap? In large part it is because corporate worship and service were based on the Spirit gifting each and every member of the local church for "the work of the ministry" (*eis ergon diakonias*, not the NIV's "works of service," Eph. 4:11–12; cf. 1 Cor. 12:11).[14] The nature of early Christian worship is succinctly spelled out in 1 Corinthians 14:26: "When you come together," Paul states, "everyone has a hymn, a teaching [*didachēn*], a revelation, a tongue, or an interpretation. All of these must be done for the strengthening of the church" (author's translation, hereafter AT). The gender-inclusive character of Paul's statement is not to be overlooked, nor is the public and verbal nature of this gifting. It was assumed that both women and men were actively involved in worship in didactic ways.

One of the ministries for which women in the church became renowned was that of *patronage*. To use Paul's language, "If it

---

[13]See *Aegyptische Urkunden aus den königlichen Staatlichen Museen zu Berlin: Griechische Urkunden* 4.1061.10—"his wife Thenapunchis, a door-keeper [*thyrouron*] of Euhemeria in the division of Themistes."

[14]The English translation, unless otherwise indicated, is the New International Version, Inclusive Language Edition (NIVI).

[your gift] is contributing to the needs of others, then give generously" (Rom. 12:8). It has long been noted that women alone are mentioned as the source of financial support for both Jesus and the Twelve. The Gospel writer, Luke, recounts that a group of women traveled from place to place with Jesus and the Twelve and "supported them out of their own means" (Luke 8:3). The imperfect tenses show that this was an ongoing activity and not a mere excursion or two. These women "continuously followed him [*ēkolouthoun autō*] and repeatedly ministered to him [*kai diēkonoun autō*]" (Mark 15:41 AT; cf. Luke 8:3).

While this fits with the increased mobility of women at this time in the Roman Empire, within Jewish society it is quite striking. Yet it rarely gets noted by traditionalists. Attention is alternatively directed to the fact that none of the Twelve was a woman. But the truly amazing detail is that Jesus welcomed women into his itinerant group and allowed them to make the same radical commitment in following him that the Twelve did. That two are identified as married women is especially striking (Joanna, the wife of Herod's steward, and Salome, the wife of Zebedee [Luke 8:1–3; Mark 15:40–41]).

Women are also singled out as patrons of house churches. Two women were sufficiently well-off to own their own homes, which they in turn offered as meeting places for the local believers: Mary in Jerusalem (Acts 12:12) and Nympha in Laodicea (Col. 4:15). A third woman, Lydia—a businesswoman from Thyatira—opened her home in Philippi to Paul and his converts as a base of operations (Acts 16:15). Offering one's home as a meeting place involved more than cleaning the house and making the coffee. The homeowner in Greco-Roman times was in charge of any and all groups that met under their roof. This was essential, since they were legally responsible for the group's behavior (see, for example, Jason's responsibility to post bond [Acts 17:7]).[15]

Women in the early church assumed other patronage roles. Paul refers to Phoebe in Romans 16:1–2 as a *prostatis* of many, including himself. Translations are wide-ranging in their rendering of this Greek word. They include "succourer" (KJV), "helper" (RSV, NIV, NASB, NLT, NKJV), "of great assistance" (PHILLIPS), "a help to many" (NAB), "a good friend" (TEV, NEB, REB),

---

[15]For further discussion, see Wayne Meeks, *The First Urban Christians: The Social World of the Apostle Paul* (New Haven, Conn.: Yale Univ. Press, 1983), 76.

"has looked after" (JB), and "a respected leader" (CEV). Sociologists, historians, and linguists, however, have shown that a *prostatis* was a "benefactor" (NRSV, REVISED NAB). Benefactors in the first century did more than write a check to cover expenses. They welcomed their clients to their house, rendered assistance as called for, and offered legal aid as needed.[16]

Women were also recognized for their apostolic labors. Junia, for instance, is commended as a woman whom Paul considered "outstanding among the apostles" (Rom. 16:7). Some traditionalists translate the Greek text as "esteemed by the apostles." But this introduces an idea totally foreign to Paul's thinking. Paul would surely say "we apostles" (1 Cor. 4:9; cf. Gal. 1:17, 1 Thess. 2:6), as he does elsewhere, not "the apostles" (thereby excluding himself). This translation also overlooks the surrounding context, which points to a role distinctly comparable to Paul's. Junia was Paul's co-patriot and co-prisoner—not to mention the fact that she was "in Christ" before Paul was. Perhaps she was among "all the apostles" (1 Cor. 15:7) or one of the five hundred to whom Christ appeared (1 Cor. 15:6 [pre-Pauline tradition]).

Priscilla and Aquila are also spoken of in ways that suggest apostolic activity. Their joint tentmaking operation with Paul in Corinth (Acts 18:1–3) and "risking their lives" for him to the benefit of "all the churches of the Gentiles" (Rom. 16:3–4) are easily understood in this fashion.

The presence of female apostles is noteworthy. Apostleship stands at the head of two New Testament lists of spiritual gifts

---

[16]Jason, for instance, posted bond to ensure the good behavior of his client Paul (Acts 17:5–9), and the Philippian church sent Paul money as the need arose (Phil. 4:10–19; cf. 1 Cor. 9:15–18 and 1 Thess. 2:9). For a concise treatment of Greco-Roman patronage, see Everett Ferguson, *Backgrounds of Early Christianity* (Grand Rapids: Eerdmans, 1987), 45.

Apphia could also justifiably be called a patron. Although we speak of "the letter to Philemon," it is actually addressed to three individuals: "Paul . . . and Timothy our brother, to Philemon our dear brother and fellow worker, to Apphia our sister, to Archippus our fellow soldier and to the church that meets in your home" (verses 1–2). "The church that meets in *your* [plural] home" certainly includes Apphia. What's more, Timothy ("our brother") and Apphia ("our sister") are referred to in exactly the same way. Too, the letter was a public one (addressed to the church) rather than a private one (addressed to three personal friends). So Paul is not extending a greeting to Philemon's family members but recognizing the leaders of the Colossian church (cf. "to all the saints in Christ Jesus at Philippi, together with the overseers and deacons" [Phil. 1:1]; also Rom. 16:1–24; Col. 4:7–18).

("Christ gave some to be apostles," Eph. 4:11; cf. 1 Cor. 12:28) and, along with prophet, is viewed as foundational to the establishment and growth of the church (Eph. 2:20). The latter reference points to the function of an apostle in the early church as the equivalent of today's church planter. This is clear from the immediate context where the Pauline term appears. Barnabas, Silas, Timothy, and Titus, for example, are named apostles in texts that stress their role as coworkers in planting churches (1 Cor. 9:5–6; 2 Cor. 8:16–21; 1 Thess. 2:7–9 [cf. 1:1]).

Some traditionalists have questioned the female gender of the Greek name *Iounian* in Romans 16:7. Yet there is no reason to read *Iounian* in any way but feminine. Both older and more recent translations render *Iounian* as the feminine "Junia" (KJV, ASV, NKJV, NRSV, NLT, REB, REVISED NAB, NIVI)—and rightly so. The masculine name "Junias" simply does not occur in any inscription, on any tombstone, in any letterhead or letter, or in any literary work contemporary with the New Testament writings. In fact, "Junias" does not exist in any extant Greek or Latin document of the Greco-Roman period. On the other hand, the feminine name Junia is quite common and well attested in both Greek and Latin inscriptions. Over 250 examples to date have been documented in Rome alone.[17]

Add to this the fact that none of the early versions of the Greek New Testament considered *Iounian* as anything but feminine. For example, the Vulgate (the standard Latin translation of the Western church) has "Junia . . . well-known among the apostles." Plus, the only variation in the ancient manuscripts is also feminine ("Julia"). The fact of the matter is that no translator or commentator prior to the Middle Ages understood *Iounian* as anything other than feminine. John Chrysostom (bishop of Constantinople in the fourth century), for instance, said: "How great is the devotion of this woman [Junia] that she should be even counted worthy of the appellation of apostle."[18]

---

[17]See Bernadette J. Brooten, "'Junia . . . Outstanding among the Apostles' (Romans 16:7)," in *Women Priests*, eds. Leonard Swidler and Arlene Swidler (New York: Paulist Press, 1977), 141–43; G. W. H. Lampe, "Iunia/Iunias: Sklavenherkunft im Kreise der vorpaulinischen Apostel (Rom. 16:7)," in *Zeitschrift für die neutestamentliche Wissenschaft* 76 (1985): 132; and Richard S. Cervin, "A Note Regarding the Name 'Junia(s)' in Romans 16:7," *New Testament Studies* 40 (1994): 464–70.

[18]John Chrysostom, *Homilies on Romans* 31 (on Romans 16:7).

Yet English translations from the 1950s to the early 1970s typically do not have "Junia." Instead, the Greek accusative *Iounian* is taken as a contraction of the masculine name *Iounianus* and translated "Junias" (as in TEV, NASB, NAB, NIV, JB, NEB, RSV, and PHILLIPS).[19] This is a complicated way of saying that Junias was a nickname or shortened form of Junianus.

There can be only one reason for this historical lapse. The presumption was that the term "apostle" could not be used of a woman; hence, the Greek must be construed as masculine. Yet the church fathers did not resort to such linguistic gymnastics. In fact, all the church fathers up to the twelfth century who quote Romans 16:7 have the name Junia (the majority) or Julia (a minority).

If there was one gift that women consistently possessed and exercised throughout the history of God's people, it was the gift of *prophecy*. As already noted, there are numerous examples of women prophets stretching back to the time of Moses. Anna continues this tradition in the New Testament period. Luke calls her a "prophetess," for she "spoke about the child to all who were looking forward to the redemption of Jerusalem" (Luke 2:36–38). Philip, one of the leaders of the Hellenistic wing of the Jerusalem church, had four daughters who were prophets (Acts 21:9; Eusebius, *History of the Church* 3.39).[20] Women in the church at Corinth exercised the gift of prophecy in public worship (1 Cor. 11:4–5), and their contributions were affirmed ("I praise you for remembering me in everything and for holding to the teachings, just as I passed them on to you" [1 Cor. 11:1–2]).[21]

Paul exhorted the Corinthian believers to "eagerly desire spiritual gifts, especially the gift of prophecy" (1 Cor. 14:1). A brief overview of the prophet's role in the early church shows why. Although prophecy is sometimes assumed to be predictive in nature (see, for example, Acts 21:10–11), the primary task of the New Testament prophet was comparable to the forthtelling role of the Old Testament prophet in reminding God's people of

---

[19]See Ray Schulz, "Romans 16:7: Junia or Junias?" *Expository Times* 98 (1987): 109.

[20]Proclus (third-century leader of the Phrygian Montanists) places the prophetic ministry of Philip's daughters in Hierapolis, Asia.

[21]Another female prophet during New Testament times was a Philadelphian woman named Ammia (Eusebius, *History of the Church* 5.17.2–4). Second-century Montanists, Priscilla and Maximilla, used women like Ammia and Philip's daughters to legitimize their own prophetic office (Eusebius, *History of the Church*, 5.17.4).

their covenant obligations. Done in the context of public worship ("when you gather," 1 Cor. 14:26), prophecy served to convict of sin (1 Cor. 14:24), to instruct (14:19 [*katecheo*]), to exhort (14:31), to encourage (Acts 15:32), and to guide in the decision-making process (Acts 13:3–4; 16:6). Just how consequential it was can be gauged from the fact that prophecy alone calls for examination of falseness or truthfulness by those with the gift of discernment (1 Cor. 14:29–30; 1 Thess. 5:20–21). Also, the prophet, along with the apostle, is viewed as foundational in the establishment and growth of the church (Eph. 2:20).

Another gift exercised by women in New Testament times was that of *teaching*. Priscilla, for example, instructed Apollos in the "way of the Lord" (Acts 18:25). The older women in the church at Crete were expected to teach the younger women (Titus 2:3–5). Teaching was also a part of what a prophet did. "You can all prophesy in turn," Paul says to the Corinthians, "so that everyone might learn and be urged along" (1 Cor. 14:31 AT [*manthanosin ... parakalontai*]; cf. 14:19 "instruct" [*katecheo*]). Since there were female prophets at Corinth (1 Cor. 11:5), instruction was most definitely part of their role.

The gifting of women as teachers in the early church was quite countercultural. Both women learners and teachers were comparatively rare. In Greek society the education of women beyond the elementary grades was not thought to be all that practical or necessary. The education of Roman women began to be taken more seriously in the centuries before Christ. But even so, there were still relatively few women teachers in the public arena during New Testament times (still playing catch-up, so to speak). Within Judaism especially, women learners and teachers were a rarity. This makes Jesus' instruction of Mary and the inclusion of female disciples particularly noteworthy (Luke 10:38–42). It also set the stage for women to have an instructional role in the church.[22]

Female teachers continued into the post-apostolic period. Women were especially at the forefront in exposing and condemning heretics. Perhaps the best known was Marcella, who was praised by Jerome for her ability to confront heretical error.[23]

---

[22]See my *Women Leaders and the Church: Three Crucial Questions* (Grand Rapids: Baker, 2000), 58–59, 87–96.

[23]Jerome, *Epistle* 127:2–7. For further discussion, see Walter Liefeld's article "Women and Evangelism in the Early Church," *Missiology* 15 (1987): 297.

What about evangelistic ministries? Here, too, women were actively engaged. This was especially the case in the Roman church. Paul commends Priscilla as a "coworker" (Rom. 16:3 AT) and singles out Tryphena, Tryphosa, and Persis as "hard laborers in the Lord" (16:12 AT). This is missionary language. Paul uses exactly the same language of his own and other male colleagues' missionary labors. The men are "fellow prisoners" (Rom. 16:7; Col. 4:10), "coworkers" (Rom. 16:3, 9, 21; 1 Cor. 3:9; 16:16–17; 2 Cor. 8:23; Phil. 2:25; 4:3; Col. 4:11; 1 Thess. 3:2; Philem. 1, 24), and "hard laborers" (1 Cor. 4:12; 16:16; 1 Thess. 5:12) who "risked their lives" for Paul (16:3) and "contended for the gospel" at his side (Phil. 4:3). The women are equally "coworkers" (Rom. 16:3–4; Phil. 4:3) and "hard laborers" (Rom. 16:6, 12) who "risked their lives" for Paul (Rom. 16:3) and "contended for the gospel" at his side (Phil. 4:2–3). Paul's joint imprisonment with Junia and Andronicus indicates that they, too, were engaged in some sort of evangelistic activity (Rom. 16:7; cf. Acts 16:19–24; 2 Cor. 11:23).

Syntyche and Euodia were active female evangelists. Paul says that they "contended side by side" with him "for the cause of the gospel" (Phil. 4:3). Some traditionalists say that Paul is merely acknowledging their financial support or hospitality. The language indicates otherwise. The term Paul uses to describe their role is a strong one. *Synathleō* ("contend side by side") describes the athlete who strains every muscle to achieve victory in the games.[24] Also, the language is missiological. "Coworker" and "colaborer" is the role of a Timothy (1 Cor. 4:12), a Titus (2 Cor. 8:23), an Epaphroditus (Phil. 2:25), and a Clement (4:3).

Female apostles, prophets, teachers, and evangelists can be grouped under the rubric of ministries of "the word" (*tē diakonia tou logou*, Acts 6:2). There is also another grouping of gifts that can be broadly classified as ministries of "serving" (literally, "to serve tables" [*diakonein trapezais*], Acts 6:2). This also fits the distinction between ministries of "speaking" and ministries of "serving" found in 1 Peter 4:11.

Those engaged in service ministries primarily attended to the physical needs of the local body of believers (Acts 6:1–6;

---

[24]See H. G. Liddell, R. Scott, and H. S. Jones, *A Greek-English Lexicon*, s.v. "*synathleō*."

11:27–30; Rom. 2:7).[25] The title "deacon" was the early church's recognition of the leadership such believers provided. In the church at Philippi, for instance, one of two identified leadership positions in the church was that of deacon (Phil. 1:1).

Women are readily labeled deacons in the New Testament. Phoebe, for example, is commended by Paul as a "deacon of the church at Cenchrea" (Rom. 16:1 AT).[26] From the list of qualifications for women deacons in 1 Timothy 3:11, it is plain that this was not an isolated role: "[Male] deacons, likewise, are to be worthy of respect, not double-tongued, not indulging in much wine, not greedy for gain.... Women [deacons], likewise, are to be worthy of respect, not malicious talkers, but temperate and trustworthy in everything" (1 Tim. 3:8, 11 AT).[27]

The post-apostolic church not only recognized the role of women deacons but continued the tradition with enthusiasm. Pliny (governor of Bithynia in the early years of the second century) tried to obtain information by torturing two female deacons (*Letters* 10.96.8). In the third, fourth, and fifth centuries virtually every Eastern father and church document mentions women deacons with approval.[28] The *Didascalia Apostolorum* (a third-century book of church order) spells out their duties. The

---

[25]Although the noun *diakonos* is not used in Acts 6:1–6, the activity of caring for those with material needs is certainly present.

[26]That Paul is using *diakonos* for an official capacity is clear from the technical language of commendation: "I commend to you our sister Phoebe, a deacon of the church at Cenchrea." Cf. 1 Corinthians 16:15–18, 2 Corinthians 8:18–24, and Philippians 2:19–30. See my article "A Letter of Apologetic Self-Commendation: 2 Corinthians 1:8–7:16," *Novum Testamentum* 31 (1989): 142–64.

[27]Some translate *gynaikas* in 1 Timothy 3:11 as "their wives." This is highly unlikely for several reasons. First, the grammar does not support it. If Paul were turning to the wives of deacons, he would have written "*their* women likewise" (*gynaikas tas autōn hosautōs*) or have included some other indication of marital status. Second, there are no parallel requirements for the wives of overseers in the immediately preceding verses. Why would Paul highlight the wives of one group of leaders and ignore the wives of another? Third, to read "likewise their wives must ..." is to assume that all deacons' wives possessed the requisite gifting and leadership skills. This plainly contradicts Pauline teaching elsewhere (see 1 Cor. 12:11). For further discussion, see my *Women Leaders and the Church*, 60–64.

[28]Women were also ordained to the diaconate in Italy and Gaul, but their numbers did not match those in the Eastern churches. For further discussion, see P. Hünermann, "Conclusions Regarding the Female Diaconate," *Theological Studies* 36 (1975): 329.

Apostolic Constitutions (a fourth-century work about pastoral and liturgical practice) includes an ordination prayer for them (9.82; 16.134–136). And *Canon #15* of the Council of Chalcedon (fifth century) details the ordination process for women deacons and places them in the ranks of the clergy.[29]

The practicality of the work of female deacons is not to be overlooked. Women could gain entry into places that were taboo for men and perform activities that would be thought inappropriate for a male minister.[30] The duties of female deacons in the post-apostolic period were quite varied. They taught children and youth, evangelized unbelieving women, discipled new believers, visited the sick, cared for the ailing, administered communion to the shut-ins, and disbursed funds to the needy. In the worship service they served as doorkeepers, assisted with the baptism of women, and administered communion as the occasion arose.[31]

Another group of women singled out for their distinctive service to the life of the Ephesian church is that of widows: "No widow may be put on the list of widows unless she is over sixty, the wife of one husband, known for her good works, such as raising her children, showing hospitality, washing the feet of the saints, helping those in trouble, and devoting herself to every kind of good deed" (1 Tim. 5:9–10 AT).

There is every reason to think that Paul is describing a ministerial role. To start with, he lists requirements that parallel the qualifications for an overseer (or bishop), elder, and deacon. The widow must have been the wife of one husband, raised her children well, be well-known for her good deeds, and have a repu-

---

[29]We also possess fourth- through sixth-century inscriptions that name women deacons from a range of geographical locations. Two are from Jerusalem, two are from Italy and Dalmatia, one is from the island of Melos, one is from Athens, and ten are from the Asian provinces of Phrygia, Cilicia, Caria, and Nevinne. See R. Gryson, *The Ministry of Women in the Early Church* (Collegeville, Minn.: Liturgical Press, 1976), 90–91; and D. R. MacDonald, "Virgins, Widows, and Paul in Second Century Asia Minor," *Society of Biblical Literature Seminar Papers* 16 (Atlanta: Scholars Press, 1979), 181, note 11.

[30]Women in the early centuries were able to take advantage of their greater social mobility to visit friends and set up networks for evangelism. See Wendy Cotter, "Women's Authority Roles in Paul's Churches: Countercultural or Conventional," *Novum Testamentum* 36 (1994): 369.

[31]See *Didascalia Apostolorum.*

tation for hospitality (cf. 1 Tim. 3:2, 12; Titus 1:6, 8). Also, these widows are designated by the technical term for the official enrollment of a recognized group (*katalegesthō*, verse 9; see the RSV, JB, REB; versus the NIV "a list").[32] Moreover, Paul instructs that these widows be financially compensated for their time (verse 3, *timaō* = "to reward," "to pay";[33] see 1 Tim. 5:17); and he speaks of "broken pledges," suggesting that these women took a vow of widowhood in which they pledged full-time service to Christ (1 Tim. 5:11–12).

The corrective nature of Paul's instruction in 1 Timothy 5 indicates that a widows' ministry had been in place for some time. The length of Paul's corrective reveals that the ministry had gotten off track (perhaps because of an unexpected growth in the number of widows at Ephesus) and was in need of clear protocols.

Paul's list of qualifications provides an insight into the nature and scope of ministering widows. Among the good deeds listed are showing hospitality, washing the feet of the saints, and helping those in trouble (1 Tim. 5:10). Hospitality was something the church became well-known for early on—especially since there was little by way of decent accommodations for the average traveler. Foot washing was a common courtesy extended to guests attending a meal in one's home. The order of hospitality followed by foot washing suggests that one piece of the widow's job description included providing food and lodging for Christians on the road. "Helping those in trouble" can be more literally translated "helping those persecuted for their faith" (*thlibō* = "to press," "to oppress").[34] What form this help took is difficult to determine. It could have involved visiting and caring for those in prison, providing shelter for those fleeing persecution, or meeting the basic needs of those who had lost family and jobs because of their commitment to Christ.[35]

The widow's job description may also have included caring for orphans, which would explain the good-parenting

---

[32]See Liddell, Scott, and Jones, *A Greek-English Lexicon*, s.v. "*katalegō*."

[33]See Liddell, Scott, and Jones, *A Greek-English Lexicon*; W. Bauer, F. W. Danker, W. F. Arndt, and F. W. Gingrich, *A Greek-English Lexicon of the New Testament and Other Early Christian Literature*, 3d ed., s.v. "*timaō*."

[34]See Liddell, Scott, and Jones, *A Greek-English Lexicon*, s.v. "*thlibō*."

[35]See my *Women Leaders and the Church*, 65–67.

requirement. House-to-house visitation is suggested by Paul's criticism that younger widows (with too much time on their hands) were "going about from house to house . . . saying things they ought not to" (1 Tim. 5:13). "Saying things they ought not to" points to a teaching role, perhaps along the lines of what is found in Titus 2:3–4. Some traditionalists think that Paul is targeting female busybodies in 1 Timothy 5:13. The typical Greek idioms are, however, missing. "To mind one's own affairs" (*prassein ta idia*, 1 Thess. 4:11), "to meddle in the affairs of others" (*periergazesthai*, 2 Thess. 3:11), or similar phraseology is what one would have expected if mere nosiness were the problem.

Ministering widows flourished in the post-apostolic period. The nature of their ministry was decidedly pastoral. Their duties included praying for the church, teaching the basics of the faith, showing hospitality, caring for the sick, fasting, prophesying, and caring for the needs of destitute widows and orphans.[36] Polycarp called them "God's altar" (*To the Philippians* 4:3), and Clement of Alexandria ranked them after elders, bishops, and deacons (*Paidagōgos* 3.12.97; *Homily* 9.36.2).

The early church was not unique in recognizing the ministry potential of its seniors. Older women (and men) took up leadership roles in the Essene communities ("the woman [shall raise her voice and say] the thanksgivings . . . and she shall stand in the council of the elder men and women").[37]

WOMEN LEADERS IN THE BIBLE

Gifting, however, does not necessarily make a leader. While women appear in a variety of ministry roles in the Bible, the key questions are whether these roles warrant the label of leadership—especially leadership over men—and whether the community of faith affirms women in these roles. The answer on both accounts is a decided yes!

---

[36]See *Canons of Hippolytus*, Canon #59, *Didascalia Apostolorum*, and *Apostolic Constitutions* 2.35.2; 3.3.2. For further discussion, see B. Thurston, *The Widows: A Women's Ministry in the Early Church* (Minneapolis: Fortress, 1989), 54.

[37]Dead Sea Scrolls *Ritual of Marriage* (4Q502, fragment 24). The church's charitable support of widows was a natural outgrowth of Judaism's concern for and ministry to the orphan, the widow, and the sojourner. See Bruce Winter, "Providentia for the Widows of 1 Timothy 5:3–16," *Tyndale Bulletin* 39 (1988): 31–32, 87.

Women Leaders in Old Testament Times

As early as Mosaic times, women were affirmed as leaders _under Moses_ of God's people. Miriam, for example, was sent by the Lord (along with her two brothers) to "lead" (Masoretic Text, _he^{ce}litîkā_; Septuagint, _anēgagon_) the people of Israel during the wilderness years (Mic. 6:4). She was held in such high regard as a leader that the Israelites would not travel until she was at the helm (Num. 12:1–16). Micah 6:4 is particularly important because it shows that Miriam's role was traditionally and historically understood as a leadership role by the community of faith for some five hundred years.

Deborah's role during the pre-monarchical period is described in leadership language. According to Judges 4:4–5, she held court in the hill country of Ephraim between Ramah and Bethel, and men and women alike came to her to have their disputes settled. Her stature as a judge was high and her leadership exemplary. She adjudicated intertribal quarrels and local disputes that proved too difficult for the tribal judges. Her ability to command was also a matter of record. When the tribes of Israel were incapable of unifying themselves against their northern Canaanite oppressors, Deborah not only united them but also led them on to victory (Judg. 4:5–24). The commander of her troops simply refused to go into battle without her (4:8). In her honor, the community of faith named the site of her ministry _mer d^ebôrâ_ or "Palm of Deborah" (4:5).

Huldah provided similar leadership during the time of the divided monarchy. Although there were other prestigious prophets around (such as Jeremiah and Zephaniah), it was Huldah's counsel concerning the Book of the Law that King Josiah sought out. And it was her warning to obey everything written therein that brought about the well-known religious reforms of the seventh century B.C. (2 Kings 22; 2 Chron. 34:14–33).

During the postexilic period the female prophet Noadiah was one of a number of Jewish prophets hired by Sanballat to thwart Nehemiah's efforts to rebuild the temple walls (Neh. 6). The fact that Noadiah is only one of two prophets mentioned by name in Israel's traditions is indicative of her stature as a prophetic leader at that time (6:14, albeit not an exemplary leader, but then neither was her male colleague, Shemaiah [6:10–13]).

Women in the ancient Near East provided political leadership. Some were heads of state. Athaliah, for example, ruled Israel from 842–836 B.C., and Salome Alexandra reigned from 76–67 B.C. Egypt and Ethiopia had a long history of queens as reigning monarchs. Two of the best known are Cleopatra, the effective ruler in Egypt from 51–31 B.C., and Candace, the queen of Ethiopia in the first century A.D. (see Acts 8:27).

Politically astute women are likewise easy to identify. The appeal of Zelophehad's daughters for a woman's right to inherit matched the best legal argumentation of the day (Num. 36:1–13). Bathsheba's efforts to gain the kingship for Solomon showed fine diplomacy. Jezebel, daughter of the priest-king of Tyre and Sidon and wife of Israel's reigning king (Ahab), was infamous for her political maneuverings. The Queen of Sheba's savvy as a negotiator was legendary (1 Kings 10:1–10; 2 Chron. 9:1–9), and Queen Esther's word commanded instant obedience (Est. 4:15–17; 9:29–32).

It is common for traditionalists to refer to such women as "exceptions." When God could not find a willing man to lead (so the argument goes), he resorted to using women. It is true that there were far fewer women leaders than their male counterparts. But this was not because of any intrinsic inferiority, basic incompetence, or gender unsuitability. There is no hint in the Bible that female leadership is wrong. The reality was that their domestic chores (especially the bearing and raising of children) left women little time to pursue public roles. Those involved in the public arena were generally upper-class women who were able to delegate their domestic tasks to other women in the household.[38]

Women Leaders in New Testament Times

There was also no lack of women leaders in the early church. This is not surprising, given the many women who responded to the gospel message. Luke records Mary the mother of Jesus and "the women" as among the 120 empowered by the Holy Spirit for witness in Jerusalem, in Judea and Samaria, and beyond (Acts 1:7–8, 14–15; 2:1–4). This empowerment fulfilled what was spoken by the prophet Joel: "In the last days, God

---

[38]See my *Women Leaders and the Church*, 94–96.

says, I will pour out my Spirit on all people. Your sons and daughters will prophesy.... Even on my servants, both men and women, I will pour out my Spirit in those days" (Acts 2:17, quoting Joel 2:28).

Male leaders were more numerous, but virtually every leadership role that names a man also names a woman. The only role lacking specific female names are overseer/bishop (unless the overseer/bishop was the leader of the house church). *But then male names are lacking as well.* In fact, there are more women named as leaders than men: Phoebe as "deacon" (Rom. 16:1–2), and Mary (Acts 12:12), Lydia (16:15), Chloe (1 Cor. 1:11), and Nympha (Col. 4:15) as overseers of house churches. This was partly a carryover from the involvement of women in the top leadership positions in the cults. For example, women served continuously as high priests of the imperial cult in Asia from the first century A.D. until the middle of the third century. Since there was only one high priest in any single city at one time, the consistent naming of women in this leadership role is especially significant. For example, during Paul's church-planting efforts in Ephesus, Iuliane served as high priestess of the imperial cult in Magnesia, a city fifteen miles southeast of Ephesus.[39] Women also served as civil servants and public officers. For instance, Menodora (first century A.D.) at one time or another served as magistrate, priestess, and *dekaprotos* (an official concerned with public revenues and the collection of taxes) of the city of Sillyon (Pisidia, Asia).[40]

---

[39]Inscriptions dating from the first century until the mid-third century place these women in Ephesus, Cyzicus, Thyatira, Aphrodisias, Magnesia, and elsewhere. See R. A. Kearsley, "Asiarchs, Archiereis, and the Archiereiai of Asia," *Greek, Roman and Byzantine Studies* 27 (1986): 183–92.

[40]A recent traditionalist essay by Steven M. Baugh ("A Foreign World: Ephesus in the First Century," in *Women in the Church: A Fresh Analysis of 1 Timothy 2:9–15*, eds. Andreas J. Köstenberger, Thomas R. Schreiner, and H. Scott Baldwin [Grand Rapids: Baker, 1995], 43–44) contends that female high priestesses of Asia were young girls who did not serve in and of their own right. Their position (he claims) was analogous to the private priestesses of Hellenistic queens (that is to say, not a public role serving both genders) and was merely honorific (a nominal position of no real substance given to the daughters and wives of the municipal elite).

Epigraphical evidence indicates otherwise. Iuliane, for example, served as high priestess of the imperial cult long before her husband did. Also, many inscriptions naming women as high priestesses do not name a father or husband. In the case of those that do, there was prestige attached to being a relative of a high priestess (and hence the naming of husbands, sons, and so forth). Then too, the majority of

For women in the early church, location played a signifi-cant role. The more Romanized the area, the more visible the leadership of women.[41] Since Paul's missionary efforts focused on the major urban areas of the Roman Empire, it is not at all surprising that most of the women named as leaders in the New Testament surface in the Pauline churches.[42]

Patron of a House Church

Most of the ministry roles in the early church had a leader-ship dimension to them. The *patron* of a house church had dis-tinct leadership responsibilities. As noted earlier, the homeowner in Greco-Roman times was in charge of any group that met in his or her domicile and was legally responsible for the group's activities. Moreover, households in the first century included not only the immediate family and relatives but also slaves, freed-men and freedwomen, hired workers, and even tenants and partners in a trade or craft. This meant that the female head of the house had to possess good administrative and management

---

women who served as high priestess were hardly young girls. Vestal virgins were the single exception. Delphic priestesses, on the other hand, had to be at least fifty years old; they came from all social classes and served a male god and his adher-ents. See Riet Van Bremen, "Women and Wealth," in *Images of Women in Antiquity*, eds. A. Cameron and A. Kuhrt (Detroit: Wayne State Univ. Press, 1987), 231–41. Finally, the position of high priestess was hardly nominal. Priests and priestesses were responsible for maintaining the sanctuary, carrying out its rituals and cere-monies, and protecting its treasures and gifts. Liturgical functions included ritual sacrifice, pronouncing the prayer or invocation, and presiding at the festivals of the deity. See Kearsley's carefully documented study, mentioned in the previous note.

The primary difficulty with Baugh's study (which confined itself to Ephesian inscriptions and data) is that it is not broad enough to accurately reflect the religious and civic roles of first-century women in either Asia or in the Greco-Roman Empire as a whole. To ignore the oriental cults (especially Isis) and their impact on women's roles is particularly egregious. See the detailed discussion and presentation of the evidence in my *Women Leaders and the Church*, 31–38.

[41]See Meeks, *The First Urban Christians*, 23–25.

[42]Virtually all the churches Paul planted were in heavily Romanized cities, where the population was a mix of Latin- and Greek-speaking people. Thessalonica, Corinth, and Ephesus, for instance, were provincial capitals. Philippi was a leading city in the province of Macedonia. Cenchrea housed a Roman naval station. Rome was the hub of the empire, so it should come as no surprise that so many of the lead-ers Paul greeted in the Roman church were women (Rom. 16). See my *Women Lead-ers and the Church*, 50.

skills. Paul, for this reason, places great emphasis on a person's track record as a family leader, for it is a definite indicator of church leadership potential (1 Tim. 3:4–5; 5:14). In fact, the term used for the female head of the household (*oikodespotein*, "to be household master" or "to be a ruler over the house," 1 Tim. 5:14) is much stronger than that used of the male (*prostēnai*, "to lead," "to guard," "to protect," "to care for," 1 Tim. 3:5).[43]

Prophet

Prophet was also a recognized leadership role. It was not an impromptu, uncontrollable movement of the Spirit (as some have argued). Luke makes this plain when he identifies the leadership of the church in Antioch as "prophets and teachers" (Acts 13:1–3). Moreover, Paul teaches that prophecy was subject to the control of the prophet (1 Cor. 14:29–33).

Some traditionalists claim that prophecy was a less "authoritative" activity (to use their language) than other forms of ministry (such as teaching, discernment of spirits, pastoring, or administration), and so women were able to prophesy in the early church. Yet the biblical evidence indicates otherwise. Prophecy was exercised in the context of public (not private) worship ("when you [both men and women] gather," 1 Cor. 14:26). And the prophet's job description included such corporate leadership activities as conviction of sin (1 Cor. 14:24), instruction (1 Cor. 14:19, *katēcheō*), exhortation (1 Cor. 14:31), and guidance (Acts 13:3–4; 16:6). In point of fact, it was to "God's holy apostles and prophets" that "the mystery of Christ has now been revealed by the Spirit" (Eph. 3:5). In a very real sense, therefore, the New Testament prophet carried on the "Thus saith the Lord" task of the Old Testament prophet. This is why Paul can call their utterances "revelation" (*apokalyphthē*, 1 Cor. 14:29–30) and why the fourth-century church historian Eusebius ranked Philip's four daughters "among the first stage in the apostolic succession."[44]

Some traditionalists argue that first-century female prophets were subject to the male leadership of the church. Yet Paul treats the prophetic activity of women as identical to the prophetic activity of men (1 Cor. 11:4–5). Plus, he states that

---

[43]See Liddell, Scott, and Jones, *A Greek-English Lexicon*, s.v. "*prostēnai*."

[44]Eusebius, *History of the Church* 3.37.1.

prophecy is subject to the control of the individual prophet (and not to some outside source, 1 Cor. 14:32).

Other traditionalists claim that the New Testament prophet differed from the Old Testament prophet in that the word of the latter was wholly authoritative and that of the former was not; the fact that the New Testament prophet had to be evaluated (1 Cor. 14:29) indicates that his or her word was merely a Spirit-prompted utterance with no guarantee of divine authority in its details.[45] To say this, however, is to overlook the equal (if not stricter) testing of the Old Testament prophet. The word of an Old Testament prophet was not true under the following circumstances: if it did not come to pass (Deut. 18:21–22), if it conflicted with God's covenant with Israel (Deut. 13:1–5), if it did not encourage obedience and moral living (Mic. 3:11), or if it contained a message of peace and prosperity (Jer. 28:8–9). The testing of Hananiah in Jeremiah 28 is a classic example of the evaluative process in Old Testament times.

Teacher

The question of whether there were women in the early church who publicly taught men is the primary bone of contention between traditionalists and egalitarians. This is because traditionalists identify public teaching with authoritative, official activity.

There most definitely were *women teachers* around in Paul's time. Priscilla instructed Apollos in the "way of the Lord" (Acts 18:24–26), the female prophets at Corinth instructed the congregation (cf. 1 Cor. 11:5 and 14:19), and the older women in the Cretan church taught the younger women (Titus 2:3–5).

The leadership component of the New Testament teacher is unmistakable. The gift of teaching comes after apostleship and prophecy in one spiritual gift list (1 Cor. 12:28), is inseparably linked with the gift of pastoring (literally "shepherding") in another ("pastor-teacher," Eph. 4:11),[46] and is part of the job

---

[45]See D. A. Carson, "'Silent in the Churches': On the Role of Women in 1 Corinthians 14:33b–36," in *Recovering Biblical Manhood and Womanhood*, 153.

[46]Pastoring in the New Testament is inseparable from teaching. This is clear from Ephesians 4:11, where the two nouns *poimenas* and *didaskalous* have a single article and are connected by *kai*. This arrangement of the grammatical pieces serves to conceptually unite the two ideas and should be translated "pastor-teachers." For discussion, see Maximilian Zerwick, *Biblical Greek* (Rome: Pontifical Biblical Institute, 1963), #184.

description of a prophet in still another ("to instruct" [*katēcheō*], 1 Cor. 14:19).

So how does one avoid the conclusion that women instructed men? Some traditionalists do so by distinguishing between public and private, authoritative and nonauthoritative, and formal and informal types of instruction—female teaching being of the latter sorts. Priscilla's instruction of Apollos was private, teaching was only incidental to the prophetic role at Corinth (and hence nonauthoritative), and the instruction provided by the older women at Crete was informal (so the argument goes).

Such distinctions, however, are decidedly modern ones. The New Testament knows no such distinctions. Teaching was an integral part of every facet of church life. Everyone in the congregation was expected to be able to teach (Col. 3:16; Heb. 5:12). Also, to make such distinctions is to lose the essentially charismatic nature of the New Testament teaching role. When the church at Corinth gathered for worship, it was taken for granted that both men and women would *verbally* instruct one another ("a hymn, a teaching, a revelation, a tongue, or an interpretation," 1 Cor. 14:26 AT).

Some traditionalists would make a distinction between the Greek term *didaskō* (which, it is argued, denotes authoritative, official teaching) and other Greek terms for instruction (*katēcheō*, *ektithemai*). One difficulty, though, is that once again the New Testament itself draws no such distinctions. At Corinth both men and women are instructed to bring a teaching (*didachē*) to the worship service. The congregation at Colosse is called to be teaching (*didaskontes*) one another (Col. 3:16). Timothy is instructed to devote himself to teaching (*didaskalia*) the church at Ephesus (1 Tim. 4:13). Antioch chose its missionaries from among the ranks of prophets and teachers (*didaskaloi*, Acts 13:1–2). The older women at Crete are told to teach well (*kalodidaskalous*) the younger women (Titus 2:3). And an overseer was expected to be able to teach (*didaktikon*, 1 Tim. 3:2).

It is true that Priscilla is said to have "expounded" (*exethento*), not "taught" (*edidaxe*), the way of God to Apollos (Acts 18:26). But this is the same term Luke uses for Paul's preaching to Jews in Rome ("he expounded" [*exetitheto*], Acts 28:23). It is also true that the term for prophetic instruction in

1 Corinthians 14:19 is *katēcheō*, not *didaskō*. But *katēcheō* and *didaskō* are virtual synonyms in the New Testament. Paul, for example, speaks of being taught (*katēchoumenos*) by the law (Rom. 2:18), and he commands the Galatian believers to share all good things with their teacher (*ho katēchoumenos*, Gal. 6:6). Luke uses *katēcheō* and *didaskō* interchangeably in Acts 18:25. Apollos had been taught" (*katēchēmenos*) the way of the Lord, and he in turn taught (*edidasken*) about Jesus. So to draw a distinction between different Greek terms for instruction at this particular stage in the church's development is exegetically wrongheaded.

Deacon and Overseer

Were there any female deacons or overseers? Euodia and Syntyche are described in language that places them squarely in the ranks of one of these two positions in the Philippian church: "To all the saints in Christ Jesus at Philippi, together with the overseers and deacons" (Phil. 1:1). Otherwise Paul would have had no need to make a public appeal to a third party (the enigmatic "yokefellow") to help these women work out their differences: "I plead with Euodia and I plead with Syntyche to agree with each other in the Lord. Yes, and I ask you, loyal yokefellow, help these women" (4:2–3 NIV). To begin with, it is very rare for Paul to name names in his letters. For him to do so here is indicative of the stature of these two women within the community of faith. Paul speaks early on in the letter about the current disunity of the Philippian congregation (2:1–18). For him to go on and specifically urge Euodia and Syntyche (whom he names as coworkers and partners in the work of the gospel) to be of "the same mind in the Lord" (4:2 NRSV) indicates that their role was so distinctly a leadership one that their disagreement put the unity of the church in jeopardy.

In similar fashion Paul explicitly salutes Phoebe as a deacon of the church in Cenchrea: "I commend to you Phoebe our sister, who is a deacon [*diakonon*] of the church in Cenchreae" (Rom. 16:1 NRSV). Yet one would not know it from reading some translations. The KJV, NKJV, NASB, TEV, and NIV translate *diakonon* as "servant." But this misses the official character of Paul's statement. Phoebe is the person Paul chose to deliver his letter to the Roman church—which is why Paul commands the

Roman church to "receive her in the Lord" and provide for her needs (16:2). Acceptance into a Christian community in Paul's day required the presentation of credentials. Paul does this quite consistently with other colleagues (2 Cor. 8:16–24; Eph. 6:21–22; Phil. 2:25–30; Col. 4:7–9), but it was especially important in Phoebe's case because Paul himself had never visited Rome.[47]

"Servant" would therefore hardly suffice.[48] "Fellow worker" (Phil. 2:25; 2 Cor. 8:23), "faithful servant" (Eph. 6:21–22), and "faithful minister" (Col. 4:7) might do for familiar leaders like Tychicus, Titus, and Epaphroditus (2 Cor. 8:16–24; Eph. 6:21–22; Col. 4:7–9). But "a deacon of the church in Cenchrea" (NLT) would have been essential for a virtual unknown like Phoebe (see also NEB, "who holds office in"; CEV, "a leader in").

Some traditionalists protest that the Greek term *diakonos* is masculine. But this overlooks the fact that there was simply no feminine form in use at this time ("deaconess" [*diakonissa*] is post-apostolic). Nor was it needed, for the masculine singular in Greek often did double duty. This was especially the case with nouns that designated a particular leadership role. Context made the gender clear.[49]

This was certainly the way the church fathers understood it. In the third century Origen states, "This text teaches with the

---

[47]One of the letter carrier's responsibilities was to read the letter to the congregation and to answer questions afterward. The carrier's credentials were, therefore, vitally important. They meant the difference between the person's ultimately being accepted or rejected.

[48]The Revised English Bible's "minister" for *diakonon* also falls short. "Minister" was not the officially recognized position it is today. Another unlikely translation is "deaconess" (RSV, JB, NJB, PHILLIPS), for the feminine term *diakonissa* was not in use until the Council of Nicea in A.D. 325 (Canon #19 of Nicea).

For further discussion, see A. A. Swidler, "Women Deacons: Some Historical Highlights," in *A New Phoebe: Perspectives on Roman Catholic Women and the Permanent Diaconate*, eds. V. Ratigan and A. Swidler (Kansas City, Mo.: Sheed & Ward, 1990), 81; V. V. FitzGerald, "The Characteristics and Nature of the Order of the Deaconess," in *Women and the Priesthood*, ed. Thomas Hopko (Crestwood, N.Y.: St. Vladimir's Seminary Press, 1983), 78.

[49]The leadership list in Ephesians 4:11 is a good example of the gender inclusivity of the Greek masculine: "Christ gave some to be apostles [*tous apostolous*], some to be prophets [*tous prophētas*], some to be evangelists [*tous euangelistas*], and some to be pastor-teachers [*tous poimenas kai didaskalous*] ..." AT. Women are named in each of these roles (Junias [Rom. 16:7]; Philip's daughters [Acts 21:9]; Syntyche and Euodia [Phil. 4:2–3]; and elderly widows at Ephesus [1 Tim. 5:9–10]).

authority of the apostle that even women are instituted deacons in the church" (*Homilies on Romans* [on Romans 10,17]). John Chrysostom (fourth century) observes that Paul "added her rank by calling her a deacon [*diakonon*]" (*Homilies on Romans* 31 [on Rom. 16:1]).

The Ephesian church most certainly had female deacons: "Women [deacons], likewise, are to be worthy of respect, not slanderers, temperate, and trustworthy in everything" (1 Tim. 3:11 AT). That Paul is speaking of women in a recognized leadership role is apparent not only from the listing of credentials but also from the fact that these credentials are the exact duplicates of those listed for male deacons in 1 Timothy 3:8–10. Also, the Greek word order of verses 8 and 11 is identical: "[Male] deacons likewise must be worthy of respect, not double-tongued, not given to much wine [*diakonous hosautōs semnous, mē dilogous, mē oinō*]. . . . Women likewise must be worthy of respect, not slanderers, temperate [*gynaikas hosautōs semnas, mē diabolous, nēphalious*]" (AT).

The post-apostolic writers understood Paul to be speaking of women deacons. Clement of Alexandria (second and third centuries) says, "For we know what the honorable Paul in one of his letters to Timothy prescribed regarding women deacons" (*Stromata* 3.6.53). And John Chrysostom (fourth century) talks of women who held the rank of deacon in the apostolic church (*Homilies on Timothy* 11 [on 1 Tim. 3:11]).

What about female elders? There are good reasons for thinking that Paul is talking about just such a leadership role in 1 Timothy 5:9–10. First, Paul limits the role to women age sixty or older (verse 9), which fits the primary Greek meaning of *presbyteros* as "elderly." This is a carryover from Judaism, where the elders of the town (a civic role) were those who were considered wise by virtue of their age.[50] Second, he lists requirements that parallel the qualifications for elders found elsewhere in his writings. The widow must have been the wife of one husband, have raised her children well, be well-known for her good deeds, and

---

[50]The primary function of Jewish elders was that of community leaders. They held no official status in the local synagogue. This is quite different from Christian elders, who seem to have had some official standing in the early church. See Emil Schürer, *The History of the Jewish People in the Age of Jesus Christ*, rev. ed. (Edinburgh: T&T Clark, 1979), 3:87–107.

have a reputation for offering hospitality (cf. Titus 1:6, 8). Third, like an elder, she is to be remunerated for her ministry (verse 3, *timaō* = "to reward," "to pay";[51] cf. 1 Tim. 5:17).

Traditionalists typically argue that there are certain leadership qualifications that exclude women. "Able to teach" (1 Tim. 3:2) is only problematic for those who would say that women in the early church were forbidden from teaching men. "The husband of one wife" (AT), as a qualification for overseers (1 Tim. 3:2), deacons (1 Tim. 3:12), and elders (Titus 1:6), needs a closer look. Would Paul include such a qualification if he envisioned women serving in these capacities? The question is a good one. But a knowledge of the mores of a Greek city like Ephesus sheds important light. Greek married women simply were not prone to multiple marriages or illicit unions. But Greek men were. In fact, extramarital affairs were par for the Greek male but not tolerated for Greek women (because of the concern for legitimate sons). Also, the divorce rate among Greek men rivaled ours today.[52]

So the fact that Paul includes this qualification for male deacons (1 Tim. 3:12) and omits it for female deacons (1 Tim. 3:11) is exactly what one would expect. Anything else would be surprising—unless, of course, Paul had the widow in view. A widow back then was inclined to remarry—as Paul himself acknowledged (1 Cor. 7:8–9). Therefore Paul includes "the wife of one husband" for them (1 Tim. 5:9, NRSV text note). It was the widow who was content to remain a widow who would serve the church with the kind of single-minded devotion that effective ministry in the first century required (1 Cor. 7:32–35).

Beyond "the husband of one wife" there are no qualifications that are male-specific. Elderly widows and female deacons are called to exhibit the same character and lifestyle qualities as their male counterparts (1 Tim. 3:8–9, 11). In fact there are some traits more likely to be possessed by women than by men. For instance, hospitality would be more natural for Greco-Roman

---

[51]See Liddell, Scott, and Jones, *A Greek-English Lexicon;* Bauer, Danker, Arndt, and Gingrich, *A Greek-English Lexicon,* s.v. "*timaō.*"

[52]For further discussion, see J. Neuffer, "First Century Cultural Backgrounds in the Greco-Roman Empire," in *Symposium on the Role of Women in the Church,* ed. J. Neuffer (Plainfield, N.J.: General Council of the Seventh-day Adventist Church, 1984), 69.

women. The ability to care for one's household (as indicative of ability to care for the church) would also be a good fit. In fact (as was noted earlier), the term used for the leadership role of the woman of the household (*oikodespotein*, "to be household master," 1 Tim. 5:14) is much stronger than the term applied to the man (*prostēnai*, "to lead," "to guide," "to care for," 1 Tim. 3:5).

So if there were no first-century leadership activities that were distinctively male in character, why the current impasse with reference to women in leadership? And if there were no qualifications that would prohibit women from serving as leaders, why do some persist in excluding them today?

WOMEN AND AUTHORITY

The issue for many traditionalists is not whether the Spirit gifts women in the same way that he gifts men, but whether a particular activity is authoritative or not. If it is, then women are excluded. To publicly teach is to exercise authority; to publicly preach is to exercise authority; to corporately lead is to exercise authority (whether one gives to the leader the name "elder," "deacon," "bishop," "pastor," "chairperson," or "president"). Therefore, women cannot publicly teach, preach, or lead in any way. Why? Because God created the male alone to lead, and to lead is to exercise authority. To be male, then, is to possess and exercise authority, and to be female is not to possess and exercise authority.

But is this truly the case from a biblical perspective? It is one thing to hold a conviction; it is another thing to find biblical support for it. And quite frankly, one is hard-pressed to find a biblical link between local church leadership and "authority" (*exousia*).[53] The New Testament writers simply do not make this

---

[53]Some traditionalists associate the Greek term *proistēmi* with "exercise of rule" or "authority" and cite 1 Thessalonians 5:12, 1 Timothy 3:4–5, and 1 Timothy 5:17 as examples. However, there is no lexical basis for this association. Johannes Louw and Eugene Nida (*Greek-English Lexicon of the New Testament: Based on Semantic Domains*, s.v. "*proistēmi*") list as meanings (1) "to guide," (2) "to be active in helping," (3) "to strive to." Cf. Bauer, Danker, Arndt, and Gingrich, *A Greek-English Lexicon*; Liddell, Scott, and Jones, *A Greek-English Lexicon*, s.v. "*proistēmi*."

The Greek term means literally "to stand before" or "to lead." It is used in contexts where the main idea is to shepherd or care for God's people (that is, it has a pastoral association). For example, in Romans 12:8 *proistēmi* is grouped with the spir-

connection. In fact, no leadership position or activity in the New Testament is linked with authority—with one exception. In 1 Corinthians 11:10 Paul states that a female's head covering is her "authority" (*exousia*) to pray and prophesy in corporate worship.[54]

Since the Greek term *exousia* ("authority") appears frequently in the New Testament (some one hundred times), the

---

itual gifts of offering practical assistance to those in need ("to give generously," "to show mercy"). Also, in 1 Timothy 3:4–5 to *proistamenon* the church is "to care for" (*epimelēsetai*) it. This fits with the role of a *prostatis* ("patron," "protector") in the culture of the day. See Liddell, Scott, and Jones, *A Greek-English Lexicon*, s.v. "*prostatis*."

[54]The Greek of 1 Corinthians 11:10 is quite straightforward: "For this reason a woman [who prays or prophesies] ought to have authority on her head [*exousian echein epi tēs kephalēs*] because of the angels." Interpretations, on the other hand, have been wide-ranging. They include theologically improbable ones like the following: A woman's head covering is (1) a shield from the prying eyes of angels, visitors, or other men in the congregation, (2) a charm or phylactery to ward off evil spirits or jealous angels, or (3) a sign of the woman's subjection to her husband (a grammatical and lexical impossibility). Those interpretations that rightly fit the context are the following: A woman's head covering is (1) a badge of her own dignity and power (to move about in public) or (2) a sign of her God-given authority (to pray and prophesy in worship).

Two things, however, are clear. First, 1 Corinthians 11:10 in its plain grammatical sense speaks of an authority that a woman herself possesses. Second, Paul's basic concern in the passage is with the proper attire of women when they pray or prophesy in public. This makes head covering as a sign of a woman's authority (or freedom) to engage in ministry activities the better option by far. It also fits with "because of the angels." The presence of angels as maintainers of order and propriety during worship was a commonly held Jewish belief (Dead Sea Scrolls *Charter for Israel in the Last Days* [1QSa 2.3–9]).

Some would argue that Paul is speaking of a woman's (or wife's) "control over her head" (that is, to keep the appropriate covering on it). The rationale is that every other New Testament use of the three-word construction—noun *exousia* + preposition *epi* + the genitive—means "to have authority *over*" (versus "to have authority *upon*"; see, for example, Craig Blomberg, *1 Corinthians*, The NIV Application Commentary Series [Grand Rapids: Zondervan, 1994], 212). One difficulty, however, is that this three-word construction appears only here in Paul's letters, so that there is no fair Pauline comparison to be made. Second, *exousia* + *epi* + the genitive in the Gospels does *not* have the uniform meaning of "to have authority over." When it is used of a physical location, it actually means "upon" and answers the question "Where?" Question: "Where does the Son of Man have authority to forgive sins?" Answer: "Upon earth" (Matt. 9:6; Mark 2:10; Luke 5:24). Matthew 28:18 makes this especially clear. Jesus tells his disciples that all authority has been given to him. Where? "*In* heaven" and "*on* earth." Third, "authority over her head" does not fit Paul's line of argument in 1 Corinthians 11:7–10. "A man," Paul argues, "ought not to have *a covering down over* his head because he is God's image and glory. The woman, however, is man's glory ... therefore, she ought to have *authority on* her head."

absence of a link with local church leadership is significant. Traditionalists might make the connection between local church leadership and authority, but the closest we come to it in the New Testament is Titus 2:15. This is where Paul tells Titus to "rebuke" the Cretan congregation "with all authority" (NIV). Even so, Titus's prerogative is not *exousia* ("authority"), but *epitagē* ("command"). Furthermore, Titus possessed this prerogative solely as Paul's deputy and not as a local church leader. Plus, because the Greek term *pas* (NIV, "all") lacks the article, the emphasis is on "each and every kind." So a better translation would be: "Rebuke with every form of command at your disposal."

A look at the relevant New Testament texts shows that it is the *church* that possesses authority and not particular individuals (or positions, for that matter). It is to the church that Jesus gives the "keys of the kingdom" (Matt. 16:19) and the authority to "bind" and "loose" (that is, enforce and waive, Matt. 18:18). It then becomes the church's responsibility to test and weigh prophetic utterances (1 Thess. 5:19–22; 1 Cor. 14:29), to choose missionaries (Acts 13:1–3) and church delegates (Acts 15:22–23; 20:4–5), to discipline (Matt. 18:20; 1 Cor. 5:4), and to reinstate (2 Cor. 2:7–8; cf. Matt 18:10–14). The church's authority comes from the power of the Lord Jesus present with believers gathered in his name (1 Cor. 5:4; Matt. 18:20) and from corporate possession of the "mind of Christ" (1 Cor. 2:16).[55]

Churches can, to be sure, choose individuals to represent their interests and to work on their behalf (Acts 6:1–7; 13:1–3; 15:2–3; 20:1–6). But in no way do these individuals exercise authority over the congregation. They are, rather, empowered to minister to the congregation and to equip it for ministry. As Paul states, "Christ gave some to be apostles, some to be prophets, some to be evangelists, and some to be pastor-teachers [*tous de poimenas kai didaskalous*], to prepare God's people for the work of the ministry [*eis ergon diakonias*]" (Eph. 4:11–12 AT).

The most frequent New Testament use of the Greek term *exousia* ("authority") is with reference to secular rulers. Both Paul and Peter call their respective congregations to submit to the political powers in authority over them ("ruling authorities" [*archais*

---

[55]See my article on "authority," *Dictionary of Paul and His Letters*, eds. Gerald F. Hawthorne, Ralph P. Martin, and Daniel G. Reid (Downers Grove, Ill.: InterVarsity Press, 1993), 54–59.

exousiais], Titus 3:1; "supreme" [*hyperechonti*], 1 Peter 2:13–17). For example, Paul tells the Roman church: "Everyone must submit themselves to the governing authorities [*exousiais hyperechousais*].... For rulers hold no terror for those who do right, but for those who do wrong" (Rom. 13:1, 3). Even here, though, the authority is divinely delegated. The authorities that exist have been established by God ("for there is no authority [*exousia*] except by God," Rom. 13:1; cf. John 19:10–11, "given from above").

What about the twelve apostles? Didn't Jesus invest them with authority? All three Gospel writers do record that the Twelve were sent out by Jesus with authority. But interestingly enough, it was an "authority [*exousian*] to drive out demons and to heal every disease and sickness" (Matt. 10:1; Mark 3:15; 6:7; Luke 9:1; 10:19) and not to preach and teach. The Twelve *were* sent out "to preach the good news" (Mark 3:14; Matt. 10:7; Luke 9:2), but authority is not mentioned in conjunction with this preaching. Yet it is all too common today to say that preaching is an authoritative activity.

What about the apostle Paul? Certainly he laid claim to apostleship and hence to authority, didn't he? He did indeed. Yet Paul rarely claims or makes reference to his apostolic authority. There are only two places where he does so—both in 2 Corinthians. "The Lord," Paul states, "gave [me] the authority [*exousian*] for building up the church and not for tearing it down" (2 Cor. 10:8; 13:10 AT). Also, while Paul does not hesitate to command when necessary (see 2 Thess. 3:6), his usual modus operandi is "to urge" (*parakaleō*) and not "to command" (*parangellō*). Moreover, although Paul does refer to his apostleship at the beginning of nine of his letters (Romans, 1–2 Corinthians, Galatians, Ephesians, Colossians, 1–2 Timothy, and Titus), he also declares himself to be a "slave" of Christ Jesus at the beginning of four (Romans, Philippians, Titus, and Philemon). Two letters, in fact, start with "Paul a slave" *and* Paul "an apostle" (Rom. 1:1, Titus 1:1)—which would suggest that "apostle" and "slave" (not "apostle" and "ruler") are two sides of the same coin.

Why is there so little mention of Paul's authority? The explanation is easy to find. Paul (along with the other New Testament writers) simply refused to buy into the top-down leadership style of the day. In 2 Corinthians 1:24 Paul told the Corinthians that his aim was not "to rule over" (*kyrieuomen*) their faith but "to work alongside" (*synergoi*) them. Peter similarly exhorted the leadership of the Asian churches to be "shepherds of God's flock ... *not* ruling over [*katakyrieuontes*] them but being examples to the flock" (1 Peter 5:2–3 AT, emphasis added).

In this respect, Paul and the other apostles are merely being obedient to the teaching of Jesus. For when James and John came to Jesus to ask for positions of power in his future kingdom, Jesus reminded his disciples that Roman leaders "rule over" (*katakurieuousin*) and "exercise authority over" (*katexousiazousin*) them. But it was not to be that way with them (Matt. 20:25–26). Traditionalists would claim that Jesus was warning against a misuse or abuse of power. But neither the Greek terms nor the context suggests this. A negative sense is not inherent in either term. Both merely denote the possession and exercise of authority (*katakurieuō* = "to gain or exercise dominion over or against someone"; *katexousiazō* = "the exercise of rule or authority").[56]

But doesn't Paul himself call for submission to local church leadership? And doesn't submission assume the exercise of authority? There are indeed two New Testament passages that call for congregational submission. In Paul's first letter to the Corinthians, the congregation is called on "to submit" (*hypotassesthe*) to "such as these" (the household of Stephanas, 1 Cor. 16:16). In the letter to the Hebrews, the readers are instructed "to remember" (*mnēmoneuete*), "follow" (*peithesthe*), and "yield to" (*hypeikete*) their "leaders" (*hēgoumenoi*, Heb. 13:7, 17).[57]

What is sometimes overlooked, however, is the reason for the submission. In neither instance is the submission based on the possession of authority or the holding of an office. It is, rather, the appropriate response to the exercise of pastoral care. The "such as these" to whom the Corinthians were to submit were "everyone who joins in the work, and labors at it" (1 Cor. 16:16). And the leaders to whom the Hebrews were to submit were those who "keep watch over" (*agrypnousin*) them (Heb. 13:17).[58]

---

[56]Louw and Nida, *Greek-English Lexicon*; Liddell, Scott, and Jones, *A Greek-English Lexicon*, s.v. "*katakurieuō*" and "*katexousiazō*."

[57]*Hypeikō* is found only here in the New Testament. The verb means "to give way," "to yield." For example, in Homer's *Iliad* 16.305 it means "to make room for another person by yielding one's seat." "Obey" is therefore not an accurate translation.

[58]*Agrypneō* means "to watch over," "to stay alert," with the implication of continuous and wakeful concern. See Louw and Nida, *Greek-English Lexicon*, s.v. "*agrypneō*."

Undoubtedly this is why the New Testament writers do not use the Greek verb *hypakouō* ("to obey"). Instead, they use words that denote a voluntary deferring to another's wishes (see, for example, 1 Cor. 16:16, *hypotassēsthe* = "a voluntary act [middle voice] of deferring to the wishes of an equal"; Heb. 13:17, *peithesthe* = "to follow" and *hypeikete* = "to give way to").[59] The distinction is an important one. Obedience can be willingly or unwillingly given. It can also be demanded by someone of a person in a lesser position (for example, by one's boss). Submission, on the other hand, is the voluntary act of a free agent.

Does this speak to the issue of the ordination of women? Unfortunately, it does not. Both the term and the concept are lacking in the New Testament—with respect to both men and women. The idea of "commissioning" (setting apart, dedicating) for a particular ministry is what we find (generally through the laying on of hands). For example, the church at Antioch commissioned Saul and Barnabas as missionaries (Acts 13:1–3), elders were commissioned at Ephesus (1 Tim. 5:22), Timothy was commissioned as an evangelist (1 Tim. 4:14; 2 Tim. 1:6), and Paul was commissioned as an apostle to the Gentiles (Acts 9:17–19; 22:12–16). But this is a far cry from how churches use the term *ordain* today. In my denomination, for example, ordination authorizes a person to "preach the Word, administer the sacraments, and bear rule in the church."[60]

WOMEN LEADERS AND BIBLICAL LIMITS

If biblical authority resides in the church and not the leader and if women are commended in the New Testament as church leaders, on what basis do traditionalists exclude women from leadership? The Council on Biblical Manhood and Womanhood lists five primary New Testament passages: Matthew 10:1–42, 1 Corinthians 14:33–35, 1 Timothy 2:12, 1 Timothy 3:1–7, and Titus 1:5–9.[61] Matthew 10:1–42 is the passage where Jesus calls

---

[59]See Liddell, Scott, and Jones, *A Greek-English Lexicon*, s.v. "hypotassomai"; "peithomai"; "hypeikō"; Ceslas Spicq, *Theological Lexicon of the New Testament*, 3:424.

[60]*The Covenant Book of Worship*, Evangelical Covenant Church (Chicago: Covenant Press, 1981), 298.

[61]*CBMW News* 1 (2/1995): 1.

his twelve disciples to him and gives them authority to drive out evil spirits and to heal every disease and sickness. How exactly one gets from driving out evil spirits and healing diseases to the exclusion of women from leadership roles is far from clear. If these twelve men had been given authority to preach or teach, one could see the Council's logic (although one might not necessarily agree with it). But Jesus' disciples are not given this kind of authority. So the ambiguity remains.

Traditionalists typically argue that the very fact that Jesus was male and that the twelve people Jesus chose to be with him were males legislates male leadership for the church.[62] Although this is a common way of thinking today, once again it is not particularly logical. For Jesus did not merely choose twelve men but twelve *Jewish* men; he himself was not merely a male but a *Jewish* one. Yet no one argues that Jewish leadership is thereby legislated. *of Ruth, man. He chose Jews for a reason.*

There is also the biblical symbolism of twelve Jewish males to represent the twelve tribes. The twelve tribes of Israel will be judged by the Twelve (Matt. 19:28; Luke 22:30). The new Jerusalem will have twelve gates, twelve angels, and twelve foundations, and will rest on the foundations the names of the Twelve (Rev. 21:12, 14). Following traditionalist logic, future judgment of the *non*-Israelite would then be in the hands of the male leadership of the church. But it is not. Male leaders will not serve as judges in the future. Nor, for that matter, will female leaders. "Do you not know," Paul says, "that *the saints* will judge the world . . . and will judge angels?" (1 Cor. 6:2–3, emphasis added). But then this is what we saw in the previous section. The *church* possesses authority, and church leaders do not—be they male or female.

The Council on Biblical Manhood and Womanhood similarly points to the qualifications for overseers and elders in 1 Timothy 3:1–7 and Titus 1:5–9 as being gender-exclusive. But again, it is difficult to see how this excludes women. "Husband of one wife" has already been dealt with (see page 103). "Able to teach" and "to refute those who oppose sound teaching" (AT) are not gender-exclusive activities. The post-apostolic church

---

[62]See, for example, James I. Packer, "Let's Stop Making Women Presbyters," *Christianity Today* 35 (11 February 1991): 20; see also James A. Borland, "Women in the Life and Teachings of Jesus," in *Recovering Biblical Manhood and Womanhood,* 120.

esteemed a number of women who were gifted in doing just that (take Marcella, for example).[63]

To be honest, there are really only two New Testament passages that are worthy of consideration: 1 Corinthians 14:34–35, where women are commanded to be silent in the church, and 1 Timothy 2:12, where women (according to the NIV rendering) are not permitted to teach or to have authority over men. Of these two, 1 Timothy 2:11–15 is the one on which traditionalists typically fix their attention. For instance, a recent traditionalist publication offers the promising title *Women in the Church* but has as its subtitle *A Fresh Analysis of 1 Timothy 2:9–15*.[64] Hopefully, we have not reached the point where 1 Timothy 2:9–15 is the lone biblical text that informs and defines this issue.

1 Corinthians 14:34–35

These two verses certainly deserve attention, for they command the silence of women in the churches:

> Women should remain silent in the churches. They are not allowed to speak, but must be in submission, as the Law says. If they want to inquire about something, they should ask their own husbands at home; for it is disgraceful for a woman to speak in the church.

I cite the text in full here because traditionalists often stop at the end of verse 34 and miss the important qualifiers that follow. All of chapter 14 must also be looked at, or else Paul ends up flatly contradicting what he says earlier in the letter. According to 1 Corinthians 11:2–5, women were anything but silent, and Paul commends them for it: "I praise you [Corinthians] for remembering me in everything and for holding to the teachings, just as I passed them on to you. . . . Every woman who prays or prophesies . . ."

Some traditionalists dismiss the prophetic activity of women in 1 Corinthians 11: (1) Paul (in their opinion) was speaking only hypothetically, (2) the setting was not a formal one (and

---

[63]See Jerome, *Epistle* 127:2–7.

[64]*Women in the Church: A Fresh Analysis of 1 Timothy 2:9–15*, eds. Köstenberger, Schreiner, and Baldwin (Grand Rapids: Baker, 1995).

hence the prophecy not authoritative),[65] or (3) prophetic activity was vertical (talking to God and for God) versus horizontal (exercising authority over another person). Yet there is nothing at all hypothetical about the grammar, for Paul puts everything in the indicative (the mood of fact) and not in the subjunctive (the mood of possibility). Also, the setting is most assuredly formal (that is, public corporate worship). "We have no other practice— nor do the churches of God" (1 Cor. 11:16) indicates as much. Plus, there is nothing particularly vertical about prophetic activity. Prophecy, by definition, is a spiritual gift intended to build up the church (1 Cor. 14:4); it is exercised when believers "gather as a church" (1 Cor. 11:17; 14:26–33). Tongue speaking (without interpretation) may be vertical: "Those who speak in a tongue," Paul states, "do not speak to people but *to God*.... But those who prophesy speak *to people*" (1 Cor. 14: 2–3, emphasis added). So the burden of the interpreter is to explain what Paul means (and does not mean) by "women should remain silent in the churches" (1 Cor. 14:34).

Several things are clear from the context. First, the setting is public worship. "When the whole church gathers in one place" is the context for Paul's instruction (1 Cor. 14:23 AT; cf. 1 Cor. 14:26 and 11:17–18; 12:7). Second, the command for silence is not absolute. "When you gather," Paul states, "*each* has a psalm, a teaching, a revelation, a tongue, or an interpretation" (14:26a, emphasis added; cf. 1 Cor. 1:5). Had Paul intended to limit public involvement to men, he surely would have said so here. Instead, he emphasizes that women and men alike are to contribute to the upbuilding of the church (14:26b).

Third, Paul's comments are corrective (versus informational) in nature. The topic is the *orderly* speaking of participants during worship, and the problem is the current *disorderly* state of affairs. Paul begins and ends this block with a command that everything be done in a fitting and orderly way that ultimately strengthens the church (1 Cor. 14:26, 40), "for God is not a God of disorder but of peace" (14:33). At the top of Paul's agenda is the orderly contribution of verbal gifts (14:26, hymns, teachings, revelations, tongues, interpretations). Two or three at the most can

[65]See F. W. Grosheide, *The First Epistle to the Corinthians* (Grand Rapids: Eerdmans, 1953). Grosheide states that "women are allowed to prophesy but not when the congregation officially meets" (341–43).

speak, and then only one at a time. If the speaking is in tongues, there must be someone to interpret. If there is no interpreter, the speakers must speak only to themselves and God (14:26–28). If the speaker is a prophet, "the others" should weigh carefully what is said (14:29).[66] If a prophetic revelation comes to someone who is sitting down, the first speaker must yield the floor to that person (14:30–31).

Paul concludes with a word of rebuke addressed to the entire congregation. The pronouns are plural: "Did the word of God originate with *you*? Or are *you* the only people it has reached?" (1 Cor. 14:36 AT, emphasis added). Paul clearly foresees that some at Corinth will reject his correction because they think they are spiritually superior: "If someone thinks [*ei tis dokei* is a condition of fact] he or she is a prophet or spiritually gifted ..." (1 Cor. 14:37 AT). He therefore challenges the so-called spiritual elite to use their gifting to affirm that what he has been saying about orderly worship is "the Lord's command."

So what kind of disorderly speaking were the Corinthian women engaging in? Scholars lean toward one of three interpretations. Some think in terms of some form of inspired speech. Thus, Paul is restraining women from mimicking the ecstatic frenzy of certain pagan cults.[67] Or he is silencing women who speak in tongues without interpretation ("If there is no interpreter, the speakers should keep quiet in the church and speak to themselves and God" [1 Cor. 14:28]).[68] Or yet again, he is prohibiting women from taking part in evaluating prophetic speech

---

[66]It is not clear who "the others" are. They could be other prophets, the rest of the congregation, or those with the gift of discernment. The latter two options find support elsewhere in Paul's writings. In his first letter to the Thessalonians, he urges the congregation to test prophecies (with the intent to prove their genuineness, see 1 Thess. 5:21). And he pairs the gift of discernment with the gift of prophecy in 1 Corinthians 12:10.

Based on the context, the last option is the likely one. It is Paul's expectation that speaking in tongues will be followed by interpretation (1 Cor. 14:27–28), so it makes sense to think that prophecy would in turn be subjected to the scrutiny of those gifted to determine whether the speaking is truly from God.

[67]See Richard and Catherine Kroeger, "Pandemonium and Silence at Corinth," in *Women and the Ministries of Christ*," eds. Roberta Hestenes and Louis Curley (Pasadena, Calif.: Fuller Theol. Sem., 1979), 49–55; Richard and Catherine Kroeger, "Strange Tongues or Plain Talk," *Daughters of Sarah* 12 (1986): 10–13.

[68]See Joseph Dillow, *Speaking in Tongues: Seven Crucial Questions* (Grand Rapids: Zondervan, 1975), 170.

("Two or three prophets should speak, and the others should weigh carefully what is said" [1 Cor. 14:29]). Traditionalists tend to gravitate toward the last of these, for to evaluate the prophecies of men (so it is argued) would be for the woman to usurp the man's created role as leader.[69]

Others opt for some form of disruptive speech. The Corinthian women were publicly contradicting or embarrassing their husbands by questioning a particular prophecy or tongue.[70] Or women were chattering during worship and thus disturbing those around them.[71] Or yet again, women were flouting the social conventions of the day by assuming the role of a teacher.

One rather recent interpretation is that 1 Corinthians 14:34–35 is the traditionalist position of certain members of the Corinthian congregation, which Paul cites ("Let the women in the churches be silent") and then responds to in verse 36 ("What! Did the word of God originate with you Corinthians? Or are you the only people it has reached?" AT).[72]

---

[69]See James Hurley, "Did Paul Require Veils or the Silence of Women? A Consideration of 1 Corinthians 11:2–16 and 1 Corinthians 14:33b–36," *Westminster Theological Journal* 35 (1973): 190–220; E. Earle Ellis, "The Silenced Wives of Corinth (1 Corinthians 14:34–35)," in *New Testament Textual Criticism*, eds. E. J. Epp and Gordon Fee (Oxford: Clarendon, 1981), 216–18; Wayne Grudem, *The Gift of Prophecy in 1 Corinthians* (Lanham, Md.: University Press of America, 1982), 249–55; and Carson, "Silent in the Churches," 152.

[70]See W. F. Orr and J. A. Walther, *1 Corinthians*, Anchor Bible (Garden City, N.Y.: Doubleday, 1976), 312–13; C. K. Barrett, *A Commentary on the First Epistle to the Corinthians*, 2d ed., Harper's New Testament Commentaries (New York: Harper & Row, 1971; reprint ed. Peabody, Mass.: Hendrickson, 1987), 332. Cf. L. Ann Jervis, "1 Corinthians 14:34–35: A Reconsideration of Paul's Limitation of the Free Speech of Some Corinthian Women," *Journal for the Study of the New Testament* 58 (1995): 60–73.

[71]See G. Engel, "Let the Women Learn in Silence. Part II," *Expository Times* 16 (1904–05): 189–90; and Scott Bartchy, "Power, Submission, and Sexual Identity Among the Early Christians," in *Essays on New Testament Christianity*, ed. C. Wetzel (Cincinnati, Ohio: Standard, 1978), 68–70.

[72]See Neal Flanagan and Edwina Snyder, "Did Paul Put Down Women in 1 Corinthians 14:34–36?" *Biblical Theology Bulletin* 11 (1981): 1–12; Chris Ukachukwu Manus, "The Subordination of the Women in the Church: 1 Corinthians 14:33b–36 Reconsidered," *Revue Africaine de Theologie* 8 (1984): 183–95; David Odell-Scott, "Let the Women Speak in Church: An Egalitarian Interpretation of 1 Corinthians 14:33b–36," *Biblical Theology Bulletin* 13 (1983): 90–93; David Odell-Scott, "In Defense of an Egalitarian Interpretation of 1 Corinthians 14:34–36: A Reply to Murphy-O'Connor's Critique," *Biblical Theology Bulletin* 17 (1987): 100–103; Gilbert Bilezikian, *Beyond Sex Roles: What the Bible Says About a Woman's Place in Church and Family*, rev. ed. (Grand

Which is the correct interpretation? A closer look at
1 Corinthians 14:34–35 helps to narrow the options. It is clear
that Paul is addressing married women. The women who were
creating the disturbance are those who could "ask their own
husbands at home" (14:35). Some claim that "women should
remain silent" includes all women (married or otherwise).[73] This,
however, is not technically correct. While the Greek term *gynē*
can mean either "wife" or "woman," only the context determines which is correct. Here the context explicitly states that
these women were married (*ei de* + the indicative ["and since
they want" = the women of 14:34]).

It is further clear that Paul was targeting married women
as a subset of the Corinthian women as a whole. A quick look at
1 Corinthians 7 shows that the women of the church included
the married (1 Cor. 7:2–5), widows (7:8–9), divorcées (7:11, 15–
16), the engaged (7:36), and the never married (7:27–28). It is also
plain that the desire of these married women was to learn:
"Since they want to *learn* something" (*ei de* + *ti mathein thelousin*
= a condition of fact, 1 Cor. 14:35 AT). This rules out tongues,
prophecy, and the like. Paul is not addressing women who were
exercising their spiritual gifts by contributing a teaching, a revelation, a tongue, or other Spirit-inspired gift to the worship
experience (14:26). Nor is he speaking to women who were exercising their gift of discernment in evaluating the truthfulness of
the prophetic word (14:30). These were, rather, married women
in the congregation who were asking questions because they
wanted to learn ("let them ask," 14:35). Their fault was not in

Rapids: Baker, 1985), 151–52; Linda McKinnish Bridges, "Silencing the Corinthian
Men, Not the Women," in *The New Has Come*, eds. A. T. Neil and V. G. Neely (Wash-
ington, D.C.: Southern Baptist Alliance, 1989); Charles Talbert, "Biblical Criticism's
Role: The Pauline View of Women as a Case in Point," in *Unfettered Word*, ed. R. B.
James (Dallas: Word, 1987), 62–71.

Verse 36 begins with the particle *ē* (translated "What!" in the KJV and RSV),
which (it is argued) Paul uses to reject or refute what has come before. See Daniel
Arichea, "The Silence of Women in the Church: Theology and Translation in
1 Corinthians 14:33b–36," *Bible Translator* 46 (1995): 101–12. One difficulty is that there
is no indication that verses 34–35 are a quotation (as one finds elsewhere in 1 Corinthians [1 Cor. 6:12–13; 7:1b; 8:1b; 10:23]). In addition, while the particle *ē* can express disapproval, it is the double *ē ē* that functions in this way and not the single *ē* as in
1 Corinthians 11:36. See Liddell, Scott, and Jones, *A Greek-English Lexicon*, s.v. "*ē*."

[73]See, for example, Carson, "Silent in the Churches," 147, 151.

the asking per se, but in the corporate disorder that their asking was producing.

It is likewise plain that the questions of these women were directed at men other than their husbands, for Paul instructs them to ask their *own* men (*tous idious andras*). While today we might look askance at someone interrupting the preacher at a confusing spot in the sermon, at Corinth it would have involved interrupting a teaching, revelation, tongue, and the like (1 Cor. 14:26). To do so would have been considered shameful behavior in Greco-Roman society. Questions blurted out by women were not tolerated during pagan worship. Because the native cults were strictly regulated, such activity would most certainly have been frowned on. Even in the oriental cults, matters of worship were in the hands of the professional clergy (the priests and priestesses) and not the laity.[74]

Why would married women be the ones asking the questions? Wouldn't all women want to learn? The key is in grasping the educational limits of married Greco-Roman women. Formal instruction stopped for most girls at the marriageable age of fourteen (Greek) or sixteen to eighteen (Roman). Greek boys, by contrast, continued their education well into their twenties and did not marry until their thirties. A good liberal arts education was seen as crucial, if boys were going to develop into responsible male citizens. This meant that men brought a maturity to the marriage relationship that women did not have and that they were in a position to "rule," while women were not. Lower-class women, in particular, would not have been in a position to pursue a career path that involved formal instruction ("not many of you are wise by worldly standards," 1 Cor. 1:26). Add to this the all-consuming task of raising children and running a household, and we have a group who, tasting freedom in Christ to expand their minds, grabbed the opportunity—albeit in a less than suitable fashion.[75]

The fact that Paul concludes this section with a congregational rebuke regarding orderliness indicates that the Corinthian

---

[74]For further discussion, see my *Women Leaders and the Church*, 32.

[75]D. A. Carson calls this "unbearably sexist" ("Silent in the Churches," 147), but it is only so if judged by modern educational standards. It is crucial to read the text in light of first-century Greco-Roman culture and not twenty-first-century Western culture. For further cultural background, see my *Women Leaders and the Church*, 31–32.

leaders were encouraging a disorderly exercise of gifts and the questions that came in their wake. Consequently, the solution is not to fixate on one aspect of Paul's corrective ("Women should remain silent in the churches") and ignore the rest ("If they [the married women] want to inquire, they should ask their own husbands at home"). While the Corinthian women in their eagerness to learn may have been at fault back then, it could easily be a different group today.

This is as far as a plain reading of the text goes. There are several other aspects, however, that beg for clarification. First, what does "as in all the congregations of the saints" go with (1 Cor. 14:33b)? If it goes with what follows, then Paul is saying that the silence of women in the church is a matter of universal practice: "As in all the congregations of the saints, women should remain silent in the churches." If it goes with what precedes, then Paul is stating that orderly worship is a matter of universal practice: "God is not a God of disorder but of peace, as in all the congregations of the saints." Readers of the NIV will not know that this is an issue, for this version begins Paul's correction with "As in all the congregations of the saints" (14:33b) and does not even provide a footnote indicating a genuine ambiguity.[76]

Second, Paul does not specify to what or to whom these inquisitive women should "be in submission" (1 Cor. 14:34). And he states that women are to submit "as the law [*nomos*] says,"

---

[76]Both writing styles are equally Paul's practice. See, for example, Ephesians 5:1: "Be imitators of God, therefore, *as dearly loved children*"; and Ephesians 5:8: "*As children of light*, so walk" (emphasis added). Yet Paul's other appeals to universal practice appear only as a concluding point (emphasis added in these citations). "Timothy," Paul says, "will remind you of my way of life in Christ Jesus, *as I teach them everywhere in every church*" (1 Cor. 4:17 NRSV). "Each one should retain the place in life that the Lord assigned . . . and *so I command in all the churches*" (1 Cor. 7:17 AT). "If anyone wants to be contentious about this, we have no other practice—*nor do the churches of God*" (1 Cor. 11:16). "For God is not a God of disorder but of peace, *as in all the congregations of the saints*" fits this pattern exactly (1 Cor. 14:33b). Also, to begin a new paragraph at verse 33b would produce an awkward redundancy: "As *in all the churches* of the saints, let the women *in the churches* be silent" (AT). Why repeat "in the churches" in the same sentence? Plus, "Let the women . . ." is a typical Pauline start to a new paragraph (see Eph. 5:22; Col. 3:18).

It is thus wrongheaded for traditionalists to treat as a given the start of a paragraph at 1 Corinthians 14:33b and assume the universality of Paul's injunction in verse 34. Carson, for instance ("Silent in the Churches," 147), does just that when he states, "Paul's rule [of silence] operates in *all* the churches."

but he does not specify whether this is Mosaic law, church law, or the laws of the land. Paul's brief remarks undoubtedly made sense to the Corinthians (as part of his continuing instruction). But to a modern ear listening to one half of a conversation carried on almost two millennia ago, the best that can be done today is to hazard an educated guess or to graciously admit ignorance.[77]

The problem comes when traditionalists have difficulty admitting ignorance (or even ambiguity), and treat these matters as plain and factual. All too often it is simply assumed that Paul is commanding women to submit to their husbands, as the so-called law of Genesis 3:16 states: "And he will rule over you." Yet this is a most improbable (if not impossible) interpretation.

---

[77]The sudden spotlight on married women, the awkward change of subject ("When *you* [plural] gather" [1 Cor. 14:26–33] ... "Let *them* [the women] be silent" [14:34–35] ... "Did the word of God originate with *you* [plural]" [14:36–40]), and the seeming contradiction between verse 34 and 1 Corinthians 11:5 were difficult for copyists in the early centuries. This is obvious from the different places these verses appear in the textual tradition. In some early manuscripts and versions, verses 34–35 follow the final verse of chapter 14 (D F G Itala, a Vulgate manuscript). In other early manuscripts and versions, verses 34–35 come after verse 33 (p⁴⁶ ℵ A B ψ K L Itala, Vulgate, Syriac, Coptic, and others). Also there is a bar-umlaut text-critical siglum in Codex Vaticanus indicating awareness of a textual problem, and P⁴⁶, ℵ A, D, and 33 have a breaking mark at the beginning of verse 34 and at the end of verse 35. Codex Fuldensis (a sixth-century manuscript of the Vulgate) has a scribal siglum directing the reader to the text of verses 36–40 in the margin. (It does not move verses 34–35 to the end of the chapter, as Carson asserts ["Silent in the Churches," 141].) It would appear that the copyist is thereby directing the liturgist to omit verses 34–35 when reading the lesson. See Bruce Metzger, *A Textual Commentary on the Greek New Testament*, 2d ed. (Stuttgart: German Bible Society, 1994), 499–500.

The paragraphing at 1 Corinthians 14:33b and then again at verse 37 is therefore highly misleading in the UBS and Nestle-Aland Greek New Testament editions. For a detailed treatment, see Philip Payne, "Fuldensis, Sigla For Variants in Vaticanus, and 1 Corinthians 14.34–5," *New Testament Studies* 41 (1995): 240–62; and Philip Payne, "MS. 88 as Evidence for a Text without 1 Corinthians 14.34–5," *New Testament Studies* 44 (1998): 152–58.

The textual tradition and versional evidence have led some scholars to conclude (with understandable justification) that 14:34–35 are not original to 1 Corinthians. See, for example, Gordon Fee, *The First Epistle to the Corinthians*, New International Commentary on the New Testament (Grand Rapids: Eerdmans, 1987), 699–705; Jacobus Petzer, "Reconsidering the Silent Women of Corinth: A Note on 1 Corinthians 14:34–35," *Theologia Evangelica* 26 (1993): 132–38; Peter Lockwood, "Does 1 Corinthians 14:34–35 Exclude Women from the Pastoral Office?" *Lutheran Theological Journal* 30 (1996): 30–37; Payne, "Fuldensis," 240–62.

For one thing, neither Genesis 3:16 nor any other Old Testament text commands women to submit to their husbands. Would Paul take an Old Testament text that is descriptive of a post-Fall, dysfunctional marital relationship (Gen. 3:16) and cite it as prescriptive for the husband-wife Christian relationship? He does not do so elsewhere. Why would he do so here? In fact, when the topic of marital relationships surfaces, Paul cites Genesis 2:24 as prescriptive (Eph. 5:31–32), and not Genesis 3:16.[78]

Actually, the immediate context offers the better clues. In 1 Corinthians 14:32 Paul states that the spirits of the prophets are *submissive* to the prophets. So when another prophet receives a revelation, the first prophet is to sit down and *be silent*. Those who speak in tongues are also commanded to be silent if there is no one to interpret. If one follows Paul's thinking carefully, "submission" and "silence" are two sides of the same coin. To be silent is to be submissive—and to be submissive (in the context of worship) is to be silent. Control over the tongue is most likely what Paul is talking about. The speaker (be they tongue speaker, prophet, or inquirer) must "bite his/her tongue" for the sake of orderly worship.[79]

"As the law says" could then easily be understood as Roman law. Official religion of the Roman variety was closely supervised. The women who participated were carefully organized and their activities strictly regulated. The unrestrained activity and inclusive nature of oriental cults (such as the popular cult of Isis) made them immediately suspect, if for no other reason than the fear that such uninhibited behavior would adversely affect the family unit and erupt in antisocial behavior.[80]

While we must leave room for some uncertainty, enough is clear about 1 Corinthians 14:34–35 to form an intelligent reconstruction: Married women, in exercising their newly acquired freedom to learn alongside the men, were disturbing the orderly flow of things by asking questions during the worship service. Paul instructs them to ask these questions of their own husbands

---

[78]Carson agrees that Paul is citing Genesis 2:24 ("Silent in the Churches," 152). Yet to forsake existing loyalties, cleave to one's spouse, and become "one flesh" is the language of mutuality, not hierarchy.

[79]Other suggestions include submission to (1) the elders of the church, (2) those who evaluate prophecies, and (3) one's own spirit.

[80]See my *Women Leaders and the Church*, 36–38.

at home (14:35) so that worship could progress in an orderly fashion ("everything should be done in a fitting and orderly way," 14:40). Eugene Peterson's *The Message* captures the sense with his paraphrase: "Wives must not disrupt worship, talking when they should be listening, asking questions that could more appropriately be asked of their husbands at home."

Sometimes in the heat of debate several aspects of 1 Corinthians 14 are overlooked. It is important to notice that Paul affirms the right of women to learn and be instructed. This, in and of itself, is a progressive, not a restrictive, attitude. Paul also affirms the right of women to ask questions. He does not question the *what* (women asking questions) but the *how* and *where* (in a disruptive manner during the worship service). Then too, it was not merely inquiring women who were silenced but also unintelligible speakers (14:27–28) and long-winded prophets (14:29–30). Paul's target was anyone and anything that would compromise the internal edification and external witness of the church (14:12, 23, 32, 40).

1 Timothy 2:11–15

These verses also deserve some attention—not because traditionalists tend to start here (and, for some, also end here), but because the passage deals with teaching roles in a seemingly prohibitive fashion. Using language somewhat similar to 1 Corinthians 14:34–35, Paul states (to quote the NIV):

> A woman should learn in quietness and full submission. I do not permit a woman to teach or to have authority over a man; she must be silent. For Adam was formed first, then Eve. And Adam was not the one deceived; it was the woman who was deceived and became a sinner. But women will be saved through childbearing—if they continue in faith, love and holiness with propriety.

The first step in getting a handle on 1 Timothy 2:11–15 is to be clear about the letter as a whole. Why was Paul writing to Timothy? It certainly was not to provide routine instruction. His stance throughout is a *corrective* one. Paul is reacting to a situation that had gotten out of hand. False teachers needed silencing (1:3–7, 18–20; 4:1–8; 5:20–22; 6:3–10, 20–21). Two church leaders had been expelled (1:20), and the men of the congregation had become angry and quarrelsome (2:8). Women were dressing inap-propriately (2:9) and learning in a disruptive manner (2:11–12). Some widows were going from house to house, speaking things they ought not to speak (5:13). Other widows had turned away from the faith altogether to follow Satan (5:15). Certain elders needed public rebuking because of their continuing sin ("Those continuing to sin are to be rebuked publicly so that the others may take warning" [5:20 AT]).[81] The congregation had turned to malicious talk, malevolent suspicions, and perpetual friction (6:4–5), and some members of the church had wandered from the faith (6:20–21). Overall, it was an alarming scenario.

Paul is also responding to a specific situation in 1 Timothy 2. The opening "I urge, then [*oun*], first of all" ties what follows back to the false teaching of the previous chapter and its divisive influence (1:3–7, 18–20). The subsequent "I want, then [*oun*]" (2:8, AT) does the same. *Congregational contention* is the keynote of chapter 2. A command for peace (as opposed to disputing) is found four times in the space of fifteen verses. Prayers for secular governing authorities are urged, "that we may live peaceful and quiet lives" (2:2). The men of the church are enjoined to lift up hands in prayer, without anger or disputing (2:8). The women are commanded to behave properly (2:9, 15) and quietly (2:12), and to learn in a peaceful (not quarrelsome) fashion (2:11).

Who were these women? Some interpret *anēr* and *gynē* in 1 Timothy 2:11–15 as "husband" and "wife." This is reflected in the NRSV text note on verse 12: "I permit no wife to teach or to have authority over her husband; she is to keep silent." Yet "husband" and "wife" do not fit the broader context of congregational worship. "I want, then, the men ... to pray" (*boulomai oun proseuchesthai tous andras*, 2:8 AT) and "I also want women to ..." (2:9–10) simply cannot be limited to husbands and wives. Nor can the verses that follow be read in this way. There is no indication whatsoever that Paul is shifting at verse 11 from women in

---

[81]The NIV translation of 1 Timothy 5:20, "Those who sin are to be rebuked publicly, so that the others may take warning," is misleading. The tense and mood are present indicative. So Paul is not treating a hypothetical possibility ("Should any sin, they are to be rebuked publicly") but a present reality ("Those who are continuing to sin must be rebuked publicly").

general to married women in specific. It is true that Paul does refer to Adam and Eve in verses 13–14, but it is to Adam and Eve as the prototypical male and female, not as a married couple.

What were these women doing? One pointer is Paul's command that women learn quietly (*en hēsychia*, 1 Tim. 2:11) and behave quietly (*einai en hēsychia*, 2:12; PHILLIPS, NEB, REB, NLT, NASB). This suggests that women were disrupting worship. The men were too (they were praying in an angry and contentious way, 2:8). Since Paul targets women who teach men (2:12) and uses the example of Adam and Eve as a corrective, it would be a fair assumption that there was a bit of a battle of the sexes going on in the congregation.

Traditionalists commonly translate the Greek term *hēsychia* as "silent," and they understand Paul to be prohibiting women from all forms of public speaking. In public (it is argued) women are to learn "in silence" and "be silent" (KJV, NKJV, RSV, NRSV, TEV, CEV, NIV, JB; cf. "keep quiet," 1 Tim. 2:12 TEV). This is problematic on a number of grounds. For one, it makes no sense in an instructional context. Silence is not compatible with the Socratic dialogical approach to learning in Paul's day. Also, Paul does not use the Greek term in this way elsewhere. When he has absence of speech in mind, the word he chooses is *sigaō* (Rom. 16:25; 1 Cor. 14:28, 30, 34). When he has calm, quiet behavior in view, he uses *hēsychia* and its cognate forms (see 1 Thess. 4:11; 2 Thess. 3:12; 1 Tim. 2:2). In fact, the adjective *hēsychion* appears nine verses earlier with this very sense. "I urge ... that requests, prayers, intercession and thanksgiving be made ... for kings and all those in authority, that we may live peaceful and *quiet* lives in all godliness and holiness" (1 Tim. 2:1–2, emphasis added).[82]

Women are encouraged to learn not merely quietly but also (according to the NIV) in "full submission" (1 Tim. 2:11). In full submission to whom or to what is the question. Traditionalists usually take submission to a husband as a given. But on what grounds? "Let a woman learn" does not suggest anything of the sort. In a learning context, it is logical to think in terms of sub-

---

[82]This is also the case for the rest of the New Testament. See *sigaō* in Luke 9:36; 18:39; 20:26; Acts 12:17; 15:12–13; see *sigē* (the noun) in Acts 21:40; Revelation 8:1. For *hēsychia* (and related forms), meaning "calm" or "restful," see Luke 23:56; Acts 11:18; 21:14; 1 Thessalonians 4:11; 2 Thessalonians 3:12; 1 Peter 3:4. For the sense "not speak," see Luke 14:4; perhaps Acts 22:2.

mission either to teachers or to oneself (in the sense of having self-control; see 1 Cor. 14:32). Submission to a teacher well suits a learning context, but so does self-control. A calm, submissive spirit was a necessary prerequisite for learning back then.[83]

What about the teaching prohibition in 1 Timothy 2:12? There are several aspects of verse 12 that make the plain sense difficult to determine. One problematic feature is Paul's choice of verb form. Paul's command in verse 11 sets the reader up to expect an imperative in verse 12, especially since verse 12 is set in contrast with verse 11. The initial *de* ("but") makes this quite clear: "Let a woman learn in a quiet and submissive fashion *but* do not let her teach" is what we expect. Instead we have the indicative: "Let a woman learn . . . but *I do not permit* her to teach" (AT, emphasis added). Some have suggested that the present indicative is used because it allows Paul to give a temporary restriction: "I am not permitting at this time." This has some merit. "Let a woman not teach" (imperative) would certainly communicate a universal norm. If this were not Paul's intent, then a shift from a present imperative (*manthanetō*) to a present indicative (*epitrepō*) would make sense.

The exact wording of Paul's restriction needs to be carefully examined. What kind of teaching is Paul prohibiting at this point? Traditionalists often assume it is a teaching office or other position of authority. But teaching in the New Testament period was an activity and not an office (Matt. 28:19–20), and it was a gift and not a position of authority (Rom. 12:7; 1 Cor. 12:28; 14:26; Eph. 4:11). It was something *every* believer was called to do, not merely church leaders (Heb. 5:12; Col. 3:16).

There is also the assumption that authority resides in the act of teaching (or in the person who teaches). In point of fact, it resides in the deposit of truth ("the truths of the faith," 1 Tim. 3:9; 4:6; "the faith," 4:1; 5:8; 6:10, 12, 21; "what has been entrusted," 6:20) that Jesus passed on to his disciples and that they in turn passed on to their disciples (2 Tim. 2:2). The Greek term for "authority" (*exousia*) is simply not used of either local church leadership or the activity of teaching (see above). Teaching is subject to evaluation, just like any other ministry role. This is why Paul instructed Timothy to publicly rebuke (1 Tim. 5:20)

---

[83]For further discussion, see Kevin Giles, "Response," in *The Bible and Women's Ministry: An Australian Dialogue*, ed. A. Nichols (Canberra: Acorn Press, 1990), 73.

anyone who departed from "the sound instruction of our Lord Jesus Christ" (6:3).

Traditionalists often counter with the claim that teaching in 1 Timothy takes on the more official sense of "doctrine" and that teaching doctrine is something women can't do. Yet "doctrine" as a system of thought is foreign to 1 Timothy—traditions, yes; doctrines, no. While Paul urged Timothy to "command and teach these things" (1 Tim. 4:11; 6:2), these "things" are not doctrines. They included matters like avoiding godless myths and old wives' tales (4:7), engaging in godly training (4:7–8), believing that God is the Savior of all (4:9–10), and urging slaves to treat their masters with full respect (6:1–2). The flaw therefore lies in translating the Greek phrase *hygiainousē didaskalia* as "sound doctrine" instead of "sound teaching" (1:10; 4:6; cf. 1 Tim. 6:1, 3; 2 Tim. 4:3; Titus 1:9; 2:1).

Without a doubt, the most difficult phrase to unpack in 1 Timothy 2:12 is *oude authentein andros* (variously translated "nor to dominate a man" or "not to exercise authority over a man"). In order to unpack its meaning two questions must be answered. First, what is the sense of *authentein*? Does it mean "to exercise authority" (that is, to carry out one's official duties)? Or is its sense "to dominate," "to get one's way," as a growing number of New Testament scholars say? A second, equally important question is the function of the "neither ... nor" (*ouk ... oude*) construction. In general, it serves to define a single coherent idea. But defining the exact coherent idea in the case of 1 Timothy 2:12 needs careful attention.

It cannot be stressed enough that in *authentein* Paul has picked a verb used nowhere else in the Protestant Bible. Two cognate nouns each appear once in the Apocrypha, but the usage does not easily fit our passage ("parents who *murder* [*authentas*] helpless lives," Wis. of Sol. 12:6; "former limited *status* [*authentia*]," 3 Macc. 2:29). This alone should give us pause in opting for a translation such as the NIV's "to have authority over." If Paul had wanted to speak of the ordinary exercise of authority, he could have chosen any number of words, the most common one being *exousia/[kat]exousiazō*.[84] But he did not. The

---

[84]Among the many words in the New Testament that mean "to rule" or "to exercise authority over," the most common are *[kat]exousiazō, krinō, katakyrieuō, archō,* and *hēgeomai*. Yet Paul uses none of these in 1 Timothy 2:12.

term *authentein* must therefore carry an essential nuance that other more commonly used words do not.

So what is this nuance? The first thing to note is that the predominant usage of the noun up to the second century A.D. is the committing of a crime or act of violence (such as murder, suicide, or sacrilege). For example, first- and second-century B.C. historians Diodorus (robbing a sacred shrine, 16.61.1.3) and Polybius (the massacre at Maronea, 22.14.2.3) use it of those who perpetrate a foul deed. Instances of the verb are scant (including the verbal noun [infinitive] and verbal adjective [participle]). Range of meaning is as follows: (1) "to commit an act of violence,"[85] (2) "to take matters into one's own hands," (3) "to exercise mastery over," or (4) "to hold sway over someone or something."[86] For instance, one first-century-B.C. letter has "And I had my way with him [*kamou authentēkotos pros auton*], and he agreed to provide Calatytis the boatman with the full payment within the hour."[87] The first-century-B.C. rhetorician Philodemus speaks of certain orators who "fight with powerful lords" *(authent[ou]sin an[axin])*.[88] And second-century astronomers talk about Saturn "dominating [*authentē-sas*] Mercury and the moon."[89]

The one meaning that does not seem to be in evidence during this period is the routine exercise of authority.[90] Consequently, the NIV's "to have authority over" must be understood in the sense of holding sway or mastery over another.[91] This is

---

[85]See *Scholia Graeca* in Aeschylus, *Eumenides* 42a (first century B.C.).

[86]See Liddell, Scott, and Jones, *A Greek-English Lexicon*, s.v. "*authenteō*." For a detailed study, see Leland Wilshire, "The TLG Computer and Further Reference to *Authentein* in 1 Timothy 2.12," *New Testament Studies* 34 (1988): 120–34, and his more recent article "1 Timothy 2:12 Revisited: A Reply to Paul W. Barnett and Timothy J. Harris," *Evangelical Quarterly* 65 (1993): 43–55.

[87]*Aegyptische Urkunden* 1208.

[88]*Rhetorica* II Fragmenta Libri [V] fr. IV line 14.

[89]Ptolemy, *Tetrabiblos* III.13 [#157]. For further discussion on this issue, see my *Women Leaders and the Church*, 175–76.

[90]One first begins to see in the writings of the second-century church fathers *authentēs* used of a mundane exercise of authority. See, for example, Shepherd of Hermas, *Vision* 9.5.6, "Let us go to the tower, for the *owner* of the tower is coming to inspect it." A mundane use of the verb does not appear until well into the third and fourth centuries A.D.

[91]Cf. J. H. Moulton and G. Milligan, *Vocabulary of the Greek New Testament*, rev. ed. (Peabody, Mass.: Hendrickson, 1997), s.v. "*authenteō*."

supported by the grammar of the verse. If Paul had a routine exercise of authority in view, he would have put it first, followed by teaching as a specific example. Instead, he starts with teaching, followed by *authentein* as a specific example. Given this word order, *authentein* meaning "to dominate" or "to gain the upper hand" provides the best fit in the context of 1 Timothy 2. Early Latin versions, such as the fourth-century Vulgate ("to dominate a man," *dominari in virum*), share a similar opinion.

But where do we go from here? The correlative construction "neither ... nor" (*ouk ... oude*) is what links the infinitives "to teach" and "to dominate." So it is important to establish the nature of this linkage. In biblical Greek (and Hebrew) "neither ... nor" is a poetic device that normally sets in parallel two or more natural groupings of words, phrases, or clauses (for example, "will neither slumber nor sleep," Ps. 121:4). It is not so in English, however, and this is where it's easy to get off track. In English "neither" and "nor" are coordinating conjunctions that connect elements of equal *grammatical* rank but not necessarily related activities. For example, if I want to be grammatically proper in punishing my son, I will say, "You can play with neither your Game Boy nor a friend." Two unrelated activities of equal grammatical rank are thereby prohibited. In biblical Greek, however, "neither ... nor" correlates similar or related *ideas* without the need for equal grammatical parts. For example, in Acts 17:24–25 Paul states that God neither dwells in temples made with human hands nor is served by human hands as though he needed anything (*ouk en cheiropoiētois naois katoikei oude hypo cheirōn anthrōpinōn therapeuetai prosdeomenos tinos*).

"Neither ... nor" constructions in the New Testament serve to pair or group *synonyms* ("neither despised nor scorned," Gal. 4:14), *closely related ideas* ("neither of the night nor of the dark," 1 Thess. 5:5), or *antonyms* ("neither Jew nor Greek, neither slave nor free," Gal. 3:28). They also function to move from the general to the particular ("wisdom neither of this age nor of the rulers of this age," 1 Cor. 2:6), to define a natural progression of related ideas ("neither sow nor reap nor gather into barns," Matt. 6:26), or to define a related purpose or a goal ("where thieves neither break in nor steal [that is, break in to steal]," Matt. 6:20).[92]

---

[92]Other examples include: (1) *Synonyms*: "neither labors nor spins" (Matt. 6:28); "neither quarreled nor cried out" (Matt. 12:19); "neither abandoned nor given up"

Of the options listed above, it is obvious that "teach" and "dominate" are not synonyms, closely related ideas, or antonyms. If *authentein* did mean "to exercise authority," we might have a movement from general to particular. But the word order would need to be "neither to exercise authority [general] nor to teach [particular]." They do not form a natural progression of related ideas either ("first teach, then dominate"). On the other hand, *to define a purpose or goal* actually provides quite a good fit: "I do not permit a woman to teach in order to gain mastery over a man," or "I do not permit a woman to teach with a view to dominating a man."[93] It also results in a good point of contrast with 1 Timothy 2:12b: "I do not permit a woman to teach a man in a dominating way but to have a quiet demeanor" (literally, "to be in calmness").[94]

Paul would then be prohibiting teaching that tries to get the upper hand (not teaching per se). A reasonable reconstruction would be as follows: The women at Ephesus (perhaps encouraged by the false teachers) were trying to gain the upper hand over the men in the congregation by teaching in a dictatorial fashion. In response, the men became angry and resisted what the women were doing. This interpretation fits the broader context of 1 Timothy 2:8–15, where Paul aims to correct inappropriate

---

(Acts 2:27); "neither leave nor forsake" (Heb. 13:5); "neither run in vain nor labor in vain" (Phil. 2:16). (2) *Closely related ideas*: "neither the desire nor the effort" (Rom. 9:16); "neither the sun nor the moon" (Rev. 21:23). (3) *Antonyms*: "neither a good tree nor a bad tree" (Matt. 7:18); "neither the one who did harm nor the one who was harmed" (2 Cor. 7:12). (4) *General to particular*: "you know neither the day nor the hour" (Matt. 25:13); "neither consulted with flesh and blood nor went up to Jerusalem" (Gal. 1:16–17). (5) *A natural progression of closely related ideas*: "born neither of blood, nor of the human will, nor of the will of man" (John 1:13); "neither the Christ, nor Elijah, nor the Prophet" (John 1:25); "neither from man nor through man" (Gal. 1:1). Finally, (6) *Goal or purpose*: "neither hears nor understands" (that is, hearing with the intent to understand, Matt. 13:13); "neither dwells in temples made with human hands nor is served by human hands" (that is, dwelling with a view to being served, Acts 17:24). See my *Women Leaders and the Church*, 176–77.

[93]Along somewhat similar lines, Donald Kushke suggests that *oude* introduces an explanation: "to teach in an authoritative fashion." See his article "An Exegetical Brief on 1 Timothy 2:12," *Wisconsin Lutheran Quarterly* 88 (1991): 64.

[94]Philip Payne highlighted the importance of the "neither . . . nor" construction in a paper presented at the Evangelical Theological Society's annual meeting on November 21, 1986. His own position is that "neither . . . nor" in this verse joins two closely associated couplets (like, "hit n'run": "teach n'domineer").

behavior on the part of both men and women (2:8, 11). It also fits the grammatical flow of 2:11–12 (AT): "Let a woman learn in a quiet and submissive fashion. I do not, however, permit her to teach with the intent to dominate a man. She must be gentle in her demeanor."

Why might the Ephesian women have been teaching in a dictatorial manner? One explanation is that they were influenced by the cult of Artemis, where the female was exalted and considered superior to the male. The importance of this cult to the citizens of Ephesus in Paul's day is evident from Luke's record of their two-hour chant, "Great is Artemis of the Ephesians!" (Acts 19:28). Artemis, it was believed, was the child of Zeus and Leto (and sister of Apollo), who sought the company of a male human rather than the gods. Artemis appeared first and then her male consort. This made Artemis and all her female adherents superior to men.[95]

An Artemis influence would certainly explain Paul's correctives in 1 Timothy 2:13–14. It was Adam who appeared first, then Eve (*Adam gar prōtos eplasthē, eita Eua*, 2:13).[96] And Eve was deceived to boot (2:14)—hardly a basis on which to claim superiority. It would also explain Paul's statement that "women will be kept safe through childbearing" (2:15 NIV 1973 ed.), for Artemis was the protector of women. Women turned to her for safe travel through the childbearing process.[97]

---

[95]For more detail, see Sharon Gritz, *Paul, Women Teachers, and the Mother Goddess at Ephesus: A Study of 1 Timothy 2:9–15 in Light of the Religious and Cultural Milieu of the First Century* (Lanham, Md.: University Press of America, 1991), 31–41; "Artemis," in *Encyclopaedia Britannica Online* at http://www.eb.com.

[96]Traditionalists typically interpret *gar* at the beginning of 1 Timothy 2:13 as causal rather than explanatory, and so they see it as introducing a "creation order" dictum: Women must not teach men *because* men, according to the order of creation, were intended to lead, and Eve's proneness to deception while taking the lead demonstrates this. This reading of the text is problematic for a number of reasons. First, there is nothing in the context to support it. In fact, 1 Timothy 2:15 is against it. "Women must not teach men *because* Eve was deceived, but she will be saved through childbearing" is nonsense. Second, although some are quick to assume a Creation-Fall ordering in 2:13–14, virtually all stop short of including "women will be saved [or kept safe] through childbearing" (2:15). To do so, though, is to lack hermeneutical integrity. Either all three statements are normative, or all three are not.

[97]As the mother goddess, Artemis was the source of life, the nourisher of all creatures, and the power of fertility in nature. Maidens turned to her as the protector of their virginity, barren women sought her aid, and women in labor turned to

Traditionalists claim that by naming Adam as "first" in the process of creation, Paul is saying something about male leadership ("For Adam was formed first, then Eve," 1 Tim. 2:13). Yet "first-then" (*prōtos-eita*) language in Paul (and, for that matter, in the New Testament) does nothing more than define a sequence of events or ideas (for example, Mark 4:28; 1 Cor. 15:46; 1 Thess. 4:16–17; James 3:17). In fact, ten verses later Paul uses it in this very way. Deacons, he states, "must first [*prōton*] be tested, and then [*eita*] . . . let them serve" (1 Tim. 3:10 AT).

What about Eve's seniority in transgression? Isn't Paul using Eve as an example of what can go wrong when women usurp the male's created leadership role ("And Adam was not the one deceived; it was the woman who was deceived and became a sinner," 1 Tim. 2:14)?[98] But this is without scriptural support. Eve was not deceived by the serpent into taking the lead in the male-female relationship. She was deceived into disobeying a command of God, namely, not to eat the fruit from the tree of the knowledge of good and evil. She listened to the voice of false teaching and was deceived by it. Paul's warning to the Corinthian congregation confirms this: "I am afraid that just as Eve was deceived by the serpent's cunning, your minds may somehow be led astray from your sincere and pure devotion to Christ" (2 Cor. 11:3).

The language of deception calls to mind the activities of the false teachers at Ephesus. If the Ephesian women were being encouraged to assume the role of teacher over men as the superior sex, this would go a long way toward explaining 1 Timothy 2:13–14. The relationship between the sexes was not intended to be one of female domination and male subordination. But neither was it intended to be one of male domination

---

her for help. See Gritz, *Paul, Women Teachers, and the Mother Goddess*, 31–41. Baugh takes issue with the premise that Artemis worship involved a fusion of a fertility cult of the mother goddess of Asia Minor and the Greek virgin goddess of the hunt ("A Foreign World," 28–33). However, the fourth-century B.C. "Rituals for Brides and Pregnant Women in the Worship of Artemis" (*Lois sacrées des cités grecques: supplément* 15) and other literary sources support such a fusion. See F. Sokolowski, *Lois sacrées de l'Asie Mineure* (Paris, 1955).

[98]See, for example, Michael Stitzinger, "Cultural Confusion and the Role of Women in the Church: A Study of 1 Timothy 2:8–14," *Calvary Baptist Theological Journal* 4 (1988): 34; and James Hurley, *Man and Woman in Biblical Perspective* (Grand Rapids: Zondervan, 1981), 216.

and female subordination. Such thinking is native to a fallen creation order (Gen. 3:16).

We must not lose track, however, of Paul's flow of thought in these verses. Paul affirms a woman's right to learn and to be instructed. "Let a woman learn" is the way 1 Timothy 2:11–15 begins. *How* they are to learn is the issue at hand, not their right to do so. It is reasonable, then, to think that *how* they taught was the actual issue behind Paul's statement in 2:12.

THE RELATIONSHIP OF MALE AND FEMALE

What the foregoing demonstrates is that what fundamentally separates traditionalists and egalitarians is a different understanding of the created order of male and female. While 1 Timothy 2:11–15 (with rare exceptions) is the starting point for traditionalists, the reason for this is easily missed. It is not a belief that women are not to teach, for Paul himself instructed that the older women in the Cretan congregation "teach well" (*kalodidaskalous*) the younger women (Titus 2:3–5). Nor is it a belief that women are not to teach publicly—although this is a common traditionalist conclusion. It is rather a belief that women are not to lead *men*—not in the family, not in the workplace, not in the community, and not in the church. For instance, a woman who is asked by a male passerby for directions must provide them in such a way that the man's leadership is not compromised.[99] To do otherwise (so it is argued) is to reverse God's created order and to blur the basic distinction between male and female: Men are created to lead; women are created to submit.

Gender hierarchy is what is behind the egalitarian challenge that appeared in the March 1998 newsletter of the Council on Biblical Manhood and Womanhood.[100] The Council's president, Wayne Grudem, challenged egalitarians either to answer six questions or to admit once and for all that an egalitarian (that is to say, an equal and mutual) relationship of male and female is not a biblical one. The challenge was to produce one extrabiblical text where (1) the Greek term *kephalē* is used of one person

---

[99]See Piper, "A Vision of Biblical Complementarity," 50–51.

[100]Wayne Grudem, "An Open Letter to Egalitarians," *Journal for Biblical Manhood and Womanhood* (March 1998): 1, 3–4.

being the "source" (versus "ruler") of another, (2) the Greek term *hypotassō* is used of mutual (versus one-directional) submission, (3) the Greek particle *ē* introduces a negative response ("What!" versus "or") to the previously stated position of the reader, (4) the Greek verb *authenteō* bears the sense "to domineer" or "to usurp authority" (versus "to exercise authority over"), and (5) the verbs in the Greek construction "neither + [verb 1] + nor + [verb 2]" can be antonyms (versus synonymous or parallel ideas). The sixth challenge was to show that women teaching false doctrine at Ephesus was the problem Paul addressed in 1 Timothy.

One difficulty with such a challenge is that egalitarians could easily produce a similar list of questions that pose an equal challenge. Egalitarians, for example, could challenge traditionalists to produce one extrabiblical text prior to the third century A.D. where (1) the Greek reciprocal pronoun *allēlous* means "some to others" (versus "one another," Eph. 5:21), (2) *Iounian* is the masculine "Junias" (versus the feminine "Junia," Rom. 16:7), (3) the Greek word *authentein* is used of the routine exercise of the authority of one person (or group) over another (1 Tim. 2:12), and (4) the Greek correlative *ouk . . . oude* requires equal grammatical parts (versus similar or parallel ideas, 1 Tim. 2:12). If examples are not forthcoming, then traditionalists would need to admit that a hierarchical relationship of male and female is not the divine standard.

Another difficulty is how the questions are framed. The Council's challenge fails to recognize two key facts. First, Christianity is by nature countercultural. Just because mutual submission was not the Greco-Roman way (and so not found in extrabiblical first-century texts) does not mean it was not the Christian way (and consequently found in biblical texts).[101] Second, the Council's challenge ignores two basic principles in interpreting biblical texts: (1) *Context* determines meaning, and (2) *Scripture* interprets Scripture. If these two principles are

---

[101]Every Greek lexicon I've consulted states that Ephesians 5:21 has no secular parallel. See, for example, Bauer, Danker, Arndt, and Gingrich, *A Greek-English Lexicon*, s.v. "*hypotassō*"; and Spicq, *Theological Lexicon*, 3:424–26. Even the New Testament concept of *submission* has no secular parallel. "To spontaneously position oneself as a servant toward one's neighbor in the hierarchy of love . . . is absolutely new" (Spicq, *Theological Lexicon*, 3:426).

applied to the Council's six questions, then answers are easy to come by. We'll begin with the second question and save the discussion of *kephalē* for last.

Mutual Submission

Even a cursory look at Paul's writings shows that mutual submission is basic to his understanding of how believers are to relate to one another (over against Greco-Roman hierarchy). "Each of you should look not only to your own interests," Paul states, "but also to the interests of others" (Phil. 2:4). The addition of the reciprocal pronoun *allēlois* ("to one another") to Paul's command for submission ("submit yourselves" [*hypotassomenoi*]) in Ephesians 5:21 makes this absolutely clear. *Allēlois* simply cannot bear any other lexical meaning but a reciprocal one.[102]

Also, the grammar and syntax of Ephesians 5:18–21 demand the idea of mutual submission. The main verb (and therefore the main command) is in verse 18: "Do not get drunk on wine.... Instead, be filled with the Spirit." What follows in verses 19–21 (the English verbs are actually Greek participles) are examples of Spirit-filled congregational life and worship, namely, "speaking to one another with psalms, hymns, and spiritual songs; singing and making music in your heart to the Lord; always giving thanks to God the Father for everything ...; submitting to one another out of reverence for Christ" (AT). It is hence wrong for Grudem to translate *hypotassomenoi* as a passive verb ("to be subject to"). It is the last of a series of participles that spell out the how of Paul's command ("Be filled with the Spirit *by* speaking ... singing ... giving thanks ... submitting to one another"). Moreover, the first and fourth participles are modified by pronouns that are reciprocal in meaning ("speaking psalms and hymns and spiritual songs to each another [*lalountes heautois*] ... submitting to one another

---

[102]See Liddell, Scott, and Jones, *A Greek-English Lexicon*, s.v. "*allēlōn*." Wayne Grudem's claim that *allēlous* [sic] in Ephesians 5:21 takes the "common" meaning "some to others" (as opposed to "each to the other," "mutually" [Bauer, Danker, Arndt, and Gingrich, *A Greek-English Lexicon*, s.v. "*allēlōn*"]) boggles the lexical imagination (see Grudem's "An Open Letter to Egalitarians," 3). And how exactly Galatians 6:2 ("Carry *each other's* burdens"), 1 Corinthians 11:33 ("When you come together to eat, wait for *each other*"), and Revelation 6:4 ("To make the people [on earth] slay *each other*") support such a "common meaning" is likewise incomprehensible.

[*hypotassomenoi allēlois*]")—making clear that the specified activities are two-directional as opposed to one-directional.[103]

How, then, can Grudem translate Ephesians 5:21 as "be subject some to others in authority"? This smacks of an act of desperation to avoid the conclusion that the wife's submission immediately following in verses 22–24 is one example of mutuality and the husband's love in verses 25–33 another. Because verse 22 lacks a verb (the text merely reads, "wives to your husbands"), the preceding participle and reciprocal pronoun (verse 21, "submitting one to the other") must be supplied. Translations such as the NIV that begin a new paragraph at verse 22 destroy the essential connection with what goes before.

The Greek Particle Ē

The Council's third challenge is rather puzzling. I know of very few evangelicals who argue that the Greek particle *ē* in 1 Corinthians 14:36 is Paul's signal that he is responding to the Corinthian position ("Let the women in the churches be silent"). The simple fact is that while *ē* can denote an exclamation expressing disapproval, the standard *Greek-English Lexicon* of Hellenistic Greek lists only two instances, and in both cases there is a double *ē ē* ("Hey, hey!" as in, *ē ē siōpa* ... ["Hey, hey! Be quiet, don't say anything so childish!"])[104] and not the single *ē* we have in 1 Corinthians 14:36 (which is surely why the revisions of the KJV and the RSV drop the "What").

Authenteō

The Council's challenge to produce extrabiblical texts where the Greek word *authenteō* bears the sense "to domineer" is easily met. In fact, all known extrabiblical instances of *authenteō* prior to the second century A.D. (usage contemporaneous with or prior to Paul), without exception have to do with power or domination ("to overpower," "to dominate").[105]

---

[103]*Heautōn* (Greek reflexive pronoun) functions as a reciprocal pronoun in Ephesians 5:19. It already is used this way in classical times. *Allēlōn* and *heautōn* often appear alongside one another (see, for example, Luke 23:12; 1 Cor. 6:7; Col. 3:13, 16). See F. Blass, A. Debrunner, and R. Funk, *A Greek Grammar of the New Testament and Other Early Christian Literature*, sec. 287.

[104]Aristophanes, *Nubes* 105; see Liddell, Scott, and Jones, *A Greek-English Lexicon*, s.v. "*ē*."

[105]See Wilshire, "1 Timothy 2:12 Revisited," 46–47.

1. *Scholia Graeca* in Aeschylus, *Eumenides* 42a (first century B.C.): "'His hands were dripping with blood [*haimati stazonta cheiras*]; he held a sword just drawn. . . .' 'Were dripping': The murderer [*ho phoneutēs*], who had just committed an act of violence [*(ton) neōsti ēuthentēkota*]."

2. *BGU* 1208 (first century B.C.)[106]: "I had my way with him [*kamou authentēkotos pros auton*], and he agreed to provide Calatytis the boatman with the full payment within the hour."

   This Berlin papyrus recounts a simple disagreement between the speaker and another individual regarding the fare that should be paid to the boatman. "I exercised authority over him" hardly fits the mundane details of the text. (Surely we don't "exercise authority over" another person about a taxicab fare.) Nor can the preposition *pros* be construed as "over." It must mean something like "I had my way *with* him"—or perhaps following Friedrich Preisigke (*Wordbook of the Greek Papyri*): "I took a firm stand [*fest auftreten*, 'to stand firm']."

3. Philodemus, *Rhetorica* II Fragmenta Libri [V] fr. IV line 14 (first century B.C.): The Philodemus text is too fragmented to be certain about the exact wording. What we have is: *hoi rhētores . . . diamachontai kai syn authent[ ]sin an[ ]*. The editor's guess is *authent[ou]sin an[axin]*. The text would then read: "These orators . . . even fight with *powerful* lords."

4. Ptolemy, *Tetrabiblos* III.13 [#157] (second century A.D.): "Therefore, if Saturn alone takes planetary control [*tēn oikodespotian . . . labōn*, literally 'household despot'] of the soul and dominates [*authentēsas*] Mercury and the moon [who govern the soul], if Saturn has an honorable position toward both the solar system and its angles [*ta kentra*],[107] then he makes [them] lovers of the body. . . ."

---

[106]*Aegyptische Urkunden aus den königlichen Staatlichen Museen zu Berlin: Griechische Urkunden.*

[107]George Knight misreads the Loeb translation "angles" as "angels" ("*AUTHENTEŌ* in Reference to Women in 1 Timothy 2:12," *New Testament Studies* 30 [1984]: 145). H. Scott Baldwin duplicates this mistake, showing that he is merely citing Knight rather than doing a fresh analysis, as the book's title claims ("Appendix 2: *Authenteō* in Ancient Greek Literature," in *Women in the Church: A Fresh Analysis*, 275).

What warrant, then, do traditionalists have in persisting to translate *authentein* as "to exercise authority" and to understand Paul in 1 Timothy 2:12 to be speaking of the carrying out of one's official duties? What makes the situation even more problematic is that the scholarship of traditionalists has not always been of a responsible sort. Many have merely quoted the flaws of George Knight's 1984 work and have ignored subsequent scholarly corrections. What's more, traditionalists have not translated and analyzed the primary sources themselves; otherwise they would have observed the error in Knight's paraphrase of *diamachontai kai syn authentousin anaxin* in Philodemus, *Rhetorica* II Fragmenta Libri [V] fr. IV line 14. The Greek text translates, "they [orators] even fight with powerful [or perhaps 'overbearing'] lords" and not Knight's "men who incur the enmity of those in authority." The most recent traditionalist work on *authenteō* not only repeats Knight's error but also misquotes the Greek text.[108]

"Neither ... Nor" Constructions

Current traditionalist scholarship is also flawed in its understanding of the Greek correlative *ou(k) ... oude* ("neither ... nor"). In English "neither" and "nor" are coordinating conjunctions that connect sentence elements of equal *grammatical* rank.[109] In biblical Greek, however, "neither ... nor" connects similar or related *ideas*, like the Lord who watches over Israel will "neither slumber nor sleep" (Ps. 121:4).[110] What we are dealing with is a poetic device. And so to do a study of the Greek construction "neither + [verb 1] + nor + [verb 2]" (as Köstenberger does) is to ignore both the literary form and the nature of

---

[108]Baldwin (see previous note) confuses the situation by citing dozens of Greek texts and writings of the church fathers that either lack the verb *authenteō* or postdate Paul by hundreds of years. The simple fact is that Baldwin includes only four pre-third-century A.D. texts where the verb or its participial form occur. Much more work needs to be done in analyzing the verb (and verbal forms) in primary sources that are contemporaneous with Paul. Baldwin likewise overlooks early versions. The fourth-century Latin Vulgate, for instance, has "But I permit a woman to neither teach nor domineer over a man" (*docere autem mulieri non permitto neque dominari in virum*).

[109]See M. D. Shertzer, *The Elements of Grammar* (New York: Macmillan, 1986), 45–46.

[110]See Blass, Debrunner, and Funk, *A Greek Grammar*, sec. 445.

Greek correlatives.[111] Moreover, the most recent traditionalist study of syntactical parallels to 1 Timothy 2:12 looks only for correlated verbs. But 1 Timothy 2:12 correlates *infinitives* (verbal nouns), not verbs. The infinitive may have tense and voice (as a verb does), but it functions predominantly as a noun or adjective.[112] The verb in verse 12 is actually *epitrepō* ("I permit"). "To teach" modifies the noun "a woman," and it answers the question "What?"[113] It would be logical, then, to look for correlated nouns or adjectives. But since the Greek correlative pairs ideas, the grammatical form is really unimportant.

Does the Greek correlative pair *opposites*? Of course it does. "Neither Jew nor Greek [*ouk . . . oude*], neither slave nor free [*ouk . . . oude*]" in Galatians 3:28 is a perfect example. Does the Greek correlative pair *a particular then a general idea* (such as "neither to teach nor to exercise authority over")? No, it does not. In every instance in the New Testament it pairs *a general then a particular idea*, as in 1 Corinthians 2:6: neither wisdom "of this age" nor "of the rulers of this age."[114] So if Paul had the exercise of authority in mind, he would have put it first, followed by *teaching* as a specific example (namely, "I permit a woman neither to exercise authority over nor to teach a man").

False Teaching and the Women of Ephesus

Grudem claims that there are no explicit examples of female false teachers in 1 Timothy, and he is correct. The cumulative picture of the activities of women in 1 Timothy may well *imply* the existence of female false teachers, but there is no explicit reference to such. Yet we must not overlook the standard interpretive principle of considering the historical situation: What

---

[111]See Andreas J. Köstenberger, "A Complex Sentence Structure in 1 Timothy 2:12," in *Women in the Church: A Fresh Analysis*, 81–103.

[112]See Nigel Turner (*Syntax*, in *Grammar of New Testament Greek*, ed. N. Turner [Edinburgh: T&T Clark, 1963], 3:134), who classifies infinitives as "noun forms."

[113]See James A. Brooks and Carlton L. Winbery, *Syntax of New Testament Greek* (Lanham, Md.: University Press of America, 1979), especially "The Infinitive as a Modifier of Substantives," 141–42. Köstenberger does not seem to recognize that the infinitive is a verbal *noun* (see "A Complex Sentence Structure," 81–103).

[114]Cf. "you know neither the day nor the hour" (Matt. 25:13 AT); "neither did I consult with flesh and blood nor did I go up to Jerusalem to meet with those who were apostles before me" (Gal. 1:16–17 AT).

prompted Paul to write this letter? Was false teaching the primary problem? Of course it was. Why else would Paul begin by instructing Timothy to stay in Ephesus so that he may command certain persons not to teach false doctrines any longer (1 Tim. 1:3)? In fact, false teaching consumes 35 percent of Paul's explicit attention in this letter.

Women also receive a great deal of attention in 1 Timothy. In fact, there is no other New Testament letter in which women figure so prominently. Paul deals with how women who pray in public are to attire themselves (1 Tim. 2:9–11), the kind of behavior that befits women in the worship service (2:12–15), qualifications for women deacons (3:11), appropriate pastoral behavior toward older and younger women (5:2), the credentials of widows in ministry (5:9–10), and the correction of younger widows (5:11–15). All told, 20 percent of the letter focuses on women.

Were any of the affected leaders women? "Going about from house to house . . . saying things they ought not to" (1 Tim. 5:13), "already turned away to follow Satan" (1 Tim. 5:15), and "always learning but never able to acknowledge the truth" (2 Tim. 3:7) certainly suggest that they were. At a minimum, Paul's language points to some sort of proselytizing activity (similar to Jehovah's Witnesses today). It would therefore be foolish indeed (not to mention misleading) not to read 1 Timothy 2 against the backdrop of false teaching (though traditionalists would rather we didn't). In fact, "they [the false teachers] forbid marriage" (1 Tim. 4:3 AT) alone explains Paul's otherwise obscure comment that "women will be saved [or 'kept safe'] through childbearing" (1 Tim. 2:15) and his seemingly inconsistent command that younger widows marry and raise a family (1 Tim. 5:14, against Paul's advice in 1 Cor. 7).

Kephalē

The real bone of contention between traditionalists and egalitarians is over the meaning of the Greek word kephalē, for this goes to the heart of the male-female relationship. What does Paul mean when he speaks of the man as kephalē of the woman? The extrabiblical meanings of "source" and "leader" do exist, but both, quite frankly, are rare. In a Jewish work that is contemporary with Paul's writings, the author has Eve speaking of "desire" as "the source [*kephalē*] of every kind of sin" (*The Life of Adam and Eve* 19), and the first-century Greek historian and moralist Plutarch recounts Catiline's plan to become the "leader" (*kephalē*) of the Roman Republic (*Cicero* 14.5). For the most part, however, biblical and extrabiblical nonliteral uses of *kephalē* have to do with the idea of "chief" or "prominent"—like the top of a mountain (Gen. 8:5), the foremost position in a column or formation (Job 1:17), the capstone of a building (Ps. 117:22), or the end of a pole (2 Chron. 5:9). What this means is that uses of *kephalē* in Paul (the only biblical writer to use this language) must be decided on a case-by-case basis.

Does Paul use *kephalē* to mean "source"? He most certainly does. Paul's four references to Christ as *kephalē* of his church without a doubt mean "source." Paul's language is thoroughly biological. The church is a living organism that draws its existence and nourishment from Christ as *kephalē*. Christ is *kephalē* and "savior" of the church, "his body" (Eph. 4:16; 5:22–23; Col. 1:18; 2:19);[115] he is its "beginning" and "firstborn" (Col. 1:18). "From him" [*ex hou*] the church is "supported, held together and grows" (Eph. 4:16; Col. 2:19). As *kephalē* of the church, Christ "feeds and cares for it," as a person does for his own body (Eph. 5:29).

Biology shapes Paul's usage in each instance. But theology is ultimately what explains it. *Kephalē* as "source" goes back to the creation of male and female. It derives from the theological notion of the first man as the "source" (*kephalē*) of the first woman. So it would be wholly inappropriate to seek parallels in Greco-Roman literature (as egalitarians are challenged by Grudem to do). "For we [the church] are members of his [Christ's] body, of his flesh, and of his bones (Eph. 5:30 KJV, NKJV).[116] The allusion to Genesis 2:21–23 and the creation of the woman from the rib of the man is unmistakable. And so is the notion of *source*. The church is the Eve of the second Adam, "bone of [his] bones

---

[115]In Ephesians 5:22–23 the lack of articles with *kephalē* and *sōtēr* is significant. If the text read "*the* head" and "*the* Savior" of the church, we might think in terms of a chief executive officer. However, the absence of articles means that these two nouns describe rather than define (that is, they point not to a specific person or thing, but rather to its nature or quality; so not "the Savior" (a title), but "savior," "deliverer," "preserver"). For further discussion, see Zerwick, *Biblical Greek*, #171–73.

[116]Ephesians 5:30 in the Western and Byzantine families of manuscripts and in the church fathers from the second century on reads, "For we are members of his body, of his flesh and of his bones."

and flesh of [his] flesh" (Gen. 2:24). How this comes to be, Paul rightly says, is "a profound mystery" (Eph 5:32).

Traditionalists would argue that Paul is speaking of the church's submission to Christ as chief executive officer. But this would certainly not constitute a profound mystery at all. This is simply the way of the Greco-Roman world—as Jesus reminded his disciples on more than one occasion (see, for example, Matt. 20:25–26). It is the church as Christ's flesh and bone, that is the mystery, as early church tradition echoes.[117] This is not to say that Christ is not Lord of the church. Undeniably he is. The fact that Paul greets all his churches with the "grace of our Lord Jesus Christ" drives this home as a point of first importance. But the premise that lordship is what Paul means by the term *kephalē* is contextually unsupportable. While our modern-day thinking might lead us in this direction, the theology of Ephesians 5:23–33 does not.

It is important to keep before us the real crux of the matter. What these six questions posed to egalitarians in March 1998 bring to light is a *patriarchal* view of society. The male was created as the "ruler" (*kephalē*) who "exercises authority over" (*authentei*) a woman. The woman was created to "submit" (*hypotassesthai*) to the male's authority. Women, therefore, are to be silent in the church; they are not permitted to lead men (as the women at Ephesus were trying to do). An egalitarian view, by contrast, is *organic* ("constituting a whole whose parts are mutually dependent or intrinsically related").[118] It sees the male as the "source" (*kephalē*) of the female, whom God created "from him" to be his "partner." The divinely ordained relationship of male and female is, therefore, a mutually submissive one (*hypotassesthai*). Neither the male nor the female is to lead in a "domineering" (*authentein*) fashion (as the women at Ephesus were trying to do).

The Creation Narratives

The starting point is therefore not 1 Timothy 2:11–15, but the creation narratives. Paul's first letter to Timothy comes into play only insofar as Paul uses these creation narratives to explicate the

---

[117]See previous note.

[118]*Webster's Third New International Dictionary*, s.v. "organic," 5b(1).

male-female relationship. A close look at Genesis 1–2 is therefore in order. Do these narratives put forward a divinely instituted gender hierarchy, as traditionalists claim? Or do they teach a male-female relationship of mutuality, as egalitarians contend?

Although traditionalists claim that male leadership is intrinsic to God's creation of male and female, support is hard to come by from the biblical texts themselves. To be sure, there *is* distinction. God created two sexually distinct beings ("male and female he created them," Gen. 1:27). And this distinction was a deliberate, calculated act on God's part ("Let us make," Gen. 1:26).

What was the purpose, though? The propagation of the human race was decidedly one reason ("Be fruitful and increase in number"), and rapid increase of the human race was essential for dominion over the earth (Gen. 1:28). Yet fruitfulness and dominion were not the primary, long-term reasons for sexual diversity. Their absence from New Testament discussions of human sexuality make this plain. Instead, what the New Testament writers affirm as God's essential purpose is that "the two [male and female] will become one flesh" (Matt. 19:5; Mark 10:8; Eph. 5:31, quoting Gen. 2:24). The Western mind-set has the tendency to understand "one flesh" solely in terms of sexual intimacy. But the Hebrew concept has more to do with that which is "mortal" or "human" (cf. "flesh and blood"). A "one flesh" union, then, has to do with the joining of one human being with another. As Jesus states, "So they are no longer two, but one" (Matt. 19:6). In fact, for Paul the oneness of male and female is a type of the union between Christ and the church (Eph. 5:32).[119]

So there is distinction. But the primary thrust of Genesis 1–2 is the sameness of male and female. Both were formed from the *ᵃdāmâ* ("earth," "reddish-brown soil"), and so both were appropriately named *ᵓādām* (Gen. 5:2, "he called them '*ᵓĀdām'* "). Both were created in God's image ("in the image of God he created them," Gen. 1:27). Although there is a great deal of theological speculation about what creation in God's image means, Genesis 1 unmistakably affirms that male and female equally share it. After all, this is what the first male recognized when he exclaimed, "This is now bone of my bones and flesh of my

[119]For further discussion, see John Oswalt, "*Bāśār*," *Theological Wordbook of the Old Testament*, eds. R. L. Harris, G. L. Archer, B. K. Waltke (Chicago: Moody Press, 1980), 1:136; Claus Westermann, *Genesis 1–11* (Minneapolis: Augsburg, 1981), 233.

flesh," and then called the female "wo-man" (*ʾiššâ*), for she was "taken out of man" (*ʾîš*, Gen. 2:23).

There is also sameness of function. Both male and female are commanded to exercise dominion over the earth—to "rule over" all of it (Gen. 1:26, 28) and to "subdue" it (Gen. 1:28). The language is significant. The Hebrew word *rādâ* ("rule") is used twenty-two times in the Old Testament with reference to human dominion (see, for example, Ps. 110:2; Isa. 14:2, 6). The Hebrew word *kābaš* ("subdue") occurs fifteen times in the Old Testament, in each instance with the meaning "to bring into submission by brute force" (see, for example, 2 Chron. 28:10; Neh. 5:5; Jer. 34:11, 16).[120] No separate spheres of rule are specified (for example, private versus public). There is not even a division of labor (for example, domestic versus nondomestic).

Although male and female can decide on practical grounds how to divide the labor, the assumption of the creation accounts is that both have what it takes to rule and subdue the entirety of what God has created. This stems from the fact of their creation in God's image. The sequence of ideas in Genesis 1 shows it is God's image that enables male and female to rule and subdue. "Let us make *ʾādām* in our image" comes first. "And let them rule over all the earth" comes second (Gen. 1:26 AT).

There is also sameness of family function. Both male and female are given joint responsibility in the bearing and rearing of children. The idea that the woman's job is to produce and raise the children and the man's job is to work the land is simply not found in the creation accounts. *Both* are called to be fruitful. And *both* are called to enjoy the produce of the land. The pronouns are plural throughout: "God blessed *them* and said to *them*, 'Be fruitful and increase in number. . . . I give *you* [plural] every seed-bearing plant on the face of the whole earth and every tree that has fruit with seed in it. They will be *yours* [plural] for food'" (Gen. 1:28–29, emphasis added).

There is likewise sameness in God's sight. Both male and female are created as spiritual equals. Both are blessed by God (Gen. 1:28). Both relate directly to God ("the LORD God called to the man . . . the LORD God said to the woman," Gen. 3:9, 13). And both are held personally accountable by God ("To the woman he said . . . To Adam he said," Gen. 3:16–17).

---

[120]See Oswalt, "*Kābaš*," *Theological Wordbook of the Old Testament*, 1:430.

The portrayal in Genesis 1–2 of male and female as personal, social, and spiritual equals is compelling. Where, then, is the gender hierarchy of the traditionalist? Four things are typically highlighted. The first is in Genesis 2, where the female is created as a help for the male: "It is not good for the man to be alone. I will make a help corresponding to him" (Gen. 2:18 AT). Traditionalists typically translate the Hebrew term *ʿēzer* as "helper" (NIV, NASB, NKJV, RSV) and argue that implicit in the term is the notion of subordination. The one who receives help (it is claimed) has a certain authority over the one who gives help.[121]

Many scholars have pointed to the fatal flaw in this line of thinking. All of the other nineteen occurrences of *ʿēzer* in the Old Testament have to do with the assistance that someone of strength offers to someone in need, namely, help from God, a king, an ally, or an army. Moreover, fifteen of these nineteen references speak of the help that God alone can provide (Ex. 18:4; Deut. 33:7, 26, 29; Ps. 20:2; 33:20; 70:5; 115:9–11 [3x]; 121:1–2 [2x]; 124:8; 146:5; Hos. 13:9). Psalm 121:1–2 is representative (emphasis added): "I lift up my eyes to the hills—where does my *help* come from? My *help* comes from the LORD, the Maker of heaven and earth." Help given to one in need fits Genesis 2:18 quite well. The male's situation was that of being "alone"; God's evaluation was "not good" (Gen. 2:18). The woman was hence created to relieve the man's aloneness through "strong partnership."

Some traditionalists counter with the argument that in offering help, God becomes the human's subordinate or servant.[122] Divine accommodation, maybe—but divine subordination, hardly. And what about the other uses of *ʿēzer*? Judah's allies would hardly have thought of themselves as Judah's subordinates. Nor would Judah under the circumstances have viewed itself as "in charge." When Jerusalem was besieged by the Babylonians and Egypt came to the city's "help," it was as one with superior strength (Isa. 30:5). And when Judah sought again the "help" of allies, these allies hardly came to Judah's aid in a subordinate capacity (Ezek. 12:14).

Neither is there any warrant here for female superiority. The woman was created as a help "in correspondence to" (*kenegdō*)

---

[121]See Raymond C. Ortlund Jr., "Male-Female Equality and Male Headship," in *Recovering Biblical Manhood and Womanhood*, 104.
[122]Ibid.

the man. This, once again, is the language of sameness, not superiority. The "she" is the personal counterpart in every way to the "he." Therefore, "partner" (REB, CEV)—and not "superior" or "helper"—accurately captures the sense of the Hebrew term ʿēzer.

A second traditionalist indicator of gender hierarchy is the fact that the male names the female. "She shall be called 'woman,'" the male said, "for she was taken out of man" (Gen. 2:23). It is argued that by naming the female, the male exercises his rightful authority over her and demonstrates his created role as leader in the relationship.[123] Yet right before this, the male states, "This is now bone of my bones and flesh of my flesh"—hardly something that someone would say about a subordinate (although some traditionalists resort to the language of "paradox").[124]

But perhaps with the recognition of sameness came the attempt to put the female in her place. This assumes, however, that there is power in naming. Traditionalists frequently say this, but biblical scholarship has shown otherwise.[125] Naming in antiquity was a way of memorializing an event or capturing a distinctive attribute. It was not an act of control or power. For instance, Isaac names the well he had dug in the Valley of Gerar *Esek* ("Dispute") because he and the herdsmen of Gerar had argued about who owned it (Gen. 26:20; see also 26:21–22). Hagar names a well *Beer Lahai Roi* ("well of the Living One who sees me") to commemorate the place where God spoke to her in the desert (Gen. 16:13–14). The son of Hagar is named *Ishmael* ("God hears") as a reminder of God's intervention on Hagar's behalf (Gen. 16:11).[126]

What about the naming of the animals? Isn't this the male exercising his God-given role as leader? Yes, the man names the animals—but not as an exercise of male initiative. The text is quite clear. Naming was the means by which the man sought to discern an associate from among the animals. It is worth noting that the Hebrew of Genesis 2:20 states that the man found no "counterpart" (*kenegdō*) to relieve his aloneness, and not that he

---

[123]Ibid., 102–103.

[124]Ibid., 99–100.

[125]See Anthony Thiselton, "The Supposed Power of Words in the Biblical Writings," *Journal of Theological Studies* 25 (1974): 283–99; and George Ramsey, "Is Name-Giving an Act of Domination in Genesis 2:23 and Elsewhere?" *Catholic Biblical Quarterly* 50 (1988): 33.

[126]See my *Women Leaders and the Church*, 102–103.

found no "subordinate" to follow his lead or "helper" to accept his direction. Here finally was "bone of [his] bones and flesh of [his] flesh." Simply put, "wo-man" is the language of sameness, and the male's naming is the recognition of this fact (that is to say, the naming describes, not prescribes).

A third traditionalist indicator of gender hierarchy is the name ʾādām ("man") in Genesis 1:26–27. One traditionalist even states that it "whispers male headship."[127] This is a rather puzzling claim, for there is a scholarly consensus that ʾādām is not a term that denotes gender.[128] In Genesis, it is connected with ᵃdāmâ ("earth," "reddish-brown soil") and is properly translated with a generic term like "human" or "humankind." When gender comes into play in the creation narratives, the Hebrew terms zākār ("male") and nᵉqēbâ ("female") are used, as in the last part of Genesis 1:27: "male and female he created them." That ʾādām is a gender-inclusive term is clear from the repeated reference to ʾādām as a "them" (Gen. 1:26, 27; 5:2). God named the created male and female ʾādām (Gen. 5:1–2)—a point conveniently passed over by some traditionalists. The Septuagint's consistent choice of the generic Greek term anthrōpos ("person," "human") to translate ʾādām points to the same thing.

A fourth (and often definitive) traditionalist indicator of gender hierarchy is the fact that the male was created before the female (Gen. 2:7–23). Surely, the male's temporal priority is God's way of saying that the man must take the lead. That "first is best and second is less" is undeniably the way Americans are educated to think. But is this what God intended? Jesus' teaching that many who are first will be last, and the last first, should caution against this line of thinking (Mark 10:31 and parallels). The account in Genesis 2 certainly attaches no significance to the order "male—then female." The creation of the animals prior to the male obviously has none.

What Genesis 1–2 does emphasize is the human completeness that occurs after the creation of woman. The male alone is "not good"; male + female is "very good." If there is any subordination in the creation accounts, it is not that of the female to the male, but that of both the female and male to God. It is God

---

[127]Ortlund, "Male-Female Equality and Male Headship," 98.

[128]See article on "ʾādām," *New International Dictionary of Old Testament Theology and Exegesis*, ed. W. A. VanGemeren (Grand Rapids: Zondervan, 1997), 1:264.

who commands, and it is the male and the female who are expected to obey.

The dangers of a traditionalist line of thinking become especially apparent in looking at a number of biblical firsts. If "first" in the divine plan designates the "leader," then the followers of John the Baptist (Mandaeans) were right in elevating John over Jesus; Mary (and not Peter) should have been the leader of the apostles, since Jesus appeared first to her (Mark 16:9); and "the dead in Christ" should be the leaders of Christ's future kingdom, since they are to be raised "first" and only "then" those who are living at Christ's return (1 Thess. 4:16–17).

Traditionalists typically appeal to Paul's use of "Adam was formed first, then Eve" (1 Tim. 2:13) as the definitive biblical support that God intended the male to lead. Yet "first ... then" (*prōton ... epeita*), meaning "leader ... follower," doesn't fit New Testament usage, for "first ... then" elsewhere merely defines a sequence of events in time or thought (Mark 4:28; 1 Cor. 15:46; 1 Thess. 4:16–17; 1 Tim. 3:10; James 3:17; Heb. 7:2). In fact, as noted earlier, Paul uses *prōton ... epeita* in this very way just ten verses later. Deacons, he states, must be tested "first" (*prōton*), and "then" (*eita*) let them serve (1 Tim. 3:10).

To sum up: There simply is no explicit statement of male leadership or male-female hierarchy in Genesis 1–2. Some have recognized the futility of squeezing hierarchy out of the creation accounts and have turned instead to Genesis 3:16b: "Your desire will be for your husband, and he will rule over you." If it is not there before the Fall, it is certainly there afterward (so it is argued). The idea of "male rule" plays such a prominent role in evangelical thinking and is so often treated as a factual statement about the way God intends things to be between a man and a woman that a brief look at Genesis 3:16 is in order.

Genesis 3:16

The first thing to note is that "male rule" finds no place in the theology of the Bible. Adam's sin is noted (Rom. 5:12–19; 1 Cor. 15:20–22), as is Eve's deception (2 Cor. 11:3; 1 Tim. 2:14), but the man's rule over the woman is not cited even once (not even for the husband-wife relationship). The simple fact is that male rule does not reappear in the Old Testament beyond Genesis 3:16. The woman is nowhere commanded to obey the man (not even her husband). And the man is nowhere commanded to rule the woman (not even his wife). On the other hand, the fact that male rule is part of the fallen condition does indicate something of the direction that human nature will incline, given any encouragement.

The second thing to note is that what the rest of Scripture lifts up as normative is not Genesis 3:16, but Genesis 1:27 and 2:23–24. Male and female relations are to be lived out not in light of the Fall, but in light of God's intent to create two sexually distinct beings in partnership. This is clear from Jesus' declaration that God from the beginning had made them male *and female* (Greek emphasis; see Matt. 19:4; Mark 10:6). Jesus also makes it clear that the marriage relationship is a functional "oneness," not a hierarchical "two-ness." In God's sight, "they are no longer two, but one" (Matt. 19:6; Mark 10:8).

The third thing to note is the nature of the female's disobedience. Some traditionalists are quick to state that Eve disobeyed in taking the lead and then forcing the male's hand.[129] This is simply not the case. Nowhere is it stated (or implied) that the female's desire was to take the lead. On the contrary, the text explicitly states that her desire in eating was to be wise like God. The male followed suit, obviously because of a similar desire (Gen. 3:4–5). A divine command had been given ("you must not eat from the tree of the knowledge of good and evil," Gen. 2:17). Disobedience on the part of both the man and the woman followed (3:6–7). And both had a price to pay as a result of their desire for knowledge (3:14–19).

The fourth thing to note is the consequence of this act of disobedience. Two statements are made. The first is a statement about the woman's marital desires: "Your desire will be for your husband" (Gen. 3:16). Some take this to be some sort of punishment. Yet God's intent that the two become one flesh surely indicates that sexual desire was a key element of the pre-Fall relationship (2:24). Part of the difficulty is that the Hebrew term *t᷐šûqâ* ("desire," "yearning") is found only two other times in the Old Testament, and neither is an exact parallel. In Genesis 4:7 God says to Cain that sin is like a crouching beast *hungering* for him. The other use of the term can be found in Song of Songs 7:10, which speaks of the bridegroom's *desire* for his beloved.

---

[129]See Ortlund, "Male-Female Equality and Male Headship," 109.

Traditionalists commonly argue that the woman's desire is to dominate her husband. Personal intimacy, however, is what links all three Old Testament uses of the Hebrew term *tᵉšûqâ*. Even more, a yearning for personal intimacy is what makes sense in the context. Since the immediately preceding clause has to do with childbearing ("with toil you will give birth to children" AT), it is quite natural to think in these terms.

What about "and he will rule over you" (Gen. 3:16b)? What does the male's postdisobedience role entail? Some traditionalists think that "rule over" is simply the husband requiring the female's obedience to his decision making. Headship (so it goes) is God's way of keeping the post-Fall woman faithful and submissive.[130] But this interjects an idea that has little connection with the immediate context. Furthermore, this would make Genesis 3:16 prescriptive, and there is nothing prescriptive about the text. Roles are prescribed in Genesis 1:28 ("God blessed them and said to them: 'Be fruitful and increase in number.... Rule over the fish ...'"). The facts regarding sin's impact are what one finds in Genesis 3. And these facts do not include role distinctions.

Other traditionalists think that to "rule" is to dominate the wife. The male will gain her submission by brute force. This does not fit with the meaning of the Hebrew term for "rule," though. *Māšal* is the standard term for "rule" or "reign" (occurring some eighty times in the Old Testament). It is not inherently negative (see Gen. 4:7, "you must master it [sin]"; cf. Gen. 45:8). We are not, therefore, talking about a term that refers to brute force—like the term *kābaš* ("to subdue") in Genesis 1:28 does. This speaks against Genesis 3:16 having to do with the corruption of a benevolent rule given to the male at creation. If this were the case, then the word "rule" would be modified by an adjective like "harsh" or "domineering." And all we have is the word "rule." A better fit with the context is that the male's rule takes the form of sexual demands.[131] This provides a good link with what precedes (childbirth, yearning for her husband). The translation would then be: "Your desire will be for your husband, and he will rule over that desire."

---

[130]See Susan Foh, "A Male Leadership View," in *Women in Ministry: Four Views*, 75–76; and Ortlund, "Male-Female Equality and Male Headship," 107.

[131]See Gordon Wenham, *Genesis 1–15*, Word Biblical Commentary (Waco, Tex.: Word, 1987), 81.

The context of Genesis 3 is human disobedience and its impact, so it is difficult not to see the male's rule as something different from the divine intent of Genesis 1–2. The divine intent was that of a partnership—a co-dominion over the earth, a co-responsibility to bear and raise children, and a co-duty to till the land. Dominion of one over the other was not the intent. This is gender dysfunction, not gender normalcy. It is a sad state of affairs, indeed, when one must seek biblical warrant for gender hierarchy in a male-female relational dysfunction that resulted from disobeying God.

QUESTIONS FROM THE EDITORS

Should we fear, as many hierarchalists suggest, that adoption of an egalitarian approach will lead to the adoption of homosexuality as an acceptable lifestyle?

There is a vast difference between being pro-mutuality (that is, egalitarian) and pro-gay. Biblical support for the former is easily found, while the latter is without biblical foundation whatsoever. It is only if one understands *egalitarian* to mean sexless or unisexual (believing there is no distinction between male and female) that a step in the direction of the viability of same-sex relations can be taken.

But this is not what Scripture teaches. Anyone committed to Scripture as the definitive rule for faith, doctrine, and practice will recognize this, for no sexual union other than a heterosexual one is affirmed in Scripture—and this despite numerous changes in the cultural setting. That male + female is the universal biblical norm is clear from both the creation narratives and subsequent biblical affirmations. Genesis 1:27 makes it plain that, when God created human beings in his image, he created *them* "male and female"— two sexually distinct human beings, not a single bisexual one. Moreover, "Let us make humankind in our image" points both to the purposeful nature of God's activity and to the distinctiveness of this step in the creation process (Gen. 1:26). This distinctiveness is further underlined by the elevated language of Genesis 1:27 and the climactic character of the final strophe: "male and female he created them." All this serves to emphasize that sexual distinction is basic to God's intent for human beings (not an afterthought) and intrinsic to our humanness (not a biological happenstance).

Jesus himself affirms the normativity of heterosexuality for the human race when he states, "From the beginning of creation 'God made them male and female'" (Mark 10:6 NRSV). This means that sexual distinction is not merely for the purpose of procreation and earthly dominion (Gen. 1:28). The divine intent is that "a man will cleave to his wife and they will become one flesh" (Gen. 2:24 AT). That "one flesh" encompasses more than sexual intimacy is clear from Jesus' statement that the union of a man and a woman means that "they are no longer two, but one"

(Matt. 19:6; Mark 10:8). Paul goes even further. The two [male + female]-become-one-flesh is a type of no less than the union of Christ and his church (Eph. 5:31–32).

Actually, the term *homosexuality* is something of a misnomer, especially if it is equated with lust or sexual craving. If current research is accurate, the appropriate terminology is *same-sex ambivalence*, with same-sex attraction indicative of an underlying pathology.[132] What clinicians have found to be common to the experiences of many of those who struggle with same-sex identity issues is the absence of sexual formation through same-sex parental identification during early childhood. This disruption can take the form of physical absence, emotional remoteness, or personal disapproval. Another common thread is the resistance on the part of the child to reattach to the parent. The sexual growth process comes to a halt and resumes only when bonding with a heterosexual parental figure (or surrogate) occurs.[133]

This means that there is no link whatsoever between an egalitarian perspective and same-sex attraction. If anything, it is a hierarchical family structure that has the potential to thwart child-parent bonding, and it is a mutually submissive familial structure that has the potential to facilitate child-parent bonding. That is why Paul in Ephesians 6:1–4 counsels fathers not to be heavy-handed with their children (*mē parorgizete*, 6:4a). Instead, they are to nourish them (5:29)—not sparing correction but being sure it is divine in character ("in the way the Lord corrects and rebukes," 6:4b AT). Parents in turn will earn praise from their children (6:2) and not simply grudging obedience (6:1). When children realize that their parents' nurture is carried out with a view to prolonging their lives (6:3), personal and sexual development will take its divinely intended course.

Your assertion that authority resides with the church rather than with its leaders is a fresh approach. Why haven't we seen much discussion of this view?

Many churches and denominations lag behind society on this point. My denomination, the Evangelical Covenant Church,

---

[132]See Elizabeth Moberly, *Homosexuality: A New Christian Ethic* (Cambridge, UK: James Clarke & Co., 1983), 20–21.

[133]See Joseph Nicolosi, *Reparative Therapy of Male Homosexuality: A New Clinical Approach* (Northvale, N.J: Jason Aronson, Inc., 1991), 25–57.

tackled the topic of biblical leadership a decade ago. The result was the commissioning of eighteen essays, a variety of study guides, and numerous workshops.[134] Even so, we were well behind the corporate world. As Walt Wright points out, Christians who have not studied organizational leadership models are prone to miss the fact that a major shift in corporate leadership paradigms has taken place.[135] The operative word in corporate management since the early 1980s has been *empowerment*—the process of developing persons into mature, contributing members of the organization—not *exercise authority over*. Rosbeth Moss Kanter, in her books *Men and Women of the Corporation* and *The Change Masters*, stresses that people at all levels of an organization are a company's most important resource and need to be involved in production innovation and improvement. The managerial role is thus one of empowering the people to be all that they can be. This is a theory of management that has been widely embraced by such leadership theorists as Thomas Peters and Robert Waterman (*In Search of Excellence*, a national best-seller), Max DePree (*Leadership Is an Art*), and Peter Block (*The Empowered Manager*). In particular, the view of DePree (former chairman and chief executive officer of furniture giant Herman Miller, Inc.) that the art of leadership is *liberating people to do what is required of them in the most effective and humane way possible* is very close to the Pauline definition of the leader as one who empowers God's people for the work of the ministry (Eph. 4:12).

It is important to be clear about this. The issue is *not* the fact of leadership. The Jerusalem church had deacons (Acts 6) and elders (Acts 11:30; 15:2–6, 22; 16:4; 21:18) from its inception. Right at the start Paul appointed elders in the churches he founded (Acts 14:23). He also instructed Titus while in Crete to appoint elders in every town, as he had directed him (Titus 1:5). His letter to the Philippians is addressed not only to the congregation but also to its overseers and deacons (Phil. 1:1). Leadership was a fact of life in first-century churches. The issue, rather, is how one goes about the task of leading. On this

---

[134]See *Servant Leadership,* eds. J. Hawkinson and R. Johnston, 2 vols. (Chicago: Covenant Publications, 1993).

[135]See Walter Wright, "The Covenant Church and Contemporary Leadership Paradigms," in *Servant Leadership,* 2:19–32.

issue first-century culture said one thing, while the New Testament writers proposed another—a distinctly countercultural alternative.

It is truly unfortunate that the biblical paradigm of empowering leadership is to be found predominantly in the corporate world and that the first-century cultural model of "exercise authority over" and "lead by force of will" is the one that still operates in many of our churches and denominations. It is surely time for the church to reclaim its New Testament heritage.

But the task will not be an easy one. Quite frankly, consensus of the whole is a more difficult thing to achieve than governance by the one, two, or few. Similarly, carrying out Paul's principle of "mutual consent" in the marriage relationship takes much more work than "decisions by the one" (1 Cor. 7:5). Ultimately, however, we are called to operate by the biblical norm that decision making falls to the corporate whole (Matt. 18:17–18)—hard though it may be. It may be an inefficient way to operate from a managerial standpoint, but that doesn't make it any less biblical.

You do not discuss extensively 1 Corinthians 11. Do you conclude it is not germane to the gender discussion?

This passage is very germane to discussions concerning gender relations. But the topic of this volume is *women in ministry*—a practice Paul affirms quite clearly in 1 Corinthians 11. Women in public worship at Corinth plainly functioned as prophets and prayer leaders (11:5). And their contributions were praised ("I praise you for remembering me in everything") and affirmed by Paul ("and for holding to the teachings, just as I passed them on to you," 11:2).

Moreover, the language throughout 1 Corinthians 11:2–16 is the language of gender equality and partnership. Both male and female bear the image of God (11:7). Both were created to be mutually dependent on one another (11:11). And both historically find their origin in each other. The first woman's physical origin is by virtue of creation "out of" (*ek* + the genitive) the first male (11:8), while all men subsequently come "through" (*dia* + the genitive) the woman (11:12).

The one Pauline distinction between male and female is the word "glory" (1 Cor. 11:7)—or in the vernacular of the day, "praise" or "honor." The details of 1 Corinthians 11 are wrought with cultural ambiguity. But the issue is not: When women publicly lead in prayer or prophecy, they must wear the proper headgear (11:6). Whether this headgear is of the natural sort (that is, hair) or of an unnatural kind (that is, a scarf) is endlessly debated (*katakalyptomai* literally means "to be down from the head").[136] Cultural customs and the biblical context seem to point in the direction of an artificial head covering. For example, in 1 Corinthians 11:15 hair and appropriate headgear are clearly distinguished by the Greek construction *anti* + the genitive ("in place of"). Hair is *nature's equivalent* to a head covering, not the head covering itself. This fits with the Greco-Roman custom of men and women pulling up their toga to the middle of the ear when carrying out official functions.[137] But the real issue for Paul is a theological, not a sociological, one: When the women pray to God, they must wear a head covering (11:13).

Why should it matter? Again the problem is theological in nature. Men by virtue of creation reflect the "glory" of God; women by virtue of creation reflect the "glory" of the male (1 Cor. 11:7). The object of worship, however, is God, not the male. Paul thrice repeats this. "Whatever is done, is to be done so as to glorify God" (10:31 AT); "a man who prays or prophesies with his head uncovered glorifies God" (11:7 AT); "everything comes from [*ek*] God ... and every act of worship is to be directed to God" (11:13 AT). A woman therefore must cover the male's glory, so that all worship and praise go to God, the Creator, and not to the male, the creature.

It is within this context that the term *kephalē* must be interpreted. The key word once again is "glory" (*doxa*). "The *kephalē* of the woman is the male" (1 Cor. 11:3) and "the woman is the glory of the male" (11:7) are two sides of the same coin. To be "the glory of the male" is for the woman to direct attention and praise to the male. This puts the male in a position of "prominence" or "pride of place"—the most common metaphorical use of *kephalē* inside and outside the Bible.[138]

---

[136]Liddell, Scott, and Jones, *A Greek-English Lexicon,* s.v. "*katakalyptomai.*"

[137]See my *Women Leaders and the Church,* 126–31.

[138]See Liddell, Scott, and Jones, *A Greek-English Lexicon,* s.v. "*kephalē*"; also my *Women Leaders and the Church,* 126–31.

What is missing from Paul's entire treatment is any notion of hierarchy. The female is "the glory of the male" by virtue of her creation "from" him and "for" him (1 Cor. 11:7–9), not by virtue of an act or gesture of subordination (such as covering the head). And the male has "pride of place" by virtue of the female coming "from" him and being created "for" him, not by virtue of having authority over the female.

Paul's may be a difficult line of argument to follow by modern standards, but this does not give us the right to change the argument to our liking. If one brings a belief in a hierarchical ordering of male and female to this passage, then the language of "head" (*kephalē*), "from," and "for" can be made to fit a top-down management paradigm. But if one understands the creation ordering of male and female to be one of relational mutuality, then "head" (*kephalē*), "from," and "for" will be understood against the biblical emphasis on source, sameness, and partnership found in Genesis 2:18–24.

Chapter Three

REFLECTIONS ON EGALITARIAN ESSAYS

by the Editors

REFLECTIONS
ON EGALITARIAN ESSAYS

by the Editors

Drs. Keener and Belleville have provided us with two spirited essays outlining the biblical support undergirding an egalitarian understanding of women in ministry. Both essays are compactly written and consist of material summarizing their writing in previously published books as well as providing fresh and new material they have developed subsequent to their previous work.[1] In some cases their positions have changed on certain issues, as in Keener's view on the nature of teaching in 1 Timothy 2. In other instances they have done additional work on related matters, such as Belleville's answers to the six rather well-known complementarian challenges.

Both authors have interacted with the egalitarian and hierarchicalist scholarship that appeared during the 1990s, as well as earlier scholarship. As such, the essays are representative of current thinking in the ongoing debate. In addition, both essays have given us fresh material that has not previously appeared in print. Belleville, for example, expands on the important work of Andreas Köstenberger regarding the "neither x nor y" construction of 1 Timothy 2:12[2] by arguing that one must add grammatical

[1]See primarily Craig S. Keener, *Paul, Women and Wives: Marriage and Women's Ministry in the Letters of Paul* (Peabody, Mass.: Hendrickson, 1992); and Linda L. Belleville, *Women Leaders and the Church: Three Crucial Questions* (Grand Rapids: Baker, 2000).

[2]Andreas J. Köstenberger, "A Complex Sentence Structure in 1 Timothy 2:12," in *Women in the Church: A Fresh Analysis of 1 Timothy 2:9–15*, eds. Andreas J. Köstenberger, Thomas R. Schreiner, and H. Scott Baldwin (Grand Rapids: Baker, 1995), 81–103.

forms other than verbs into this formula in order to understand its function properly. And Keener adds a large amount of historical background material to support the idea that the women in 1 Corinthians 14 were interrupting with inappropriate questions due to their lack of education. These both reflect cutting-edge, fresh, and important contributions to the gender-in-ministry debate. Having made these preliminary observations, we would now like to make some additional background observations and then highlight more general and specific features of these two egalitarian essays.

Readers of this volume who are familiar with scholarly New Testament literature will recognize that both of our authors have produced essays that reflect current argumentation styles in the field. Other readers who do not regularly read academic argumentation by biblical scholars may occasionally get lost in the material. Perhaps some background information will be helpful. To determine the meaning of difficult texts, scholars must make decisions regarding the literary form and purpose of the documents, the larger context of the material, the immediate context (including the logical flow of the author's thought), the grammar and construction in the original language, the meanings and nuances of the words used, and how all of this fits with larger patterns reflected in the writings of that author. And this list is only an abbreviated summary of the processes that sometimes need to be brought to the interpretive task when problematic passages are scrutinized.[3] At each step in this long chain of tasks, decisions are made that direct as well as influence the balance of the process. As a result, two egalitarian scholars, such as the two writing for this volume, might both come to a prototypical egalitarian position on a certain passage, yet arrive at that decision after having made quite a different set of interpretive decisions en route. To use an analogy, there are many ways to build a garden wall. A garden wall by definition provides boundaries and protection for a certain plot of land, but it may be comprised of a great variety of types, shapes, and colors of stones put together in various patterns and sequences. We have seen in these two essays examples of very similar egalitarian conclusions reached, however, often by different routes. At

---

[3]See further William W. Klein, Craig L. Blomberg, and Robert L. Hubbard Jr., *Introduction to Biblical Interpretation* (Dallas: Word, 1993), especially 155–214.

the same time, discussion of the array of women's leadership roles in the Bible, the roles of Phoebe and Junia, and numerous other details closely coalesce.

The complexity of dealing responsibly with difficult passages accounts for the great variety of positions evangelical scholars can reach regarding various interpretive details. And this very same complexity belies the naive belief that there is one, and only one, set of correct interpretive decisions for evangelical believers on 1 Timothy 2:11–15, on 1 Corinthians 11:2–16 and 14:33–38, or on some other central passage to the debate. What is by far the more important consideration is to ensure that the scholar making the myriad of decisions, when working with difficult passages, is informed, honest, thorough, and faithful in the process. For evangelicals this standard means that our commitment to the authority and inspiration of Scripture is a strong and central component of our hermeneutic. Once one determines the meaning of a passage as best one can, one will accept it as true and authoritative at the appropriate level of contemporary application. The two egalitarian authors of these essays clearly and consistently meet this standard.

In fact, we must note again that the debate surrounding issues of women in ministry is not one of orthodoxy versus liberalism, faithfulness to Scripture versus departure from the faith, or truth versus heresy. Evangelicals with the strongest of views regarding the inspiration and authority of Scripture, the supremacy of the work of Christ, and the all-sufficiency of Christ's salvation for our sin-cursed world can subscribe to either egalitarian or hierarchicalist understandings of the roles of women in ministry. The two egalitarian essays in this volume represent positions fully within the orbit of doctrinally sound evangelicalism, as well as within the boundaries of sound New Testament scholarship.[4]

---

[4]We may also add that these essays do not include the so-called hermeneutical oddities that some hierarchicalist authors have identified in the evangelical egalitarian literature. For example, neither of our writers defends the view that 1 Corinthians 14:33–38 is in any way a Corinthian slogan that Paul then refutes. Neither author attempts to take part or all of these verses as absent from the original text of 1 Corinthians. Neither tries to define *authentein* in 1 Timothy 2:12 as "to murder," "to engage in fertility rites," or "to proclaim oneself the author of." Nor do they attempt to turn the "helper suitable for him" of Genesis 2:18 into someone actually superior to the man, as the occasional feminist scholar has tried to do.

These essays are thus fundamentally distinct from broader egalitarian approaches among liberal Christian or non-Christian scholars. In addition to the evangelical egalitarian who is committed to synthesizing all of the biblical material on the topic, there is the approach that reflects an outright rejection of Christianity or the Bible as irredeemably *androcentric*, a label that comes from David Clines's article on Genesis 1–3[5] but which is perhaps most famously represented by Mary Daly.[6] In this camp, too, are those who have abandoned the Judeo-Christian tradition in favor of religions they believe to be more amenable to feminism, especially forms of ancient paganism that help them revive goddess worship.[7] Then there is the common liberal Christian feminist approach that sees the Bible as containing contradictory strands, a dominant patriarchal tradition modified by a minority liberationist motif. Perhaps Elizabeth Schüssler Fiorenza's book *In Memory of Her: A Feminist Theological Reconstruction of Christian Origins* (New York: Crossroad, 1983) and subsequent work best reflects this tradition.[8] It does not reject Christianity or Scripture outright but prefers the minority liberating voice as the only one applicable for today. It also is often bound up with the view that sees the oldest New Testament witness and sources as being the most egalitarian, with subsequent writers re-patriarchalizing the Christian faith. This approach can then be linked with views of pseudonymous authorship of works like the Pastoral Epistles in the second or third generation of Christianity. Clearly these are not the approaches of Keener or Belleville.

Now to some general comments about the two essays in this section of our volume. At the heart of the gender-in-ministry debate is the ministry of prophecy as found in both Testaments,

---

[5]David J.A. Clines, "What Does Eve Do to Help? and Other Irredeemably Androcentric Orientations in Genesis 1–3," in *What Does Eve Do to Help? and Other Readerly Questions in the Old Testament*, ed. David J.A. Clines (Sheffield: Sheffield Academic Press, 1990), 25–48.

[6]See especially Mary Daly, *The Church and the Second Sex* (Boston: Beacon, 1985).

[7]See Naomi R. Goldenberg, *Changing of the Gods: Feminism and the End of Traditional Religions* (Boston: Beacon, 1979).

[8]For a largely Old Testament counterpart to this classic New Testament study, see Phyllis Trible, *Texts of Terror: Literary-Feminist Readings of Biblical Narratives* (Philadelphia: Fortress, 1984). For a standard systematic-theological approach, see Rosemary Radford Reuther, *Sexism and God-talk: Toward a Feminist Theology* (Boston: Beacon, 1983).

including its features related to office and gifting, its purpose and function in the unfolding of God's plan, and its importance and connection to modern expressions of ministry. Both of our authors give a more prominent role to this issue than do many egalitarians. Keener begins his argument with a rather extensive review of prophecy and gender, and he contends that women functioned without limits in this important role. Belleville likewise notes that women functioned as prophets during every era of Israel's history, though she finds the core issue in the debate to be the question of whether or not women can lead men. Both writers note that in both the Old and New Testaments female and male prophets alike delivered God's word to his people and that this role in the New Testament was a leadership role, was expressed in the public worship of the church, and was foundational to the very establishment of the church.

Hierarchicalists, however, are more likely to argue, at least with reference to Paul's letters, that apostles (read "missionaries" or "church planters") and prophets (those who proclaimed God's word charismatically) were actually exercising spiritual gifts, not occupying the duly acknowledged offices of ongoing church leadership.[9] Consequently, the observation that women possessed the gift of prophecy and participated in the leadership of God's people does not lead to the conclusion that all church offices are now open to them.[10] For hierarchicalists, the more institutionalized role of overseer (bishop)/elder is actually the "highest" authoritative leadership position in the church—and women did not participate in that office.[11] One can deny that

---

[9] See especially Wayne A. Grudem, *The Gift of Prophecy in 1 Corinthians* (Lanham, Md.: University Press of America, 1982).

[10] Over against Keener, the numerical ranking in 1 Corinthians 12:28 need not be hierarchical but may simply be chronological. See further Craig L. Blomberg, *1 Corinthians*, The NIV Application Commentary Series (Grand Rapids: Zondervan, 1994), 247.

[11] "Overseer" and "bishop" are simply two alternate English renderings of the Greek *episkopos*. "Elder" renders *presbyteros*. The equating of these terms reflects standard congregationalist church polity, especially in light of their overlapping leadership roles in 1 Timothy 3:1–7 and 5:17–20. First Timothy 3:1 uses the cognate noun *episkopē*; in Philippians 1:1 the *episkopos* is linked with the *diakonos* (both in the plural) as the leaders of the church. Presbyterian and episcopal models would, of course, distinguish the various terms somewhat differently. Congregationalists also often equate "pastor" with this cluster of terms, particularly in light of their apparent interchangeability in Acts 20:17–31. But they would also distinguish the "office" of pastor from the "gift" of pastoring (or shepherding).

the concept of office existed in the New Testament, but it remains true that Paul in 1 Timothy and Titus refers to elders (or overseers) and deacons as positions that people occupied in the church with specific criteria for selecting those who would fill them—a quite different approach from a person faithfully recognizing and exercising his or her spiritual gifts, which God's Spirit distributes according to his will (1 Cor. 12:11). And "overseer" and "elder" never appear on any biblical writer's list of spiritual gifts. On the other hand, against these hierarchicalist positions both Keener and Belleville argue that biblical evidence is lacking to support the contention that the role (or office) of overseer/elder is a "higher" position than that held in the early church by the apostles or in both the Old and New Testaments by prophets. If anything, they would argue that the latter are more foundational and hence more important.

The discussions in the gender debate regarding prophecy highlight two further problems. First, how do we translate first-century polity and practice into twenty-first-century church forms? Or to put it another way, what is the contemporary equivalent of the office of overseer/elder? Conversely, what is the New Testament equivalent of today's senior pastor or other positions within a church staff? What sort of church leader today carries the same authority as that exercised by Paul? The questions are nearly endless. The complexity of linking the ancient to the modern in terms of gifts and roles builds on and is an extension of the debate that has raged throughout church history as to which system of church governance is the "most biblical." One can find evangelical defenders of the three major types of polity that have emerged: congregational, presbyterian, and episcopal forms. Few churches seek to imitate exactly what is arguably the predominant New Testament model by meeting only in homes with one elder per house church, having multiple home congregations in one community that make up "the local church," and utilizing itinerant missionaries or apostles in additional leadership roles over them.[12] Yet nearly everyone today strives to implement the principles underlying New Testament church government forms,

---

[12]See especially Bradley Blue, "Acts and the House Church," in *The Book of Acts in Its Graeco-Roman Setting*, eds. David W. J. Gill and Conrad Gempf (Grand Rapids: Eerdmans, 1994), 119–222. Even this historical reconstruction, however, has been challenged.

even though egalitarians and hierarchicalists disagree at several important points as to just what those principles are with regard to gender. Egalitarians tend to see the ministry of women as prophets in the New Testament as in keeping with Old Testament practice and a foundation for the full participation of women in church life today. Hierarchicalists are more likely to note the consistent gaps in both Testaments—no women priests in the Old Testament, no women apostles in the ministry of Jesus, no women overseers/elders in the New Testament church—as implying that the highest office of spiritual leadership is always reserved for men.

A second major issue at the heart of the gender-in-ministry debate revolves around how we should determine which features of New Testament church life are transcultural and which require changed applications to be faithful to their underlying principles because of the changes in the culture from then until now.[13] Here the gender debate touches a vast range of issues from decorum to social custom to apparel to head coverings to jewelry. All parties would likely agree that some material in the New Testament is cultural, with the balance falling under the general heading of transcultural. Again, almost all parties in the gender debate would also say that the principles underlying the cultural material that is no longer necessary to replicate continue to be relevant and important. Passages like 1 Corinthians 11 and 14 as well as 1 Timothy 2 all contain elements that are grist for the cultural-transcultural mill. Keener's essay discusses at some length the apostle Paul's ad hoc use of Old Testament material, including early Genesis material, to support an argument the apostle was making. The importance of the argument is clearly seen when we realize that many interpreters automatically assume that, when the apostle summons supporting material from Genesis 1–2 (so-called creation ordinances) or even Genesis 3 (the way life has been mandated since the fall of Adam and Eve), the argument must necessarily involve transcultural practices. Keener argues that Paul at times uses these (and other) Scriptures in an ad hoc way without intending to set down a principle for all time, and while hierarchicalists will no doubt vigorously disagree, his argument is an important one that merits the attention of all parties in this debate.

---

[13]For an introductory methodological discussion, see Klein, Blomberg, and Hubbard, *Introduction to Biblical Interpretation*, 401–26.

Now to some more specific comments about these two egal-itarian essays. We can identify two broad positions among evan-gelical egalitarians, one somewhat more common in the United States and the other perhaps more common in the British Com-monwealth. The former involves arguing that the best exegesis of the New Testament texts traditionally seen to prohibit women's roles in certain respects in fact shows that they were more egalitarian even in their original contexts than has often been recognized.[14] The latter tends to argue that these texts did imply rather widespread prohibitions on women's leadership in the first-century world, but they were due to specific circum-stances within that world that largely no longer obtain today.[15] In keeping with their American ethos, both Keener and Belleville fall closer to the former position, though each clearly does appeal to both kinds of arguments at different points along the way. Thus, for all of Keener's extensive and helpful research into the historical background of the controversial New Testament texts, his position on 1 Corinthians 14:33–38 is ultimately that Paul was forbidding only the intrusive questions of uneducated women in church. Similarly, 1 Timothy 2:12 in its original setting prohibited the Ephesian women from teaching or having authority over men because these women were promoting heresy. In a context where this was not a problem, Paul would not have made the same prohibition. These are quite different approaches from what both hierarchicalist and liberal feminist authors have most com-monly argued, namely, that Paul was absolutely prohibiting women from certain senior leadership roles throughout the entire church of his day. Then, of course, these two groups radically diverge as to whether such a policy should remain in force in our day. Belleville focuses more on 1 Timothy 2:12 as prohibiting *dom-ineering* teaching over men, while more closely following Keener with respect to 1 Corinthians 14. One does wonder, however,

---

[14]Here one thinks especially of the many works of Richard Clark Kroeger and Catherine Clark Kroeger, ably summarized in their *I Suffer Not a Woman: Rethinking 1 Timothy 2:11–15 in Light of Ancient Evidence* (Grand Rapids: Baker, 1992). It has been largely American scholars who have proposed what the Council on Biblical Man-hood and Womanhood calls "hermeneutical oddities," such as those noted in foot-note 4 above.

[15]See R. T. France, *Women in the Church's Ministry: A Test Case for Biblical Inter-pretation* (Grand Rapids: Eerdmans, 1995). Cf. already F. F. Bruce, *1 and 2 Corinthians* (London: Marshall, Morgan, & Scott, 1971), 137.

whether it is not historically and exegetically more plausible to argue simply that the biblical writers were more sweeping in their prohibitions than American evangelicals of almost all theological stripes, but that we all (to varying degrees) recognize that cultural elements, no longer as pervasive in our world today as then, call for changed applications.[16]

Both Keener's and Belleville's reconstructions of 1 Corinthians 14 and 1 Timothy 2 seemingly require us to believe that all women were part of the problem, even at these two local levels, and that no men were any part of the problem, with the result that Paul feels comfortable restricting all women in these two congregations and none of the men.[17] Nevertheless, many men were illiterate and uneducated, as well as the women, and thus just as likely to ask disruptive questions and be just as easily seduced by heresy.[18] And, in fact, in the Pastoral Epistles it is only the men who are ever explicitly said to teach heresy (though it is not unnatural to imagine the women being influenced by their false teaching). Egalitarians tend to argue that heretical teaching and misunderstandings on the part of women are clearly in the background of these two passages, but hierarchicalists argue that because such female behavior is not explicitly mentioned, we cannot assume it was present.

---

[16]See Clark H. Pinnock, "Biblical Authority and the Issues in Question," in *Women, Authority and the Bible*, ed. Alvera Mickelsen (Downers Grove, Ill.: InterVarsity Press, 1986), 55, commenting on Colossians 3:18 and similar texts: "The issue is not just whether there is a way to make verses such as 'wives, be subject to your husbands, as is fitting in the Lord' (Col. 3:18) and similar texts say something other than they seem to say. It is the practical problem of getting people at large to believe that they do. The radical feminists and the traditionalists both argue that such texts are not feminist in content, and I suspect that their view, agreeing as it does with the 'plain sense' reading so widely held, will prevail and not be successfully refuted by biblical feminists. Of course, the biblical feminist interpretation is possible; the problem is that it does not strike many people, either scholarly or untutored, as plausible."

[17]Belleville explicitly affirms that men were active in promoting the heresy, but does not deal with this resulting tension in Paul's prohibition.

[18]D. A. Carson ("'Silent in the Churches': On the Role of Women in 1 Corinthians 14:33b–36," in *Recovering Biblical Manhood and Womanhood: A Response to Evangelical Feminism*, eds. John Piper and Wayne Grudem [Wheaton, Ill.: Crossway, 1991], 147) thus calls the approach that silences the women in these two passages simply because of supposed cultural factors "unbearably sexist"! Belleville's response (above, page 116, note 75) suggests that she has not understood Carson's point here.

These two authors approach the subject of gender roles in the home differently. While not part of the contributors' assignment in this book, the issue is nevertheless addressed by Keener, who takes a view on roles in the home that matches his view on roles in the church. But he notes exceptions, and it is worth stressing that there are scholars who adopt a hierarchicalist approach to the family and an egalitarian perspective in the church.[19] Belleville does not directly address the domestic question here, presumably believing the topic of gender roles in ministry can be adequately addressed on its own. But her recent book, *Women Leaders and the Church: Three Crucial Questions*, goes into the question in detail as part of her larger helpful discussion of the roles women can play in society.

These two essays also differ from many egalitarian discussions both in what they do or do not emphasize and in their sequence of arguments. Neither of our authors makes much at all of Galatians 3:28, whereas that text has often been a flash point or even starting point for egalitarian discussion on this topic. Neither author *begins* with Genesis 1–2 as demonstrating egalitarian patterns in creation that should be preserved or restored in the new creation of life in Christ (although well into her essay Belleville argues that this is the proper starting point and deals with these chapters in detail).[20] Neither author does much with 1 Corinthians 11, and what they do discuss avoids the more nuanced treatments of both timeless and cultural rationales for the various commands Paul gives in verses 2–16. It is at least arguable that the appeals to custom and common practice dictate the specifics of head coverings, while the appeal to creation governs the broader principle of wifely submission.[21] And neither author quite addresses the issue of the ongoing pattern of one particular office or role of leadership being prohibited to women throughout the sweep of the biblical revelation, as noted above. Both Keener and Belleville acknowledge that in the New

---

[19]See, for example, Grant R. Osborne, *The Hermeneutical Spiral: A Comprehensive Introduction to Biblical Interpretation* (Downers Grove, Ill.: InterVarsity Press, 1991), 328–30.

[20]On both of these points, see Gilbert Bilezikian, *Beyond Sex Roles: What the Bible Says About a Woman's Place in Church and Family*, rev. ed. (Grand Rapids: Baker, 1985); and Aída B. Spencer, *Beyond the Curse: Women Called to Ministry* (Nashville: Nelson, 1985).

[21]See Blomberg, *1 Corinthians*, 207–26, especially 214–20.

Testament we simply have no named examples of either gender serving in the role or office of overseer/elder, while Belleville constructs an argument for women elders being positively in view in 1 Timothy 5. Keener cites important precedents for women in ministry leadership throughout church history but fails to note, with egalitarians Tucker and Liefeld in their magisterial survey of church history, that, of all the leadership roles women have held and the more institutionalized the church has become in any place, the more likely the office or ongoing role of chief pastoral leadership has been reserved for men.[22] Both of our authors do address these issues piecemeal, talking about priests here, synagogue leaders there, elders in other places, but neither specifically addresses the issue of the apparently transcultural pattern throughout both Testaments and most of church history that reserves certain roles for men.

Hierarchicalists also often add to the above line of reasoning by pointing out that egalitarian understandings of basic New Testament texts such as these two essays have examined are fairly recent when compared to the long sweep of church history. If these approaches to 1 Timothy 2, 1 Corinthians 14, or Galatians 3 have rarely, if ever, appeared in the history of Christian thought before the twentieth century, can we not conclude that they are novel, modern innovations that would be entirely foreign to the authors of the New Testament documents—and thus out of step with the intended meaning of these passages? Keener addresses this line of thinking briefly, but we may explore the issue further. "Recency" arguments are powerful but, at the same time, limited in their value. For example, many evangelicals have used recency arguments to cast aspersion on pretribulationalism and dispensational theology. Many of the arguments for a literal six-day creation and a young earth are ironically products of the post-Enlightenment, post-evolutionist era, and there was a larger diversity among the church fathers on how to interpret Genesis 1 than most modern conservatives realize.[23] The same is true of the debate over the final destiny of the unevangelized. The so-called restrictivist position is used as

---

[22]Ruth A. Tucker and Walter L. Liefeld, *Daughters of the Church: Women and Ministry from New Testament Times to the Present* (Grand Rapids: Zondervan, 1987).

[23]On both of these issues see Mark A. Noll, *The Scandal of the Evangelical Mind* (Grand Rapids: Eerdmans, 1994), 114–39, 177–208.

a litmus test by many modern evangelicals, when, in fact, no less than five major approaches to this question have prevailed among orthodox theologians throughout church history.[24] It is not at all clear, therefore, that the argument of recency in and of itself is damning. At least there are many who appeal to this argument quite selectively!

The egalitarian cause could in fact be bolstered by the observation that openness to women in ministry prevailed in numerous nineteenth- and early twentieth-century contexts that, in fact, adopted more restrictive positions after the fundamentalist-modernist controversy in the 1920s. One thinks, for example, of schools like Moody Bible Institute in Chicago, Illinois, or denominations like the Evangelical Free Church of America (see our introduction, footnote 9). It is simply not a true historical statement to claim that most or all of the cultural forces leading to modern evangelical egalitarianism have come from the secular culture; Christians have at times led the way on these issues. Conversely, secular cultural forces have in part contributed to the ascendancy of hierarchicalism, or a retrenchment from more open positions.[25] On the other hand, secular forces have clearly contributed powerfully at various times and places to shaping the forms of egalitarianism, as Belleville stresses at the beginning of her essay. Moreover, we can cite instances where relatively modern concepts have been adopted by almost all wings of the American church, even though such approaches might have been totally foreign to first-century Christians. We must thus ask if this is necessarily bad. Might the availability of general revelation to all humans in some contexts preserve truths that the church has not always adequately stressed?

Take political democracy and economic capitalism as examples. Democracy can trace its roots to ancient Greece, but for most of human history democracy was not a primary governmental form among the nations of the world. The rise of democracy among the political states of the modern world has even influenced the church, with the result that certain forms of

---

[24]See especially John Sanders, *No Other Name: An Investigation into the Destiny of the Unevangelized* (Grand Rapids: Eerdmans, 1992).

[25]On both of these points see Rebecca Merrill Groothuis, *Women Caught in the Conflict: The Culture War Between Traditionalism and Feminism* (Grand Rapids: Baker, 1994).

church government are predicated on democratic principles.[26] Certain economic trends in the first-century Roman Empire resembled a primitive capitalism, but the full-blown system would await Adam Smith and the eighteenth century.[27] Yet many conservative writers, including many who are equally conservative with respect to gender roles, believe that enough biblical teaching lays the groundwork for democracy and capitalism that these systems should be accepted, even if their primary ancient stimuli were Greek and Roman, not Jewish or Christian, and even if their modern development involves significant impetus from secular social forces.[28] Thus the recency of a concept may or may not be a valid reason for us to jettison its employment. Church history is informative, instructive, valuable, and influential, but it is not inspired or infallible.

The gender-in-ministry debate revolves around leadership in the church, a topic that inevitably leads to a discussion of authority. Throughout Scripture God has clearly invested leaders with authority, be they Moses and Paul, king and priest, or prophet and apostle. Scripture is also clear that authority and how it is used changes in the kingdom of God that Jesus came to proclaim and establish. In most discussions revolving around this topic the parties are likely to assume that authority is invested in the leaders of local church congregations, that this authority is a necessary component of leadership, and that authority, when used properly, can further the work of the kingdom and bring honor and glory to God. What is more debatable involves who has the authority and whether it is shared between men and women or whether it is the primary domain of males only. But Belleville's discussion of authority goes beyond the more common argument of egalitarians who point out that authority in the church is service and servanthood and is not domination or power.[29] She

---

[26]For a balanced overview of Christian and other ideological impacts on the foundational philosophy of the United States, see Mark A. Noll, *Christians in the American Revolution* (Grand Rapids: Christian Univ. Press, 1977).

[27]On the economics of the first-century Roman Empire, see William R. Herzog II, *Parables as Subversive Speech: Jesus as Pedagogue of the Oppressed* (Louisville: Westminster John Knox, 1994), 53–73.

[28]See especially Ronald H. Nash, *Poverty and Wealth: The Christian Debate over Capitalism* (Westchester, Ill.: Crossway, 1986). See also E. Calvin Beisner, *Prosperity and Poverty* (Westchester, Ill.: Crossway, 1988).

[29]See also Bilezikian, *Beyond Sex Roles*, 104–18.

suggests that *exousia* ("authority") is granted by the Lord of the church to the congregation of believers rather than to their leaders.

Here Belleville is following the trajectory of discussions of whether it is even appropriate to speak of authority in the church invested in a single office or in shared leadership and whether ordination (a ceremony often held to convey such authority) finds a clear biblical mandate.[30] Belleville argues that New Testament authors simply do not link *exousia* with the preaching and teaching ministry of individual leaders. Rather, she contends that authority is given to the church as a whole. In this way she moves the debate into a new arena, because if authority is granted to the entire church, then it is shared equally by all members of the church, both male and female. Furthermore, if authority rests with the corporate expression of the body of Christ, it is not associated with role or office or gift. Hierarchicalists, on the other hand, will object to separating authority from leadership, role, and office, because this connection is central to their position. It also seems somewhat artificial for Belleville to argue that since authority is only specifically mentioned in the context of the disciples' ministry of exorcism and healing (Matt. 10:1–4), their accompanying ministry of preaching and teaching was not similarly invested with Jesus' authority. After all, in the immediately preceding passage (Matt. 9:35–38), Jesus' own ministry, which the disciples are commissioned here to replicate, links teaching and preaching the gospel of the kingdom inseparably to healing every kind of disease.

Our final observation deals with the broader social issues that sometimes get involved in this debate, namely, slavery and homosexuality. The former consumed the energy of the American church 150 years ago and was as acrimonious as the gender debate can now sometimes be. The latter is a current issue about which, however, evangelicals have comparatively little disagreement. Egalitarians often point to the slavery issue as argued by abolitionists as a debate that has some remarkable similarities to the current gender debate.[31] Scholars argued over the lexical meaning of

---

[30]See, respectively, Walter L. Liefeld, "A Plural Ministry View," in *Women in Ministry: Four Views*, eds. Bonnidell Clouse and Robert G. Clouse (Downers Grove, Ill.: InterVarsity Press, 1989), 127–53; Marjorie Warkentin, *Ordination: A Biblical-Historical View* (Grand Rapids: Eerdmans, 1982).

[31]See especially Willard M. Swartley, *Slavery, Sabbath, War and Women* (Scottdale, Pa.: Herald, 1983).

Hebrew and Greek words, over the explicit versus implicit meaning of texts, and over the ramifications of such significant social change on the stability and future of society—all issues, by the way, that appear in current gender debates. Egalitarians argue that we should learn from the slavery debates of the nineteenth century and realize that the gospel contains seeds of change that were not fully expressed in the first century but which have germinated and borne fruit centuries later. The abolition of slavery was not a viable social change possible in the first century, but it became just that in the nineteenth (and to a lesser degree in certain other times and cultures in church history).[32] On the other hand, the hierarchicalist may protest that, strictly speaking, the equivalent to abolishing the institution of slavery would be abolishing the institution of marriage, which is *not* an egalitarian objective!

The relationship of homosexuality to the gender debate is considerably different. Even though evangelicals speak with a fairly united voice on the topic, namely, that the practice of homosexuality violates the moral standards of God, hierarchicalists strongly contend that altering the traditional understanding of gender roles in home, church, and society will almost inevitably lead to wider acceptance of homosexuality as a legitimate lifestyle and to an erosion of biblical standards of what is moral or immoral. Clearly there are examples of this slippery slope among conservative Christians in recent church history. Christians for Biblical Equality was in fact formed in part as a reaction to a larger evangelical egalitarian movement, some strands of which were beginning to move in this direction. But both authors of our egalitarian essays strongly and rightly contend that equality between the sexes involves issues so sufficiently different from those in the homosexuality debate that the slippery slope scarcely proves inevitable. While all parties agree that there are numerous biblical texts that present women in a positive light, no biblical passage treats homosexuality at all positively.[33]

---

[32]For a detailed discussion of slavery in the New Testament world, see Thomas Wiedemann, *Greek and Roman Slavery* (Baltimore: Johns Hopkins Univ. Press, 1981). For a full history of abolitionist movements over the years and the roles Christianity at times played within them, see David B. Davis, *Slavery and Human Progress* (Oxford: Oxford Univ. Press, 1984).

[33]The best book-length evangelical treatment of both the biblical and contemporary issues remains Thomas E. Schmidt, *Straight and Narrow? Compassion and Clarity in the Homosexuality Debate* (Downers Grove, Ill.: InterVarsity Press, 1995).

Keener and Belleville have thus put readers who hold a wide variety of theological positions in their debt by these cogently argued cases for an evangelical egalitarian approach to gender roles in ministry. We now turn to two equally cogent hierarchicalist essays and will resume our commentary following their presentations.

Part Two

WOMEN IN MINISTRY
THE COMPLEMENTARIAN VIEW:
TWO PERSPECTIVES

Chapter Four

WOMEN IN MINISTRY

**Thomas R. Schreiner,
The Southern Baptist Theological Seminary**

WOMEN IN MINISTRY

Thomas R. Schreiner

I believe the role of women in the church is the most controversial and sensitive issue within evangelicalism today. This isn't to say that it is the most important controversy, for other debates—the openness of God, and inclusivism versus exclusivism, for example—are more central. Nonetheless, "the women's issue" generally sparks more intense debate, probably because women who must defend their call to pastoral ministry feel that their personhood and dignity are being questioned by those who doubt the validity of their ordination. Men who support the ordination of women are often passionate about the issue, both for exegetical reasons and because they feel compassion for women who have shared their stories with them.[1] Most women who feel called to ministry have experienced the pain of speaking with men who have told them that their desires are unbiblical.

I am as affected by our cultural climate as anyone, and thus I would prefer, when speaking with women who feel called to pastoral ministry, to say that they should move ahead and that they have God's blessing to do so. It is never pleasant to see someone's face fall in disappointment when they hear my view on this matter. On the other hand, I must resist the temptation to please people and instead must be faithful to how I understand Scripture. And I understand Scripture to forbid women

---

[1]It is clear, for example, that Craig Keener (*Paul, Women and Wives: Marriage and Women's Ministry in the Letters of Paul* [Peabody, Mass.: Hendrickson, 1992], 3–4, 120) is influenced significantly by the sense of call that many women feel.

from teaching and exercising authority over a man (1 Tim. 2:12). In this essay I will try to explain what is involved in this prohibition. Following the lead of others, I will call my view the *complementarian* view, and I will call the view that believes all ministries should be open to women the *egalitarian* view.

HISTORY, HERMENEUTICS, AND TERMINOLOGY

Before I undertake an explanation of the biblical text, I want to say something about history, hermeneutics, and accurate terminology. Let me begin with history. Throughout most of church history women have been prohibited from serving as pastors and priests.[2] Thus, the view I support in this essay is "the historic view." I readily admit that those supporting the historic view have sometimes used extreme and unpersuasive arguments to defend their views, and that low views of women have colored their interpretations. Nor does the tradition of the church prove that women should be proscribed from the pastorate, for as evangelicals we believe in *sola scriptura*. Nonetheless, evangelicals must beware of what C. S. Lewis called "chronological snobbery." The tradition of the church is not infallible, but it should not be discarded easily. The presumptive evidence is against a "new interpretation," for we are apt to be ensnared by our own cultural context and thus may fail to see what was clear to our ancestors. An interpretation that has stood the test of time and has been ratified by the church in century after century—both in the East and the West and in the North and the South—has an impressive pedigree, even if some of the supporting arguments used are unpersuasive.[3] Moreover, the view that women should not be priests or pastors has transcended confessional barriers. It has been the view throughout history of most Protestants, the vari-

---

[2] See Daniel Doriani, "A History of the Interpretation of 1 Timothy 2," in *Women in the Church: A Fresh Analysis of 1 Timothy 2:9–15*, eds. Andreas J. Köstenberger, Thomas R. Schreiner, and H. Scott Baldwin (Grand Rapids: Baker, 1995), 213–67.

[3] Karen Jo Torjeson (*When Women Were Priests: Women's Leadership in the Early Church and the Scandal of Their Subordination in the Rise of Christianity* [San Francisco: HarperSanFrancisco, 1993], 9–87) argues that women actually functioned as priests in the earliest part of church history. Ruth A. Tucker and Walter L. Liefeld (*Daughters of the Church: Women and Ministry from New Testament Times to the Present* [Grand Rapids: Zondervan, 1987], 63, 89–127), who are egalitarian scholars, are more careful and persuasive in their analysis of the evidence.

ous Orthodox branches of the church, and the Roman Catholic Church. All of these groups could be wrong, of course. Scripture is the final arbiter on such matters. But the burden of proof is surely on those who promote a new interpretation, especially since the new interpretation follows on the heels of the feminist revolution in our society. Despite some of the positive contributions of feminism (for example, equal pay for equal work and an emphasis on treating women as human beings), it is scarcely clear that the movement as a whole has been a force for good.[4] The final verdict is not in, but I am not optimistic about the outcome.

A brief word on hermeneutics is also necessary. We are keenly aware that all interpreters are shaped by their previous history and culture.[5] No one encounters a text with a blank slate, without presuppositions. A detached objectivity is impossible, for we are finite human beings who inhabit a particular culture and a specific society. On the other hand, we must beware of thinking that we can never transcend our culture. Otherwise, we will always and inevitably read into texts what we already believe. If we are ensnared by our own histories and social location, then we can dispense with reading any books, though we may enjoy reading those that support our current biases. If we can never learn anything new and if we invariably return to our own worldview, then there is no "truth" to be discovered anyway. Every essay in this volume would simply represent the cultural biases of the contributors, and your response as a reader would be your own particular cultural bias. If we are trapped by our past, we might as well relish who we are—and conclude that we're simply wasting our time in reading anybody else's opinion anyway.

The idea that we are completely bound by our past is hermeneutical nihilism. Instead, awareness of our cultural background and presuppositions may become the pathway by which

---

[4]See Mary A. Kassian, *The Feminist Gospel: The Movement to Unite Feminism with the Church* (Wheaton, Ill.: Crossway, 1992); Robert W. Yarbrough, "The Hermeneutics of 1 Timothy 2:9–15," in *Women in the Church: A Fresh Analysis*, 155–96; Harold O. J. Brown, "The New Testament Against Itself: 1 Timothy 2:9–15 and the 'Breakthrough' of Galatians 3:28," in *Women in the Church: A Fresh Analysis*, 197–211. From a secular point of view, see Nicholas Davidson, *The Failure of Feminism* (Buffalo, N.Y.: Prometheus, 1988).

[5]For a helpful analysis of common hermeneutical errors on both sides, see Andreas J. Köstenberger, "Gender Passages in the New Testament: Hermeneutical Fallacies Critiqued," *Westminster Theological Journal* 56 (1994): 259–83.

we transcend our past. People do change, and we can with dili-
gent effort understand those who are different from us. Similarly,
comprehending texts that are distant from us is possible, and we
may even accept such a "foreign" world as the truth. Indeed,
hermeneutical nihilism is really a form of atheism, for evangelicals believe in a God who speaks and who enables us to understand his words. The Spirit of God enables us to comprehend and
embrace the truths of his word (1 Cor. 2:6–16), truths we rejected
when we were unregenerate. Christians are confident that God's
word is an effective word, a word that creates life (John 6:63).
Naturally, this does not mean that Christians now have perfect
knowledge, nor does it imply that we will agree on everything;
neither am I denying that some texts are difficult to interpret. We
"know in part" (1 Cor. 13:12) until the day of redemption.[6] And
yet we can gain a substantial and accurate understanding of the
Scriptures in this age. I approach this issue, therefore, with the
confidence that God's word speaks to us today and that his will
on the role of women can be discerned.

Another hermeneutical matter must be discussed at this
juncture. Occasionally the debate between the complementarian
and egalitarian views is framed as a choice between fundamental texts. For example, one author uses the ordination of women
as an illustration in discussing the millennium, declaring the following about the role of women:

> The crucial question becomes which passages control the
> discussion: the passages where no limits seem to be
> expressed or those that do. Different sides take different
> positions based on whether they regard the nonrestric-
> tive texts to be more fundamental to determining the
> view or the restrictive texts.[7]

I simply want to say at the outset that I categorically reject
the dichotomy expressed here. I do not believe that the issue
relates to which texts are "more fundamental" or which texts
"control the discussion." Such a view assumes that one set of
texts functions as a prism by which the other set of texts is

---

[6]Unless otherwise noted, Scripture citations are taken from the updated New
American Standard Bible (NASB).

[7]Darrell L. Bock, "Summary Essay," in *Three Views on the Millennium and
Beyond,* ed. D. L. Bock (Grand Rapids: Zondervan, 1999), 280. Incidentally, this is not
a criticism of Bock's overall view, for I believe he is a complementarian.

viewed. All of us are prone, of course, to read the Scriptures through a particular grid, and none of us escapes such a tendency completely. But this way of framing the issue assumes that the decision on women's ordination is arrived at by deciding which set of texts is more fundamental. If this perspective is correct, it is hard to see how one could possibly say that 1 Timothy 2:11–15 is more fundamental than Galatians 3:28. The game seems to be over even before it begins. I am convinced that the complementarian view is correct, not because 1 Timothy 2:11– 15 is "more fundamental" or that it "controls the discussion" when interpreting Galatians 3:28. Rather, complementarians, in my opinion, have done the most justice to both Galatians 3:28 and 1 Timothy 2:11–15 when these texts are interpreted in context. Neither text should have priority over the other. Both must be interpreted carefully and rigorously in context.

I have often heard egalitarians make another hermeneutical statement quite similar to what was noted above. They will say that Galatians 3:28 is a *clear* text, and the texts that limit women from some ministries are *unclear*.[8] Then they proceed to say that clear texts must have sovereignty over unclear ones. Who could possibly disagree with this hermeneutical principle when it is abstractly stated? I also believe that clear texts should have priority. However, the claim that Galatians 3:28 is the clear text begs the question. Both Galatians 3:28 and texts that limit women in ministry yield a clear and noncontradictory message. Those who preceded us in church history did not think that 1 Timothy 2:11–15 was unclear and that Galatians 3:28 was transparent. Our ancestors did not perceive the same tension between the two texts that many feel today. The texts strike us as polar because a modern notion of equality is often imported into Galatians 3:28. My own position is that the main point in both Galatians 3:28 and the texts that limit the role of women is clear. I am not arguing that every detail in texts like 1 Corinthians 11:2–16 and 1 Timothy 2:11–15 is transparent, but the basic teaching is not hard to understand, nor is the main truth in Galatians 3:28 difficult to grasp.

A word about terminology is also in order. Even though I use the phrase "ordination of women" for convenience, the real

---

[8]So Gretchen Gaebelein Hull, *Equal to Serve: Women and Men in the Church and Home* (Old Tappan, N.J.: Revell, 1987), 183–89.

issue is not ordination but whether women can function in the pastoral office. The language of ordination is not regularly used in the New Testament of those who serve as leaders in the church.[9] The New Testament refers to *presbyteroi* ("elders") and *episkopoi* ("overseers") who serve as leaders in the early church. That elders and overseers constitute the same office is evident from Paul's address to the Ephesian leaders at Miletus (Acts 20:17–35). In Acts 20:17 they are designated as "elders," while in verse 28 the same group is described as "overseers." The term "elders" probably designates the office, while the term "overseers" refers to function, the responsibility to watch over the church. Verse 28 also contains a pastoral metaphor, for the overseers are responsible to *poimainein* ("shepherd") God's flock. Here we have an indication that pastors, overseers, and elders refer to the same office.

Titus 1:5–9 also supports the idea that "elders" and "overseers" refer to the same office. Paul charges Titus to appoint elders in every city (Titus 1:5) and then proceeds to describe the requisite character (1:6). In verse 7 he shifts to the word "overseer." The singular use of the word "overseer" (*episkopon*) does not designate another office, but is generic. The "for" (*gar*) connecting verses 6–7 indicates that a new office is not in view, since Paul continues to describe the character required of leaders. Indeed, the very same word (*anenklētos*, "above reproach") is used in both verses 6 and 7, functioning as further evidence that "overseers" and "elders" refer to the same office. Peter's first letter (1 Peter 5:1–4) provides confirmatory evidence as well. Peter addresses the elders (*presbyterous*) in verse 1, calling on them to shepherd (*poimanate*) the flock. The participle *episkopountes* ("overseeing") is also used (verse 2), and so I conclude that shepherding (pastoring) and overseeing are the responsibilities of elders.[10]

Nor is it the case that elders and overseers were exceptional in the New Testament. Paul and Barnabas appointed elders in

---

[9] For a study of ordination, see Marjorie Warkentin, *Ordination: A Biblical-Historical View* (Grand Rapids: Eerdmans, 1982).

[10] Over against the normal presbyterian view that distinguishes ruling and teaching elders in 1 Timothy 5:17. Of course, whether "elders" refers to an office is also debated. R. Alastair Campbell (*The Elders: Seniority within Earliest Christianity* [Edinburgh: T&T Clark, 1998]) has recently proposed that an office is not designated by the term. Supporting the notion that an office is in view is the dissertation by Ben Merkle, *The Elder and Overseer: One Office in the Early Church* (Ph.D. diss., The Southern Baptist Theological Seminary).

every church planted on their first missionary journey (Acts 14:23).[11] "Overseers and deacons" (Phil. 1:1) comprise the two offices in Philippi. Leaders in the church at Jerusalem are designated as "elders" (Acts 15:2, 4, 6, 22, 23; 16:4). We have already seen that Paul instructed Titus to appoint elders in Crete (Titus 1:5). The qualifications and responsibilities of overseers and elders are also explained in 1 Timothy 3:1–7 and 5:17–25. Peter's reference to "elders" (1 Peter 5:1) indicates that elders were appointed in the churches in Pontus, Galatia, Cappadocia, Asia, and Bithynia (1 Peter 1:1). When James refers to the leaders of the church, he calls them "elders" (James 5:14). This brief survey reveals that elders and overseers were common in the New Testament church. Elders are not limited to Paul's letters but are also found in the writings of James, Peter, and Luke. Geographically, elders and overseers stretch from Jerusalem to Philippi to Crete. The terminology, of course, is not fixed. Leaders of churches are also referred to without the use of the titles "elders" or "overseers" (1 Cor. 16:15–16; Gal. 6:6; 1 Thess. 5:12–13).

My thesis in this essay is that women were not appointed to the pastoral office. Sometimes we ask, "Are women called to the ministry?" I used that very language in introducing this essay. But such language is too imprecise. *All* believers, including women, are called to ministry. There are a multitude of ministries that women can and should fulfill. Similarly, the question is not whether women should be ordained, since ordination is not the central issue in the New Testament. The question I want to raise in this essay is quite specific: Are women called to function as pastors, elders, or overseers? My answer to this question is no, and this essay will explain why.

THE DIGNITY AND SIGNIFICANCE OF WOMEN

We are apt to misunderstand the Scriptures if we immediately delve into texts that limit women from the pastoral office, for the dignity and significance of women is constantly taught in the Bible. Genesis 1:26–28 teaches that both men and women

---

[11]The appointing of elders in "every church" indicates a plurality of leadership in local churches. So also Acts 20:17 refers to *presbyterous tēs ekklēsias*, showing that there were plural elders for a single church. This is the most plausible way of reading Philippians 1:1 and the other texts regarding elders as well.

are made in God's image, and together they are to rule over the world God created. Not only are both males and females made in God's image, but also they are *equally* made in his image. No evidence exists that males somehow reflect God's image more than females. Stanley Grenz provides no evidence for saying that contemporary complementarians deny that both men and women equally share God's image.[12] Anyone who has read the literature knows that such an allegation is not true of the vast majority of complementarians.

The dignity of women is often portrayed in the Old Testament. We think of the courageous life of Sarah (Gen. 12–23), the faith of Rahab (Josh. 2), the commitment of Hannah (1 Sam. 1–2), the devotion of Ruth (Ruth 1–4), Abigail's gentle but firm rebuke of David (1 Sam. 25), the humble faith of the widow of Zarephath (1 Kings 17) and the Shunammite woman (2 Kings 4), and the risk-taking faith of Esther (Est. 1–10). As the author of Hebrews says, "time will fail me" (Heb. 11:32) were I to narrate the lives of these Old Testament women and others whom I have skipped over.

It has been noted often and rightly that Jesus treated women with dignity and respect and that he elevated them in a world where they were often mistreated. He displayed courage and tenderness in speaking to the Samaritan woman when it was contrary to cultural conventions (John 4:7–29). The compassion of Jesus was evident when he raised from the dead the only son of the widow of Nain (Luke 7:11–17), for that son would likely have become her only means of support. He lovingly healed the woman who had suffered from a hemorrhage of blood for twelve years (Mark 5:25–34) and delivered the woman who had been unable to stand up straight for eighteen years (Luke 13:10–17), even though he was criticized in the latter instance for performing such a healing on the Sabbath. Jesus' tender firmness toward women in bondage to sin was remarkable, as is evidenced in the woman caught in adultery (John 8:1–11) and the sinful woman who washed his feet with her tears and dried them with her hair (Luke 7:36–50). Jesus healed

---

[12]Stanley J. Grenz with Denise Muir Kjesbo, *Women in the Church: A Biblical Theology of Women in Ministry* (Downers Grove, Ill.: InterVarsity Press, 1995), 169. Amazingly, Grenz cites Ruth Tucker, who is an egalitarian, in support but cites no primary sources to prove his charge.

women who were hurting, such as the daughter of the Syrophoenician woman (Mark 7:24–30) and Peter's mother-in-law (Mark 1:29–31). When suffering agony on the cross, he was concerned for his mother's welfare and requested John to care for her (John 19:26–27).

Jesus often used women or the world of women as examples in his teaching. He commended the queen of Sheba (Matt. 12:42), likened the kingdom of heaven to leaven which was put in dough by a woman (Matt. 13:33), told the parable of the ten virgins (Matt. 25:1–13), and defended his ministry to sinners with the parable of the lost coin of a woman (Luke 15:8–10). The necessity of steadfastness in prayer is illustrated by the widow who confronts the unjust judge (Luke 18:1–8). Jesus upheld the dignity of women by speaking out against divorce, which particularly injured women in the ancient world (Mark 10:2–12). Nor are women simply sex objects to be desired by men, for Jesus spoke strongly against lust (Matt. 5:27–30). Jesus also commended the poor widow, who gave all she owned, more than the rich, who gave lavish gifts out of their abundance (Luke 21:1–4).

Women were also prominently featured in the ministry of Jesus. His ministry was financed by several women of means (Luke 8:1–3), and it is likely that some of these women traveled with him during at least some of his ministry. Jesus commended Mary for listening to his word, in contrast to Martha, who was excessively worried about preparations for a meal (Luke 10:38–42). The account is particularly significant because some in Judaism prohibited women from learning Torah, but Jesus encouraged women to learn the Scriptures.[13] His close relationship with Mary and Martha is illustrated by the account of the raising of Lazarus (John 11:1–44) and his anointing for burial by Mary (John 12:1–8). The devotion of women was also apparent in their concern for Jesus, even on his way to the cross (Luke 23:27–31; cf. Mark 15:40–41). Finally, Jesus appeared to women and entrusted them to be his witnesses when he was raised from the dead (Matt. 28:1–10; Mark 16:1–8; Luke 24:1–12; John 20:1–18), even though the testimony of women was not received by courts. What is particularly striking is that Jesus appeared to

---

[13]On the topic of women learning Torah, see the balanced appraisal of Ben Witherington III, *Women and the Genesis of Christianity* (Cambridge: Cambridge Univ. Press, 1990), 6–9.

women first, showing again their significance and value as human beings.

The importance of women was not relinquished by the early church after Jesus' ministry. Women participated with men in prayer before the day of Pentecost (Acts 1:12–14). Widows who were lacking daily provisions were not shunted aside, but specific plans were enacted to ensure that their needs were met (Acts 6:1–6; 1 Tim. 5:3–16; see also James 1:26–27). Tabitha was commended for her loving concern for others (Acts 9:36–42), and Luke features the conversion of Lydia, who worked as a merchant (Acts 16:14–15). Concern for women is illustrated in the eviction of the demon from the slave girl (Acts 16:16–18). Her owners were concerned for profits (Acts 16:19–21), but Paul desired her salvation and deliverance.

All of these texts confirm the teaching of Galatians 3:28, "There is neither Jew nor Greek, there is neither slave nor free man, there is neither male nor female; for you are all one in Christ Jesus."[14] Both women and men, slave and free are valuable to God. Women are made in God's image and thus possess dignity as his image bearers. The fundamental purpose of Galatians 3:28 *in context* is to say that both men and women have equal access to salvation in Christ. The Judaizing opponents had rocked the Galatian churches, causing them to wonder if one had to be circumcised to be saved (Gal. 5:2–6; 6:12–13). Paul reminded them that one belongs to the family of Abraham by faith alone (Gal. 3:6–9, 14, 29). One does not need to become a Jew and receive circumcision in order to qualify for membership in the people of God. Nor are the people of God restricted to males. Anyone who believes in Christ, whether male or female, is part of God's family.

Klyne Snodgrass argues that Galatians 3:28 cannot be confined to salvation but also has social implications.[15] Jews and Gentiles, for instance, now relate to each other differently because of their oneness in Christ. I believe Snodgrass is correct. The main point of Galatians 3:28 is that all people, including

---

[14]Some scholars see this verse as containing an early baptismal formula, but the prehistory of the text need not detain us here.

[15]Klyne R. Snodgrass, "Galatians 3:28: Conundrum or Solution?" in *Women, Authority and the Bible*, ed. Alvera Mickelsen (Downers Grove, Ill: InterVarsity Press, 1986), 161–81.

both men and women, have equal access to salvation in Christ. Nonetheless, it is also true that such a truth has social consequences and implications. However, we must read the rest of what Paul says to explain accurately what these social implications are. It is extraordinarily easy to impose on the biblical text our modern democratic Western notions of social equality.[16] As we proceed, we will attempt to discern Paul's own understanding of the social implications of Galatians 3:28.

The late F. F. Bruce's understanding of Galatians 3:28 was fundamentally flawed, for he read into it his own philosophical conception of equality: "Paul states the basic principle here; if restrictions on it are found elsewhere in the Pauline corpus ... they are to be understood in relation to Galatians 3:28, and not vice versa."[17] Bruce's assertion begged the question. He assumed that all the verses were to be interpreted through the lens of Galatians 3:28, but thereby he ensured that his own notions of equality would be read into the verse. Nothing Paul writes elsewhere can qualify or limit his view of Galatians 3:28. Let me apply Bruce's logic to the issue of homosexuality.[18] What if I were to say, "Galatians 3:28 is Paul's fundamental statement on what it means to be male and female. Any verse written elsewhere on the matter must be read in light of Galatians 3:28. Therefore,

---

[16]Rebecca Merrill Groothuis (*Good News for Women: A Biblical Picture of Gender Equality* [Grand Rapids: Baker, 1997], 46) falls into this very error in defining equality. She does not derive her definition from Scripture but from classical liberal thought. For a persuasive critique of Snodgrass and egalitarian interpretations of Galatians 3:28, see Köstenberger, "Gender Passages," 274–79; and the insightful work of Richard W. Hove, *Equality in Christ? Galatians 3:28 and the Gender Dispute* (Wheaton, Ill.: Crossway, 1999).

[17]F. F. Bruce, *Commentary on Galatians*, New International Greek Testament Commentary (Grand Rapids: Eerdmans, 1982), 190. Judith M. Gundry-Volf would draw different conclusions than I would from Galatians 3:28, but she rightly argues that Galatians 3:28 does not abolish all gender differences. See "Christ and Gender: A Study of Difference and Equality in Galatians 3:28," in *Jesus Christus als die Mitte der Schrift: Studien zur Hermeneutik des Evangeliums*, eds. C. Landmesser, H. J. Eckstein, and H. Lichtenberger (Beihefte zur Zeitschrift für die neutestamentliche Wissenschaft 86 [Berlin/New York: Walter de Gruyter, 1997]), 439–77.

[18]I am not saying that the issues of women in ministry and homosexuality are of equal clarity or importance, for I am persuaded that anyone who thinks homosexuality is acceptable is no longer an evangelical. The scriptural teaching on homosexuality is clearer than its teaching on the role of women. Nonetheless, the very principle propounded by F. F. Bruce could logically lead to the result I point out above.

those verses in Paul's letters that proscribe homosexuality are to be read in light of Galatians 3:28. Paul says that whether one is a male or female is of no significance to God. Therefore, whether one marries a male or female is irrelevant." Evangelicals would rightly protest that such an exegesis reads modern notions of sexual relations into the text. My point is that precisely the same kind of question-begging exegesis is being employed in egalitarian interpretations of Galatians 3:28. Women have equal access to salvation, and there are social consequences to this truth, to be sure, but we need to read Paul and the rest of the Scriptures to determine what those implications are.

At this juncture we need to remind ourselves of the teaching of Galatians 3:28. The Bible does not teach that men or masters or Jews are somehow closer to God. Males and females, masters and slaves, and Jews and Greeks all have equal access to salvation. It certainly follows that we should treat every human being, whether male or female, with dignity and respect. We also proclaim the gospel to all people groups and both genders in the hope of their salvation.

Since men and women have equal access to salvation, they are also joint heirs "of the grace of life" (1 Peter 3:7). Peter teaches here that both men and women have an equal destiny; both will receive an inheritance on the day of the Lord. The Bible does not teach that women will have a lesser reward than men, that men will somehow rule over women in heaven, or that women will have a lesser place in heaven. Men and women are equally heirs to the salvation God has promised.

WOMEN IN MINISTRY

It would be a fundamental mistake to so concentrate on the Scripture passages that limit women in ministry that we fail to see the many ministries in which women were engaged in Bible times. My purpose in this section is to show the variety of ministries involving women and also to explain how such participation in ministry does not contradict the view that women are prohibited from serving in the pastoral office.

The Scriptures clearly teach that women functioned, at least occasionally, as prophets. In the Old Testament Miriam (Ex. 15:20–21), Deborah (Judg. 4:4–5), and Huldah (2 Kings 22:14–20) are prominent. Anna in the New Testament also functions like an Old Testament prophet, since she exercised her gift before Jesus' public ministry (Luke 2:36–38). In Peter's Pentecost sermon he emphasized that Joel's prophecy has been fulfilled and that the Spirit has been poured out on both men and women (Acts 2:17–18). Philip's four daughters were prophets (Acts 21:9), and women in Corinth apparently exercised the gift as well (1 Cor. 11:5). The spiritual gift of prophecy belongs to women as well as men (Rom. 12:6; 1 Cor. 12:10, 28; Eph. 4:11). Egalitarians often argue that prophecy is actually ranked above teaching (1 Cor. 12:28), and thus if women have the right to prophesy, then they must also be able to teach and preach because they possess all the spiritual gifts.

To handle this issue adequately we must define the gift of *prophecy*. Some define prophecy as preaching.[19] If this definition is accurate, it is hard to see how women can be banned from the pastoral office, since one of the fundamental roles of elders is preaching that involves teaching (1 Tim. 3:2; 5:17; Titus 1:9). There are good reasons to conclude, however, that prophecy is *not* preaching. In 1 Corinthians 14:29–32 Paul indicates that prophecy involves the spontaneous reception of revelation or oracles from God.[20] This is evident from verse 30, for a revelation is suddenly given to a prophet who is seated. Clearly a prepared message is not involved, for the person sitting down receives a revelation from God without warning and stands to deliver this spontaneous word of God to the congregation. Such a definition of prophecy fits with Agabus's prophecies in Acts. The Lord revealed to him that a famine would spread over the world (Acts 11:27–28), and he also prophesied that Paul would be tied up and handed over to the Gentiles (Acts 21:10–11). These prophecies are hardly prepared messages, but are oracles

---

[19]See, for example (surprisingly), J. I. Packer (*Keep in Step with the Spirit* [Old Tappan, N.J.: Revell, 1984], 215), who essentially defines prophecy as "preaching."

[20]For studies of prophecy that support this basic view, see David E. Aune, *Prophecy in Early Christianity and the Ancient Mediterranean World* (Grand Rapids: Eerdmans, 1983); Wayne A. Grudem, *The Gift of Prophecy in 1 Corinthians* (Lanham, Md.: University Press of America, 1982); Graham Houston, *Prophecy: A Gift for Today?* (Downers Grove, Ill.: InterVarsity Press, 1989), 82–86; Christopher Forbes, *Prophecy and Inspired Speech in Early Christianity and Its Hellenistic Environment* (Wissenschaftliche Untersuchungen zum Neuen Testament 2/75 [Tübingen: Mohr, 1995]), 218–21; Max Turner, *The Holy Spirit and Spiritual Gifts*, rev. ed. (Peabody, Mass.: Hendrickson, 1996), 185–220.

that come supernaturally and unexpectedly from God. The oracular nature of prophecy is also evident in the prophecies of Huldah (2 Kings 22:14–20) and Deborah (Judg. 4:4–9), for they deliver God's specific word in response to particular situations. I conclude that prophecy is not to be equated with preaching. It also follows that prophecy is distinct from the gift of teaching. Teaching involves the explanation of tradition that has already been transmitted, whereas prophecy is *fresh* revelation.[21]

It is not the purpose of this essay to resolve whether prophecy still exists as a gift today.[22] What must be observed is that the presence of women prophets does not neutralize the prohibition against women serving as pastors. God has raised up women prophets in the history of the church, but it does not follow that women should serve as elders or overseers of God's flock. In the Old Testament women served occasionally as prophets but never as priests.[23] Similarly, in the New Testament women served as prophets but never as pastors or overseers or apostles. Not a single New Testament example can be adduced that women served as pastors, elders, or overseers. When we examine 1 Corinthians 11:2–16 in more detail later, we will also see that Paul instructs women to exercise their prophetic gift with a submissive demeanor and attitude, since man is the head of a woman (1 Cor. 11:3). Another difference between prophecy and teaching must be noted. Prophecy is a *passive* gift in which oracles or revelations are given by God to a prophet. Teaching, on the other hand, is a gift that naturally fits with leadership and a settled office, for it involves the transmission and explanation of tradition.[24] I am not arguing that prophecy is a lesser gift than teaching, only that it is a distinct gift.

---

[21]See Gerhard Friedrich, *Theological Dictionary of the New Testament*, 6:854, s.v. *"prophētēs"*; David Hill, *New Testament Prophecy* (Atlanta: John Knox, 1979), 131–33; Heinrich Greeven, "Propheten, Lehrer, Vorsteher bei Paulus," *Zeitschrift für die neutestamentliche Wissenschaft* 44 (1952–53): 29–30; Forbes, *Prophecy and Inspired Speech*, 225–29; Turner, *The Holy Spirit and Spiritual Gifts*, 187–90, 206–12.

[22]For a discussion of this issue, see *Are Miraculous Gifts for Today? Four Views*, ed. Wayne A. Grudem (Grand Rapids: Zondervan, 1996).

[23]For development of this argument, see Gordon J. Wenham, "The Ordination of Women: Why Is It So Divisive?" *Churchman* 92 (1978): 310–19.

[24]Previously I argued that the gift of prophecy by women was not exercised as publicly as it was by men. See my essay "The Valuable Ministries of Women in the Context of Male Leadership: A Survey of Old and New Testament Examples and

Isn't there a flaw in the above argument? For women have the gift of teaching as well as men. When the spiritual gifts are listed (Rom. 12:6–8; 1 Cor. 12:8–10, 28–30; Eph. 4:11; 1 Peter 4:10–11), no hint is given that women lack the gift of teaching. In fact, Priscilla and Aquila together instructed Apollos more accurately about the things of the Lord (Acts 18:26), and the listing of Priscilla first may signal that she was more learned than her husband. Paul also testifies to the powerful ministry of this couple, calling them fellow workers in the gospel and referring to a church that met in their home (Rom. 16:3–5; 1 Cor. 16:19; cf. 2 Tim. 4:19). Some egalitarians also point to Titus 2:3, where the teaching of women is commended.

In many respects I agree with egalitarians here. Sometimes complementarians have given the impression that women are unintelligent and that they lack any ability to teach. Such a view is clearly mistaken, for some women unquestionably have the spiritual gift of teaching. Men should be open to receiving biblical and doctrinal instruction from women. Otherwise, they are not following the humble example of Apollos, who learned from Priscilla and Aquila. Moreover, women should be encouraged to share what they have learned from the Scriptures when the church gathers. The mutual teaching recommended in Colossians 3:16 and 1 Corinthians 14:26 is not limited to men. Sometimes we men are more chauvinistic than biblical.

Nonetheless, the above Scripture texts do not indicate that women filled the pastoral office or functioned as regular teachers of the congregation. All believers are to instruct one another, both when the church gathers and when we meet in smaller groups of two or three (Col. 3:16; 1 Cor. 14:26). To encourage and instruct one another is the responsibility of all believers. But such mutual encouragement and instruction is not the same thing as a woman being appointed to the pastoral office or functioning as the regular teacher of a gathering of men and women.

Complementarians can easily go too far and think that women cannot teach them anything from Scripture, when the example of Priscilla says otherwise. On the other hand, a single occasion in which Priscilla taught Apollos in private hardly

Teaching," in *Recovering Biblical Manhood and Womanhood: A Response to Evangelical Feminism*, eds. John Piper and Wayne Grudem (Wheaton, Ill.: Crossway, 1991), 216. I now have some reservations about the validity of this argument.

demonstrates that she filled the pastoral office. Let me use an example from today. If a man from my church named Jim took aside another person in my congregation and explained something from the Bible to him, it does not follow that Jim was actually functioning as a teacher or a pastor in our church. Other information would be needed to clarify Jim's precise role. Egalitarians can be tempted to read more into the Priscilla account than it actually says. And egalitarians are sometimes disingenuous about Titus 2:3, for the context reveals that Paul encourages the older women to instruct *younger women*.[25] It is eisegesis to use this text to defend the belief that women can teach men in pastoral ministry, for the ministry of older women to younger women is what is commended here.

Paul celebrates the contribution of women in ministry. One of his favorite terms for those who assist him in ministry is *synergos* ("coworker," "fellow worker"). The lineup of coworkers is impressive: Timothy (Rom. 16:21; 1 Thess. 3:2; Philem. 1), Apollos (1 Cor. 3:9), Urbanus (Rom. 16:9), Titus (2 Cor. 8:23), Epaphroditus (Phil. 2:25), Aristarchus (Col. 4:10; Philem. 24), Mark (Col. 4:11; Philem. 24), Jesus Justus (Col. 4:11), Epaphras (Philem. 24), Demas (Philem. 24), and Luke (Philem. 24). But coworkers are not limited to men. Priscilla is called a *synergos* ("fellow worker") in Romans 16:3. Euodia and Syntyche are commended as coworkers in Philippians 4:3, and Paul says they struggled together with him in spreading the gospel.

Paul also often uses the verb *kopiaō* ("to labor") to designate those involved in ministry (1 Cor. 16:16). Indeed, the term *kopiaō* often describes his own ministry (1 Cor. 4:12; 15:10; Gal. 4:11; Phil. 2:16; Col. 1:29; 1 Tim. 4:10). In some texts leaders are said to labor, or work hard (1 Cor. 16:16; 1 Thess. 5:12; 1 Tim. 5:17). What is remarkable is that a number of women are noted by Paul as having worked hard: Mary (Rom. 16:6) and Tryphaena, Tryphosa, and Persis (Rom. 16:12). Egalitarians conclude from this evidence that women functioned as leaders in the early church. We ought not to miss a point that both egalitarians and complementarians can agree on: Women were obviously significantly involved in ministry. And they worked hard in their ministries. But the evidence does not clearly indicate that women functioned as leaders, for the terms are fundamentally vague on

---

[25]See Grenz, *Women in the Church*, 129.

the matter of leadership. We know women worked hard in ministry, but these terms do not tell us that they functioned as pastors. The flaw in such reasoning is easily apparent if we consider the case of the apostle Paul. Let me construct a simple syllogism:

> Paul the apostle often describes his ministry as labor, or hard work.
> A number of women are said to labor in ministry.
> Therefore, women functioned as apostles.

The logical flaw here is immediately apparent, for "labor" is not unique to or distinctive of apostles. People can labor in ministry without being apostles. Similarly, women labor in ministry without necessarily functioning as leaders. In my own church many women are working hard and laboring in the ministry, but they do not fill pastoral leadership roles. The reader should note carefully what I am *not* saying. I am not arguing that the terms "fellow worker" ("coworker") and "labor" ("work hard") clearly exclude women from pastoral leadership. I am merely saying that the terms do not demonstrate that they functioned as such.

Did women serve as deacons in the New Testament period? The debate centers on Romans 16:1 and 1 Timothy 3:11. Many complementarians are persuaded that women were not deacons. Unfortunately, the text is unclear, so certainty is precluded, and we are limited to a study of two verses! On balance I think that women did serve as deacons and that we should encourage them to fill this office in our churches. The word for "deacon" (*diakonos*) often refers to service in general, with no specific office being intended. Nevertheless, it seems that Phoebe filled an office in Romans 16:1, for she is spoken of as a "deacon of the church at Cenchreae" (NRSV). The addition of the words "of the church at Cenchreae" after the word *diakonos* suggests an official position, for it appears that she filled a particular role in a specific local church.

It is possible that 1 Timothy 3:11 refers to the wives of deacons instead of women deacons, but a reference to women deacons is more likely for a number of reasons. First, the women in 3:11 are introduced with the term "likewise." This is the same term used to introduce male deacons in 3:8, so it is most reasonable to think that Paul is continuing to describe offices in the church. Second, some English versions translate the word "women" (*gynaikas*) here as "wives" (KJV, NKJV, NIV), but the

Greek language does not have a separate word for "wives," and the term could just as easily be translated "women" (NASB, NRSV, RSV). In fact, the reference would clearly be to wives if Paul had written "their wives" (requiring simply the addition of the Greek word *autōn*) or "the wives of deacons" (requiring simply the addition of the Greek word *diakonōn*). Since neither of these terms is used, women deacons rather than wives are probably in view.[26] Third, the qualifications for these women are identical or similar to the qualifications of male deacons and elders. The similarity of the qualifications suggests an office, not merely a status as the wives of deacons. Fourth, why would Paul emphasize the wives of deacons and pass over the wives of elders, especially if elders (see below) had greater responsibility in the act of governing the church? Failure to mention the wives of elders is mystifying if that office carried more responsibility. A reference to women deacons, however, makes good sense if women could serve as deacons but not as elders (more on this below).

I conclude that women did serve as deacons in the New Testament and that they should serve as such in our churches today. We see once again that women were vitally involved in ministry during the New Testament era, and churches today are misguided if they prohibit women from doing what the Scriptures allow.

But if women served as deacons when the New Testament was written, how can they be prohibited from governing and teaching roles today? One of the problems in the contemporary church is that many churches have deviated from the biblical pattern in which there were two offices: elders/overseers and deacons (Phil. 1:1; 1 Tim. 3:1–13). In many modern churches the deacons function as the governing board of a church. This is unfortunate, for deacons are nowhere identified with or made a subcategory of elders in the New Testament. The offices of deacon and elder are distinct.[27] And appointing women as deacons does not affect the validity of the complementarian view at all, for elders/overseers—*not* deacons—are responsible for leadership

---

[26]In support of a reference to wives, see George W. Knight III, *The Pastoral Epistles: A Commentary on the Greek Text*, New International Greek Testament Commentary (Grand Rapids: Eerdmans, 1992), 170–73.

[27]I discussed the evidence for elders previously in this essay (pages 182–83).

and teaching in the church. Two qualities demanded of elders, namely, being able to teach (1 Tim. 3:2; 5:17; Titus 1:9) and governing the church (1 Tim. 3:5; 5:17; Acts 20:28), are nowhere required of deacons. The elders, not the deacons, have the responsibility for the doctrinal purity and leadership of a church. The deacons are responsible for ministries of mercy and service in the church, and they do not exercise leadership in teaching and in governing the church. It is significant, then, that 1 Timothy 2:12 prohibits women from teaching and exercising authority over men. Notice that women are prohibited from doing the two activities that distinguish elders from deacons (teaching and exercising authority). I conclude, then, that women can and should serve as deacons, but they should not occupy the pastoral office, which involves teaching and exercising authority.[28]

Egalitarians are convinced that women did serve as leaders in the early church. They identify Junia as a woman apostle in Romans 16:7. Some believe that women functioned as leaders because John wrote in his second letter to "the chosen lady" (2 John 1), and this lady is understood to be an individual woman leading the church.[29] Others think that women served as elders because Paul refers to women elders in 1 Timothy 5:2 (cf. Titus 2:3). Many egalitarians point to Phoebe in Romans 16:2, understanding the word *prostatis* to refer to a leader.[30] Still others say that women must have functioned as leaders because churches met in their houses, and as the patrons of these houses they would have been leaders—for example, Mary the mother

---

[28]Sometimes people appeal to the New Testament accounts of Stephen and Philip and argue that their ministries show that deacons functioned as leaders and were not restricted to "service" ministries (Acts 6:1–8:40). I have space for only a few brief comments. First, we are not absolutely sure that Stephen and Philip functioned as deacons, for the title is not used of those appointed in Acts 6:1–6, though the noun *diakonia* is used of the need (6:1) and the verb *diakonein* (6:2) of the task to be fulfilled. On balance I think the Seven were deacons, but certainty eludes us. Second, the preaching ministry of Stephen and Philip hardly proves that it is part of the ministry of deacons to preach, for the Seven are appointed so that the Twelve will not abandon the ministry of the word (6:2, 4). Third, simply because some deacons did more than required (Stephen and Philip served *and* preached), it does not follow that *all* deacons can or should teach and preach. Luke features Stephen and Philip precisely because they were exceptional.

[29]See Aída B. Spencer, *Beyond the Curse: Women Called to Ministry* (Nashville: Nelson, 1985), 109–12; Tucker and Liefeld, *Daughters of the Church*, 74–75.

[30]See Keener, *Paul, Women and Wives*, 238–40; Spencer, *Beyond the Curse*, 113–17.

of John Mark (Acts 12:12–17), Lydia (16:13–15), Chloe (1 Cor. 1:11), Priscilla (Rom. 16:3–5), and Nympha (Col. 4:15).[31]

The arguments of egalitarians in the preceding paragraph are remarkably weak. Some argue that women should preach because they bore witness to the resurrection. We should not reason, however, that Mary Magdalene was qualified to be a leader because Jesus appeared to her.[32] Nor is there any evidence elsewhere that she functioned as such. Seeing the risen Lord and bearing witness to his resurrection was a great joy and privilege, to be sure, but it does not logically follow that such women should serve as leaders or teachers. Indeed, if Jesus had appointed female apostles, then it would be clear that all ministry roles are open to women. We know, however, that Jesus appointed only male apostles. Now I do not believe that a male apostolate settles the issue on the role of women. But if Jesus were as egalitarian and bold and radical as egalitarians make him out to be, it is passing strange that he did not appoint any female apostles, especially since these same egalitarians see Paul as commending female apostles (Rom. 16:7). Jesus seems to accommodate to the culture more than Paul—when he could have made a bold statement that would have resolved the whole issue definitively. A male apostolate does not prove that women should not serve as leaders, but when combined with the other evidence, it does serve as confirmatory evidence for the complementarian view.

Nor is it at all compelling to say that women patrons functioned as leaders of house churches. No convincing evidence supports such a view. Does anyone really believe that Mary the mother of John Mark was one of the leaders of the church in Jerusalem simply because the church met in her house (Acts 12:12)? Acts makes it clear that the leaders were Peter, John, and James the brother of the Lord (in addition to the other apostles and elders). No correlation can be drawn between the church meeting in Mary's house and the assuming of a leadership role.

Similarly, not even a hint is given of Chloe functioning as a leader in Corinth. The church, in fact, is exhorted to be subject

---

[31]This appears to be the view of Grenz, *Women in the Church*, 90–91.

[32]Over against Grenz (*Women in the Church*, 79), who also supports women as leaders on the basis of Rhoda telling the others that Peter was at the door of the house (Acts 12:14)!

to the house of Stephanas (1 Cor. 16:15–16), and Chloe is left out. Nor is it persuasive to define the word *prostatis* as "leader" in Romans 16:2. What Paul says in this verse is that the Romans should *parastēte* ("assist") Phoebe wherever she needs help because she has been a *prostatis* ("helper") of many, including Paul himself.[33] The play on words between *parastēte* and *prostatis* is obvious. Phoebe is commended here as a patroness. Paul is scarcely suggesting that she functioned as his leader or as the leader of the church. Paul did not even agree that the Jerusalem apostles were his leaders (Gal. 1:11–2:14), and so it is impossible to believe that he would assign such a role to Phoebe!

The evidence that women served as elders is practically nonexistent and unpersuasive. For example, it is obvious in Titus 2:3 that the office of elder is not in view, for Paul refers to older men (2:2), older women (2:3), younger women (2:4–5), and younger men (2:6). The mention of the various age groups reveals that Paul refers to age rather than office. The same argument applies to 1 Timothy 5:2. In verses 1–2 Paul gives Timothy advice about how to relate to older men, older women, younger men, and younger women. Any notion of office has to be read into the text here, and virtually all commentators agree that age (not office) is intended. Nor does "chosen lady" in 2 John refer to a woman leader or elder.[34] Almost all commentators agree that it is a reference to the church as a whole. The plurals in verses 6, 8, 10, and 12 indicate that John writes to the church as a whole, not simply to one person. Referring to the church as a "lady" comports with the rest of Scripture, for both Paul and John describe the church as Christ's bride (Eph. 5:22–23; Rev. 19:7). And Israel is also portrayed as a woman in the Old Testament (Isa. 54:1; Jer.

---

[33]For further discussion on Phoebe, including a bibliography citing alternative views, see my commentary *Romans*, Baker Exegetical Commentary on the New Testament (Grand Rapids: Baker, 1998), 786–88.

[34]Grenz, *Women in the Church*, 91–92. Grenz admits that the evidence is ambiguous, but he fails to inform the reader that virtually all the commentators agree a specific woman is not in view. The sources he mentions (see his book, page 242, notes 95 and 96) are a commentator from 1888, another commentary without a date, and Spencer, *Beyond the Curse*. The standard commentaries all stand in agreement against him. See, for example, Raymond E. Brown, *The Epistles of John*, Anchor Bible (Garden City, N.J.: Doubleday, 1982), 651–55; Stephen S. Smalley, *1, 2, 3 John*, Word Biblical Commentary (Dallas: Word, 1984), 318; John R. W. Stott, *The Epistles of John*, Tyndale New Testament Commentaries (Grand Rapids: Eerdmans, 1964), 200–201.

6:23; 31:21; Lam. 4:3, 22). Readers would naturally understand the metaphor of the church as a lady to refer to Christ's church. The distinction between the lady and her children should not be used to say that a woman was the leader and the children were the congregation. The lady designates the church as a whole, and the children refer to the individual members of the church.

The support for women serving as elders or leaders vanishes when closely examined. The most plausible argument for the egalitarian view comes from the example of Junia, for she and Andronicus are identified as apostles in Romans 16:7.[35] But the verse is far too ambiguous to make a case. It is hermeneutically akin to finding support for baptism for the dead from 1 Corinthians 15:29, for the purpose of the verse is not to speak to women in leadership roles. The text is ambiguous at three levels: First, is Paul referring to a man or a woman? Second, are Andronicus and Junia(s) outstanding in the eyes of the apostles, or are they outstanding apostles themselves? Third, is the term "apostle" used as a technical term, or is it used nontechnically to refer to missionaries?

Scholars continue to debate whether the reference is to a man or a woman (Junias or Junia). If it is the male Junias, then we have a contraction of the name Junianus. Personally, I believe a woman is in view. This was the majority view in the history of the church until at least the thirteenth century. Moreover, a contraction of Junianus is nowhere else found in Greek literature, and so I think we can be confident that Junia was a woman.

Second, is Paul saying that Andronicus and Junia were "outstanding among the apostles," or "outstanding in the eyes of the apostles"? The former is the view of almost all commentators. Michael Burer and Daniel Wallace, however, recently conducted an intensive search and analysis of the phrase, compiling significant evidence to support the idea that "noteworthy in the eyes of the apostles" is the best translation.[36] Their research indicates that it is unlikely that Junia is identified as an apostle here,

---

[35]For a careful assessment of the evidence, see the essay by Andreas J. Köstenberger, "Women in the Pauline Mission," in *The Gospel to the Nations: Perspectives on Paul's Mission*, eds. Peter G. Bolt and Mark Thompson (Downers Grove, Ill.: InterVarsity Press, 2000), 221–47. For further discussion on Junia see my commentary *Romans*, 795–97.

[36]Michael H. Burer and Daniel B. Wallace, "Was Junia Really an Apostle? A Reexamination of Romans 16:7," *New Testament Studies*, forthcoming.

and hence the verse says nothing about women serving in the apostolic office.

If, however, for the sake of argument we accept the idea that Junia was a woman and that she is identified as an apostle, then are not the egalitarians vindicated? If women served as apostles, then can any leadership role be ruled out for them? But here the third consideration arises. Paul is not assigning Andronicus and Junia a place with the Twelve. The term *apostolos* is not always a technical term (see 2 Cor. 8:23; Phil. 2:25).[37] The term can also be used in a nontechnical sense to refer to missionaries. Biblical commentator Rudolf Schnackenburg wrote, "The apostles referred to in Romans 16:7, without further qualification, could hardly have been anything else but itinerant missionaries."[38] In the Apostolic Fathers *apostolos* is used of itinerant evangelists.[39] If Junia was an apostle, she probably functioned particularly as a missionary to women. Ernst Käsemann observed that "the wife can have access to the women's areas, which would not be generally accessible to the husband."[40] In the culture of Paul's day the reading of Käsemann and Schnackenburg is much more likely than the modern view that Junia was an apostle in the technical sense. To sum up, the verse does not clearly identify Junia as an apostle, and even if this view is incorrect, "apostle" is not used in a technical sense.

Egalitarians, however, detect a contradiction when complementarians say that women can function as missionaries but not as pastors. I think Romans 6:7 and Philippians 4:2–3 indicate that women did indeed function as missionaries, and complementarians should celebrate and encourage such a ministry. But I fail to see the contradiction, for the very same Paul who

[37]See Wolf-Henning Ollrog, *Paulus und seine Mitarbeiter: Untersuchungen zu Theorie and Praxis der paulinischen Mission* (Wissenschaftliche Monographien zum Alten und Neuen Testament 50 [Neukirchen-Vluyn: Neukirchener Verlag, 1979]), 79–84.

[38]Rudolf Schnackenburg, "Apostles before and during Paul's Time," in *Apostolic History and the Gospel: Biblical and Historical Essays Presented to F. F. Bruce on His Sixtieth Birthday*, eds. W. W. Gasque and R. P. Martin (Grand Rapids: Eerdmans, 1970), 294; so also E. Earle Ellis, *Pauline Theology: Ministry and Society* (Grand Rapids: Eerdmans, 1989), 66.

[39]*Didache* 11:3–6; Shepherd of Hermas, *Vision* 13.1 and *Similitude* 92.4; 93.5; 102.2.

[40]Ernst Käsemann, *Commentary on Romans* (Grand Rapids: Eerdmans, 1980), 413; so also Peter Stuhlmacher, *Paul's Letter to the Romans* (Louisville, Ky.: Westminster John Knox, 1994), 249.

celebrated women missionaries also prohibited them from serving as pastors/overseers/elders. If there is a contradiction, it exists in Paul himself, and no evangelical would want to say this. Paul, moved by the Holy Spirit, barred women from the pastoral office and permitted them to be missionaries. Many women missionaries in the history of the church have agreed with the complementarian view, and once the church was planted in a particular mission field, male leaders were appointed. I am not, however, baptizing everything women missionaries have done in the field throughout history. Very likely some roles were fitting and others questionable. We derive our view of what women missionaries can and should do from Scripture, not from what they have in fact done. We would not want to claim that everything male missionaries have done throughout history has been right either. Nonetheless, many women missionaries throughout history have actually held the complementarian view and ministered and preached the gospel in such a way that this view was not violated.

DIFFERENT ROLES FOR MEN AND WOMEN

Different Roles Established in Genesis 1–3

We have already seen that men and women equally are made in God's image (Gen. 1:26–27) and are thus of equal value and significance as God's creatures. But I would also contend that there are six indications in Genesis 1–3 of a role differentiation between men and women. By role differentiation I mean that Adam has the responsibility of leadership and Eve has the responsibility to follow his leadership. Before explaining these six points I must make a crucial comment: *Equality of personhood does not rule out differences in role.* For moderns the tension between these two truths (equality of personhood and differences in role) is nearly unbearable. For instance, the basic point of Rebecca Merrill Groothuis's book *Good News for Women* is that one cannot logically posit both equality of personhood and differences in role. Groothuis, however, simply reveals that she imbibes the modern enlightenment view of equality, which insists that equality must involve equality of *function*. Anyone familiar with American society knows that this notion of equality continues to exert tremendous influence on our society.

The biblical view, however, is very different. God is not an equal opportunity employer—at least as far as installation into ministry is concerned. God decreed that priests could come *only from the tribe of Levi*, but all Israelites had equal worth and dignity before God.[41] Similarly, the pastoral role is reserved for men only, and yet women have equal dignity and value as persons created in God's image. Groothuis and other egalitarians are faced with the daunting prospect of saying that Israelites who could never serve as priests are of less dignity and value than those who were qualified for the priesthood.[42] Complementarians are spared such a problematic conclusion, for we acknowledge that a difference in role that is permanent (the tribe of Joseph could never serve as priests) does not mean that that those who cannot fill that role (descendants of Joseph) are of lesser worth or dignity.

The six indications that Adam had a special responsibility as a leader are these:

1. God created Adam first, and then he created Eve.
2. God gave Adam the command not to eat from the tree of the knowledge of good and evil.
3. God created Eve to be a helper for Adam.
4. Adam exercised his leadership by naming the creature God formed out of Adam's rib "woman."
5. The serpent subverted God's pattern of leadership by tempting Eve rather than Adam.
6. God approached Adam first after the first couple had sinned, even though Eve sinned first.

I am not suggesting that every one of these arguments is of equal weight or clarity. Arguments two and five, for example, are plausible only if the other arguments are credible. They cannot stand alone as decisive arguments for the interpretation proposed. Each argument needs to be investigated briefly.

First, the responsibility for leadership belonged to Adam (and hence to males) because Adam was created before Eve (Gen. 2:7, 21–24). I am unpersuaded by those who argue that Adam was neither male nor female, a sexually undifferentiated being,

---

[41]See James B. Hurley, *Man and Woman in Biblical Perspective* (Grand Rapids: Zondervan, 1981), 44–45.

[42]Grenz (*Women in the Church*, 152) faces the same problem.

before the creation of Eve.[43] When Yahweh fashioned the woman out of the man, he made a person who was suitable *for the man* (Gen. 2:18), and Adam recognized her as a fitting counterpart (Gen. 2:23). What the text emphasizes is the creation of Adam first and the act of the woman being formed from the man's rib (Gen. 2:21–23). Nothing is said about *ha-ʾādām* suddenly becoming male. Nor does the creation account in Genesis 2 abandon the theme of equality, for, as Adam said, the woman was "bone of my bones and flesh of my flesh" (Gen. 2:23). The man and woman were united in a love relationship as partners (Gen. 2:24).

The narrative in Genesis 2, however, adds a dimension that is missing in chapter 1.[44] Contemporary scholars rightly emphasize that the narrative was written carefully and artistically to convey a message to readers.[45] The discerning reader observes that the man was created before the woman and that the woman was even fashioned from part of the man. The narrator writes with great skill, summoning us to ponder thoughtfully the elements of the story. Why does the narrator bother to tell us that the man was created first and then the woman? That the woman shares full humanity and personhood with the man is evident, as we have already seen, from Genesis 2:23–24. But if the only point of the story were the equality of men and women, then creation at the same point in time would be most fitting. An egalitarian message would be communicated nicely by the creation of man and woman at the same instant. I believe the narrator relays the creation of man *first* to signal that Adam (and hence males in general) had a particular responsibility to lead in his relationship with Eve. Correspondingly, Eve had a responsibility to follow Adam's leadership.

Egalitarians object to this interpretation by saying that such logic would lead us to think that animals should rule over human beings, since animals were created before humans.[46] This objection has always struck me as a clever debating point instead of as a substantive argument. The narrator did not worry about readers drawing such a conclusion, since it is patently obvious

---

[43]Over against Phyllis Trible, *God and the Rhetoric of Sexuality* (Philadelphia: Fortress, 1978), 80, 98.

[44]I believe the two creation accounts are complementary, not contradictory.

[45]See Robert Alter, *The Art of Biblical Narrative* (New York: Basic Books, 1981).

[46]See, for example, Paul Jewett, *Man as Male and Female: A Study of Sexual Relationships from a Theological Point of View* (Grand Rapids: Eerdmans, 1975), 126–27.

that human beings are distinguished from animals, insofar as humans are the only creatures made in God's image (Gen. 1:26–27). But readers *would* be inclined to ask this question: "Why is the human race differentiated into male and female, and why is the male created first?" A more serious response could be that females were created last as the crown of creation, and if anything, females rather than males would assume leadership. Such a reading would fit the pattern of Genesis 1, where human beings are created last and are responsible to rule the world for God. This latter reading suffers, however, from imposing the narrative pattern of Genesis 1 on Genesis 2. Instead, the Hebrew reader would be disposed to read the second creation account in terms of *primogeniture.*[47] The firstborn male has authority over the younger brothers. The reversal of primogeniture explains why the stories of Jacob's primacy over Esau (Genesis 26–36) and Joseph's rule over his brothers are so shocking (Genesis 37–50).

Egalitarians, of course, face another problem with their particular reading of Genesis 2—a canonical one. Paul forbids women to teach and exercise authority over a man because Adam was created before Eve (1 Tim. 2:12–13). Many egalitarians, when interpreting Genesis 2, fail to mention 1 Timothy 2:12–13. The most natural reading of the words of Paul in 1 Timothy 2:11–15 supports the complementarian interpretation of Genesis 2: Men bear the responsibility to lead and teach in the church *because* Adam was created before Eve (see also 1 Cor. 11:8–9).

Second, the command to refrain from eating from the tree of the knowledge of good and evil was given to Adam, not to Eve (Gen. 2:16–17). This argument for male leadership is not decisive but suggestive. God likely commissioned Adam to instruct Eve about this command, signaling Adam's responsibility for leadership and teaching in the relationship. Closely connected is the injunction given to Adam to cultivate and take care of the Garden of Eden (Gen. 2:15). It is possible, of course, that nothing should be made of the fact that the prohibition in Genesis 2:16–17 was given only to Adam. On the other hand, the story could have been constructed so that the command was given to the husband and wife. I believe the narrator is providing a hint of male leadership by revealing that the restriction was communicated only to Adam.

---

[47]See Hurley, *Man and Woman in Biblical Perspective*, 207–208.

The third indication of male leadership is that Eve was created as a "helper" (*ʿēzer*) for Adam (Gen. 2:18, 20). The standard egalitarian objection is that Yahweh is often designated as Israel's helper, and yet he is clearly not subordinate to Israel.[48] Yahweh surely *is* Israel's helper in that he saves and delivers Israel—so how can complementarians possibly think that describing Eve as Adam's helper *supports* the case for male headship? If anything it seems that the argument could be reversed. Yahweh was Israel's helper *and leader*. The objection appears to be a strong one, and it has the merit of precluding a simplistic argument for the complementarian view.

The egalitarian interpretation, however, is also in danger of promoting a simplistic argument that is not contextually grounded. Anyone who has read the Old Testament knows that Yahweh was often portrayed as Israel's helper, and thus the term "helper" alone does not signify male leadership in Genesis 2. And yet words are assigned their meanings in context, and in the narrative context of Genesis 1–3 the word "helper" signifies that Eve was to help Adam in the task of ruling over creation. Indeed, in some contexts in the Old Testament, the word "help" designates those who assist a superior or ruler in accomplishing his task.[49] For instance, in 1 Kings 20:16 thirty-two kings, who have less power than Ben-hadad, helped him in war. Indeed, the verb "to help" is used of warriors who helped David militarily (1 Chron. 12:1, 22–23), and it is clear that David was the leader and they were assisting him. Similarly, David exhorted leaders to help Solomon when he was king (1 Chron. 22:17), in which case there is no doubt that these leaders were assisting Solomon in his leadership over the nation. An army also helped King Uzziah in a military campaign (2 Chron. 26:13). Yahweh pledged that he would nullify those who helped the prince in Jerusalem (Ezek. 12:14; cf. 32:21), and those who helped were obviously subordinates of the prince. These examples show that context is decisive in determining whether the one who helps has a superior or inferior role. Egalitarians cannot dismiss the comple-

---

[48]For this argument, see Trible, *God and the Rhetoric of Sexuality*, 90.

[49]So also David J.A. Clines, "What Does Eve Do to Help? and Other Irredeemably Androcentric Orientations in Genesis 1–3," in *What Does Eve Do to Help? and Other Readerly Questions in the Old Testament*, ed. David J.A. Clines (Sheffield: Sheffield Academic Press, 1990), 31–32.

mentarian view simply by saying that Yahweh helped Israel, for in other texts it is clear that leaders were helped by those who were under their authority.

I believe there is contextual warrant in Genesis 1–3 for the idea that women help men by supporting the leadership of the latter. If we read Genesis carefully, we see that the rule of human beings over creation, which is a call to careful stewardship (not exploitation), is combined with the injunction to have offspring who will in turn exercise dominion over the earth for God's glory (Gen. 1:26, 28). One of the ways women help men, therefore, is by bearing children, as David J. A. Clines rightly argues. I am not suggesting that this is the only way women function as helpers, but the difference in roles between men and women is established at creation in that only women bear children. We are not surprised to learn that the curse on Adam focuses on his work in the fields, so that thorns and thistles grow as a consequence of his sin (Gen. 3:17–19). Correspondingly, Eve is cursed in her sphere, so that she experiences pain in the bearing of children (Gen. 3:16).[50] It is important to notice that the distinct role of women—bearing children—is not the result of the Fall. The consequence of the Fall is an *increase in pain* during childbirth, but the actual bearing of children, which is the distinct task of the woman, was established before sin entered the world.

A contemporary observation is appropriate here. The support of abortion rights by radical feminists is closely linked with the goal of changing the role of women. Radical feminists rightly perceive that pregnancy and giving birth to children distinguish women from men. If women are liberated so that sexual relations are severed from motherhood, then women can enjoy the same rights as men. I would contend that such feminist aspirations run counter to God's created intention, for God himself decreed that women, and not men, would bear children.

Once again a canonical reading of Scripture confirms the interpretation adopted here. In 1 Corinthians 11:8–9 Paul reflected on the narrative in Genesis 2, for in 1 Corinthians 11:8 he observed that man did not come from woman, but woman from man. Then in verse 9 he declared, "For indeed man was not created for the woman's sake, but woman for the man's sake." How do we explain Paul's words in this verse? I think it

---

[50]See Clines, "What Does Eve Do to Help?" 33–36.

is quite likely that he was reflecting on the word "helper" in Genesis 2:18, 20. We know that the creation account in Genesis 2 was in his mind, and the notion that woman was created "for the man's sake" is almost certainly a Pauline commentary on the word "helper." The woman was created for Adam's sake to help in ruling the world for God's glory. Such an interpretation of 1 Corinthians 11:9 fits the context of that chapter nicely, since man is designated here as the "head" of the woman (1 Cor. 11:3). We have strong Pauline evidence, therefore, that "helper" refers to the subordinate role of women.

I am now prepared to assert my fourth argument from Genesis—the naming of the woman by Adam. A prefatory comment is in order. For clarity each of the arguments presented is separated from the other, but we need to remember that each one is closely linked in the narrative. For example, the narrator linked the naming of the animals with the man's need for a helper (Gen. 2:18–20). The narrator wanted us to perceive that a suitable helper was not found among the animals. Adam needed a partner who was bone of his bones and flesh of his flesh (Gen. 2:23) to assist him in his task of cultivating and caring for God's garden. A unique creative work of God was needed in order to provide a woman for him. Adam perceived, when naming the birds, wild animals, and domestic animals, that none of these was a suitable partner. The intertwining of the various parts of the narrative actually functions as an argument for the complementarian view, for we must see that the word "helper" appears in a context in which animals are named by Adam.

What is the significance of the naming of the creatures God made (Gen. 2:18–20)? The link in the text is obvious, for this was certainly one of the means by which Adam exercised his rule over the creatures according to God's mandate (Gen. 1:26, 28; 2:15).[51] God exercised his rule and sovereignty in calling the light "day" and the darkness "night" (Gen. 1:5), and in naming the firmament "heaven" and the dry land "earth" (Gen. 1:8, 10). Similarly, Adam exercised his rule, under God's lordship, by naming the animals. Even today the scientific study of species consists in classification and naming. We distinguish dogs from cats and whales from seals. Naming the animals was not a whimsical and arbitrary game for Adam. He named the animals

---

[51]See Hurley, *Man and Woman in Biblical Perspective*, 210–12.

so that their names corresponded to their nature. It is significant that Adam named the animals, and not vice versa! The narrator signals that Adam was beginning to fulfill God's mandate to exercise dominion over the world and God's garden.

The naming of the woman occurs in Genesis 2:23, suggesting that Adam had the responsibility for leadership in the relationship. It would be easy to misconstrue my argument here. I am certainly not suggesting that Eve was comparable to the animals! The very point of the narrative is that she was remarkably different, wholly suitable to function as his helper. Contrary to the animals, she was taken from the man and was bone of his bones and flesh of his flesh. The man instantly and gladly perceived the difference (Gen. 2:23)! As noted before, the mutuality and equality of man and woman are also communicated in the narrative. Nonetheless, the leadership role of Adam is also reflected in the narrative. He perceived that she was different from the animals and *qārā*ʾ ("called") her by the name *ʾiššâ* ("woman," Gen. 2:23), using the same verb for the naming of animals in Genesis 2:19–20. The assigning of a name to the woman in such an abbreviated narrative is highly significant. Yahweh could have reserved such a task for himself and removed any hint of male leadership. Of course, the woman is remarkably different from all the other creatures God made, but Adam's naming of the woman signifies that he bears the leadership role. There is no exegetical warrant for assigning a different significance to the naming of the animals and the woman. We need to be very careful here. In both instances naming is a symbol of rule, but it would be unwarranted to deduce that the rule is precisely the same or that women are like animals. The entire narrative illustrates that there was both continuity and discontinuity between Adam's rule over woman and his dominion over God's creatures.

The most significant objection to this interpretation is found in the work of Phyllis Trible.[52] She says that the notion of naming is only present when the verb *qārā*ʾ ("call") is joined with the noun *šēm* ("name"), pointing to a number of texts in which "name" is joined with the verb "call" (for example, Gen. 4:17, 25–26). The naming of animals, according to Trible, signified Adam's power and authority over them, but no parallel can be

---

[52]See Trible, *God and the Rhetoric of Sexuality*, 99–100.

drawn to Genesis 2:23, since the woman was not named there. Trible's argument is unpersuasive.[53] She is correct that the noun "name" is usually linked with "call" in naming formulas, but she mistakenly concludes that the noun "name" must be present in order for naming to occur. Such a conclusion demands more precision from language than is warranted, for we must not demand in advance that naming occurs only when a predetermined pattern is followed. The repetition of the verb *qārā³* (Gen. 2:19–20, 23) links the naming of the woman with the naming of the animals so that the reader naturally recognizes the parallel between the two accounts. Adam perceived that she was "woman" precisely because she was taken from the man, revealing that his classification was in accord with reality and that he understood the remarkable difference between woman and the animals.

Trible's more substantive objection is that calling this person *ʾiššâ* ("woman," Gen. 2:23) cannot be equated with naming, for "woman" is "not a name; it is a common noun, not a proper noun. It designates gender; it does not specify a person."[54] Trible's comment reveals that she misunderstood the parallel between the naming of the animals and the naming of the woman. When Adam named the animals, he did not give them personal or proper names. He classified the animals into distinct groups, presumably distinguishing between, say, lions, tigers, and bears. He did not name any tigers Tony. He identified them as tigers over against bears. So too, it is completely irrelevant that a personal or proper name is lacking for the woman in Genesis 2:23. In naming the woman, Adam was classifying her, in effect distinguishing her from the other creatures named. He recognized her distinctiveness and aptly captured it with the name "woman," thereby noticing how closely related she was to himself as a man. To conclude, male leadership is communicated by the naming of the woman, and the parallel with naming the animals stands, even though the biblical nar-

---

[53]Over against Trible's view, see Clines, "What Does Eve Do to Help?" 37–40 (especially 39, footnote 3). George W. Ramsey ("Is Name-Giving an Act of Domination in Genesis 2:23 and Elsewhere?" *Catholic Biblical Quarterly* 50 [1988]: 24–35) maintains that naming is linked only with discernment, not domination. But this view ignores the connection between the injunction to rule the world and the act of naming.

[54]Cited in Clines, "What Does Eve Do to Help?" 100.

rator hardly suggests that animals and women are parallel in every way.[55]

The fifth indication of male leadership is that the serpent, which was exceedingly astute, approached Eve rather than Adam in the temptation (Gen. 3:1–7). Thereby he subverted the pattern of male leadership, as Paul himself hints at in 1 Timothy 2:14. I do not want to make too much of this argument, and my case hardly depends on it. I acknowledge forthrightly that it could be incorrect, but in any case it would not affect the other arguments presented. I mention it because I am persuaded that what actually occurred (and what did not occur) in the narrative is significant.

Finally, the responsibility of men is indicated by the fact that Adam was rebuked before Eve (Gen. 3:8–12). If God were truly egalitarian, Eve would have been reprimanded first, since she ate the fruit before her husband and presumably convinced Adam to eat of it as well. Yahweh spoke to Adam first because he bore primary responsibility for what occurred in the garden. In Romans 5:12–19 Paul confirms this reading of the narrative, for the sin of the human race was traced to Adam, not to Eve. I am not suggesting that Eve bore no responsibility for her sin. Yahweh censured her actions as well and judged her for what she did (Gen. 3:13, 16). Greater responsibility, however, is assigned to Adam as the leader of the first human couple.

It is crucial to see that these six arguments relate to the relationship between Adam and Eve before the Fall. God instituted role distinctions between men and women before sin ever entered the world. Even the two arguments I presented from Genesis 3 depend on a role difference established before the Fall. If Adam and Eve possessed different roles before the Fall, then the distinct roles of men and women are not the result of sin. They stem from God's intention in creation, and everything that God created is good. Male leadership is not the result of the Fall, but it is God's good and perfect will for man and woman.

The doctrine of creation is of enormous significance for the debate on the roles of men and women. We know from Jesus

---

[55]Incidentally, Trible's view that the naming of Eve (Gen. 3:20) is an inappropriate act of male dominance (*God and the Rhetoric of Sexuality,* 133–34) is unconvincing, for the text provides no clue that an abuse of power is involved. Instead, this word is linked in the narrative with the promise of life (Gen. 3:20–21). For a critique of Trible, see Clines, "What Does Eve Do to Help?" 39.

himself that marriage is to be permanent because permanence in marriage was God's intent in creating us male and female (Gen. 1:26–27; 2:24; Matt. 19:3–12). We know that homosexuality is prohibited because it counters God's creational intent (Rom. 1:26–27). We know that food is to be eaten with thanksgiving because God created it (1 Tim. 4:1–5). Similarly, we know that role differences between men and women are not the result of the Fall, but are part of the fabric of God's good and perfect created order. Sin has entered the world and distorted how men and women relate to one another. Men transgress by turning their responsibility to lead into a privilege so that they tyrannically abuse their authority or abdicate their responsibility and descend into abject passivity. Women try to subvert male leadership by contesting their leadership or by responding with an obsequiousness that is not fitting.[56] Similarly, we can see how sin has thwarted God's intent that a man and woman should remain married for life, with the result that divorce is all too common. But differences in role, like the permanence of marriage, remains God's intention. And such differences in role are good and beautiful and, through the redemption accomplished by Christ, can be lived out today in a beautiful, albeit not perfect, way.

Different Roles Confirmed in Marriage Texts

We are debating the role of women *in ministry* in this book, not whether husbands and wives have different functions within a marriage. And yet this latter issue cannot and must not be neglected, for the biblical teaching about the family forms the fabric and background for what is said about women in ministry. If role differences exist in the family, they plausibly exist in the church as well. Indeed, in 1 Timothy 3:15 Paul compares the church to God's household, and in 1 Timothy 5:1–2 Paul exhorts Timothy to treat other church members as he would a father or a mother, a brother or a sister.[57] We must note that Paul does not

---

[56]My view here depends on my interpretation of Genesis 3:16, which I do not have space here to explain. See Susan T. Foh, "What Is the Woman's Desire?" *Westminster Theological Journal* 37 (1975): 376–83.

[57]For an illuminating study on the relationship between the church and the family, see Vern S. Poythress, "The Church as Family: Why Male Leadership in the Family Requires Male Leadership in the Church," in *Recovering Biblical Manhood and Womanhood*, 233–47.

instruct Timothy to treat everyone with undifferentiated sameness. The wise person responds differently when speaking to an
older man rather than to a younger man, in a way that shows
more deference and respect for the older man's experience. If
God has assigned husbands a particular responsibility as leaders of their homes, it would make sense that he has also
ordained that men should bear responsibility in the leadership
of the church. Ministry and family should not be segregated
rigidly from one another. The two spheres interpenetrate, and
what is true of the one is generally accurate in the other.

When we examine the biblical texts on husbands and wives,
it is clear that husbands have a responsibility to exercise loving
leadership, and wives are called on to submit (Eph. 5:22–33; Col.
3:18–19; Titus 2:4–5; 1 Peter 3:1–7). Space precludes a detailed
analysis of these texts, and thus only a few major issues can be
addressed here, particularly those areas where egalitarians question the complementarian view. We should note at the outset that
husbands are exhorted to love their wives, to refrain from all bitterness, and to treat them gently. The Bible nowhere suggests that
the husband's leadership is to be used as a platform for selfish-
ness or for abuse of his wife. Rather, the husband should pattern
himself after Christ, exercising a loving leadership on the wife's
behalf. I want to add only that the love and tenderness of a husband is still exercised *in leadership*. Christ served the church by
giving his life for it, and yet he remains the leader and lord of the
church. We ought not to think, therefore, that the leadership of
husbands is canceled out in the call to serve.

Many egalitarians appeal to Ephesians 5:21 ("Be subject to
one another in the fear of Christ") to support mutual submission
in marriage, but the argument is unpersuasive.[58] When the verse
is interpreted in context, it is doubtful that mutual submission
in marriage is intended. Verse 21 is transitional, bridging the gap
between Ephesians 5:18–20 and the household exhortations in
5:22–6:9. It is doubtful, though, that the content of Ephesians
5:21 should be read into the exhortations that follow. Otherwise,
Paul would be suggesting that parents and children (Eph. 6:1–
4) and masters and slaves (Eph. 6:5–9) should mutually submit
to each other. It is highly implausible that parents would be

---

[58]See, for example, Grenz, *Women in the Church*, 115, 178; Keener, *Paul, Women
and Wives*, 159, 168–72.

encouraged to submit to children, or masters to submit to slaves.[59] While such an idea might appeal to some people today, it would scarcely enter into the mind of someone writing two thousand years ago. We look in vain for any clear indication elsewhere in the Scriptures that parents should submit to children, or masters to slaves.[60] Nor do the Scriptures ever call on husbands to submit to their wives, but they consistently summon wives to submit to their husbands.

How, then, should we interpret Ephesians 5:21? What Paul has in mind is the relationship we have with one another in the church (see Eph. 5:19–21), one in which believers mutually submit to one another. These words cannot be imposed on the marriage relationship, but refer instead to a corporate setting in which believers praise God in song and submit to one another in the community.[61]

Others contest the complementarian view by disputing the meaning of *kephalē* ("head"). Egalitarians typically define it to mean "source" instead of "authority over."[62] The meaning of the term *kephalē* can be established only by a careful analysis of its use in biblical and extrabiblical literature. Wayne Grudem and Joseph Fitzmyer have demonstrated conclusively that "authority over" in many contexts is the most likely meaning of the term.[63] It may

---

[59]So also Hurley, *Man and Woman in Biblical Perspective*, 158.

[60]Keener (*Paul, Women and Wives*, 186–88) acknowledges that mutual submission is not demanded of children, showing his inconsistency, for if this is the case, Ephesians 5:21 does *not* function as the introduction to all of Ephesians 5:22–6:9. Nor do I find Keener's view (*Paul, Women and Wives*, 206) that Ephesians 6:9 teaches submission for masters to be persuasive. The persistent fact is that husbands, parents, and masters are never told to submit to wives, children, and slaves respectively.

[61]I am not suggesting, incidentally, that husbands never follow the advice of their wives. Wise husbands do so often, but they do so as leaders.

[62]See, for example, Gilbert Bilezikian, *Beyond Sex Roles: What the Bible Says About a Woman's Place in Church and Family*, rev. ed. (Grand Rapids: Baker, 1985), 215–52; Berkeley Mickelsen and Alvera Mickelsen, "What Does *Kephalē* Mean in the New Testament?" in *Women, Authority and the Bible*, 97–110; Catherine Clark Kroeger, "The Classical Concept of *Head* as 'Source,'" in Hull, *Equal to Serve*, 267–83. For another complementarian view, see Richard S. Cervin, "Does *Kephalē* Mean 'Source' or 'Authority' in Greek Literature? A Rebuttal," *Trinity Journal* 10 (1989): 85–112. For the weaknesses in Cervin's view as well, see the second article listed under Grudem in the next note.

[63]Wayne Grudem, "Does *Kephalē* ('Head') Mean 'Source' or 'Authority Over' in Greek Literature? A Survey of 2,336 Examples," *Trinity Journal* 6 (1985): 38–59;

well be, however, that *kephalē* in some contexts denotes both "authority over" and "source," as Clinton Arnold argues.[64] The definitions "authority over" and "source" make sense of Colossians 2:19 and Ephesians 4:15, where Christ as the Head both reigns over and provides for the church.

In any case, even if *kephalē* should be defined only as "source" (which is very unlikely), it would still support male leadership. Let me explain. In Ephesians 5:22–24 Paul exhorts wives to submit to their husbands in everything. What reason is given for such a command? Paul provides the rationale in Ephesians 5:23 (note the *hoti*): "For the husband is the head of the wife, as Christ also is the head of the church." If the word *kephalē* means "source," then Paul exhorts wives to submit because their husbands are their source. So even if *kephalē* means "source," wives are to fulfill a supportive and submissive role, and husbands, as the "source," are to function as leaders.

The same argument obtains in 1 Corinthians 11:2–16. If *kephalē* means "source," then women are to defer to their source by adorning themselves properly. The idea that the source has particular authority hearkens back to Genesis 2:21–25, where the woman comes from the man (see 1 Cor. 11:8). Similarly, children should obey their parents because parents are the source of their existence. Nonetheless, the meaning "authority over" cannot be exorcised from Ephesians 5:22–24, for the call for wives to submit to their husbands as the church submits to Christ indicates that the *authority* of Christ as head is in view (cf. Eph. 1:22; Col. 1:18; 2:10). I am not denying that there may be an idea of *source* as well, since husbands are to nourish and care for their wives, just as Christ has tenderly loved the church. In any case, the husband's special role as the leader of his wife cannot be explained away in Ephesians 5:22–33.

Occasionally a few egalitarians maintain that the word "submit" (*hypotassō*) does not connote the idea of obedience. For instance, Gretchen Gaebelein Hull suggests that *hypotassō* means

Wayne Grudem, "The Meaning of *Kephalē* ('Head'): A Response to Recent Studies," in *Recovering Biblical Manhood and Womanhood*, 425–68, 534–41; Joseph A. Fitzmyer, "*Kephalē* in 1 Corinthians 11:3," *Interpretation* 47 (1993): 52–59.

[64]Clinton E. Arnold, "Jesus Christ: 'Head' of the Church (Colossians and Ephesians)," in *Jesus of Nazareth: Lord and Christ. Essays on the Historical Jesus and New Testament Christology*, eds. J. B. Green and M. Turner (Grand Rapids: Eerdmans, 1994), 346–66.

"to identify with" rather than "to obey."[65] Certainly there is no suggestion that husbands should compel their wives to submit. Submission is a voluntary and glad response on the part of wives, and husbands are commanded to love their wives, not to see to it that they submit. Nor is it fitting if a wife's submission is conceived of in terms of a child's obedience to parents, for the relationship of a husband and wife is remarkably different from the relationship between a parent and a child. Indeed, Paul can speak of the mutual obligations husbands and wives have to one another (1 Cor. 7:3–5), emphasizing that the husband ultimately does not have authority over his own body and that the wife has authority over his body. Complementarians have too often made the mistake of envisioning the husband-wife relationship in one-dimensional terms, so that any idea of mutuality and partnership is removed, and wives are conceived of as servants (or even as slaves) of husbands. Such a militaristic conception of marriage is foreign to the biblical perspective, and 1 Corinthians 7:3–5 reminds us that mutuality also characterizes the marriage relationship.

On the other hand, we cannot dismiss the particular calling of the wife to submit, and such submission does involve obedience. In the Bible submission is required to God's law (Rom. 8:7), to the government (Rom. 13:1, 5; Titus 3:1; 1 Peter 2:13), of slaves to masters (Titus 2:9; 1 Peter 2:18), and of younger people to their elders (1 Peter 5:5). The submission of Christ to the Father (1 Cor. 15:27–28) and of demons to Christ (Eph. 1:21; 1 Peter 3:22) is also described. The above examples illustrate that the concept of obedience *is* involved in submission. Indeed, 1 Peter 3:5–6 removes any doubt, for Peter commends the holy women of the past, who were "submissive to their own husbands; just as Sarah obeyed Abraham." Notice the "just as" connecting the word "submissive" to the verb "obeyed." When Peter describes the submission of Sarah, he uses the word "obey" to portray it. Such submission should not be construed as demeaning or as a denial of a person's dignity or personhood, for Christ himself submits to the Father (1 Cor. 15:27–28), and as the Son, he did what the Father commanded, yet there is no idea that the Son lacks dignity or worth. To say that those who submit are of less worth and dignity is not a bib-

---

[65]Hull, *Equal to Serve*, 195.

lical worldview but a secular worldview that serves only to guide our highly competitive society.[66]

Is it possible, though, that the submission required of wives is an example of cultural accommodation? In the contexts where wives are exhorted to submit to husbands we also see that slaves are commanded to submit to their masters (Eph. 5:22–33 and 6:5–9; Col. 3:18–19 and 3:22–4:1; Titus 2:4–5 and 2:9–10; 1 Peter 2:18–25 and 3:1–7). Evangelical egalitarians accept as the word of God Paul's admonitions to slaves. In the culture of Paul's day submission to masters was fitting, for societal revolution is not the means by which a culture is transformed. Indeed, in Paul's day people would reject the gospel if they felt that it was overturning cultural norms. So, it is argued, Paul counsels submission to wives "so that the word of God will not be dishonored" (Titus 2:5).[67] Similarly, slaves are to live responsibly "so that they will adorn the doctrine of God our Savior in every respect" (Titus 2:10). But in our culture the same norms do not apply. Our contemporaries will reject the gospel, it is claimed, if women do not have the same rights as men, just as it would be a hindrance to the gospel if we recommended slavery. Egalitarians put the point even more sharply. If we insist that wives should submit today and that women cannot serve as pastors, then are we also recommending the reinstitution of slavery? Many Christians in the 1800s appealed to the Bible to defend slavery, and many egalitarians believe that those who defend the complementarian view on women's roles are making a similar mistake today.[68]

---

[66]Most egalitarians deny that there is any sense in which the Son submits eternally to the Father. See, for example, Gilbert Bilezikian, "Hermeneutical Bungee-Jumping: Subordination in the Godhead," *Journal of the Evangelical Theological Society* 40 (1997): 57–68. But Craig S. Keener ("Is Subordination within the Trinity Really Heresy? A Study of John 5:18 in Context," *Trinity Journal* 20 [1999]: 39–51), who is himself an egalitarian, properly suggests that the eternal subordination of the Son, rightly understood, is biblically probable.

[67]For this view, see Alan Padgett, "The Pauline Rationale for Submission: Biblical Feminism and the *hina* Clauses of Titus 2:1–10," *Evangelical Quarterly* 59 (1987): 39–52.

[68]For this thesis, see Willard M. Swartley, *Slavery, Sabbath, War and Women: Case Issues in Biblical Interpretation* (Scottdale, Pa.: Herald, 1983); Keener, *Paul, Women and Wives*, 184–224; Kevin Giles, "The Biblical Case for Slavery: Can the Bible Mislead? A Case Study in Hermeneutics," *Evangelical Quarterly* 66 (1994): 3–17. Unfortunately, Giles (page 4) relinquishes the Bible's authority in social relations. See the critique by Yarbrough, "The Hermeneutics of 1 Timothy 2:9–15," 189.

We must admit that this objection is a thoughtful one. I believe egalitarians are correct in saying that some of the commands and norms in Scripture are the result of cultural accommodation. Slavery is not God's ideal, and yet the Scriptures regulate and transform cultures in which slavery is practiced. The Bible does not recommend revolution to wipe out existing institutions but counsels a transformation from within. Paul, for instance, did not require Philemon to give up Onesimus as his slave, but he expected the relationship between master and slave to be transformed by their unity in Christ so that Onesimus would be treated as a brother in the Lord and not merely as a slave. If egalitarians are correct in saying that the admonitions to wives and the restrictions on women in ministry are analogous to the counsel given to slaves, then I would agree that the restrictions on women are due to cultural accommodation and are not required of believers today. Nevertheless, I think egalitarians make a crucial mistake when they draw a parallel between the exhortations given to slaves and those given to wives. The marriage relationship is not analogous to slavery, for slavery is an evil human institution regulated by Scripture. Marriage, on the other hand, is a creation ordinance of God and part of God's good will for human beings (Gen. 2:18–25). Thus, the parallel between marriage and slavery does not stand.[69]

The weakness of the parallel between slavery and marriage is obvious when the relationship between children and parents is introduced. In the household passages Paul exhorts husbands and wives, parents and children, and masters and slaves (Eph. 5:22–6:9; Col. 3:18–4:1). The inclusion of parents and children is instructive. Those who say that the admonition to wives is culturally bounded by appealing to the matter of slavery must also (to be consistent) say that the admonition for children to obey their parents no longer applies today. But there is no doubt that children are mandated by God to obey their parents, and such a command is not harmful for children but is part of God's good

---

[69]Craig Keener (*Paul, Women and Wives*, 208–209) objects that the issue is whether a wife's submission to her husband is permanently mandated, not the ordinance of marriage itself. But I would argue that Paul's argument in Ephesians 5:22–33 demonstrates that the marriage relationship mirrors Christ's relationship to the church. In addition, Genesis 2–3 indicates that role distinctions between husbands and wives was God's intention in creating man and woman.

intention for them.[70] Bearing and raising children is, from the time of creation, part of God's good intention for human beings (Gen. 1:28). Similarly, the marriage relationship stems from God's creational intent (Gen. 2:18–25). The same cannot be said for slavery! Both the marriage and parent-child relationships hearken back to creation, but slavery does not, and hence the appeal to slavery as a parallel to the relationship between men and women fails.[71]

The analogy Paul draws between Christ and the church and husbands and wives in Ephesians 5:22–33 also demonstrates that the exhortations for husbands and wives are transcultural. Husbands are to pattern their love after Christ's love for the church, and wives are to submit in the same way that the church submits to Christ. Ephesians 5:32 adds a crucial dimension to this argument. Paul remarks, "This mystery is great; but I am speaking with reference to Christ and the church." What Paul means by this is that the relationship of a husband and wife mirrors an even greater reality, namely, the relationship between Christ and the church. It is not the case that marriage was instituted first, and then God decided that marriage would function as an illustration of Christ's relationship to the church.[72] Instead, from all eternity God envisioned Christ's relationship to the church, and he instituted marriage as a picture or mirror of Christ's relationship to the church. The husband represents Christ, and the wife represents the church. We must beware, of course, of pressing the typological parallel too far, for a husband does not die for the wife or cleanse or purify her. But the typological relationship indicates that the wife's submission to the

---

[70]Of course, I am not denying that sin has affected the relationship between parents and children, with the result that no parents raise their children perfectly, and, in fact, some parents do great damage to their children.

[71]Nor is it clear from Titus 2:3–5 that wives are to submit only in order to avoid cultural scandal in Paul's day. Padgett ("The Pauline Rationale for Submission") provides no clear basis upon which certain admonitions are culturally dated and others are transcendent, for in these very verses Paul also summons wives to love their husbands and children and to be kind, sensible, and pure. These commands are given for the same reason as the command to submit to husbands, namely, so that the gospel will be honored. But, of course, no one would think that these commands no longer apply today.

[72]For an analysis of this theme, see Andreas J. Köstenberger, "The Mystery of Christ and the Church: Head and Body, 'One Flesh,'" *Trinity Journal* 12 (1991): 79–94.

husband is not merely a cultural accommodation to Greco-Roman society. Such submission mirrors to the world the church's submission to Christ.

Correspondingly, the husband's loving leadership is not a reflection of a patriarchal society, but it is intended to portray Christ's loving and saving work for his church. The institution of marriage and the responsibilities of husbands and wives within it are not culturally limited, but are God's transcendent intention for all marriages for all time, since all marriages should reflect Christ's love for the church and the church's submission to Christ. Few believers ever think of their marriages in such terms, indicating that a secular mind-set has infiltrated our view of marriage as well. How glorious and beautiful and awesome it is to realize that our marriages reflect Christ's love for the church and the church's loving response to Christ.

Different Roles in Ministry: Scripture Texts

Women Prohibited from Teaching Men: 1 Timothy 2:11–14

It is not surprising to discover that, just as there are distinct roles between husbands and wives in the family, different roles between men and women are also mandated in the church.[73] Women should not fill the role of pastor/elder/overseer. The fundamental text on this matter is 1 Timothy 2:11–15. This text is a battleground in current scholarship, and entire books are being written on it.[74] In this essay I can only "sketch in" my understanding of the passage. For a thorough treatment, I refer readers to a book I coedited (*Women in the Church: A Fresh Analysis of 1 Timothy 2:9–15*).

---

[73]Some scholars believe that Paul is addressing husbands and wives rather than men and women here. So, for example, Gordon P. Hugenberger, "Women in Church Office: Hermeneutics or Exegesis? A Survey of Approaches to 1 Timothy 2:8–15," *Journal of the Evangelical Theological Society* 35 (1992): 341–60. Such a view is not contextually convincing. For a refutation, see my essay "An Interpretation of 1 Timothy 2:9–15: A Dialogue with Scholarship," in *Women in the Church: A Fresh Analysis,* 115–17.

[74]From the egalitarian point of view, see Richard Clark Kroeger and Catherine Clark Kroeger, *I Suffer Not a Woman: Rethinking 1 Timothy 2:11–15 in Light of Ancient Evidence* (Grand Rapids: Baker, 1992); Sharon Gritz, *Paul, Women Teachers, and the Mother Goddess at Ephesus: A Study of 1 Timothy 2:9–15 in Light of the Religious and Cultural Milieu of the First Century* (Lanham, Md.: University Press of America, 1991).

Before examining 1 Timothy 2:11–14, I want to say a word about verses 9–10. Some ask why we forbid women from functioning as pastors when we do not prohibit women from wearing jewelry.[75] Let me say this: If the Scriptures (rightly interpreted) banned the wearing of jewelry, then we should cease wearing it. The Bible, not our culture, must reign supreme. On the other hand, we must interpret the Scriptures in their historical and cultural context. They were written to specific situations and to cultures that differed from our own. The prohibition regarding the braiding of hair and the wearing of jewelry would not surprise Paul's readers, for such admonitions were part of the common stock of ethical exhortation in the Greco-Roman world.[76] Discerning why a command was given is appropriate, precisely because culture has changed. We must distinguish between the principle and the cultural outworking of a principle. We do not practice the holy kiss today (1 Cor. 16:20), but we still derive a principle from it, namely, to greet one another warmly in Christ—perhaps with a warm handshake or a hug. We do not demand that people with indigestion drink wine (1 Tim. 5:23), but we do think taking an antacid is advisable for those who suffer from stomach pain. Similarly, the principle in 1 Timothy 2:9–10 is that women should dress modestly and without ostentation.[77] As a complementarian, I do not believe we should try to revert to the culture of the biblical times. I do believe we should follow the moral norms and principles taught in the Bible. As we study 1 Timothy 2:12 we must discern how its admonition applies to us today.

In 1 Timothy 2:11–12 Paul exhorts the women to learn quietly and submissively, forbidding them to teach or exercise authority over a man. It has often been observed that Paul departs from some of his contemporaries in encouraging women to learn the Scriptures. The influence of Jesus, who instructed Mary (Luke 10:38–42), is obvious here. Nevertheless, the emphasis in this context is on the *manner* in which a woman learns, that

[75]See, for example, Alvera Mickelsen, "An Egalitarian View: There Is Neither Male nor Female in Christ," in *Women in Ministry: Four Views*, eds. Bonnidell Clouse and Robert G. Clouse (Downers Grove, Ill.: InterVarsity Press, 1989), 201.

[76]See Steven M. Baugh, "A Foreign World: Ephesus in the First Century," in *Women in the Church: A Fresh Analysis*, 47–48; Keener, *Paul, Women and Wives*, 103–107.

[77]For a more detailed discussion of 1 Timothy 2:9–10 see my essay "An Interpretation of 1 Timothy 2:9–15," 114–21.

is to say, quietly and submissively. Paul assumes that women should learn. What concerns him is that some of the women in Ephesus are arrogating authority to themselves and are not learning with submission. The prohibition in 1 Timothy 2:12 further explains verse 11. Paul does not allow women to teach or to exercise authority over a man. Andreas Köstenberger has conclusively shown that the two infinitives, *didaskein* ("to teach") and *authentein* ("to exercise authority"), which are connected by *oude* ("nor"), refer to two distinct activities.[78] He establishes this case by consulting verbal forms connected by *oude* in biblical and extrabiblical literature. He also discovered that the two distinct activities are both viewed either positively or negatively when connected by *oude*. Whether the activities are positive or negative is established by the context. Köstenberger rightly notes that the verb *didaskō* ("to teach") is a positive term in the Pastoral Epistles (1 Tim. 4:11; 6:2; 2 Tim. 2:2) unless the context adds information to indicate otherwise (Titus 1:11). When Paul wants to use a verb to designate false teaching, he uses the term *heterodidaskaleō* ("to teach strange or false doctrines," 1 Tim. 1:3; 6:3). Köstenberger's study is significant for our understanding of 1 Timothy 2:12. Paul prohibits two distinct activities—teaching and exercising authority. Both teaching and exercising authority are legitimate activities in and of themselves. He does not prohibit women from teaching or exercising authority because these actions are intrinsically evil. Both teaching and exercising authority are proper activities for believers, but in this context he forbids women from engaging in such activities.

Köstenberger's study goes a long way to solving the debate on the meaning of the verb *authentein* ("to exercise authority") in 1 Timothy 2:12. In 1979 Catherine Kroeger proposed that the verb meant "to engage in fertility practices," but scholars of all persuasions dismiss this view.[79] Now the Kroegers propose that verse 12 should be translated, "I do not allow a woman to teach nor to proclaim herself the author or originator of a man."[80] Three

---

[78] Andreas J. Köstenberger, "A Complex Sentence Structure in 1 Timothy 2:12," in *Women in the Church: A Fresh Analysis*, 81–103.

[79] Catherine Clark Kroeger, "Ancient Heresies and a Strange Greek Verb," *Reformed Journal* 29 (1979): 12–15.

[80] See Kroeger and Kroeger, *I Suffer Not a Woman*, 103. Also Philip B. Payne, "Part II: The Interpretation of 1 Timothy 2:11–15: A Surrejoinder," in *What Does the Scripture Teach about the Ordination of Women?* (Minneapolis: unpublished paper,

careful and technical studies have been conducted on *authentein*, and all three demonstrate that the most natural meaning for the term is "to exercise authority."[81] Scott Baldwin, in particular, has examined virtually every use of the term and carefully separated the verb from the noun, for many scholars mistakenly blend the verb and noun together in their study of the term. Of course, it is just possible *in context* that a term with a positive meaning ("to exercise authority") could have a negative meaning ("to domineer").[82] But at this juncture Köstenberger's work applies again, for he has shown in his study of the sentence structure that both terms are either inherently positive or inherently negative. Since the term "teach" has no negative connotations, we should not read a negative sense into "exercise authority." I realize the discussion of this point has been rather technical, but my conclusion is this: Technical study has verified that complementarians have rightly interpreted this verse. Paul prohibits women from teaching or exercising authority over men.[83]

1986), 108–110, who lists five different meanings for the infinitive, which does not inspire confidence that he has any definite sense of what the infinitive means.

[81]George W. Knight III, "*AUTHENTEŌ* in Reference to Women in 1 Timothy 2:12," *New Testament Studies* 30 (1984): 143–57; Leland E. Wilshire, "The TLG Computer and Further Reference to *Authenteō* in 1 Timothy 2:12," *New Testament Studies* 34 (1988): 120–34; H. Scott Baldwin, "A Difficult Word: *Authenteō* in 1 Timothy 2:12," in *Women in the Church: A Fresh Analysis*, 65–80, 269–305. See my summary and more detailed analysis of this word in my essay "An Interpretation of 1 Timothy 2:9–15," 130–33.

[82]See, for example, Carroll D. Osburn, "*Authenteō* (1 Timothy 2:12)," *Restoration Quarterly* 25 (1982): 1–12.

[83]Some egalitarians have appealed to the phrase *ouk epitrepō* ("I do not permit") to support their case, arguing that the indicative mood demonstrates that the exhortation is not even a command and that the present tense suggests that the exhortation is merely a temporary restriction to be lifted once women are qualified to teach (see, for example, Philip B. Payne, "Libertarian Women in Ephesus: A Response to Douglas J. Moo's Article, '1 Timothy 2:11–15: Meaning and Significance,'" *Trinity Journal* 2 [1981]: 170–72; Grenz, *Women in the Church*, 127–28). Both assertions are incorrect. Paul often uses indicatives to introduce commands. For example, the famous admonition to give one's whole life to God (Rom. 12:1–2) is introduced with the indicative *parakalō* ("I exhort"). It is linguistically naive to insist that commands must be in the imperative mood (see 1 Cor. 1:10; Eph. 4:1; Phil. 4:2; 1 Tim. 2:8; 5:14; 2 Tim. 1:6; Titus 3:8). Nor can one appeal to the present tense to say that the command is merely temporary. The same argument could then be used to say that Paul desires believers to give their lives to God only for a brief period of time (Rom. 12:1) or that he wants the men to pray without wrath and dissension merely for the present time (1 Tim. 2:8), but in the future they could desist.

We have seen previously that prohibiting a woman from teaching or exercising authority over a man applies to the tasks of an elder, for elders have a unique responsibility to teach and rule in God's church. But on what basis does Paul forbid women from teaching and exercising authority? His words in 1 Timothy 2:13 provide the reason: "For it was Adam who was first created, and then Eve." The *gar* ("for") introducing this verse is best understood as a ground for the command, since a reason naturally follows the prohibition.[84] Women should not teach men or exercise authority over them because this would violate God's intention in creation. Since Paul appeals to creation, the prohibition transcends culture. Paul disallows homosexuality because it contravenes God's created order (Rom. 1:26–27). Jesus asserts the permanency of marriage by appealing to creation (Matt. 19:3–12). There is no suggestion in the 1 Timothy 2 passage, therefore, that the prohibition is temporary, nor is there any indication that the restriction is somehow due to human sin or to the limitations of women. The restriction on women stems from God's creation mandate, not from the cultural situation at Ephesus.

Egalitarians often argue that the restriction can be explained by the lack of education among the women in Ephesus, or alternatively they suggest that these women were duped by false teachers—and thus the women would be allowed to teach once their doctrinal deficiencies were corrected.[85] Both of these views are unconvincing. Paul could have easily written this: "I do not allow a woman to teach or exercise authority over a man as long as she is uneducated and unlearned." He gives no indication, however, that lack of education is the problem. In fact, egalitarians skate over the reason given (Paul's appeal to the created order) and appeal to one that is not even mentioned (lack of edu-

---

[84]Egalitarians often understand this verse to be merely an illustration. For this view, see Gritz, *Paul, Women Teachers, and the Mother Goddess*, 136; Witherington, *Women and the Genesis of Christianity*, 194–95; David M. Scholer, "1 Timothy 2:9–15 and the Place of Women in the Church's Ministry," in *Women, Authority and the Bible*, 208; Alan Padgett, "Wealthy Women at Ephesus: 1 Timothy 2:8–15 in Social Context," *Interpretation* 41 (1987): 25; Keener, *Paul, Women and Wives*, 115–17. In defense of this verse functioning as a reason for the command, see Douglas J. Moo, "The Interpretation of 1 Timothy 2:11–15: A Rejoinder," *Trinity Journal* 2 (1981): 202–203.

[85]For documentation of the egalitarian view, see my essay "An Interpretation of 1 Timothy 2:9–15," 137.

cation).[86] Furthermore, as Steven M. Baugh points out, it is not the case that all women were uneducated in Ephesus.[87] Indeed, we know from 2 Timothy 4:19 that Priscilla was in Ephesus, and she was certainly educated.

Nor is the second attempt to explain away 1 Timothy 2:12 any more persuasive. Paul could have written, "I do not permit a woman to teach or exercise authority over a man. For she is being led astray by false teachers." There are multiple problems with this hypothesis. First, why does Paul only mention women, since we know that at least some men were being duped by the false teachers as well? It would be insufferably sexist to prohibit only women from teaching and exercising authority when men were being led astray as well.[88] Second, the theory requires that *all* the women in Ephesus were deluded by the false teachers. Paul gives no indication that the restriction applies only to some women, but it is incredibly hard to believe that every single woman in Ephesus was beguiled by the false teaching. Third, egalitarian scholars have been busy remaking the background to the situation in 1 Timothy 2:11–15, but their reconstructions have been highly speculative and sometimes wildly implausible. For example, in their work on 1 Timothy (*I Suffer Not a Woman*) the Kroegers allege that Ephesus was feminist; they appeal to later evidence to vindicate their thesis and ransack the entire Greco-Roman world to sustain it. They have rightly been excoriated in reviews for producing a work that departs from a sound historical method.[89] They fall prey to Samuel Sandmel's warning against parallelomania, and they would have been wise to apply the kind of sober method recommended in John Barclay's essay

---

[86]Royce Gordon Gruenler ("The Mission-Lifestyle Setting of 1 Timothy 2:8–15," *Journal of the Evangelical Theological Society* 41 [1998]: 215–38) argues that the subordination of women is explicable from the missionary situation in 1 Timothy. But he does not really engage in an intensive exegesis of the text, nor does he persuasively demonstrate that the prohibition is due to mission. Once again, Paul could have easily communicated such an idea, but he did not clearly do so.

[87]Baugh, "A Foreign World," 45–47.

[88]See D. A. Carson, "'Silent in the Churches': On the Role of Women in 1 Corinthians 14:33b–36," in *Recovering Biblical Manhood and Womanhood*, 147.

[89]See Steven M. Baugh, "The Apostle among the Amazons," *Westminster Theological Journal* 56 (1994): 153–71; Albert Wolters, "Review: *I Suffer Not a Woman*," *Calvin Theological Journal* 28 (1993): 208–13; Robert W. Yarbrough, "*I Suffer Not a Woman*: A Review Essay," *Presbyterion* 18 (1992): 25–33.

on reconstructing the teaching and identity of opponents.[90] Bruce Barron blithely appeals to second-century gnostic sources and gives no indication that appealing to later evidence is a problem.[91] In *Paul, Women Teachers, and the Mother Goddess at Ephesus* Sharon Gritz argues that the Artemis cult is responsible for the problem in Ephesus. Her work is much more careful than that of the Kroegers, but at the end of the day she does not provide any hard data from the letter to substantiate her thesis.[92]

Speculation runs rampant among those defending the egalitarian thesis. I challenge egalitarians to demonstrate from 1 Timothy itself the nature of the false teaching instead of from later and external sources. I conclude that egalitarians have not yet provided a plausible explanation for Paul's argument from creation in 1 Timothy 2:13. In fact, they often complain that Paul's argument in this verse is unclear and hard to understand.[93] Yet most Christians throughout church history did not think the verse was so obscure, nor do I think it is hard to grasp. I would suggest that the verse seems difficult because it runs counter to our own cultural intuitions. But the Scriptures exist to challenge our worldview and to correct our way of looking at the world.

In 1 Timothy 2:14 Paul gives a second reason for the prohibition. Women are forbidden to teach because Eve was deceived, and not Adam. Egalitarians occasionally appeal to this verse to say that women were responsible for spreading the heresy in Ephesus, and that is why they are prevented from teaching.[94] When we read 1 Timothy and the rest of the Pastoral Epistles, however, the only false teachers named are men (1 Tim. 1:20; 2 Tim. 1:15; 2:17). The only evidence we have is that women

---

[90]Samuel Sandmel, "Parallelomania," *Journal of Biblical Literature* 81 (1962): 2–13; John M. G. Barclay, "Mirror-Reading a Polemical Letter: Galatians as a Test Case," *Journal for the Study of the New Testament* 3 (1987): 73–93. See also Jerry L. Sumney, "Identifying Paul's Opponents: The Question of Method in 2 Corinthians," in Journal for the Study of the New Testament: Supplement Series 40 (1990).

[91]Bruce Barron, "Putting Women in Their Place: 1 Timothy 2 and Evangelical Views of Women in Church Leadership," *Journal of the Evangelical Theological Society* 33 (1990): 451–59.

[92]See my "An Interpretation of 1 Timothy 2:9–15," 107–12, for a discussion on the setting of the text.

[93]For documentation, see my "An Interpretation of 1 Timothy 2:9–15," 136.

[94]For a detailed discussion of this verse, see my "An Interpretation of 1 Timothy 2:9–15," 140–46, though I am less certain about my previous interpretation of this verse.

were influenced by the heresy, not that they were purveyors of it (2 Tim. 3:5–9). Nor does 1 Timothy 2:14 suggest that women were disseminating false teaching, for to say that one is deceived is not to say that one is spreading error, but only that one is being led astray by it. What the verse highlights is what transpired in Eve's heart, namely, deception, and nothing is said about her giving Adam faulty instruction.

Nor is it plausible to say that 1 Timothy 2:14 highlights Eve's ignorance of God's command, and then to conclude that the women of Ephesus are prohibited from teaching because of a lack of education. The problem with this interpretation is that deception does not equate with lack of education, for the latter is remedied through instruction, while the former has a moral component. Nor does it make sense to say that Eve was ignorant of God's command given to Adam. If she were ignorant because Adam failed to inform her of the command, then the blame would surely rest with Adam. Alternatively, if Adam muddled the command and explained it poorly to Eve, this would scarcely fit with an injunction that encouraged men to teach rather than women. Presumably Adam explained the prohibition to Eve, and it is hard to see how she could not have grasped it, since it is quite easy to understand what was forbidden. If Eve couldn't understand it, then she was inherently stupid—which would explain why men should teach. But deception should not be equated with stupidity. Paul is not saying that Eve somehow lacked education or intelligence. He argues that she failed morally and was deceived by the serpent.

Egalitarians often allege that they have a better explanation of 1 Timothy 2:14 than complementarians. I would maintain that none of their explanations is persuasive, for there is no evidence in this verse that women were banned from teaching because they were spreading the heresy, nor is there any indication that they were uneducated, for deception cannot be equated with lack of education.

What then is the point of 1 Timothy 2:14? Let me acknowledge at the outset the difficulty of the verse. I believe the complementarian view stands on the basis of the clarity of verse 13 so that resolving the interpretation of verse 14 is not crucial for the passage as a whole. In the history of the church some have argued that women are less intelligent or more apt to be deceived than men. The idea that women are less intelligent is not taught elsewhere in Scripture, and Paul does not argue from lack of intelligence, but from the experience of deception. Others have suggested that the point is that Eve was deceived first, and Adam was deceived afterward. As Paul writes to his trusted coworker, he knows that Timothy will reflect on the Pauline teaching that sin has been transmitted through Adam (Rom. 5:12–19). So even though Eve sinned first, sin is traced to Adam, pointing to male headship. This is a very attractive interpretation. What militates against it is the assertion in the text that Adam was not deceived, but Eve was.

Perhaps the best suggestion is that the serpent took the initiative to tempt Eve rather than Adam, thereby subverting the pattern of male leadership.[95] I argued in a previous essay that perhaps Paul is suggesting that women are more prone to deceit than men, but this view has the disadvantage of suggesting an inherent defect in women, for the language of deceit in Scripture always involves a moral failing. Thus, I think that Paul likely reflects on the fact that the serpent subverted male headship by tempting Eve rather than Adam.[96] On this view 1 Timothy 2:14 supports the command in verse 12, providing an additional and complementary reason for male leadership in the church.

Women Exhorted to Prophesy with a Submissive Demeanor: 1 Corinthians 11:2–16

Because of space limitations, and because some elements of this passage have been discussed previously in this essay, I refer readers to a more detailed treatment elsewhere.[97] I do want to look at several issues here, beginning with the custom that is in view. How did Paul want the women to adorn themselves? We

---

[95]See also Gruenler, "The Mission-Lifestyle Setting," 217–18, 220–21.

[96]Due to space limitations I am bypassing the interpretation of 1 Timothy 2:15. For my view see "An Interpretation of 1 Timothy 2:9–15," 146–53. I do not believe that my specific interpretation affects the major teaching of the text in a decisive way (over against Keener, *Paul, Women and Wives*, 118; Scholer, "1 Timothy 2:9–15 and the Place of Women," 196). For an alternate interpretation, see Andreas J. Köstenberger, "Ascertaining Women's God-Ordained Roles: An Interpretation of 1 Timothy 2:15," *Bulletin for Biblical Research* 7 (1997): 107–43.

[97]See my essay "Head Coverings, Prophecies and the Trinity: 1 Corinthians 11:2–16," in *Recovering Biblical Manhood and Womanhood*, 124–39.

must admit immediately that complete certainty eludes us. Scholars have suggested veiling, the wearing of a shawl, or the tying of hair atop the head so that the hair didn't fall loosely onto the shoulders.[98] Whatever the custom was, the failure of the Corinthian women to abide by it was considered disgraceful. The behavior of the Corinthian women was as shocking as if they shaved their heads altogether (1 Cor. 11:6).

Even if we cannot specify the custom, why would Paul be concerned about how the women adorn themselves? We have already noted that honor and shame come to the forefront (1 Cor. 11:4–7, 13–15). Those who repudiate the custom bring dishonor upon their heads. The word "head" in verse 5 is probably a play on words, for the women who adorn themselves improperly bring dishonor on themselves *and* their husbands. It is evident that the women's adornment impinges on the relationship between men and women, since Paul introduces the whole matter by saying, "Christ is the head of every man, and the man is the head of a woman, and God is the head of Christ" (1 Cor. 11:3). I noted previously that the word *kephalē* ("head") may have both the idea of "authority over" and "source," and even if one were to adopt only the latter idea, male leadership could not be expunged from the text. Paul is concerned about the way women adorn themselves because shameful adornment is a symbol of rebellion against male leadership. A woman who is properly adorned signals that she is submissive to male headship. That woman was created to assist and help man is clear from the Pauline commentary in verses 7–9: "For a man ought not to have his head covered, since he is the image and glory of God; but the woman is the glory of man. For man does not originate from woman, but woman from man; for indeed man was not created for the woman's sake, but woman for the man's sake." We should note that the woman is required to adorn herself in a certain way because she came from the man,

---

[98]Supporting a shawl or veil is Gordon D. Fee, *The First Epistle to the Corinthians*, New International Commentary on the New Testament (Grand Rapids: Eerdmans, 1987), 506–12; Keener, *Paul, Women and Wives*, 22–31; Cynthia L. Thompson, "Hairstyles, Head-Coverings, and St. Paul: Portraits from Roman Corinth," *Biblical Archaeologist* 51 (1988): 99–115. Supporting hairstyle is Hurley, *Man and Woman in Biblical Perspective*, 254–71; David E. Blattenberger III, *Rethinking 1 Corinthians 11:2–16 through Archaeological and Moral-Rhetorical Analysis* (Lewiston, N.Y.: Mellen, 1997).

showing that an argument from source does not exclude male leadership.[99]

Paul does not merely impose restrictions on women. He encourages women to pray and prophesy in church if they are properly adorned (1 Cor. 11:5). Complementarians who relegate such prayer and prophecy by women to private meetings fail to convince, because the distinction between public and private meetings of the church is a modern invention; in Paul's day the church often met in homes for worship and instruction. Moreover, it is evident that 1 Corinthians 11:2–14:40 relates to activities when the church is gathered together. Paul commends women praying and prophesying in church, but he insists on proper adornment because such adornment signals submission to male leadership. It is also crucial at this juncture to reiterate what was said earlier. Prophecy is not preaching. Paul does not permit women to preach and teach if they are properly adorned, but he does allow them to prophesy. The permission to prophesy does not mean that women fill the office of pastor/elder/overseer. When women pray and prophesy, they must adorn themselves properly, thereby indicating that they are supportive of male leadership in the church.

We should also notice the programmatic nature of 1 Corinthians 11:3. God is the head of Christ, which signifies that God is the *authority over* the Christ. The Father commands and sends, and the Son obeys and goes. Even though the Son obeys the Father, he is equal in essence, dignity, and personhood with the Father. A difference in role does not signify a difference in worth. Some scholars are now actually arguing that the Son submits to the Father, *and the Father submits to the Son*. Stanley Grenz posits such a thesis in defense of the egalitarian view.[100] Amazingly enough, he does not provide any biblical evidence to support his assertion. He simply claims that the Father also submits to the Son. The reason he does not supply scriptural support is simple: There is no evidence in the Bible that the Father and Son mutually submit to one another. Grenz's interpretation is concocted out of nothing and proposed to the reader as though it were rooted somewhere in the Bible.

---

[99]I am not suggesting that *kephalē* means only "source" here. Probably both "authority over" and "source" are involved. My judgment on this issue represents a change from my "Head Coverings, Prophecies and the Trinity," 124–39.

[100]Grenz, *Women in the Church*, 153–54.

The parallel between Christ's submission to the Father and the deference of women to men is important. For right after Paul sets forth the distinct role of women in 1 Corinthians 11:2–10, he reminds his readers that both men and women are equal in the Lord (11:11–12). Some scholars have interpreted verses 11–12 as though Paul were now denying the male leadership taught in verses 2–10.[101] Such a reading is unpersuasive.

Paul returns to the differences between the genders in 1 Corinthians 11:13–16, and in verse 16 he reminds the Corinthians that all the other churches practice the custom that the Corinthians are resisting.[102] The text beautifully balances differences in roles with equality of personhood. Egalitarians have sometimes claimed that Paul corrects in verses 11–12 the focus on submission in verses 2–10. More likely, the themes of submission and equality are complementary. Women and men are equal in the Lord, and yet distinct roles are also demanded. Paul saw no contradiction on this point—and neither should we.

Should women wear a veil or a shawl today? A minority of complementarians thinks they should.[103] But we must remember that the Bible was written in the context of particular historical and cultural circumstances that we do not necessarily imitate today. As I noted before in the cases of the holy kiss and drinking wine for indigestion, we must distinguish between the principle and the cultural outworking of a principle. Similarly, the

---

[101]Scholars often appeal to verse 10 to support the idea that women have independent authority in prophesying. This interpretation was proposed by Morna D. Hooker ("Authority on Her Head: An Examination of 1 Corinthians xi.10," *New Testament Studies* 10 [1964]: 410–16) and has been adopted by most egalitarians (see, for example, Keener, *Paul, Women and Wives*, 38–42). But there are serious problems with this view (see my "Head Coverings, Prophecies and the Trinity," 134–37).

[102]Judith M. Gundry-Volf ("Gender and Creation in 1 Corinthians 11:2–16: A Study in Paul's Theological Method," in *Evangelium Schriftauslegung Kirche: Festschrift für Peter Stuhlmacher zum 65 Geburtstag*, ed. O. Hofius [Göttingen: Vandenhoeck & Ruprecht, 1997], 151–71) argues that Paul integrates creation, culture, and eschatological life in Christ in a complex fashion in these verses so that he in effect supports patriarchy and equality simultaneously. On the one hand, I disagree with Gundry-Volf's claim that 1 Corinthians 11:11–12 partially mutes the patriarchy of the previous verses. On the other hand, her own proposal is overly complex and does not really offer a clear way forward in the debate.

[103]See, for example, Bruce Waltke, "1 Corinthians 11:2–16: An Interpretation," *Bibliotheca Sacra* 135 (1978): 46–57; Robert Culver, "A Traditional View: Let Your Women Keep Silence," in *Women in Ministry: Four Views*, 29–32, 48.

principle in 1 Corinthians 11:2–16 is *deference to male leadership*. In our culture such deference is not signaled by wearing a shawl or a veil, or by tying one's hair into a bun atop the head. Women should read the Scriptures and pray in church with a demeanor that illustrates submission to male headship, but they should not be required to wear veils, for that confuses the particular cultural practice with the principle.

Am I trying to escape the scandal of the biblical text? In actuality I believe there is a custom in Western society that is somewhat analogous to the first-century situation. In some cases women today who refuse to take a husband's last name signal that they are "liberated." I realize there are exceptions (famous athletes or authors may want to retain name recognition). I believe if Paul were alive today, he would encourage women who marry to take the last name of their husband, signaling thereby their deference to male leadership.[104]

Is it possible that the same hermeneutical method I have applied to 1 Corinthians 11:2–16 could be related to 1 Timothy 2:11–15? In one of my classes a woman once said to me, "Is it possible that the admonition not to teach or exercise authority over a man has an underlying principle that we have missed, so that women can teach and exercise authority over men without denying the principle of 1 Timothy 2:11–15?" I replied, "Of course it is possible. But in this case it seems that the principle and practice coalesce.[105] Please explain to me what the principle is in the text if it does not relate to women teaching the Scriptures and exercising authority over other believers." I have never read any author who has successfully explained what this "other principle" might be. Thus, I am persuaded that we fulfill the admonition of 1 Timothy 2:12 when we prohibit women from filling the pastoral office and when we restrict them from teaching the Scriptures to adult males.[106]

---

[104]I am not claiming that taking a husband's last name should always be required. Our culture may change. In some cultures retaining one's maiden name may show respect for one's father. I am merely suggesting that in some cases women have desired to make a statement about their view of gender relations by not taking their husband's last name.

[105]See Köstenberger, "Gender Passages," 270.

[106]Craig Keener (*Paul, Women and Wives*, 19) thinks that if one abandons the head covering, then the limitation imposed by 1 Timothy 2:12 must be surrendered as well. But I believe I am following Keener's very principle of trying to discern the principle in each text (see *Paul, Women and Wives*, 46).

The Principle of Submission Applied to a Particular Situation:
1 Corinthians 14:33b–36

The entire matter of principle and practice comes to the forefront in this difficult text, which I can only survey briefly. Gordon Fee has argued that the verses are a later interpolation, but this view has been decisively refuted by Don Carson and Curt Niccum.[107] On first blush the passage seems to prohibit women from speaking in church at all, but this is an unpersuasive interpretation. In 1 Corinthians 11:5 Paul has already permitted women to pray and prophesy in the church. He would not bother to explain in such detail how they should adorn themselves if he thought women should desist from speaking altogether! What then is Paul prohibiting here? Scholars have suggested a plethora of interpretations that cannot be canvassed here. For instance, some have said that the text is contradictory, others that women were interrupting the worship service with questions, and still others that women were banned from assessing and passing judgment on the prophecies uttered by the prophets.[108] Virtually all acknowledge that the specific situation that called forth these words is difficult to identify.

On the other hand, we cannot simply say that the verses are restricted to the local situation at Corinth. The admonition here relates to what is practiced "in all the churches of the saints" (1 Cor. 14:33). Paul summons the women to submit, for this is what the *nomos* ("Law") requires (14:34). Paul does not specify any particular verse from the Old Testament, but "Law" in Paul virtually always refers to the Old Testament, and here we probably have a reference to the teaching of Genesis 1–2. We may

---

[107]See Fee, *The First Epistle to the Corinthians*, 699–705; Carson, "Silent in the Churches," 141–45; Curt Niccum, "The Voice of the Manuscripts on the Silence of Women: The External Evidence for 1 Corinthians 14.34–35," *New Testament Studies* 43 (1997): 242–55. See also Keener's fine survey of interpretive options (*Paul, Women and Wives*, 70–100). Philip B. Payne ("Fuldensis, Sigla for Variants in Vaticanus, and 1 Corinthians 14.34–5," *New Testament Studies* 41 [1995]: 240–62) argues that evidence from Codex Fuldensis and a "bar-umlaut" siglum in Vaticanus indicate that 1 Corinthians 14:34–35 is a later interpolation. Niccum demonstrates, however, that the evidence adduced by Payne does not really support an interpolation.

[108]For a survey of options and the view that the judging of prophecies is forbidden, see Carson, "Silent in the Churches," 145–53. For a survey that reaches another conclusion, see Forbes, *Prophecy and Inspired Speech*, 270–77.

have some uncertainty about the particular situation in Corinth, but the principle enunciated here fits with the rest of Scripture. The women are not to speak in such a way that they arrogate leadership. As in all the other churches, they are to behave submissively and reserve the exercise of the pastoral office to men.[109]

CONCLUSION

The Bible speaks with one voice on whether women should fill the pastoral office, and it also seems to me that it forbids women from teaching and exercising authority over men. I realize, of course, that even those who agree with these conclusions may disagree on how this would be worked out in the myriad of specific situations that arise in life.[110] I want to affirm in closing only that the Bible also indicates that women were vitally involved in many other ministry roles in both the Old Testament and the New Testament. Complementarians should celebrate and advocate women filling such roles. We must also constantly remind our egalitarian society that differences in function do not signify differences in worth. The world may think that way—but the church knows better.

---

[109]Keener (*Paul, Women and Wives*, 87) agrees with me that the principle in the text is *submission*, though he would apply the text differently to today.

[110]I simply cannot attempt to address the diversity of practical questions in this brief essay.

QUESTIONS FROM THE EDITORS

Your essay begins with a reminder that the standard position with regard to men and women has been complementarian throughout the past twenty centuries of church history. Yet sometimes centuries-old positions of the church have turned out to be wrong. How do we determine if the gender-roles debate is one of these?

The history of the church is certainly not determinative or conclusive in resolving the question of the role of women in ministry. As Protestants, we believe in *sola scriptura,* and hence the Scriptures constitute our final authority for both faith and practice. Nevertheless, I believe that a tradition of the church—one embraced by both Protestants and Roman Catholics and by the Orthodox branches as well—enjoys a privileged position in which the burden of proof in any debate is on its detractors. We should be open to examining and revising the cherished beliefs of our ancestors, for history is instructive, not authoritative. And yet a consensus in the history of the church should not be overturned easily. C. S. Lewis warned us about the danger of chronological snobbery, and we are prone to think that our generation exceeds in wisdom those who preceded us.

The church throughout the ages has also read the Bible carefully and reverently, and therefore it can serve us by correcting some of our blind spots. Every generation tends to think it has progressed beyond their forebears, and this is particularly true of American society, for the notions of progress and manifest destiny are still deeply embedded in our thinking. The tradition of the church calls us back to the wisdom of our ancestors, asking us to consider the ancient paths.

At the end of the day, however, the question must be resolved exegetically. The wisdom of the church must not be discarded, but neither should it be canonized. The burden of the proof is on those proposing a new interpretation, and yet it is just possible that a new interpretation is correct and that previous generations have misread the Scriptures because of their own cultural biases. We must all, therefore, be like the Bereans who examined the Scriptures carefully to verify the truth of Paul's preaching (Acts 17:11). The Scriptures, not the tradition of the church, are the final authority, and so this matter must be decided by interpreting the biblical text.

Given your points of agreement with egalitarians on several exegetical items traditionally taken in a more hierarchical fashion and given your admission that you have changed your own mind over time on a couple of these items, do you foresee a time when the complementarian position even more closely resembles the egalitarian perspective than it does now? Or do you see complementarians "carrying the day" and moving evangelicalism generally further away from egalitarianism?

I mentioned in my answer to your first question that new interpretations should provoke us to rethink accepted truths, for the Scriptures are the final authority. Egalitarian interpreters have rightly reminded us of the dignity of women and have corrected certain extremes found in traditional views. I read egalitarian interpretations to learn if there are weaknesses in my own views that need revising. On some matters, I have indeed changed my mind upon further reflection.

I do not believe, however, that the complementarian and egalitarian views will more closely resemble one another in the future. The substantive differences between the two interpretations remain, and the distance between the two views is still noteworthy. Further, these fundamental differences show that the two views are mutually exclusive at the most basic level and thus are incapable of ultimate harmony. The heart of the entire debate is whether the Scriptures forbid women from serving as pastors because of the created order. I see no evidence that this fundamental difference is being slowly modified today, and therefore I believe that the two sides will continue to promote significantly different views.

Which side will prevail? I do not wear the prophet's mantle, and so I cannot predict the near future. I am confident, though, that the complementarian view will ultimately prevail. The biblical text is an unyielding rock. It confronts every generation in all its starkness and pristine beauty. One generation may avoid it, but another will rediscover its truth, for the text is immovable and will survive the cultural movements of our day.

For unsaved contemporary women who are accustomed to enjoying equality and autonomy in society, does not the gospel (the Good News) contain some bad news, namely, that they cannot enjoy similar equal opportunity of roles or offices in the church?

I believe this question exposes why the biblical teaching on the role of women is so difficult for our generation. We live in a society where equality and autonomy are the highest virtues. America is known for its rugged individualism and for its prizing of individual freedom. The idea of equality that permeates our culture is often read into the biblical texts as well.

The question suggests that women will be happy only if our churches mirror the view of contemporary society. The fundamental issue for us, however, is what the Bible teaches. The Bible reveals God's plan and pattern for both men and women. Most important, following the Scriptures is the pathway to happiness and fulfillment. In our own human wisdom we may think that some of the Bible's teachings squelch our own quest for happiness. Trusting God means, however, that we believe his word rather than put our trust in our own judgment. God's plan for men and women in the church is beautiful and delightful, for doing God's will is always fulfilling. The pathway to joy is not autonomy and freedom; no, it is found in glad obedience to our God, knowing that he commands only what will bring us pleasures that exceed anything the world can offer.

Chapter Five

WOMEN IN MINISTRY

Ann L. Bowman,
International School of Theology

WOMEN IN MINISTRY

Ann L. Bowman

In 1981 I was one of nineteen women in a student body of approximately 1,250 at Dallas Theological Seminary. I had already spent fifteen years in professional ministry, first with a denominational mission board in Sierra Leone, West Africa, and then with a parachurch mission in California, Korea, and the Philippines. Seminary provided a respite, an opportunity to regroup spiritually, emotionally, and intellectually and to prepare myself for an even broader scope of Christian service.

During my years at Dallas Seminary and later at Talbot School of Theology, I began to ponder the nature of ministry and how I, as a woman, was called to serve. My own calling and gifting were clear to me; what I needed was the larger picture of how men and women serve together as part of Christ's body, the church.

The following is an essay on the nature of ministry in the New Testament and the multifaceted ways in which women have been involved in ministry—both then and now. I'll begin by discussing the nature of ministry and what it means to be *called* to ministry. Next, I'll look at how God prepares believers for ministry both generally and in ways tailored to each individual. Since New Testament ministry always has a clear relational context, I'll look at that as well. God equips each person for ministry, and I want to explore the resources he makes available, especially spiritual gifts. The New Testament depicts women fulfilling many different ministry roles, and I will consider these carefully. Finally, I want to examine some practical factors that affect how ministry is carried out, as well as describe some situations that can hinder or redirect the way ministry is done. At each juncture I'll include illustrations both from biblical history and from my own journey as a woman who ministers.

A NEW TESTAMENT VIEW OF MINISTRY

God has called all believers to minister. When God himself is the focus of our ministry, we often use the words "worship" and "serve." When our focus is on others, the terms "serve" and "minister" are appropriate. Four Greek terms are used to describe New Testament ministry.

Ministry to God

Two New Testament word groups are used to describe ministry to the Lord, and both are translated "serve" and "worship" (*latreuō* and *leitourgeō*).[1] The *latreuō* group appears more commonly in the New Testament.[2] For example, the writer to the Hebrews encourages his readers to "*worship* God acceptably with reverence and awe" (Heb. 12:28, emphasis added).[3] Even service to others is, first of all, an act of worship to God, and so Paul speaks of "God, whom I *serve* with my whole heart in preaching the gospel of his Son" (Rom. 1:9, emphasis added).

The comparatively few uses of the *leitourgeō* word group are usually related to Old Testament ritual worship. Nevertheless, Luke uses the verb in Acts 13:2 to describe prophets and teachers from the church in Antioch who are spending time in worship and fasting. Paul also uses various forms from the word group to refer to serving others (Rom. 15:27; 2 Cor. 9:12; Phil. 2:30).[4]

---

[1]In the Septuagint both groups refer to worship conducted by the priests and Levites. The difference is that *leitourgeō* is used exclusively for ritual worship, while *latreuō* may also refer to the worship of the people of Israel corporately and individually, both in outward temple worship and through inward devotion. See article on "serve," *The New International Dictionary of New Testament Theology*, ed. Colin Brown (Grand Rapids: Zondervan, 1976), 3:550; "*latreuō*" and "*leitourgeō*," *Theological Dictionary of the New Testament*, ed. G. Kittel (Grand Rapids: Eerdmans, 1967): 4:59–61, 219–21.

[2]See article on "*latreuō*," *Theological Dictionary of the New Testament*, 4:63–65.

[3]Unless otherwise noted, Scripture quotations are taken from the New International Version (NIV).

[4]In this sense its usage parallels the *diakoneō* word group. See article on "serve," *The New International Dictionary of New Testament Theology*, 3:551–52; "*latreuō*" and "*leitourgeō*,"*Theological Dictionary of the New Testament*, 4: 64, 227–28.

Ministry to Others

Paul refers to himself both as a *doulos* ("slave") and as a *diakonos* ("servant"). He uses the term *doulos* to emphasize the believer's complete submission to the Lord (Acts 4:29; 16:17; Rom. 1:1; Gal. 1:10; Col. 4:12). Peter also exhorts his readers to "live as free men, but do not use your freedom as a cover-up for evil; live as servants of God" (1 Peter 2:16). Although the biblical writers focus primarily on our vertical relationship with Jesus Christ, the outworking of this subjection to him will be to serve our neighbors (Matt. 20:27; Gal. 5:13).[5]

Service to others is commonly expressed through using a word from the "serve" (*diakoneō*) word group. In particular, the noun *diakonos* ("servant") primarily focuses on this horizontal aspect of service given to individuals, whether Christians or non-Christians, in the name of Christ.[6] The servant can be involved in both spiritual service and practical service. Thus Paul describes himself as a servant of the gospel (Eph. 3:7; Col. 1:23), yet he is also concerned with the collection for the poor in Jerusalem (2 Cor. 8:4). As the early church developed, groups of individuals began to be set apart to focus on the more practical aspects of ministry, and they were called deacons (*diakonos*, Phil. 1:1; 1 Tim. 3:8).

A Biblical Definition of Ministry

These brief word studies point out that New Testament ministry has both vertical and horizontal aspects. Ministry is, first and foremost, our offering of adoration, love, praise, and reverence to God. This act of worship involves freely giving ourselves to our holy, loving Father in full surrender (Rom. 12:1). In this we glorify him, for we are acknowledging that he is, in fact, God and that he is worthy of our praise (see Phil. 2:9–11).

The natural outflow of our ministry to the Lord is our service to others. Jesus himself demonstrated this lifestyle of humble

---

[5]See article on "slave," *The New International Dictionary of New Testament Theology*, 3:597–98; "*doulos*,"*Theological Dictionary of the New Testament*, 2:273–79.

[6]See article on "serve," *The New International Dictionary of New Testament Theology*, 3:548; "*diakonia*" and "*diakonos*," *Theological Dictionary of the New Testament*, 2:87–89. The picture of being a servant of Christ is present (2 Cor. 11:23; Col. 1:7; 1 Tim. 4:6), but the word especially describes service given to the church (2 Cor. 11:8; Col. 1:25) and to individuals (1 Cor. 16:15; 2 Tim. 4:11).

service when he became a slave (*doulos*) in order to pay the penalty for human sin and so provide salvation (Phil. 2:5–11). His self-giving lifestyle provides both the basis and model for Christians serving one another (Gal. 5:13; Phil 2:1–4; cf. John 13:15) and reaching out to those who have not yet experienced his free gift of salvation (Phil. 2:22).

A NEW TESTAMENT VIEW OF CALLING TO MINISTRY

God's General Call to All Believers

The Great Commission

All four Gospels, as well as the book of Acts, include some form of what is commonly called the Great Commission. Matthew's record is perhaps the best known:

> Then Jesus came to them and said, "All authority in heaven and on earth has been given to me. Therefore go and make disciples of all nations, baptizing them in the name of the Father and of the Son and of the Holy Spirit, and teaching them to obey everything I have commanded you. And surely I am with you always, to the very end of the age."
>
> MATTHEW 28:18–20

The command to go and make disciples is as relevant to believers today as it was in the first century. What's more, the call to be involved in ministry is not limited to a comparative few who are in "professional" Christian work or who at least have some title or position in a local assembly of believers. In the New Testament *all* believers are called to serve. Paul describes Christ's church as a body in Ephesians 2, and in Romans 12 and 1 Corinthians 12 he expands on this metaphor of the body. The worship assembly he describes in 1 Corinthians 14:26 had various members of the group ministering to one another as they shared their spiritual gifts. The church in Acts had widespread participation of what today would be called the laity.

No Distinction Between Clergy and Laity

As the church grew during the first three centuries after Christ's time on earth, a distinction gradually developed between professional clergy and the laity, and "the ministry" became the domain of professionals. Many streams of the Christian church have perpetuated this concept, and today the term "minister" commonly refers to one who holds a church office, especially that of pastor/elder.

In the New Testament, however, no distinction exists between clergy and laity.[7] Rather than the selective priesthood of the old covenant, the New Testament teaches the universal priesthood of believers (1 Peter 2:5, 9; 3:7; Rev. 1:6).[8] While some are appointed to take on leadership roles in the church, all are called to share in the church's ministry, both in the worship assembly and in their everyday lives.[9]

God is an equal opportunity employer. He has called all Christians to be involved in the enterprise of taking the gospel of salvation to the ends of the earth, of discipling those who believe, and of sending these disciples to reach others with the Good News. Women today do this vocationally as they translate the Scriptures for national Christians in the Republic of Togo in Africa or as they sit as hospital chaplains with grieving families in an inner-city hospital ward. Others quietly lead their children to a saving faith in Christ or give a smile and a listening ear to a sales associate in a department store. Still others find treasured time for worship and for intercession for those in need across the street and around the globe.

God's Specific Calls to Individuals

Individual Calling to Ministry

In Ephesians 2:10 Paul declares that we who have been saved by God's grace are God's workmanship. The Master Potter has carefully formed us, and he has a plan and purpose for our lives as we seek to glorify him. Specifically, the outflow of his saving grace in our lives will be good works, which he will

---

[7]Robert L. Saucy, *The Church in God's Program* (Chicago: Moody Press, 1972), 128.

[8]Eduard Schweizer, *Church Order in the New Testament* (London: SCM Press, 1961), 188–93.

[9]See article on "ministry," *Dictionary of Paul and His Letters,* eds. Gerald F. Hawthorne, Ralph P. Martin, and Daniel G. Reid (Downers Grove, Ill.: InterVarsity Press, 1993), 602–603. A helpful study of early church leadership is Kevin Giles's book *Patterns of Ministry Among the First Christians* (San Francisco: HarperSanFrancisco, 1991).

accomplish in and through us by the power of his indwelling Spirit (Eph. 5:18). Works play no role in *securing* God's salvation. But afterwards, Christians will *demonstrate* their salvation by their works. This is the same message James brings when he forthrightly states that "faith by itself, if it is not accompanied by action, is dead" (James 2:17). Salvation is intended to produce good works that attest to its reality and that ultimately glorify God.

In addition to a general call, God also issues specific calls to each of us for avenues of service. At times we may not be aware of the details of this call. Furthermore, as the seasons of our lives change, the fulfillment of the call may take different directions and may even change completely. Nevertheless, as we minister both to the Lord directly and to others, we accomplish the good works noted in Ephesians 2:10. The same heavenly Father who from eternity knew our names and called us into existence, who oversaw our development in our mother's womb, and who brought us into this world also wills to bring us into relationship with himself and into service in his kingdom (Ps. 139:13–16; Eph. 1:4–6). At times he will allow us to grasp the larger view of his purposes; at other times we will see very little. Nevertheless, we can always ask him, "Father, what is your will now? What are you doing in this situation, and how can I cooperate with your purposes in it?" (see John 5:19).

Determining Calling to Ministry

Both the Old and New Testaments provide abundant examples of individuals called into God's service. Abraham, Moses, Deborah, David, Elisha, Isaiah, and Jeremiah come quickly to mind. In the New Testament we see the twelve disciples whom Jesus called to be with him, as well as individuals such as Stephen, Philip, Paul, and Barnabas. Women such as Phoebe (Rom. 16:1–2), Priscilla (Acts 18:26), Tabitha (Acts 9:36–42), and Lydia (Acts 16:13–15) were all involved in fulfilling God's call on their lives.

In the New Testament, for example, the Lord demonstrates great variety in how he calls and directs his children. Paul was called to salvation and commissioned for ministry in dramatic fashion on the Damascus road as light flashed and a voice spoke from heaven (Acts 9:1–9). Yet that experience was not completed until three days later when Ananias bravely prayed that Paul would be healed and filled with the Holy Spirit (Acts 9:10–19).

In Acts 13:2 the Lord spoke prophetically through the Holy Spirit to the prophets and teachers in Antioch as they worshiped and fasted: "Set apart for me Barnabas and Saul for the work to which I have called them." In response to this clear word the two men set out on the first of Paul's missionary journeys. On Paul's second trip to Asia Minor the Holy Spirit somehow set boundaries to prevent Paul's progress eastward and finally, through a vision, made clear a new direction: Macedonia (Acts 16:6–10). Some years later, as Paul's life was at risk in a Roman prison in Jerusalem, and the likelihood of his fulfilling his call had dimmed, he received a clear word. "The Lord stood near Paul and said, 'Take courage! As you have testified about me in Jerusalem, so you must also testify in Rome'" (Acts 23:11).

Just as God creatively brought clarity of call and direction to Paul and others through the centuries, so he gives guidance to Christians today. My own experience of calling has been progressive, and my Father's call has come to me in many different ways. As a senior in high school I entered into a personal relationship with Jesus Christ. My decision to invite Christ into my life was quiet and very rational—and absolutely life-changing. Four years later I was transfixed by Paul's exhortation in Romans 12:1–2 to present our whole selves to God as a living sacrifice. Nothing less than Christ's total lordship in my life could be sufficient. I made this commitment, and about six months later God gave me a quiet assurance that he wanted to use me in foreign missionary service. After that it was simply a question of where and with which mission board. About two years later it became evident that the most obvious answer was the right one: my own denomination's mission work in Sierra Leone, West Africa.

After returning from three fulfilling years as a secondary school teacher in a mission school for nationals, I faced another crossroad. Should I remain with the mission, or should I seek to fulfill God's call elsewhere? This time the answer came more visually as I waited before him in prayer. As a result I joined the parachurch organization with which I have served for the past thirty years.

Four years later, while serving in Korea, I had to decide whether to accept a challenge to transfer to an administrative position in the Philippines. Although well qualified for the work, my heart's desire was to teach, and so I hesitated. I was in church the Sunday before I had to give my final answer, and the Lord spoke powerfully through his Word: "Moreover it is required in stewards, that a man be found faithful" (1 Cor. 4:2 KJV). Regardless of my personal preferences, I knew I was a steward of considerable administrative skills, so I accepted the assignment. When I later arrived in the Philippines, I discovered my job description had changed—the training center had a critical need for experienced teachers and trainers! Even as I trained a replacement in the office, I settled into my first love—teaching.

After five years in the Philippines I once again needed clear direction from the Lord. This time his answer came through a process of Spirit-directed reasoning. A friend had given me a book that posed the question "What will you be doing twenty years from now?"[10] I realized that though I had no answer, I needed one. As I pondered this question, I knew I already possessed most of the answer—for my purpose in life was clear. I knew I was on earth to glorify God as, through faith, I sought to live a holy life and to be involved in a ministry of discipleship. I reasoned that my Father would most likely want to use me in the areas in which he had obviously gifted me, notably in teaching God's Word. But in order to focus on that in the years ahead I needed two things—content and credibility. Clearly seminary was in my future, and two years later I made a smooth transition from the mission field to the seminary campus.

GOD'S OVERALL PREPARATION FOR MINISTRY

Faster computers, the Internet, automatic bread makers, cell phones, new toll roads to bypass traffic tie-ups . . . and the list could go on. The wonders of our technological age subtly teach us that any cumbersome process can be sped up or replaced. While this may be true in the arena of computer chips, it is not true in the arena of preparation for ministry.

Ministry preparation involves more than the acquisition of skills and knowledge. Undergirding these must be a life in the

---

[10]Ray and Anne Ortlund, *The Best Half of Life* (Glendale, Calif.: Regal, 1976).

process of transformation through the sanctifying ministry of the Holy Spirit. This transforming process involves the entire person, and it integrally affects how we carry out our ministry calling. In the next section I want to establish the fact that God prepares our entire person for ministry, and then I'll examine the process of sanctification and how it is fundamental to our ministry to the Lord and our service in the world.

Preparation of the Whole Person for Ministry

A Holistic View of Persons

Although biblical writers will at times focus on specific aspects of the person, such as the physical body, the mind, or the emotions, the primary focus seems to be on the person as an *integrated being*. Franz Delitzsch understood human beings to be tripartite, that is, composed of body, soul, and spirit.[11] While these are certainly key aspects of a human being, they are not separable, contrasting aspects of a person. Others have seen humankind as bipartite, having a material part (the body) and an immaterial part (the soul).[12] More recent scholarship has focused on the person as a whole, integrated being. In this view the terms "mind," "will," "emotions," "soul," "spirit," and "body" all refer to different ways of viewing the whole person.[13]

The overall construct in the Old Testament seems to follow the Hebrew view of a person as a *nepeš*. Genesis 2:7 declares that in the act of creation "the man became a living being" (*nepeš*). His *bāśār* ("flesh")[14] is imbued with his *nepeš* ("soul," or "life"). His physical being is impregnated with life that goes beyond physiological processes, for he also has the ability to reason, to

---

[11]Franz Delitzsch, *A System of Biblical Psychology*, 2d ed., trans. Robert E. Wallis (Edinburgh: T&T Clark, 1869), 118–19.

[12]James O. Buswell, *A Systematic Theology of the Christian Religion* (Grand Rapids: Zondervan, 1962), 1:243–48.

[13]George E. Ladd, *A Theology of the New Testament* (Grand Rapids: Eerdmans, 1974), 457–61; Keith J. Edwards, "The Nature of Human Mental Life," in *Christian Perspectives on Being Human*, eds. J. P. Moreland and David M. Ciocchi (Grand Rapids: Baker, 1993), 175–97; Ken Blue, *Authority to Heal* (Downers Grove, Ill.: InterVarsity Press, 1987), 139–42.

[14]See article on *"bāśār,"* *Theological Wordbook of the Old Testament*, ed. R. Laird Harris (Chicago: Moody Press, 1980), 1:136.

feel, and to communicate with God.[15] In addition, God has breathed his breath, or *rûaḥ* ("spirit"), into human beings, and it forms an element in their personalities (Gen. 45:27; 1 Sam. 30:12; 1 Kings 10:5). At times, forms such as *nepeš* and *rûaḥ* tend to overlap (Job 7:11; Isa. 26:9).[16]

In the New Testament Paul likewise sees people as integrated beings whose aspects cannot be separated. The typical Pauline term for the physical body is *sōma*, although another word (*sarx*) is sometimes used in the same way (see, for example, 2 Cor. 4:10, 11 where the terms are used in parallel statements). The term *psychē* ("soul") most commonly refers to the whole person. For example, Paul desires to share with his disciples not only the gospel but his own *psychē* (his own "soul," his own "life") as well (1 Thess. 2:8), and he is willing to spend and be expended for their *psychē* ("souls," 2 Cor. 12:15). Epaphroditus risked his *psychē* (his "soul," his "life") in service to the apostle and nearly died as a result (Phil. 2:30).

Paul's most common term for persons, however, is not *psychē* ("soul") but *pneuma* ("spirit").[17] This may well have been due to the apostle's personal experience with the Holy Spirit as a permanent, indwelling Person in his life.[18] Paul believed that all persons possess *pneuma* in the sense of self-consciousness or self-awareness (1 Cor. 2:11; 2 Cor. 2:13; 7:13).[19] Beginning at the point of conversion, the Holy Spirit renews the human spirit so that the person may enter into living fellowship with God himself.[20]

---

[15]See article on "*nepeš*," *Theological Wordbook of the Old Testament*, 2:587–91.

[16]See article on "*rûaḥ*," *Theological Wordbook of the Old Testament*, 2:836–37. W. David Stacey (*The Pauline View of Man* [London: Macmillan, 1956], 90) concludes that the term *nepeš* is most commonly used when men and women are seen in relationship to one another, while *rûaḥ* occurs most often when the reference is to a person in relationship with God. In both situations, however, the whole person is in view, including the physical body.

[17]Ernest de Witt Burton, *Spirit, Soul, and Flesh* (Chicago: Univ. of Chicago Press, 1918), 205–206.

[18]Stacey, *The Pauline View of Man*, 126–27. This view is seconded by Ladd, *A Theology of the New Testament*, 461.

[19]See article on "*pneuma*," *Theological Dictionary of the New Testament*, 6:435; Stacey, *The Pauline View of Man*, 135–36.

[20]Ladd, *A Theology of the New Testament*, 463; Stacey, *The Pauline View of Man*, 135. Stacey later states that Paul uses the term *spirit* for "the godward side of man" (137).

The Interrelatedness of Persons

This understanding allows us to appreciate more fully the Scripture passages in which writers focus on a particular aspect of an individual. Thus Paul and other writers fill their letters with exhortations to live godly lives—which is an appeal to the will. Paul accepts the validity of emotions, even strong ones, as he directs the Ephesian believers, "Be angry, and yet do not sin" (Eph. 4:26 NASB). To the Corinthians he speaks of the interaction of the body and the emotions:

> For when we came into Macedonia, this body of ours had no rest, but we were harassed at every turn—conflicts on the outside, fears within. But God, who comforts the downcast, comforted us by the coming of Titus, and not only by his coming but also by the comfort you had given him.
>
> 2 CORINTHIANS 7:5–7

Elsewhere Paul exhorts the Romans to present their bodies—representing their whole person—to God and to allow him to transform them through the renewing of their minds (Rom. 12:1–2). And the apostle prays for every aspect of the individual when he writes to the Thessalonians, "May God himself, the God of peace, sanctify you through and through. May your whole spirit, soul and body be kept blameless at the coming of our Lord Jesus Christ" (1 Thess. 5:23; see Mark 12:30).

Preparation for Ministry through Sanctification

Several years ago I worked closely with a man who had made some hard choices to turn from a life of destructive behavior. He had been through a season of focused redirection of his life and now was walking out his newfound freedom in the daily world of work and family. He had strong, supportive Christian friends to pray and counsel with him, but reversing years of bad-habit patterns was still difficult at times. His delightfully expressive face tended to mirror how the week had gone. He'd share a bit of the story and how hard it was to keep pressing on, and then, as he read the twinkle in my eyes, he would say, "I know, I know. The 'P' word!" He meant *process*, and he was right on target. And as several of us would pray with him, he would recommit himself to cooperating with the Holy Spirit in the process of sanctification in his life.

The Nature of Sanctification

Sanctification is Christ's redemptive work applied to the believer over the course of a lifetime in order to produce personal holiness. This gracious work of the Holy Spirit in our lives causes us to identify and to turn from the works of the world, the flesh, and Satan.

Paul teaches that sanctification has a past, a present, and a future aspect to it.[21] Sanctification is a positional truth that has an experiential component to it; it begins the moment we receive Christ as Savior. *Positionally* we belong to God; we are set apart as his people (Rom. 15:16; 1 Cor. 1:2; 2 Thess. 2:13).[22] Paul exhorts us, then, to *experience* sanctification through Spirit-empowered holy living (Rom. 6:19; Gal. 5:16; Phil. 2:12–13; Col. 1:10; 1 Thess. 4:7). Paul also gives strong motivation for living a sanctified life as he describes a future time when our works will be judged and rewards given (Rom. 14:10; 2 Cor. 5:10; cf. 1 Cor. 3:10–15).[23] Ultimately, the goal of sanctification is eschatological: to be presented to God in complete purity (Eph. 5:26–27; Col. 1:22; 1 Thess. 3:13; 5:23).[24]

Sanctification as a Process

Sanctification, then, is an aspect of the finished work of Christ in salvation. God does not first sanctify the soul and then the body, or vice versa. His sanctifying work affects all aspects of our being at once, beginning with the moment of initial salvation; at the same time, however, we experience it as a progressive growth in holiness empowered by the Holy

---

[21]This brief summary of Paul's theology of sanctification is revised from my earlier discussion in "Women in Ministry: An Exegetical Study of 1 Timothy 2:11–15," *Bibliotheca Sacra* 149 (1992): 208–209.

[22]The Puritan expositor John Owen (*The Holy Spirit: His Gifts and Power* [Grand Rapids: Kregel, 1954], 221) defines sanctification as "the immediate work of God upon our whole nature, proceeding from the peace made for us by Jesus Christ, whereby being changed into his likeness, we are kept entirely in peace with God, and are preserved unblamable, in a state of gracious acceptance with him to the end."

[23]Ladd, *A Theology of the New Testament*, 521–22.

[24]Bernard Ramm, *Them He Glorified* (Grand Rapids: Eerdmans, 1963), 69–73.

Spirit.[25] Paul declares that believers "are being transformed into his likeness with ever-increasing glory, which comes from the Lord, who is the Spirit" (2 Cor. 3:18).

Paul states that "those God foreknew he also predestined to be conformed to the likeness of his Son" (Rom. 8:29).[26] While the Father guarantees the outcome—conformity to Christ's image—believers experience it as a process. It involves, for example, increasing in the knowledge of God (Phil. 3:10; Col. 1:10) and growing in faith and in love for one another (2 Thess. 1:3). Paul points out to Timothy that it will produce growth in many areas: in speech, in life, in love, in faith, in purity, in the exercise of spiritual gifts (1 Tim. 4:11–15). Paul himself used the metaphor of a race whose goal was conformity to Christ's image. He had not yet reached perfection in his experience but was rather pressing on toward this goal (Phil. 3:12–14).

Our Cooperation with God in Sanctification

As several Scripture passages make clear, sanctification is a cooperative process involving both divine sovereignty and human responsibility. The initiative always rests with God (1 Thess 5:23); however, the Holy Spirit enables each of us to respond with open hands and an obedient heart (2 Cor. 7:1; Heb. 12:14; 2 Peter 1:5–7). Paul summarizes this concept in his exhortation to the Philippians: "Continue to work out your salvation with fear and trembling, for it is God who works in you to will and to act according to his good purpose" (Phil. 2:12b–13).

Sanctification of the Whole Person

The Holy Spirit's work of sanctification affects the entire person (1 Thess. 5:23–24). God is committed to the wholeness of our body, spirit, mind, will, and emotions.[27] In Romans 12:2 Paul

---

[25]Abraham Kuyper, *The Work of the Holy Spirit*, trans. Henri de Vries (Grand Rapids: Eerdmans, 1975), 469. Kuyper earlier writes, "The complete sanctification of my personality, body and soul does not imply that my holy disposition is now in contact with all the fullness of the divine holiness" (450).

[26]Abraham Kuyper (*The Work of the Holy Spirit*, 459) explains that the work of sanctification is a lifelong process, consummated at death. "Its progress cannot be measured or numbered, ten degrees now and fifteen next year. It is the reflection of Christ's form upon the mirror surface of the soul; first in dim outlines, gradually more distinct, until the experienced eye recognizes in it the form of Jesus."

[27]Kuyper, *The Work of the Holy Spirit*, 448, 450, 491.

urges believers to "be transformed by the renewing of your mind." Sanctification affects the mind, for it involves growth in wisdom and knowledge (Phil. 1:9; Col. 1:10). Our will, which is involved as we make decisions, is also affected by the process of sanctification. God will strengthen and empower each of us to make godly choices.

Emotions are touched as the fruit of the Spirit is produced (Gal. 5:22–23). We turn from loving the things of this world (1 John 2:15), and the Lord brings healing from negative emotions, such as bitterness and rage, that flow from unresolved anger (Eph. 4:31). In addition, both our spirit, the part of us that communes with God, and our physical body are also touched by God's sanctifying grace. Paul exhorts the Corinthians, "Let us purify ourselves from everything that contaminates body and spirit, perfecting holiness out of reverence for God" (2 Cor. 7:1).

Ministry That Flows from Our Whole Being

The preceding discussion leads to an observation: We minister out of who we are and who we are becoming. The activities of ministry ultimately cannot be separated from the character of the individual who performs them. My own journey is a case in point.

When I returned to the United States after fifteen years on the mission field, I went for a medical examination. The doctor found a lump; that discovery led to the first of four cancer operations. After the fourth surgery my doctor, a gracious and honest man, told me, "The percentage chances of this returning this last time were infinitesimal. I did my best, but I cannot guarantee it won't return again." Two years later God in his mercy healed me completely, and there has been no recurrence.

Today I can honestly say that I look back on the early 1980s with gratitude. First, I am grateful for God's healing power. Second, I am grateful for outstanding medical care. Third, I am grateful because it radically changed who I am and how I minister to others. As I told a friend after the last surgery, "Oh, yes—the cancer was the best thing that ever happened to me. It made me human!" As I experienced the compassion of the Lord and of others during those years, I found my own heart softened. As I learned to embrace my own weakness and to receive his healing—physical, spiritual, and emotional—God began to open doors of ministry for me to share his compassion and healing with others.

GOD'S SPECIFIC PREPARATION FOR MINISTRY

The Holy Spirit's ministry of sanctification undergirds all that our heavenly Father intends to do in our lives as we worship him and serve others. Built on this foundation are five specific areas in which God prepares his children for the work of the ministry: an intimate relationship with himself, biblical knowledge, natural abilities, training, and life experience. These areas are interrelated and ongoing, yet each has its unique dynamics.

Intimate Relationship with God Himself

Perhaps it seems strange even to mention intimacy with the Lord as an aspect of ministry preparation, yet it is the central—and often missing—element in ministry. As I'll note later on, ministry always occurs in a relational context. We readily acknowledge the horizontal aspect as we minister to others, but the vertical aspect can be easily neglected. Three of the many facets of this vertical relationship with our heavenly Father are spending time in his presence, wholly committing ourselves to him, and caring for issues of forgiveness.

Spending Time in God's Presence

We spend time in the presence of our gracious, loving Father in order to get to know him more intimately and personally than ever before. Although we may come to this time because it is a discipline we have built into our lives, God intends to fill these times of obedience with his living presence as we come to know him with increasing intimacy. Few have described this process more eloquently than J. I. Packer:

> Knowing God involves, first, listening to God's Word and receiving it as the Holy Spirit interprets it, in application to oneself; second, noting God's nature and character, as His Word and works reveal it; third, accepting His invitations

and doing what He commands; fourth, recognizing, and rejoicing in, what love He has shown in thus approaching one and drawing one into this divine fellowship.[28]

Time in Worship

Worship is our offering of adoration, love, praise, and reverence to God. Its primary purpose is to lift up the Lord God Almighty, whether we are alone or together with his worshiping community. Worship may be expressed through our singing and our spoken praise, or through the silent adoration of our hearts. Worship is about God, and not us. It involves freely giving ourselves to our holy, loving Father in full surrender. We come to him with open hands and open hearts and ask him to meet us and to change us as we wait before him.

Worship serves to bridge the gap between ourselves and God. We often come to worship with all sorts of baggage. Sometimes it involves sin, but often it simply involves the cares, the stresses, the busyness of the day. He is pleased when we come to him just as we are—eager and excited to meet him, or tired and bedraggled and wounded. He is our loving Father, and he is ready to meet us wherever we are. Our time of worship gives us the opportunity to move into his presence from wherever we are at that present moment.

Time in Meditation on God's Word

Throughout the ages writers have encouraged God's people to spend time reflecting on the treasures of Scripture in relation to their own lives. Meditation does not exclude systematic *study* of God's Word—indeed, it is based on rightly observing and interpreting that Word—but it goes beyond exegesis into the arena of *application* and resulting *life-transformation*.

God longs to communicate with us through his Word, and as we read and ponder a portion of Scripture, he illumines and gives understanding of it (1 Cor. 2:9–3:2).[29] Meditation, then, is

---

[28]J. I. Packer, *Knowing God* (Downers Grove, Ill.: InterVarsity Press, 1993), 32.

[29]John Walvoord (*The Holy Spirit* [Grand Rapids: Zondervan, 1965], 220–21) notes, "To Christians who are spiritual, i.e., filled with the Holy Spirit, it is possible for the Spirit to reveal the deep things of God. In the extended revelation of this truth in 1 Corinthians 2:9–3:2, it is clear that the deeper things of spiritual truth can be understood only by those who are qualified to be taught by the Spirit. The teaching work of the Spirit also extends to warning against error, and we are told in 1 John

the process of the reflective study of Scripture that includes complete dependence on the Holy Spirit to give understanding of its truth. The same Spirit then prompts an obedient response to this truth, and the lifelong work of inner transformation moves forward in our lives:

> Now the Lord is the Spirit, and where the Spirit of the Lord is, there is freedom. And we, who with unveiled faces all reflect the Lord's glory, are being transformed into his likeness with ever-increasing glory, which comes from the Lord, who is the Spirit.

> 2 CORINTHIANS 3:17–18

Time in Prayer

Looking back on my seminary years, a few classes stand out as especially valuable. My Hebrew, Aramaic, and Greek classes have had lasting value, both for my personal study of the Bible and for my professional work as a New Testament Greek professor. John Hannah's class in "History of Doctrine," which I took and then took again three years later, was fundamental in solidifying my understanding of Christian theology. But the class in "Theology and Practice of Prayer" I can describe only as life-changing.[30]

The academic load for this class was significant, but multiple research papers, considerable outside reading, and a final exam were the norm at my seminary. Even the keeping of a prayer journal seemed reasonable. What floored me was the unexpected requirement that for six days a week we spend at least a half hour a day in prayer. I remember thinking, *As a busy seminary student, how can I ever accomplish this; what's more, how can I think of enough things to pray for?*

The idea of praying with some semblance of structure seemed legalistic, partly because it starkly contrasted with my prior experience of prayer. One of my great delights as a new Christian had been the discovery that at last I had someone to talk to. From the beginning of my walk with the Lord it seemed

---

2:27 that the anointing of the Spirit, i.e., his indwelling, makes it possible for us to be taught the truth even without human teachers."

[30]I am grateful to Dr. Thomas L. Constable of Dallas Theological Seminary, who poured his life into our small class of surprised but grateful students in the autumn of 1982.

perfectly normal to "pray without ceasing," and that included all aspects of prayer: thanksgiving, adoration, confession, personal petition, and intercession for others. Nevertheless, my desire for a good grade overcame my reluctance, and much to my surprise, I walked into a new and deeper experience of intimacy with my heavenly Father.

Prayer is an inseparable part of an intimate relationship with God. As we come to him in prayer, we begin to know his heart, and our wills become more completely aligned with his. The psalmist David sets an example as he expresses his confidence that God will both hear and answer his requests. "In the morning, O LORD, you hear my voice; in the morning I lay my requests before you and wait in expectation" (Ps. 5:3). Paul's exhortation to the Philippian Christians rings true today:

> Do not be anxious about anything, but in everything, by prayer and petition, with thanksgiving, present your requests to God. And the peace of God, which transcends all understanding, will guard your hearts and your minds in Christ Jesus.
>
> PHILIPPIANS 4:6–7

Wholly Committing Ourselves to God

I once took a seminary class in which we explored various approaches to Christian commitment. In particular, we focused on three theological views: Keswick theology and its insistence on an experience of Christ's lordship in our lives as we consider ourselves to be dead to sin and alive to God;[31] Wesleyan-Arminian holiness theology and its focus on an experience of death to a controlling sinful nature and a new freedom to live according to God's commandments;[32] and classical Pentecostal,

---

[31]Brief overviews of this theological view may be found in the article "Keswick Convention," *Evangelical Dictionary of Theology*, ed. Walter A. Elwell (Grand Rapids: Baker, 1984), 603–604; "Keswick Higher Life Movement," *Dictionary of Pentecostal and Charismatic Movements*, eds. Stanley M. Burgess and Gary B. McGee (Grand Rapids: Zondervan, 1988), 518–19.

[32]Brief overviews of this theological view may be found in the article "Holiness Movement, American," *Evangelical Dictionary of Theology*, 516–18; "The Wesleyan Tradition," *Evangelical Dictionary of Theology*, 1165–67; "Holiness Movement," *Dictionary of Pentecostal and Charismatic Movements*, 406–409. See also Vinson Synan, *The Holiness and Pentecostal Movement in the United States* (Grand Rapids: Eerdmans, 1971), 13–93.

Charismatic, and Third Wave theology and its emphasis on an initial, but primarily ongoing, experience of empowerment to live the Christian life.[33]

My own Christian walk has led me through all three theological camps, and I've found value in each. But there is one common nonnegotiable issue in each of these approaches: a specific, ongoing submission to the lordship of Jesus Christ. Whenever that is in place, we can confidently draw upon the Holy Spirit's power to set us free from the power of besetting sin and to empower us to live a life of personal holiness and fruitful ministry. Paul sums it up in his letter to the Romans:

> Therefore, I urge you, brothers, in view of God's mercy, to offer your bodies as living sacrifices, holy and pleasing to God—this is your spiritual act of worship. Do not conform any longer to the pattern of this world, but be transformed by the renewing of your mind. Then you will be able to test and approve what God's will is—his good, pleasing and perfect will.
>
> ROMANS 12:1-2

Caring for Issues of Forgiveness

We can bring our sin, as well as that of those who have sinned against us, and leave it at the foot of the cross. When Jesus died on the cross nearly two thousand years ago, he paid the penalty for all sin—past, present, and future. And so, at the cross, we now receive the forgiveness of God (Col. 2:13–14) and extend the gift of that forgiveness to others (Eph. 4:32; Col. 3:13).

Receiving Forgiveness for Our Own Sin

When Isaiah met God in the temple, Isaiah's immediate response was an overwhelming recognition of his own sinfulness. "'Woe to me,' I cried. 'I am ruined! For I am a man of unclean lips, and I live among a people of unclean lips, and my

---

[33]Brief overviews of this theological view may be found in the article "Charismatic Movement," *Evangelical Dictionary of Theology*, 205–208; V. Synan, "Pentecostalism," *Evangelical Dictionary of Theology*, 835–39; P. D. Hocken, "Charismatic Movement," *Dictionary of Pentecostal and Charismatic Movements*, 130–60. See also Synan, *The Holiness and Pentecostal Movement in the United States*, 95–224.

eyes have seen the King, the LORD Almighty'" (Isa. 6:5). Isaiah's need was for forgiveness, and God gave it to him; one of the seraphs took a coal from the altar, touched his lips, and said, "See, this has touched your lips; your guilt is taken away and your sin atoned for" (Isa. 6:7b). King David also understood that sin stands as a barrier in a believer's fellowship with the living God:

> If I had cherished sin in my heart,
>> the Lord would not have listened;
> but God has surely listened
>> and heard my voice in prayer.
> Praise be to God,
>> who has not rejected my prayer
>> or withheld his love from me!
>
> PSALM 66:18–20

Christ offered himself as an unblemished sacrifice, and his blood cleanses our consciences from acts that lead to death so that we may serve God (Heb. 10:22). In our daily experience the Holy Spirit mediates the forgiveness Christ purchased once and for all on the cross. Perhaps the clearest statements of the need for God's cleansing are set against the background of the Old Testament sacrificial system. David, who knew much about the need for cleansing of sin, prayed, "Wash me thoroughly from my iniquity, and cleanse me from my sin" (Ps. 51:2 NKJV). This picture of cleansing from sin is carried into the New Testament. "If we confess our sins, He is faithful and just to forgive us our sins and to cleanse us from all unrighteousness" (1 John 1:9 NKJV).

I once prayed with a middle-aged woman who struggled with deep feelings of anger. She had been through a long season of healing and had confessed her bitterness toward those who had wronged her. She had forgiven them freely and had honestly dealt with the inner hurts as thoroughly as she knew how. Yet she still did not feel cleansed from the residue of the bitterness, finding that it kept returning. I prayed that the Lord would wash it off her—that she would be thoroughly cleansed from the defilement of the years of pent-up anger. When I saw her a year later, she told me what had happened. As I was praying she had begun to see the blood of Jesus coming toward her like the waves of the ocean. His blood washed over her again and again, like the crashing waves, and with each wave she felt cleaner. Since that time she had been free from the defilement and the experience of all the residual rage.

Extending Forgiveness to Others for Their Sins Against Us

We are to forgive because we have been forgiven by God: "Be kind and compassionate to one another, forgiving each other, just as in Christ God forgave you" (Eph. 4:32; cf. Col. 3:13). Our personal fellowship with God is based on our choice to forgive those who have sinned against us (Matt. 6:14–15; Mark 11:25).[34] Our unwillingness to forgive those who have hurt us creates a major barrier in our fellowship with the Lord. In fact, to use the word picture from Jesus' parable, it places us in prison (Matt. 18:21–35).

Forgiveness needs to be based on an honest acknowledgment that the offenses were wrong and hurtful. It's important to see this, because it's so easy to simply push away the pain and either say that it doesn't really matter or else make excuses for the offenders. This affirmation accurately recognizes three things: the true nature of the offenses; the emotional wounding that occurred (feeling used, shamed, worthless, abandoned, rejected); and the consequences of the offenses that have played out over time (physical or emotional injury from abuse, financial or other loss, and the like).

Forgiveness is, first and foremost, a decision of the will—a decision empowered by the Holy Spirit to act in accordance with the commands of Scripture. True forgiveness involves releasing the offenders from repayment, agreeing to live with the consequences of that sin, giving up revenge, giving up unrealistic expectations, and acknowledging and grieving the loss caused by the sin. When we extend forgiveness, we give offenders the gift they don't deserve, as we tear up the IOU we have carried against them.

Increasing Biblical Knowledge

Paul encouraged Timothy, his son in the faith, to "do your best to present yourself to God as one approved, a workman who does not need to be ashamed and who correctly handles

---

[34]Wayne Grudem, *Systematic Theology* (Grand Rapids: Zondervan, 1994), 385–86.

the word of truth" (2 Tim. 2:15). In the Bible God discloses truth—information about himself that we would otherwise have no way of knowing. The writers of the Bible received and recorded this revelation through the process of inspiration (2 Tim. 3:16). God's word is authoritative, and his commands are worthy of our obedience.

As God prepares us for ministry, an accurate, extensive, and practical knowledge of the Bible is crucial. When I became a Christian as a teenager, I immediately entered into a strong discipleship program in which the Bible was emphasized. Through my local church and through Youth for Christ, I was taught to value, memorize, and obey what is contained in the Bible. I learned basic Bible study skills, and these, along with solid teaching in a series of good churches, carried me through many years of Christian service.

As a missionary in Manila, I was blessed with a missionary pastor who was an outstanding Bible teacher. One day I realized that I could do the same research he was doing and craft a message equal to one of his, but it would take me weeks to do what he was doing on a weekly basis. Obviously, his biblical training afforded him benefits I needed if I was to continue in a teaching ministry. Soon I began to grapple with the question of future focus in my ministry. As I recognized God's call to major on teaching the Word of God, a seminary education was no longer a luxury but a necessity.

Identifying and Valuing Natural Abilities

All of us are born with natural abilities. Often these have a physiological basis. Family circumstances, educational background, culture, and other factors can enhance or diminish these abilities, but they generally do not remove them altogether. Examples could include a robust and resonant voice, a strong and healthy body, an enthusiastic and optimistic outlook on life, an aptitude in critical-logical thought, a naturally gentle demeanor, an imposing physical stature, and a natural ability to persuade others. Two especially significant areas that are part of our basic "hardwiring" are the predominant way in which we *learn* new information and the predominant way in which we *process* information.

Identifying Basic Learning Styles

Individuals have a dominant learning style—visual, auditory, or kinesthetic (touch-motion).[35] These are the channels through which a person brings in and makes sense of new information most efficiently. While each person processes information through all three channels, one normally predominates.

These learning styles can be seen in action in the process of discipleship. Visual persons often benefit most from a book or an article on a timely subject. They treasure the words on a page and enjoy returning to the sections they have underlined. Auditory learners are much more likely to appreciate a good cassette tape or a group discussion on the topic. Kinesthetic learners fare best when they are actively involved in the process of learning. Group discussions, role-playing, and even discussion while window-shopping at the mall or while jogging are beneficial.

Identifying Logical and Intuitive Abilities

Individuals continually receive and process information through both left and right brain hemispheres.[36] Nevertheless, at a given point in time, one hemisphere tends to be more involved than the other. This difference can be illustrated in the way people listen to a speaker giving a presentation. Those who are more dependent on their left hemisphere are focused on grasping a logical sequence of information—even when the speaker is unconscious of having one! These individuals need the speaker to have a logical outline and to follow the outline.

Those who are more oriented toward their right hemisphere are focused on grasping the relational and intuitive aspects of what the speaker says, especially the word pictures, illustrations,

---

[35]For a discussion of learning styles, see Paul Welter, *How to Help a Friend* (Wheaton, Ill.: Tyndale, 1978), 186–263.

[36]Mary Stewart Van Leeuwen (*Gender and Grace: Love, Work and Parenting in a Changing World* [Downers Grove, Ill.: InterVarsity Press, 1990], 102) offers a brief summary: "In virtually all right-handed people, and the majority of left-handed ones, the left brain hemisphere is more specialized for language, logical analysis, mathematics and other 'sequential' activities—that is, those that proceed a step at a time in an orderly fashion. The right hemisphere, by contrast, is more specialized for artistic and spatial abilities, and for an emotional, non-analytic, non-verbal approach to reality."

and personal experiences. Logical sequence is not a high priority; these folks tend to listen for key statements. These will be picked out either because the speaker emphasizes them or because they seem especially insightful or helpful and obviously related to the listeners' own experience. What these individuals especially remember are often the speaker's stories. They want to immediately relate to their own life experience, and someone else's personal experience enables them to do this most quickly.

Spiritual Gifts and Natural Abilities

Although I'll discuss spiritual gifts momentarily, it may be good to note here that natural abilities and spiritual gifts are not the same. Both come from the Lord, to be sure. Both may be used for godly or for selfish ends; thus both may produce good or bad fruit (Eph. 4:15–16; 1 Cor. 14:23).

Sometimes the difference between a spiritual gift and a natural ability is obvious. Within two months of becoming a Christian I was elected program chairman of my church youth group, of the Christian club at my high school, and of a school political club. I can only judge this leadership ability to be a spiritual gift, since I had previously been rather introverted and had not led any group prior to receiving Christ. Over the years God has joined this spiritual gift with others, such as teaching and pastoring, and has used me in a variety of leadership roles.

Christians are indwelt by the Holy Spirit, who is the source of spiritual gifts (Rom. 8:9, 14, 16–17; 1 Cor. 12:7). Although nonbelievers may have natural talents that the Spirit will later infuse with power, they do not have spiritual gifts prior to their conversion (1 Cor. 14:16, 23–24). The apostle Paul was a gifted leader, teacher, and speaker prior to his "Damascus road" encounter (Acts 22:3–5; Gal. 1:15–16; Phil. 3:5–6). It was only after his conversion, however, that the Holy Spirit reshaped and infused these abilities with power and gave additional gifts as well (Rom. 15:19; 1 Cor. 14:18–19; 2 Cor. 12:12).

Many pre-Christians have the ability to teach or to administer programs. However, their training and ability does not automatically ensure that they will have the spiritual gifts of teaching and administration after their conversion. The real question is whether God chooses to infuse that natural gifting with supernatural gifting and empowering so that people's lives are radically affected. Lewis Sperry Chafer aptly summarizes this point:

> Such natural ability the Spirit will doubtless employ; but a gift in the Bible's use of the word is a direct undertaking or manifestation of the Spirit working through the believer. It is the Spirit of God doing something, and using the believer to accomplish it, rather than the believer doing something, and calling on God for help in the task.[37]

Enhancing Abilities Through Training

Success in gaining a license as a physician requires a better-than-average intelligence, physical and emotional stamina, perseverance, a value on excellence and precision, and some basic people skills. These abilities, coupled with a rigorous training program, can produce the man or woman we would choose to remove a cancerous tumor from our body.

If we require such rigorous training for medical personnel, it shouldn't be surprising that we would want to enhance the natural abilities God has given us as we prepare for and carry out the work of the ministry. The glory of the Christian life is that the newest believer can be used by the Lord to lead her friend to a saving knowledge of Jesus Christ. In Christian service *everyone* gets to play, both the oldest and youngest among us. Yet, as we recognize our calling to ministry, it is right and good that we would seek to enhance the abilities God has given us.

Embracing Life's Experiences

As we grow older, we gain life experiences that shape how we think and react to life generally and to people around us. Some of those experiences are positive and encouraging, some are relatively neutral, and others are traumatic. As Christians we have the opportunity to place our trust in God's promise:

> And we know that in all things God works for the good of those who love him, who have been called

---

[37]Lewis Sperry Chafer, *He That Is Spiritual* (Grand Rapids: Zondervan, 1967), 54.

according to his purpose. For those God foreknew he also predestined to be conformed to the likeness of his Son, that he might be the firstborn among many brothers.

ROMANS 8:28–29

As unlikely as it may seem at times, nothing in our lives—not even the most tragic events—is ever wasted. Our heavenly Father remains on his throne, and he uses both the joyous and the tearful occasions of our lives to conform us to the image of his Son, Jesus.

I grew up in a typical post–World War II family, one not dissimilar to the *Leave It to Beaver* clan of television fame, except that I was the only child. At age twelve my world fell apart, as my father spent nearly a year in a tuberculosis sanitarium and then slid into alcoholism. About four years later I heard the gospel message and received Christ into my life.

After many years of fruitful Christian service I read an article about adult children of alcoholics—and was astounded. It was as though the author had read my biography, for a number of the characteristics he listed described my life. For example, I tended to be an overachiever, which served me well in graduate school and freed me to have a ministry of training another generation of pastors and missionaries. And my high value on loyalty equipped me to persevere through hard times in ministry and to see fruitfulness long after others had turned back.

Like Joseph to his brothers, I could say to the enemy of my soul, "You intended to harm me, but God intended it for good to accomplish what is now being done, the saving of many lives" (Gen. 50:20). This is not to say that I haven't needed to find healing for the wounds of the past, for I certainly have, but it is most clearly to say that as I have embraced life as I found it and submitted myself to the lordship of Jesus Christ, God has worked all things in my life into a pattern for good.

THE RELATIONAL CONTEXT FOR MINISTRY

Relationship in Community in New Testament Times

During his earthly ministry Jesus set the pattern for intimacy in community with his disciples and with the other men and women who traveled with him (Luke 8:1–3). He constantly mentored them in ministry and occasionally sent them out in pairs to minister (Mark 3:13–15; 6:6b–13). Nevertheless, they had a safe place to come home to, a community of like-minded men and women who were serving with a common purpose.

After the crucifixion these men and women were still together, and they were the first to hear the women's report of Jesus' resurrection (Luke 24:9–10). After Jesus' ascension Peter and the other disciples, Mary the mother of Jesus, the other women, and Jesus' brothers all gathered in an upstairs room. There they met together for fellowship, mutual encouragement, and prayer as they awaited the coming of the Holy Spirit at Pentecost (Acts 1:12–14; 2:1).

The early church continued this pattern of community modeled by Jesus. After three thousand were converted at Pentecost, Luke notes that all the believers were melded into a community with common experience and common purpose (Acts 2:42–47). The dispute over food distribution to widows from different ethnic backgrounds makes it clear that they didn't always live together in perfect harmony (Acts 6:1). Nevertheless, this group of men and women continued to live out Jesus' dual values of community and of outreach with the gospel message.

Relationship in Community Today

Although our cultural setting is so different from that of the first century, our need for community has not changed. God created each of us to live in relationship with him and with one another. In fact, God himself exists as a Trinity. The Father, Son, and Holy Spirit continually exist in unhindered relationship with one another. God's plan is for each of us to enjoy a renewing relationship with himself and with others.

He never intended us to live in isolation, although our woundedness from past relationships may lead us to believe that it is not safe to trust others and that we need to protect ourselves. The good news is that God is wholly committed to healing these wounded places in our lives, and he does so within the context of safe, caring relationships.[38]

---

[38]A discussion of how God does this is beyond the scope of this essay. For a helpful discussion, see Henry Cloud, *Changes That Heal* (Grand Rapids: Zondervan, 1992), 17–42. Cloud notes that such relationships are full of *grace,* as we are fully

The Value of Community for Ministry

Although God's calling in our lives is individual, we are still an integral part of the body of Christ. We are members both of the church universal and of a group of believers who are the local, visible expression of that body. If we are to have maximum effectiveness in ministry, our connection with a local body of believers is crucial. In practical terms this means that we need a group of people who will be there for us as we minister within the church and at work and at home. In addition, we need a group of people who will send us out to do ministry across the city and around the world.

Those who support us as we minister locally will very likely be a smaller group within the church, such as a home fellowship or cell group. They may also be part of a specialized team, such as a ministry outreach to nursing homes or an inner-city benevolence team. In my church I oversee a ministry of prayer counseling for those who need spiritual and emotional healing. About twenty men and women are involved in our prayer teams, who meet for three weeks with those desiring prayer. Each week our prayer teams meet and pray together. These small teams of three or four also talk and pray with each other, and we are free to call each other during the week for mutual support.

This is the same dynamic we see in the early church when Peter and John were brought before the Sanhedrin after healing the crippled beggar at the gate called Beautiful (Acts 3:1–10). The apostles' favor with the people was so great that, after the religious leaders commanded Peter and John not to speak or teach in the name of Jesus, they released them (Acts 4:1–22). Peter and John reported to the waiting church all that had happened, and the believers praised God for his sovereign ordering of events and prayed for boldness and power to continue proclaiming the gospel message and performing signs and wonders (Acts 4:23–30). Luke records the results of this prayer: "After

---

accepted as we truly are. They are also filled with *truth,* which shows us the facts of a situation and provides a basis for wise decision making. In addition, these relationships must be ones in which grace and truth are experienced over *time.* Just as it takes time for a young seedling to grow into a strong tree, so it takes time for us to grow in the experience of God's healing embrace. We need to allow God's grace and truth to touch the deep places in our lives and to transform us.

they prayed, the place where they were meeting was shaken. And they were all filled with the Holy Spirit and spoke the word of God boldly" (Acts 4:31).

We also need people who will support us as we minister in contexts not directly sponsored by our local church. The relationship I have with my local church provides an illustration. From my earliest years in parachurch ministry I understood that I was under the protection and authority of my local church. This fellowship of believers then released me to minister with my parachurch group, whether overseas or on loan to the seminary where I teach. Over the years God has blessed me with many different churches and godly pastors who have faithfully prayed for me, wept and rejoiced with me, and supported me financially.

The church in Antioch provides an example in the way they released Saul (Paul) and Barnabas for ministry:

> In the church at Antioch there were prophets and teachers: Barnabas, Simeon called Niger, Lucius of Cyrene, Manaen (who had been brought up with Herod the tetrarch) and Saul. While they were worshiping the Lord and fasting, the Holy Spirit said, "Set apart for me Barnabas and Saul for the work to which I have called them." So after they had fasted and prayed, they placed their hands on them and sent them off.
>
> ACTS 13:1–3

After their lengthy missionary journey through Asia Minor Barnabas and Saul returned to Antioch: "They gathered the church together and reported all that God had done through them and how he had opened the door of faith to the Gentiles" (Acts 14:27).

BIBLICAL FACTORS THAT SHAPE MINISTRY

In the preceding discussion I've laid out God's process of preparation for ministry. Since we often see ministry as a vocation, or at least as a segment of the work we do on earth, we tend to think that "preparation" is what we do first. Then, once we have jumped through the requisite hoops of education and apprenticeship, we will be able to minister. While this may be true for certain formal aspects of ministry, it is only part of the picture.

Ministry is an outflow of the sanctifying work of the Holy Spirit in our lives. This is a lifelong process, which includes all aspects of our being. I want to focus now on the spiritual resources that are equally available to all believers. First, I'll consider the fact that all Christians have equal standing before God. Second, I'll examine the supernatural empowering that the Holy Spirit makes available to all who serve. Third, in advance of an in-depth discussion of spiritual gifts, I'll note that spiritual gifts are available to all believers.

Equal Standing before God in Ministry

Personal Equality in Creation

The Bible teaches the absolute personal equality of man and woman as human beings created in the image of God. In Genesis 1:27 the author presents the story of the creation of man and woman in a form of Hebrew poetry called *synthetic parallelism:*

So God created man in his own image,
    in the image of God he created him;
    male and female he created them.

The second line reiterates the first, with "in the image of God" placed in the emphatic position. The third line supplements the first and second lines by giving further information about who was created. Here the writer focuses on the duality of individuals by placing "male and female" in the emphatic position. In this verse the writer of Genesis makes two points: First, God created human beings in his own image. At the very least this means that we humans are rational-moral creatures.[39] Second, because man and woman together possess the divine image, they both are equal in their relationship with God.[40]

Man and woman were equally given God's commission to be fruitful and multiply and to rule over the earth (Genesis 1:28). No subordination of roles is expressed or implied in these verses. Each has been created in God's image and each shares in the responsibility of ruling over the earth.

---

[39]See article on "*ʾādām*," *Theological Wordbook of the Old Testament*, 1:25. It is worth noting that even after the fall of humankind the term "*ʾādām*" is used to refer to human beings.

[40]August Dillman, *Genesis Critically and Exegetically Expounded*, trans. William B. Stevenson (Edinburgh: T&T Clark, 1897), 84.

Personal Equality in the New Creation

The apostle Paul affirmed the personal equality of man and woman in the new creation by stating that there is "neither ... male nor female" (Gal. 3:28). Both men and women receive salvation by grace through faith (Eph. 2:8–9; 1 Peter 1:18–19). Both are indwelt by the Holy Spirit (Rom. 8:9), who makes their bodies his temple (1 Cor. 6:19–20). All believers have equal standing before God (Rom. 5:1–2), and Paul views man and woman as equal, yet interdependent (1 Cor. 11:11–12). A woman's personal spiritual growth and ministry are ordained by God. She has access to God in prayer, as does a man (1 Cor. 11:4–5, 13), and is nurtured by the living and enduring word of God, as is a man (1 Peter 2:2).[41]

Personal Equality in the Priesthood of the Believer

Both men and women share equally in the priesthood of the believer. Each has direct access to God; no intercession by an intermediary is necessary (Heb. 4:16; 1 Peter 2:5; Rev. 1:6). The writer to the Hebrews tells us that as priests we can enter the Most Holy Place (Heb. 10:19–22), we can offer up sacrifices of praise to God (13:15), and we can expect that the sacrifice of our good works will be pleasing to God (13:16).[42] Each of us is also directly responsible to God to obey his commands. These commands include those that apply to our personal relationship with God (Phil. 3:7–17; 4:6–8; 1 Thess. 5:16–22), as well as those related to our ministry to others through evangelism, discipleship, and ministry to the poor (Rom. 12:9–21; 13:8–10; 2 Cor. 5:20–21; 1 Thess. 5:12–22).

Equal Empowering Available for Ministry

In addition to equal standing before God, men and women have equal spiritual resources available for ministry. In particular, this includes empowering for ministry. In his metaphor of the vine and the branches, Jesus emphasized the necessity of our remaining

---

[41]For a more complete discussion see Raymond C. Ortlund Jr., "Male-Female Equality and Male Headship: Genesis 1–3," in *Recovering Biblical Manhood and Womanhood*, eds. John Piper and Wayne Grudem (Wheaton, Ill.: Crossway, 1991), 95–112.

[42]See the discussion in Grudem, *Systematic Theology*, 629–30.

vitally connected to him as our source of nurture and empowering: "I am the vine; you are the branches. If a man remains in me and I in him, he will bear much fruit; apart from me you can do nothing" (John 15:5). Later Jesus pointedly told the men and women who followed him to remain in Jerusalem until they had received power from on high (Acts 1:4–5, 8). Even as the early Christians needed supernatural empowering to transform their character and do the work of the ministry, so we need it today.

The Certainty of the Spirit's Indwelling

The Holy Spirit causes a person to be born into God's family and to receive new life (John 3:6–7; 6:63; Titus 3:5), and he indwells every believer (Rom. 8:9). Part of the Spirit's ministry is to empower each one for ministry in the world. Before his ascension Jesus promised his disciples the empowering they would need for the task of world evangelization (Acts 1:8). At Pentecost that empowering was realized as the Holy Spirit came to permanently indwell them (Acts 2:1–40). As the church began to grow in numbers and influence, believers experienced other specific times in which the Holy Spirit brought needed empowering for service (Acts 4:8, 31; 6:10; 8:29; 10:44). Writers have often observed that Luke emphasizes the Spirit's work at key turning points in the early church's history (Acts 10:19–20; 11:2; 13:2–5; 16:6–10).[43] Paul himself attributed his success among the Gentiles to the Holy Spirit, for he says he ministered "by the power of signs and miracles, through the power of the Spirit" (Rom. 15:19; see also 1 Cor. 2:4–5; Gal. 3:2).

The Comprehensiveness of the Spirit's Filling

Numerous passages in the New Testament speak of the Holy Spirit's empowering, often referred to as "the filling of the Holy Spirit." Two different Greek word groups are used in these passages, and these terms are used to highlight different aspects of the Holy Spirit's ministry in our lives.[44] The first term (*pimplēmi*)

---

[43]See article on "Holy Spirit," *Dictionary of Paul and His Letters,* 408–409.

[44]Wayne Grudem (*Systematic Theology,* 782–83) discusses the divisiveness that can surround the terminology sometimes used to describe the experience of the Spirit's filling and concludes that "the filling of the Holy Spirit" is a particularly irenic label.

is used primarily in Luke and Acts to describe God's sovereign empowering of individuals for ministry. Its focus is on the event of filling rather than on the state of fullness that results, and a comparison of the passages makes it clear that this sort of empowering could happen to the same individuals more than once (Luke 1:15, 41, 67; Acts 2:4; 4:8, 31; 9:17; 13:9).[45] The second Greek word group (*plērē* or *plēroō*) is used when a writer desires to focus on the empowering necessary for character development. Charles Ryrie calls this "the extensive influence and control of the Spirit in a believer's life,"[46] and its focus is the lifestyle brought about by internal spiritual transformation (Luke 4:1; Acts 6:3, 5; 7:55; 11:24; 13:52; Eph. 5:18).[47]

Equal Spiritual Gifts Available for Ministry

God's resources for Christian service include not only the Holy Spirit's empowering but also the Spirit's gifting. Nowhere does Scripture say that gifts are gender-based; rather, all are available to men and women alike. Sometimes confusion exists on this issue because gifts have been equated with church office, but these are not the same.[48] For example, someone may possess a pastoral gift that includes leading, nurturing, mentoring, providing for, and protecting those committed to his or her care. This gift may be utilized by someone filling the role of senior pastor in a church, but it may also be used by a parent in the home, a small group Bible study leader, or a Christian college dean.

I'm reminded of Londa, who directs the Office of Student Services at my seminary. She is a remarkable young woman whose open door invites students to stop by for a visit when the stress of graduate school hits a peak and they need a listening

---

[45]Charles C. Ryrie, *Basic Theology* (Wheaton, Ill.: SP Publications, 1986), 376.

[46]Ryrie, *Basic Theology*, 376. See also Walvoord, *The Holy Spirit*, 194–95.

[47]"To be filled with the Spirit means to allow Jesus to have the fullest control that we are conscious of. Insofar as we do that, we will always be finding new areas of self-centeredness to surrender as the Lord who is Spirit possesses us more and more fully" (Michael Green, *I Believe in the Holy Spirit* [Grand Rapids: Eerdmans, 1975], 187). See also the excellent exposition of Ephesians 5:18 in D. Martin Lloyd-Jones, *Life in the Spirit in Marriage, Home and Word* (Grand Rapids: Baker, 1973), 40–54.

[48]Ryrie, *Basic Theology*, 367–68. See the helpful discussion of the relationship between gifts and offices in Grudem, *Systematic Theology*, 1020–21, note 9.

ear and someone to pray with them. This is the same young woman who plans wildly successful Super Bowl parties for the school and joins my Greek classes to cheer on the students as they do their creative presentations of the quarter's exegetical passage. While Londa has several identifiable spiritual gifts, her pastoral gift clearly stands at the top of any list.

SPIRITUAL GIFTS AS GOD'S PRIMARY EQUIPMENT FOR MINISTRY

God's primary strategy for equipping us to minister is through his provision of spiritual gifts. He makes these available to all Christians throughout the church age.[49] In his extended metaphor of the church as the body of Christ, Paul affirms the importance of each of us ministering to others through the use of our God-given gifts.

Description of Spiritual Gifts

Spiritual gifts are special abilities that God graciously gives each Christian in order to carry out ministry.[50] "Each one should use whatever gift he has received to serve others, faithfully administering God's grace in its various forms" (1 Peter 4:10).

The primary word used in the New Testament for "gift" (*charisma*) emphasizes the fact that it is graciously and freely

[49]The last century saw considerable discussion concerning which spiritual gifts are available for Christians today. Some scholars contend that all those mentioned in the Bible are still available, and others hold that some have ceased. Since nearly all scholars believe that at least some gifts are available today, the principles discussed in this essay are valid, no matter which position is preferred. A recent book (*Are Miraculous Gifts for Today?: Four Views*, ed. Wayne Grudem [Grand Rapids: Zondervan, 1996]) contrasts the possible views. Representative volumes favoring a noncessationist viewpoint include Gordon D. Fee, *The First Epistle to the Corinthians*, The New International Commentary on the New Testament (Grand Rapids: Eerdmans, 1987), 641–52; D. A. Carson, *Showing the Spirit: A Theological Exposition of 1 Corinthians 12–14* (Grand Rapids: Baker, 1987), 66–76; Jack Deere, *Surprised by the Power of the Spirit* (Grand Rapids: Zondervan, 1993), 99–143, 219–66. Those favoring a cessationist position include Thomas R. Edgar, *Miraculous Gifts: Are They for Today?* (Neptune, N.J.: Loizeaux, 1983); Richard Gaffin, *Perspectives on Pentecost* (Phillipsburg, N.J.: Presbyterian and Reformed, 1979); Robert L. Thomas, *Understanding Spiritual Gifts* (Chicago: Moody Press, 1978).

[50]This discussion of spiritual gifts is revised from my earlier treatment in "Women, Spiritual Gifts, and Ministry," *Faith and Mission* 14 (fall 1996): 61–66.

given (see, for example, 1 Cor. 12:4). Its most frequent biblical usage speaks of a gift given for spiritual service, although it may also refer to the gifts of salvation (Rom. 6:23) and God's providential care (2 Cor. 1:11).

Other terms used for gifts have slightly different emphases, and Paul uses several of them together in 1 Corinthians 12:1–7. In 1 Corinthians 12:1 and 14:1 Paul uses a term (*pneumatikos*) that emphasizes the Holy Spirit's involvement in the operation of these gifts.[51] In 1 Corinthians 12:5 the apostle uses a word (*diakonia*, "service") that is a common Greek term for all types of work. Here he emphasizes the fact that what appear to be everyday acts of service may also be spiritual gifts.[52] Spiritual gifts involve an infusion of supernatural power, and Paul's use of *energēma* ("working") in 1 Corinthians 12:6 highlights that. The term *phanerōsis* ("manifestation") in 1 Corinthians 12:7 emphasizes the fact that spiritual gifts are a visible display of the Holy Spirit's presence.[53] In Ephesians 4:7 Paul uses yet another word (*dōrea*) for "gift" that emphasizes that God gives gracious, free gifts.[54]

Purpose of Spiritual Gifts

Spiritual gifts serve at least four purposes. First, they are given to glorify God. The apostle Peter makes this clear:

> Each one should use whatever gift he has received to serve others, faithfully administering God's grace in its various forms. If anyone speaks, he should do it as one speaking the very words of God. If anyone serves, he should do it with the strength God provides, so that in all things God may be praised through Jesus Christ.
>
> 1 PETER 4:10–11

Second, spiritual gifts are tools that God gives to believers for blessing and serving others[55] and as such they are to be exercised for the common good rather than for personal gain or

---

[51]Walvoord, *The Holy Spirit*, 164.

[52]Carson, *Showing the Spirit*, 34.

[53]Fee, *The First Epistle to the Corinthians*, 589.

[54]W. Bauer, F. W. Danker, W. F. Arndt, and F. W. Gingrich, *A Greek-English Lexicon of the New Testament and Other Early Christian Literature*, 3d ed., s.v. "*dorean*."

[55]J. Oswald Sanders, *The Holy Spirit and His Gifts* (Grand Rapids: Zondervan, 1970), 110.

exaltation.[56] Third, they are given for the edification of Christ's body, the church. This process of edification will ultimately result in unity (Eph. 4:12b–13). Fourth, spiritual gifts provide a foretaste of the more complete working of the Holy Spirit that believers will experience in the age to come. Gifts of spiritual insight are received with gratitude in the present church age, but they cannot compare with the depth of spiritual knowledge and insight we will have in heaven (1 Cor. 13:8–12).[57]

Distribution of Spiritual Gifts

The Holy Spirit sovereignly distributes spiritual gifts to all believers: "All these are the work of one and the same Spirit, and he gives them to each one, just as he determines" (1 Cor. 12:11; see also 1 Cor. 12:7; 1 Peter 4:10). He decides which gifts are given to various individuals, as well as when they receive them. Nevertheless, an interplay of divine sovereignty and human responsibility is at work here, for Paul twice states that believers are to seek spiritual gifts (1 Cor. 12:31a; 14:1). What Paul pictures here is the Holy Spirit's work in the hearts of believers, motivating them to ask for particular gifts.

Variety of Spiritual Gifts

Spiritual gifts are listed in six New Testament passages (1 Cor. 12:8–10; 12:28; 12:29; Rom. 12:6–8; Eph. 4:11; and 1 Peter 4:10–11). Many familiar gifts are included more than once, such as prophecy/prophets, which appears on all five of Paul's lists. Teaching/teachers appears four times and apostles occurs three times. Other gifts, such as mercy, gifts of healing, leadership, faith, encouragement, distinguishing between spirits, and giving, illustrate the great variety of gifts available.[58]

---

[56]Fee, *The First Epistle to the Corinthians*, 589.

[57]Grudem, *Systematic Theology*, 1018–19.

[58]The choice of gifts in each list was occasioned by a special circumstance on the part of either the author or the letter's recipient, such as a doctrine or practice needing further explanation or correction. See Gordon D. Fee and Douglas Stuart, *How to Read the Bible for All Its Worth*, 2d ed. (Grand Rapids: Zondervan, 1993), 48–49, 76–77. Even in 1 Corinthians 12–14 Paul's purpose was not to write a comprehensive treatment of the doctrine of spiritual gifts. Rather, he sought to bring correction to the Corinthian church's practices, and he set the stage by first providing basic teaching on the subject.

These lists seem to be illustrative rather than exhaustive, a view encouraged by the fact that additional gifts are mentioned in other contexts.[59] Some are specifically labeled "gifts," such as celibacy and marriage (1 Cor. 7:7), and others are included in a context with terms that are elsewhere labeled gifts. These include music (1 Cor. 14:26), voluntary poverty (1 Cor. 13:3), martyrdom (1 Cor. 13:3), and hospitality (1 Peter 4:9). Craftsmanship is mentioned only in the Old Testament: "See, I have chosen Bezalel, . . . and I have filled him with the Spirit of God, with skill, ability and knowledge in all kinds of crafts" (Ex. 31:2–3).

After studying the variety of spiritual gifts available, several observations are in order. First, each list is incomplete, since it adds others not listed elsewhere, and other gifts may exist that are not specifically labeled as such. Second, the order in which the gifts are listed varies. This makes it difficult to be definitive about any order of importance,[60] although the fact that apostles and prophets appear together on three of the lists may have some significance. This is probably because they were foundational in bringing new revelation (Eph. 3:5) and thus in providing a solid foundation for the church (Eph. 2:20).[61]

A third point, closely related, is that the frequency of inclusion of some gifts may have some significance. For example, prophecy is included on all five of Paul's lists, probably underscoring how valuable Paul considered revelatory giftedness to be.[62] Fourth, the lists taken together present an interplay between the name of the gift and the person exercising the gift. For example, Paul lists both *teaching* and *teachers*, as well as *prophecy* and *prophets*. This difference seems to occur because at times the apostle focuses on the individual who consistently exercises a gift rather than on the gift itself, as in Ephesians 4:11. In that case he mentions the gifts that are especially significant in building and preserving church unity.[63]

---

[59]See article on "ministry," *Dictionary of Paul and His Letters*, 603.

[60]Carson, *Showing the Spirit*, 35–36. For example, in Paul's five lists *prophecy* appears in four different positions.

[61]Ladd, *A Theology of the New Testament*, 535.

[62]Since each of Paul's lists is representative, he may also have included the gift of prophecy because it was one with which his readers were sure to be familiar.

[63]As Herman Ridderbos notes (*Paul: An Outline of His Theology* [Grand Rapids: Eerdmans, 1975], 444), "It is not the institutional but qualitative aspect in the charismata that comes to the fore." See also Bengt Holmberg, *Paul and Power* (Lund: CWK Gleerup, 1978); Buswell, *A Systematic Theology*, 2:224.

Interdependency of Spiritual Gifts

In 1 Corinthians 12:12–31 Paul uses the picture of the church as Christ's body to explain the principles that govern the operation of spiritual gifts in the church. All Christians are members of Christ's body through the baptism in the Holy Spirit (12:12–13). Using the metaphor of a human body, Paul explains that while great diversity exists among the members, they nevertheless were designed to work together in unity (12:14–20). Furthermore, all members, no matter how seemingly insignificant, are necessary for the proper functioning of that body; they are *interdependent* (12:21–26). He then draws the parallel with the body of Christ by making two observations. First, Christ's body has *unity:* All Christians functioning together form his body (12:27a). Second, Christ's body has *diversity:* Each person has a specialized contribution to make (12:27b).[64]

Paul next gives two reasons why he can claim that the members of Christ's body are interdependent. First, each person has different, valuable gifts to contribute (1 Cor. 12:28). He lists several gifts to illustrate this point and emphasizes that it is God who makes the final decision on the distribution of spiritual gifts.[65] God alone selects various people to fulfill needed roles because he knows perfectly how the parts can best fit together at any given time. The second reason for the interdependency of believers is that no one individual has all the gifts (12:29–30). Through a series of rhetorical questions Paul emphasizes that no Christian is a com-

---

[64]The Greek phrase *melē ek merous* (rendered "each one of you is a part of it") emphasizes the body's qualitative diversity. The phrase *ek merous* is best rendered "individually" and has the substantival force of an adverb (Bauer, Danker, Arndt, and Gingrich, *A Greek-English Lexicon,* s.v. "*ek*"; A. T. Robertson, *A Grammar of the Greek New Testament in the Light of Historical Research* [Nashville: Broadman, 1934], 550). See also Frederic Godet, *Commentary on St. Paul's First Epistle to the Corinthians,* 2 vols., trans. A. Cusin (Edinburgh: T&T Clark, 1893), 648.

[65]Paul does this through his choice of the verb *etheto* ("appointed"), a term he elsewhere uses to describe God's sovereign initiative in human history. Although the verb *tithēmi* ("appointed") occurs more than a hundred times in the New Testament, Paul rarely uses it. When he does, it is to describe God's sovereign initiative in human history, whereby God has appointed individuals both to salvation (1 Thess. 5:9) and to share the news of God's reconciling activity with others (2 Cor. 5:19). Paul uses the term in relation to himself to speak of his apostolic call (1 Tim. 1:12; 2:7). See article on "*tithēmi,*" *Theological Dictionary of the New Testament,* 8:155–57; "determine," *The New International Dictionary of New Testament Theology,* 1:477.

pletely self-contained unit. Thus all believers need one another, as well as the gifts they bring as they minister together.

Paul closes his discussion of interdependency by exhorting the Corinthians to "eagerly desire the greater gifts" (1 Cor. 12:31a).[66] He has already demonstrated both the high value he places on spiritual gifts generally and the need for Christians to utilize their God-given gifts to benefit everyone. God places in believers a desire for certain gifts so that they can ask him for them. Individuals may already be exercising these gifts, or they may be new tools that are needed to fulfill his ministry call in their lives. The initiative rests with God (1 Cor. 12:11, 28) to make believers aware of which gifts to request—but once that is clear, he encourages each person to ask.

I recently led a ministry team to Scandinavia to offer training to local churches in a model of prayer counseling for the emotionally wounded. All six of us had been involved in various aspects of Christian ministry for many years, and all were leaders in both Christian and secular contexts. Because we all valued and respected the great diversity of giftedness in one another, we were able to work in harmony in unusual ministry situations, often by means of interpreters. Two of us were especially gifted in teaching, and so we supervised that area. While all of us were able to approach situations with a fair degree of spiritual insight, two were unusually gifted in dealing with those who had been involved in occult practices. Others had expertise in handling specialized situations such as post-abortion syndrome, eating disorders, and sexual abuse. We often felt we were a relay team, handing the baton of ministry to another as the need arose.

WOMEN AND MEN MINISTERING TOGETHER

Women and men ministered side by side with Jesus during his earthly ministry. He set an example for them as he ministered

---

[66]The verb *zēloute* ("eagerly desire") is best understood as appearing in the imperative mood rather than in the indicative. The primary evidence against this being in the indicative mood is that exactly the same verb form (*zēloute*) is clearly used in the imperative mood in 1 Corinthians 14:1 and 14:39. In 14:1 it is used in a resumptive sense, referring back to 12:31. As Gordon Fee notes, some have suggested that it is an imperative that stands as part of a Corinthian slogan. The lack of contextual signals and the dissimilarity with previously quoted slogans make this unlikely. See Fee, *The First Epistle to the Corinthians*, 624; Carson, *Showing the Spirit*, 53–55.

equally to those in need, regardless of gender. The early church followed this example, as men and women served together in spreading the gospel.

Women in the Ministry of Jesus

Jesus ministered to women, even if this went against cultural norms, and he accorded them honor and responsibility as they ministered to others. In contrast to accepted religious and social customs, Jesus spoke with a Samaritan woman and revealed to her the nature of true worship (John 4:7–26). Jesus cared equally for the physical infirmities of women (Mark 1:29–31; 5:25–34), and he drew attention to the devotion of an unnamed poor widow to teach a lesson in discipleship (Mark 12:41–44).

Women who had been healed by Jesus praised God publicly in the synagogue (Luke 13:13). In a male-dominated culture Jesus redressed legal situations that were weighted against women (Matt. 19:9–10; Mark 10:11–12). In a culture in which a woman's testimony was not legally valid to establish a fact, Jesus entrusted women with the great privilege of carrying the news of his resurrection to the twelve disciples (Mark 16:6–8; Luke 24:11).

Jesus also saw women as coworkers in his earthly ministry. A loyal group of women accompanied him and served him on his ministry tours (Matt. 27:55; Mark 15:41; Luke 8:1–3). He allowed Mary, Lazarus's sister, to sit at his feet and learn (Luke 10:42)—a privilege that religious teachers at the time granted only to men. At the end of his earthly ministry, Jesus gave the Great Commission to the group of faithful men and women assembled together (Matt. 28:19–20; Mark 16:15–16; Acts 1:8).

Women in the Ministry
of the New Testament Church

Women and men also served together in the New Testament church. After Jesus' ascension, men and women gathered together in prayer in an upstairs room (Acts 1:1–14); this is the group that experienced the Holy Spirit's indwelling and empowering presence on Pentecost (Acts 2:1–4). Both men and women gathered in the home of Mary the mother of John as they prayed for Peter's release from prison (Acts 12:12–17).

Women played an active role in the Corinthian church. For example, as Paul began to sum up his instructions concerning Spirit-directed order in the worship assembly, he gave a brief overview of the kinds of activities that are appropriate. As with other lists in this section, the items he mentioned did not include all possibilities. "What then shall we say, brothers? When you come together, everyone has a hymn, or a word of instruction, a revelation, a tongue or an interpretation. All of these must be done for the strengthening of the church" (1 Cor. 14:26). Both men and women are depicted as participating in these activities.[67]

Paul used the term *synergos* ("fellow worker") to refer to both men and women who served with him in the gospel ministry. Three women, Priscilla, Euodia, and Syntyche, are among the thirteen people he identifies with this term.[68] Paul is not simply using this term in a sociological sense; instead, it is a theological statement. He is saying that they are workers who serve together in the grand enterprise of extending the kingdom of God to the ends of the earth.[69]

Two other references underscore Paul's basic assumption that both men and women will serve in the gospel ministry. First, in Romans 16 ten of the twenty-nine people commended by Paul for loyal service were women (Rom. 16:1–23). No distinction in service or status is either stated or implied. Second, Paul saw a role for unmarried women in ministry, for he encouraged both unmarried men and unmarried women to remain single and to devote themselves to the Lord's service (1 Cor. 7:32–34).

---

[67]This fact is indicated, first, by the succeeding context (1 Cor. 14:27–40) in which the participation of both men and women is regulated. Second, the term *hekastos* ("everyone") in verse 26 refers to each one who is a part of a specified group—in this case, the worship assembly. Third, the vocative use of "brothers" in 1 Corinthians consistently refers to both men and women together. See Bauer, Danker, Arndt, and Gingrich, *A Greek-English Lexicon*, s.v. "*hekastos*"; Fee, *The First Epistle to the Corinthians*, 31, note 16; 52, note 22; and 690.

[68]The list includes Priscilla and Aquila (Rom. 16:3), Urbanus (Rom. 16:9), Timothy (Rom. 16:21; 1 Thess. 3:2), Titus (2 Cor. 8:23), Epaphroditus (Phil. 2:25), Euodia and Syntyche (Phil. 4:2–3), Philemon (Philem. 1), and Mark, Aristarchus, Demas, and Luke (Philem. 24).

[69]See article on "*synergos*," *Theological Dictionary of the New Testament*, 7:874.

WOMEN MINISTERING IN THEIR AREAS OF GIFTING

Teaching

Teaching is the God-given ability to explain clearly the harmony and detail of God's revelation in such a way that people learn. While prophecy involves transmitting *new* revelation from God, teaching focuses on explaining revelation that has already been given. In 1 Thessalonians 4:1–2 Paul exhorts the believers to follow the teachings he gave them "by the authority of the Lord Jesus"—a reference to instructions given to Paul as revelation and passed along to them in the form of teaching. Although all believers are empowered and illumined by the Holy Spirit to understand the Bible (1 Cor. 2:15–16; 1 John 2:27), not all have the same ability to communicate this truth to others. This gift does not necessarily require superior knowledge. It does, however, require the ability to successfully communicate and apply the truth to others.

The New Testament pictures women teaching in a variety of settings. Paul speaks highly of the quality of instruction Timothy received from his mother Eunice and his grandmother Lois (2 Tim. 1:5; 3:14–15). Since Timothy's father was a Gentile, it seems clear that Timothy's excellent background in the content of the Old Testament was gained through these godly women. In addition to teaching children, women were also to be involved in teaching other women. In Titus 2:3–5 Paul exhorts the older women to teach and to mentor the younger women.

Priscilla offers an example of a woman teacher with a more visible ministry. Priscilla and her husband, Aquila, were fellow workers with Paul (Rom. 16:3). In four of the six references to them Priscilla's name precedes her husband's (Acts 18:18, 26; Rom. 16:3; 2 Tim. 4:19). This unconventional reference is likely an indication that she was the more active of the two in ministry. They first met Paul when he made his second trip to Corinth and worked with them in their tentmaking business (Acts 18:2–3). This gave them an excellent opportunity to be personally mentored by Paul as they worked together in their business and in evangelistic outreach. They traveled with Paul to Ephesus a year and a half later and stayed there for several years (Acts 18:11, 19).

During those years they met an itinerant preacher named Apollos, who was a Jew from Alexandria. Although an eloquent expositor of the Scriptures, his understanding of the Christian message was incomplete. After hearing him preach, Priscilla and Aquila "invited him to their home and explained to him the way of God more adequately" (Acts 18:26). The word "explained" indicates that they gave him a thorough, step-by-step explanation of Christian doctrine. Priscilla was clearly involved in this teaching process. When Paul returned to Ephesus on his third missionary journey, he spoke of "the church that meets at their house" (1 Cor. 16:19), indicating their service as house-church leaders.

The New Testament pictures Priscilla as a strong, well-respected leader in the early church. She was a skilled teacher with a thorough understanding of both the Old Testament Scriptures and the gospel message. As a leader in the early church together with her husband, she made a significant contribution to the spread of the gospel.

Prophecy

Prophecy is the special ability God gives a believer to receive a message from him and communicate it to others. This message may be for his gathered people, a group among them, or any one of his people individually. Paul explains that "everyone who prophesies speaks to men for their strengthening, encouragement and comfort" (1 Cor. 14:3). Prophecy is a source of edification to those who receive it (1 Cor. 14:4–5). God can use it to disclose the secrets of the heart of an unbeliever (1 Cor. 14:22–25). Paul states that prophetic messages are to be carefully evaluated (1 Cor. 14:29; 1 Thess. 5:20–21), and so it is clear that a prophetic word cannot be raised to the same level of authority and inerrancy as Scripture.

The Holy Spirit used women in prophetic ministry. On his way to Jerusalem Paul stopped in Caesarea with Philip the evangelist, whose four unmarried daughters prophesied (Acts 21:8–9). Paul refers to the women in the Corinthian church who shared their prophetic ministry in the worship assembly (1 Cor. 11:5).

Apostle

This gift involves being sent out by God to introduce the gospel into new areas. Paul describes this area of gifting in his life when he says, "It has always been my ambition to preach the gospel where Christ was not known, so that I would not be building on someone else's foundation" (Rom. 15:20). In the New Testament an apostle's ministry was accompanied by signs and wonders (2 Cor. 12:12). Barnabas provides a clear example of how this gift operated. He was a representative between churches (Acts 11:22, 30; 15:22–25) and was used by God to strengthen local congregations (Acts 11:23). He, along with Paul, was sent out by the Holy Spirit from the church in Antioch (Acts 13:2–4, 14:14) for the purpose of planting new churches. Andronicus and Junias (a woman)—Paul's relatives and fellow prisoners—were said by Paul to be "outstanding among the apostles, and . . . in Christ before I was" (Rom. 16:7).

Service

This gift focuses on practical service to those who have needs (1 Cor. 16:15; 2 Cor. 8:4). The kind of service in view here is that which is offered without thought of recompense. Paul exhorts those who have this gift to exercise it to the fullest extent—to give themselves to it wholeheartedly (Rom. 12:7).

Women carried out various ministries of service and good works (Acts 9:36; 12:12; 16:14–15; 1 Tim. 2:10; 5:9–10). Tabitha, also called Dorcas, is an excellent example of a woman with the gift of service. Luke describes her as a disciple "who was always doing good and helping the poor" (Acts 9:36).

Hospitality

This is the God-given ability to provide an open home and a warm, loving welcome to those in need of food, lodging, and a place of emotional and spiritual rest. Lydia opened her home in Philippi to Paul and his companions and urged them to stay with her (Acts 16:15). In Corinth Paul stayed with Priscilla and Aquila, with whom he worked as a tentmaker (Acts 18:3). Women also opened their homes to be used as house churches (Acts 12:12; 1 Cor. 16:19; Col. 4:15). The early church set a high priority on showing hospitality to traveling Christians, and elders and widows were especially encouraged to fulfill this role (1 Tim. 3:2; 5:10). The writer to the Hebrews exhorted his readers to extend hospitality and even spoke of the possibility of entertaining angels without knowing it (Heb. 13:2).

WOMEN MINISTERING IN LEADERSHIP ROLES

This essay would be incomplete without a few comments on whether it is appropriate for women to serve in two roles—elder and deacon. Note that these roles are not examples of spiritual gifts. To be done well, of course, they require the Holy Spirit's ministry through the individual in multiple areas of gifting. At the very least, it seems likely that God would give someone fulfilling the role of deacon the gifts of service and possibly mercy, and someone fulfilling the role of elder would do well to have gifts of leadership, teaching, and pastoring.

Deacon

The position of deacon is generally understood to include ministry in areas of practical service. Charity and food distribution are included (Acts 6:1–6) and possibly ministry such as counseling (note the requirement in 1 Tim. 3:8–10 that deacons must be sincere and not be double-talkers or slanderers). The term translated "deacon" (*diakonos*) in 1 Timothy 3:8 and Philippians 1:1 is commonly translated as "servant" and can refer to either a man or a woman, depending on the context. For example, it is used in reference to Phoebe in Acts 16:1. In 1 Timothy 3:8 the reference is to men, but in verse 11 Paul speaks of women who are fulfilling the same role.

The identity of the women in 1 Timothy 3:11 has been variously interpreted. Some consider them to be the wives of male deacons.[70] Although the term translated "women" (*gynē*) can also mean "wives," it seems unlikely here.[71] A second view considers these women to be unmarried assistants to the men who served as deacons.[72] A third view understands the women to be

---

[70]Charles C. Ryrie, *The Role of Women in the Church* (Chicago: Moody Press, 1958), 90–91.

[71]First, the word is hardly a technical term for wives and can equally well refer to any adult female See Bauer, Danker, Arndt, and Gingrich, *A Greek-English Lexicon*, s.v. "*gynē*." Second, had deacons' wives been intended, Paul could easily have made the issue much clearer by using either a definite article or a possessive pronoun. Third, this view fails to take into account the force of the conjunction *hōsautōs* ("likewise"), which is used here to indicate a transition from one distinct class to another.

[72]While this would give the conjunction "likewise" its full force in introducing a new category, it seems to place an unnecessary restriction on the women who were clearly doing the same work as the men described in the surrounding verses. See Robert M. Lewis, "The 'Women' of 1 Timothy 3:11," *Bibliotheca Sacra* 136 (1979): 168.

a select group of women who, like the men, were set apart to perform a ministry of practical service. This group could include both single and married women, as well as widows.

I believe this is the most likely view for at least a couple of reasons. First, it adequately accounts for the use of "likewise" to introduce a new category. Second, the qualifications for the men and women in 1 Timothy 3:8–11 are practically identical:[73]

Men	Women
worthy of respect	worthy of respect
sincere	not malicious talkers
not indulging in much wine	temperate
not pursuing dishonest gain	trustworthy in everything

In connection with this discussion of women who fulfilled the role of deacons, I want to look briefly at the role of Phoebe (Rom. 16:1–2), who carried Paul's letter to the church in Rome. Paul refers to her first as "a servant of the church in Cenchrea" (Rom. 16:1). The term translated "servant" may just as well be translated as "deacon," and it seems likely that a woman of her prominence might fulfill this role.

The following verse says that "she has been a great help to many people, including me." However this translation obscures the fact that Paul literally says she has been "a protectress [*prostatis*] of many and of myself." The term "protectress" refers to someone who is a patroness or helper and carries with it the idea of leadership.[74] It probably connotes Phoebe's leadership in social and financial realms, with her social standing and wealth being used to the advantage of the church in Cenchrea. This in no way detracts from the likelihood that she served the church as a deacon; it simply clarifies the significant role she played in that fellowship.[75]

---

[73]James B. Hurley, *Man and Woman in Biblical Perspective* (Grand Rapids: Zondervan, 1981), 230.

[74]David M. Scholer, "Paul's Women Co-Workers in the Ministry of the Church," *Daughters of Sarah* 6 (July 1980): 5.

[75]For a helpful discussion of Phoebe's role, see Craig S. Keener, *Paul, Women and Wives: Marriage and Women's Ministry in the Letters of Paul* (Peabody, Mass.: Hendrickson, 1992), 237–40.

Elder

The primary leadership role discussed in the New Testament is that of elder; it is variously referred to as *presbyteros* ("elder"), *episkopos* ("overseer"), and *poimēn* ("shepherd," "pastor"). This role is generally understood to have included giving direction to the church and teaching the Scriptures (1 Tim. 3:1–7; 5:17; Titus 1:6–9). The qualifications for elders in both 1 Timothy 3:2 and Titus 1:6 state that an elder should be "the husband of but one wife." The fact that the elder is referred to as a husband carries with it the presupposition that elders would normally be both male and married. In the patriarchal culture of the Greco-Roman world of the first century this would be the normal situation.

In the New Testament no woman is cited as an example of an elder. The apostle John addresses his second epistle to "the chosen lady and her children." This is sometimes considered a reference to a woman who is serving as the pastor of a house church.[76] Others consider it a reference to the local congregation as a whole.[77] The fact remains that the reference is somewhat ambiguous, and by itself, lacking corroborating passages of Scripture, it does not provide a sufficient foundation for building a case that the New Testament church had women elders. This is not to say that it did not have women elders; it is simply to say that we have no record of it.

Delegated Authority

An important concept in church leadership is that of delegated authority.[78] God alone possesses all power and authority, and legitimate human authority is derived from him (Rom. 13:1b). As Christians we are all called to minister under Jesus' authority (Matt. 28:18–20; John 20:21).[79] God-given authority

---

[76]Stanley J. Grenz with Denise Muir Kjesbo, *Women in the Church: A Biblical Theology of Women in Ministry* (Downers Grove, Ill.: InterVarsity Press, 1995), 91–92.

[77]A. E. Brooke, *A Critical and Exegetical Commentary on the Johannine Epistles* (Edinburgh: T&T Clark, 1912), lxxxi, 168–69.

[78]See my discussion in "Women, Spiritual Gifts, and Ministry," 59–60.

[79]This concept of delegated authority is illustrated in Matthew 8:8–9, where the centurion tells Jesus that it wasn't necessary for Jesus to come to his home in order for his servant to be healed: "But just say the word, and my servant will be healed. For I myself am a man under authority, with soldiers under me. I tell this one, 'Go,' and he goes; and that one, 'Come,' and he comes. I say to my servant, 'Do this,' and he does it."

structures exist within the church, and directions are given both to those who exercise authority and to those who serve. When clear communication and mutual respect are present on both sides, these relationships operate well.

God places men and women in leadership to serve, watch over, and protect those he has committed to their care. The New Testament metaphor is that of a shepherd, and so Peter says elders are to shepherd (*poimainō*) God's flock (1 Peter 5:2–3).[80] These leaders need to be good examples of godly living—strong and secure people who have experienced substantial emotional and spiritual healing in their own lives. Whatever the specifics of their job descriptions, they are responsible to nurture, comfort, mentor, and release into ministry those entrusted to their care (1 Thess. 2:10–12; 2 Tim. 2:2). When leaders serve in this manner, they open the way for those who follow them to fulfill their own responsibilities to respect and obey their leaders.[81]

This has specific application to the issue of women serving, for example, in multiple-staff churches today. In such congregations the staff pastors typically have more focused responsibilities, such as evangelism, men's or women's ministries, youth ministry, children's ministry, administration, and small group ministry. It is not uncommon to see women effectively serving in some of these roles under the direction of a senior pastor. Like men serving in the same roles, they are serving under delegated authority.

---

[80]Addressing Peter, Jesus uses this same verb (John 21:16), and Paul uses it to describe the ministry of the Ephesian elders (Acts 20:28). The writer to the Hebrews uses the verb *agrupneō* ("to keep watch over") to emphasize being constantly watchful (Heb. 13:17; see also Mark 13:33; Luke 21:36). Paul uses the cognate noun (*agrupniais*) to refer to his own watchful concern as a leader in the early church (2 Cor. 6:5; 11:27).

[81]Paul writes the Thessalonians, "Now we ask you, brothers, to respect those who work hard among you, who are over you in the Lord and who admonish you. Hold them in the highest regard in love because of their work. Live in peace with each other" (1 Thess. 5:12–13; see Heb. 13:17). Behind these exhortations is the assumption that the leaders to whom they submit are fulfilling their roles as servant-shepherds and not abusing their authority. See Philip E. Hughes, *A Commentary on the Epistle to the Hebrews* (Grand Rapids: Eerdmans, 1977), 586–87; Homer A. Kent, Jr., *The Epistle to the Hebrews: A Commentary* (Grand Rapids: Baker, 1972), 288; Robert L. Thomas, "1 Thessalonians," in *The Expositor's Bible Commentary* (Grand Rapids: Zondervan, 1978), 11:288. See also Bo Reicke's excellent discussion on "*proistēmi*" ("to care for"), *Theological Dictionary of the New Testament*, 6:701–702.

Women as Senior Pastors

The bottom line, I think, is whether a woman can fulfill the role commonly called senior pastor or lead pastor in a church. I noted earlier that the New Testament does not offer an example of a woman carrying out this role; the real question is whether it *precludes* her from doing so. It seems to me that it comes down to a need for a clear definition of the expression "senior pastor." Typically we understand this to be the person who has final responsibility for decision making in the church. Of course, varieties of church government immediately muddy the waters. Is this the independent church plant in which the senior pastor's decision is final, or is it a denominational church where a presbytery or other governing board within or outside of the local church can make final decisions about church policy?

The Ephesian Church in 1 Timothy 2

A relevant New Testament passage here is 1 Timothy 2:11–15. Since others in this volume have discussed this passage at length, I will simply summarize what I've written elsewhere in great detail.[82]

In this chapter Paul writes to correct problems in four different aspects of the Ephesian worship assembly. Public prayer is to be offered for all, especially for those in positions of secular authority (1 Tim. 2:1–7); men are to worship with cleansed consciences (2:8); women are to dress in a manner appropriate for such an occasion (2:9–10); and women are to learn quietly and not teach or hold authority over men in the worship assembly (2:11–15).

A word about the historical situation is necessary. False teachers had arisen in the Ephesian church since Paul's last visit there (1 Tim. 1:3–11; 4:1–5; see Acts 20:17–38). Quite possibly these false teachers were within the church, and among them may have been some who were recognized as elders (Acts 20:29–30). False teaching was a consistent threat to the young church, and a few years later Paul specifically refers to men who were leading women astray through false teaching (2 Tim. 3:6–7). Here it seems likely that Paul singles out the women in verses

---

[82]See my article "Women in Ministry," 193–213.

11–15 because a problem existed with the content of their teaching.[83] Because their speaking it in the worship assembly would lend authority to their words, the problem would have to be addressed.

Paul's directive to the women in the Ephesian church (1 Tim 2:11) is positive, not negative: They are to learn (*manthanetō*) through instruction (see 2 Tim. 3:7, 14; John 7:17; 1 Cor. 14:31).[84] Furthermore, they are to learn in quietness (*hēsychia*), a term used elsewhere to mean "rest, quietness" (1 Tim. 2:2; 2 Thess. 3:12). The fact that they are to learn "in quietness and full submission" seems to underscore Paul's focus in this passage on the heart attitude that is to accompany learning.

Through an example of contrasting behavior, Paul elaborates on his directive that the Ephesian women should learn: "I do not permit a woman to teach or to have authority over a man" (1 Tim. 2:12). The word *didaskō* ("teach") and its cognates refer almost exclusively to public instruction of groups.[85] The word *authentein* ("to have authority over") is used only here in the New Testament and only rarely in secular literature before and during the New Testament period.[86] Paul's choice of an unusual word is undoubtedly significant, but we cannot be certain as to what the significance is. The simple phrase "to have authority over" rather than "to usurp authority" is probably best.

In 1 Timothy 2:13–14 Paul cites two reasons why he directs the Ephesian women to learn in quietness. In both cases he is using a rabbinic technique known as *summary citation* to refer

---

[83]Historical reconstructions generally fall into three categories. First, women may have been seeking to improperly assert authority over men in the worship assembly. Second, women may have been teaching heretical doctrine. Third, women generally were doctrinally untaught and thus in greater danger of falling into heresy. For a list of the literature supporting each view see my "Women in Ministry," 194, notes 2–4.

[84]See article on *"manthanō," Theological Dictionary of the New Testament*, 4:410; Bauer, Danker, Arndt, and Gingrich, *A Greek-English Lexicon*, s.v. *"manthanō."*

[85]Roy B. Zuck, "Greek Words for Teach," *Bibliotheca Sacra* 122 (1965): 159–60.

[86]A great deal has been written on this word in the past two decades. A sampling of the literature includes the study by George W. Knight III, *"AUTHENTEŌ* in Reference to Women in 1 Timothy 2:12," *New Testament Studies* 30 (1984): 143–57. Knight concludes that it means simply "to have authority." Other authors have argued for differing meanings. A summary of the literature may be found in my "Women in Ministry," 201, note 24. Also see Grenz, *Women in the Church*, 132–33 and 252–53, notes 192–97.

back to entire passages in Genesis 2 and 3.[87] First, he says that "Adam was formed first, then Eve," a reference to the Genesis 2 account of creation. The implication is that Adam's chronological priority carried with it some degree of authority. The Genesis 2 text does not explain how this is true, although the concept of *primogeniture* may provide some explanation.[88] Paul is not stating that the male has ontological superiority over the female, nor is he saying that his prohibition on teaching and holding authority is found in the Genesis account.[89] Rather, the unstated application of Paul's argument is that just as final authority rested with the man in creation, so he wants this order to be maintained in the church.

Paul in 1 Timothy 2:14 also argues by analogy. In this case he refers to the Genesis 3 account of the fall of humankind: "And Adam was not the one deceived; it was the woman who was deceived and became a sinner." Paul is not suggesting that women are more easily deceived than men or that they are less intelligent. Both Scripture and history witness to the ease with which both men and women are deceived in regard to doctrine. The word "deceived" simply points to Paul's citation of Genesis 3. He here highlights the reversal of roles in Genesis 3 in which Adam abdicated his authority to Eve and became responsible for bringing sin into the world by eating the fruit she offered him (Gen. 3:17; Rom. 5:12). Paul's point is that just as this role reversal caused devastation in the beginning of history, so he does not want there to be a role reversal in the church that could also have undesired results.

Many explanations have been asserted for 1 Timothy 2:15.[90] I believe it provides Paul's summary for verses 11–14, as he

---

[87]Note my lengthy discussion of this technique in my "Women in Ministry," 204, notes 35–39. For example, when Jesus uses a single statement in Luke 17:32 ("Remember Lot's wife!"), it recalls an entire pericope. To understand the implied warning it is necessary to recall the circumstances that caused Sodom's destruction (Gen. 18:22–19:11), the flight of Lot and his family from the city (19:12–25), and the sin of Lot's wife and its tragic results (19:17, 26).

[88]Hurley, *Man and Woman in Biblical Perspective*, 207.

[89]As Allen Ross notes ("The Participation of Women in Ministry and Service," *Exegesis and Exposition* 4 [1989]: 77), "His ruling would stand as authoritative whether he connected it with creation or not; but he shows how his instruction harmonizes with the design of the creator in this world."

[90]See my "Women in Ministry," 206–12.

offers what he expects the results to be if the women in the Ephesian worship assembly act appropriately, namely, that they will experience the fullness of salvation in the eschatological sense in which believers' works are judged and rewards are given (Rom. 14:10; 2 Cor. 5:10; see also 1 Cor. 3:10–15). Their rewards will be commensurate with fulfilling their proper role in life, here summarized by the term "childbearing." This figure of speech [91] represents "the general scope of activities in which a Christian woman should be involved."[92]

THREE OBSERVATIONS ABOUT WOMEN IN CHURCH LEADERSHIP

In light of what I have written about elders, about delegated authority, and about 1 Timothy 2, let me make three observations. The first comment is actually a question: Is 1 Timothy 2:11–12 describing the situation of a senior pastor? It is important to note that in the same epistle Paul refers to multiple elders and to a division of labor among those elders: "The elders who direct the affairs of the church well are worthy of double honor, especially those whose work is preaching and teaching" (1 Tim. 5:17). For this reason I think one would be hard-pressed to say that a person fulfilling the role described in 1 Timothy 2:12 was *necessarily* the senior pastor. Nevertheless, I believe that the person doing the teaching in the worship assembly typically *would* be the senior pastor, since this is the most public, influential role pictured in the local churches of the first century.

Second, it seems clear that this senior pastor—the one who was doing the teaching in the worship assembly and who had final responsibility for the affairs of the church—was a man rather than a woman. Again, this is based on the evidence that elders in the New Testament are uniformly seen to be men. In the patriarchal culture of that day, this would be wholly appropriate. In today's church I think we may also say that the role of senior pastor is reserved for men. At the same time, I see nothing that would prevent women from serving as staff pastors in the local church. Like the men who serve as staff pas-

---

[91] A synecdoche, whereby a part is put for the whole.

[92] Douglas Moo, "1 Timothy 2:11–15: Meaning and Significance," *Trinity Journal* 2 NS (1981): 72.

tors, they also are serving under the delegated authority of the senior pastor.

The third observation concerns hermeneutics and may also be phrased as a question: Does the injunction to learn in quietness (1 Tim. 2:11) automatically apply to all women at all times in church history? A basic hermeneutical principle is that if the same situation exists today, then the passage should be applied directly as it was then. Thus if a group of women are causing disruption in a present-day worship assembly through their false teaching, then it is appropriate for them to learn in quietness. After all, Paul is explicit about silencing others who are teaching false doctrine (see, for example, 2 Tim. 2:23–26; Titus 1:10–16). In the same way, if men in a twenty-first-century church are standing together in the worship assembly with hatred in their hearts toward one another, then they need to repent before the Lord and before one another because they have not been following Paul's directive in 1 Timothy 2:8.

PRACTICAL FACTORS
THAT SHAPE MINISTRY

In the preceding section I surveyed the many kinds of spiritual resources women and men need in order to minister in the ways God has uniquely ordained. In this section I want to highlight the practical factors that affect ministry in the twenty-first century.

My purpose here is not to present an exhaustive list of differences. However, I believe that two areas are especially significant: differences in each person's mixture of spiritual gifts and differences in culture. These differences *do* exist, and they must be taken into account as ministry is carried out.

Differences in Spiritual Gifts

Much has already been said in this essay about spiritual gifts, for they are the primary "tools" God gives us for Christian service. Our personal palette of spiritual gifts affects our ministry in at least five different ways.

First, all Christians have been given spiritual gifts, and while we may have several we can easily identify, often one or two are prominent. Yet even those whom God uses powerfully through the use of a specific gift can be very different from another with the same gifting. For example, Lynn, the children's pastor at my church, is remarkably gifted at teaching and pastoring children, as well as in recruiting and deploying volunteers. Under her enthusiastic direction the children's ministry has blossomed. And then there's my theology professor whom I enjoyed in the seminary classroom but who is best known for his worldwide teaching ministry through his many books and articles, all written with clarity and depth. Both of these people are gifted teachers who have spent years cooperating with the Holy Spirit as the Spirit developed their gifting. Yet each ministers in very different ways to very different constituencies.

Second, as we become more comfortable with our spiritual gifts, we begin to see how we flow freely among various gifts as we carry out ministry, and we begin to understand how these gifts interact with one another. For example, although I have both gifting and training as an administrator, I have often noted that my success in delegation can largely be attributed to two other gifts that are actually my greater strengths. As a teacher I am able to make the assignment clear, and as a pastor I am able to shepherd people as they learn and ultimately take over a new area of responsibility.

Third, because gifts are tools for ministry, we can reasonably ask and expect God to give the additional gifts we need when he leads us into new areas of ministry. About twelve years ago the Lord led me into a new area of ministry—praying with and counseling the emotionally and spiritually wounded. While my gifts as a pastor and teacher are involved in this ministry, other gifts are critical as well, such as mercy and spiritual insight. While my earlier experience with cancer had paved the way for compassion in my life, the depth of spiritual wisdom and understanding God began to develop in my life was something new.

Fourth, we can expect the Holy Spirit to develop and refine the use of spiritual gifts in our lives. Take Barry, for example. Although originally involved in vocational Christian service, Barry became convinced that God had given him the gift of giving. Since the potential to develop large amounts of resources to give seemed limited in his career at the time, he decided to transfer to a secular job. Over the past twenty years, four things have happened. First, he and his wife have reared an outstanding son and daughter who would make any parent proud. Second, he and his wife have remained actively involved in Christian leadership in their local church and in two parachurch organizations. Third, he has slowly built up a business (first in insurance and real estate, and eventually in financial planning) that has become very successful. Fourth, he has faithfully increased both the amount and percentage of his income that he regularly gives to kingdom ministry.

Fifth, we can celebrate diversity as Christians use their spiritual gifts to carry out ministry.[93] This isn't always easy in our churches or Christian organizations for at least three reasons. First, highly visible leadership roles, and the gifts associated with these roles, are generally considered to be more desirable than behind-the-scenes roles. Second, those gifts that are most directly involved in fulfilling the vision of the senior pastor or other leader may be most highly valued. Third, there may be a subtle message communicated that the gifts possessed by the leadership are the most valuable and that really "good" Christians will minister in the same way.

The truth, of course, is that *all* spiritual gifts are valuable, and all are necessary, just as Paul taught the Corinthians (1 Cor. 12:12–31). As pastors and other leaders recognize that some gifts are routinely and wrongly disparaged, they can begin to make needed corrections in their own attitudes and those of their people and to celebrate the diversity of gifting in their midst.

Cultural Differences

Accurate Communication across Cultures

When I was twenty-two years old, I went from the conservative southern region of the United States to the tropical forests of Sierra Leone, West Africa. Cross-cultural training was virtually unknown in those days; I actually never heard the term "culture shock" until I returned to the States after three years in

---

[93]See my comments in "Women, Spiritual Gifts, and Ministry," 69–70.

West Africa. Unlike my later experience in the Philippines, where I adjusted quite freely to Filipino culture and values, my adjustment in Africa was to a missionary community that at some level interacted with Sierra Leonian culture and values.

An indelible lesson in cross-cultural communication concerned taking pictures of other missionaries that might one day become part of a missionary slide show. Although it was wholly appropriate for expatriate men in this former British colony to wear walking shorts and knee-high socks, we never photographed them this way. The reason was simple: If the slide were shown in a highly conservative American church that judged such attire to be sinful, most people would not hear another word the missionary said, no matter how many Sierra Leonians had become Christians and were growing in discipleship.

During my early years with my parachurch organization I served as the first director of training for what might be described as a "Christian Peace Corps." Skilled men and women— teachers, medical personnel, engineers, contractors, and the like—were sent overseas to hold full-time jobs and work with the national church. As my team and I designed the initial training course, I had ample opportunity to reflect on the skills needed for successful cross-cultural adaptation.

These newfound skills were invaluable as I took an eight-month assignment in Korea and then moved to the Philippines for the next seven years. In an unexpected way I found this expertise useful as I returned to the States to enter the brave new world of an almost entirely male seminary.[94] I began to reflect on what was communicated by my clothing, makeup, decision to carry or not to carry a briefcase, and language (for example, whether my speech was direct versus laden with descriptive adjectives and adverbs). I became conscious of the values of this new culture and was able to make purposeful decisions about whether to adopt them as my own or simply to adapt to them. I worked hard at determining which were specifically biblical values and which were simply male. Twenty years later I am aware that I did my share of stereotyping; at the same time, I know that

---

[94]In their fascinating book *The Managerial Woman* (New York: Pocket Books, 1978), Margaret Hennig and Anne Jardim describe a woman's entry into a predominantly male business world with an extended parable detailing strategies for adapting to a totally foreign culture.

I achieved a level of objectivity that made my educational experience productive and enjoyable.

Accurate Communication between Genders

Men and women communicate differently, and both styles of communication are valid. In a real sense, this may be considered *cross-cultural communication*. In order for clear communication to occur in ministry contexts, women and men need to understand and adapt to the styles of the other gender. Inspirational Christian speaker and writer Rhonda Kelley gives a helpful summary of some key differences. For example, men often communicate as a way to maintain independence and establish status, while women speak as a way to maintain intimacy and build rapport. Men generally talk more in public, and women talk more in less formal settings. Women tend to use body language more obviously, and men less directly. These differences also appear in topics of discussion—people and feelings for women versus facts and figures for men. Men often are more focused on strategies for problem solving, and women are often more focused on supportiveness in the midst of a problem while it is being solved. Women tend to use more descriptive, emotionally laden terms, and men tend to use more precise terms.[95]

The implications for those involved in ministry are obvious. Both women and men need to recognize and respect the communication patterns used by those of the other gender. One is not better than another; they are simply different. The best communicators are those, first of all, who know who they are as a man or woman and are comfortable in their gender identity. This makes the cross-cultural jump to a new set of communication skills less threatening and more enjoyable. Second, they have been so touched by the Holy Spirit that they are willing to serve those of the other gender by taking time to learn how to communicate well with them.

---

[95]Rhonda H. Kelley, "Communication between Men and Women in the Context of the Christian Community," *Faith and Mission* 14 (fall 1996): 51–52. Two other helpful studies are Deborah Tannen, *You Just Don't Understand: Men and Women in Conversation* (New York: Ballentine, 1990); and Judith Tingley, *Genderflex: Men and Women Speaking Each Other's Language at Work* (New York: AMACOM, 1993).

FACTORS THAT HINDER OR REDIRECT MINISTRY

Three other factors deserve comment—factors that can either hinder our ministries or become the catalyst for redirecting them toward more fruitful service. *Character defects and blockages* are internal and have to do with emotional and spiritual brokenness. Externally, we may find our ministries redirected as we may face *unexpected or difficult life circumstances*. Finally, we may discover the reality of *spiritual warfare*.

Character Defects and Blockages

Most of us have known individuals who began well in the Christian life but finished poorly. We look at those who have fallen away, and our hearts are broken as we see the devastation in their lives and the loss to the kingdom of God. They meant well, but like the various types of people in Jesus' parable of the sower, they did not persevere in a lifetime of fruitfulness (Luke 8:5–15). When times of testing came, some fell away. Others were choked by life's worries, riches, and pleasures, and they did not go on to Christian maturity.

As I've worked with those who are hurting, I have come to understand that painful events happen to all of us. In a healthy relational environment, open and honest communication occurs. Opportunities are given to express our feelings, consistent love and support are given, and responsibility is clarified. Resolution comes as the situation becomes a part of our life that is neither dwelt on nor repressed. In an unhealthy relational environment, however, little or no communication occurs, and painful feelings are pushed down deep inside us, with predictable results. First, we begin to believe lies about ourselves, about other people, and about God. Next, we make vows based on these lies in order to protect ourselves from further hurt. Finally, we build fortresses and live inside them. And one day we discover that our carefully constructed fortress actually becomes a prison—and *we* are the prisoner!

Fortunately, God has made provision for releasing us from this prison, even when, through no fault of our own, its construction began when we were very young. The central element of spiritual and emotional healing is *forgiveness*—forgiveness that we extend to an offender and that we receive from the Lord as we confess our own sin. In an earlier section of this essay ("Caring for Issues of Forgiveness") I discussed this twofold aspect of forgiveness at some length. One final aspect of the healing process is to invite God's presence into the place of pain. We ask the Lord, through the power of his Spirit, to touch and heal our emotional wounds and to bring cleansing and release from them. The Holy Spirit makes real in our experience the truth of Ephesians 3:16–19 as he brings increased intimacy with our heavenly Father and with the Lord Jesus.

Life Circumstances

Nothing fully prepares us for the disruption caused by a catastrophic illness or the death of a loved one. Sudden financial reversals or an unexpected divorce can leave a person facing decisions they never expected to face. While God's grace is always sufficient, we still have to walk through these difficult situations one day at a time.

In the midst of all that God allows in our lives, he still rules in the heavenly places. Sometimes he will take us out of active ministry for a season. Sometimes he may use a change in our circumstances to completely redirect our ministries into areas we never expected. Whatever his direction for our lives, one thing stands firm: Absolutely *nothing* can separate us from his love. As Paul declares, "Who shall separate us from the love of Christ? Shall trouble or hardship or persecution or famine or nakedness or danger or sword? . . . No, in all these things we are more than conquerors through him who loved us" (Rom. 8:35, 37).

Spiritual Warfare

Whether we are aware of it or not, we live in the midst of an ongoing spiritual battle. The apostle Paul puts it this way:

> Finally, be strong in the Lord and in his mighty power. Put on the full armor of God so that you can take your stand against the devil's schemes. For our struggle is not against flesh and blood, but against the rulers, against the authorities, against the powers of this dark world and against the spiritual forces of evil in the heavenly realms.
>
> EPHESIANS 6:10–12

The apostle Peter uses even more graphic language:

> Be self-controlled and alert. Your enemy the devil prowls around like a roaring lion looking for someone to devour. Resist him, standing firm in the faith, because you know that your brothers throughout the world are undergoing the same kind of sufferings.
>
> 1 PETER 5:8–9

The good news is that Satan and his hosts were totally defeated through Jesus' finished work on the cross. After describing this atoning work, Paul says that "having disarmed the powers and authorities, [God] made a public spectacle of them, triumphing over them by the cross" (Col. 2:15). As Christians, then, we have the privilege of standing firm against the enemy's attacks. James encourages his readers, "Submit yourselves, then, to God. Resist the devil, and he will flee from you" (James 4:7). Paul concurs as he urges, "Therefore put on the full armor of God, so that when the day of evil comes, you may be able to stand your ground, and after you have done everything, to stand" (Eph. 6:13).

Since the question is not *whether*, but *when* we will experience spiritual warfare in our ministries, it is good to have a few basic principles in mind.[96] First, we need to follow Paul's and James's admonitions to be alert. Second, when we become aware of enemy attack, we need to respond by turning our attention to the Lord and focusing on his sufficiency in the situation. We can choose not to be controlled by fear (Ps. 34:4–7; Rom. 8:38–39; 1 John 4:18).[97] At the same time we can ask the Lord to reveal any attitudes and actions in our lives, any areas of sin or compromise, that offer the enemy legal ground to accuse us (Ps. 139:23–24). Third, once we have allowed the Lord to calm our hearts and clear our minds, we can ask him for his wisdom to help us handle each particular situation (James 1:5).

---

[96] A helpful discussion appears in Charles H. Kraft, *I Give You Authority* (Grand Rapids: Baker, 1997), 153–81.

[97] There will certainly be times when we experience the emotion of fear. Healthy fear is a gift from God. It serves as a red light on the dashboard of our lives that says, "Something is wrong. I need to be cautious, check this out, and take appropriate action to avoid danger."

CONCLUSION

In Matthew 28:18–20 Jesus commissioned a group of men and women to adopt and fulfill a great vision:

> Therefore go and make disciples of all nations, baptizing them in the name of the Father and of the Son and of the Holy Spirit, and teaching them to obey everything I have commanded you. And surely I am with you always, to the very end of the age.

Christians today carry the same mandate, and both women and men must participate in order to accomplish it. Focusing on the one area where Scripture has placed a limitation on women's service—the role of senior pastor—is counterproductive. In our fast-paced world we need to focus on the multifaceted opportunities that *are* available to women.

In this essay I've discussed what it means to be involved in ministry and what is involved for women in particular to participate in ministry. We have seen how the Father draws each woman into close relationship with himself and creates passion in her heart to serve the Lord Jesus as he chooses. The Spirit gives his gifts and oversees the development of these gifts in each woman. And he empowers her as she steps out to accomplish the works that he prepared in eternity past for her to do.

The Lord has called women and men to minister together in his kingdom enterprise. Let's celebrate—and all put our hands to the task!

QUESTIONS FROM THE EDITORS

Instead of focusing somewhat narrowly on specific passages that may bear directly on the gender-roles debate, you have chosen to write an essay that raises equally important but much broader concerns applicable to all people in ministry. Please explain your rationale in adopting this approach.

When I agreed to participate in this project, my understanding was that I would write an essay on women in ministry. I decided the first question to be answered was "What is ministry?" Then I needed to know what the Bible, and the New Testament in particular, had to say about ministry both generally and in relation to women in particular. I realized afresh that the New Testament has a great deal to say about Christians, both male and female, who minister. Thus, if I were to discuss women in ministry, I would need to work almost entirely with passages that apply to both men and women. For that reason, I chose to maintain the applicational focus on women through using personal illustrations.

This essay also reflects what I believe is a crucial issue in the gender-roles debate, namely, the valuing of spiritual gifts. A proper understanding of spiritual gifts increases the options for women to minister, even within the limits of a complementarian position. Rather than focusing on what women should *not* be doing, I believe it's important to focus on what they *should* be doing. Viewing ministry through the lens of spiritual gifts opens vast numbers of possibilities.[98]

If someone were to describe you as a complementarian who functions as an egalitarian, how would you respond?

I would say, "What a strange description!" While it is true that I have filled a number of what some might consider nontraditional ministry roles, I have always, without exception, filled them under appropriate male authority. For example, I earlier described a ministry trip to Scandinavia. My team and I

---

[98]For a lengthy list of the kinds of ministry opportunities available, see my article "Women, Spiritual Gifts, and Ministry," 68–69.

were sent out by my local church with the full blessing of my senior pastor and the church fellowship. We ministered in three cities by the invitation and under the covering of pastors in those cities. It seems to me that this is clearly a complementarian approach to ministry.

It may be helpful to address a variation of this question: "What are some factors that have made it possible for you to be involved in nontraditional ministry roles?" First, the Lord has given me the priceless gift of serving him in ministry as a single woman. Since I have never had a husband or children, I have been free to travel and to work odd hours—to do whatever it takes to accomplish the work of the ministry.

Second, I have been blessed with excellent mentors over the past forty years as a Christian, and all but two of the most significant ones have been men. They have brought me alongside and have modeled both ministry and interpersonal skills to me. They have believed in me, supported me, and encouraged me to take risks in ministry.

Third, I have rarely sought out new areas in which to minister. In the vast majority of cases my pastor or my parachurch director came to me and said, "We have a need here. Would you pray about filling it?" Sometimes my gifting and experience were obvious; at other times my leaders saw in me a fundamental mixture of intelligence, relational abilities, and spiritual maturity that could be developed to fill the current need. Because I was teachable and had demonstrated commitment to the ministry, they believed that God could use me in the new situation.

You speak at length in your essay about how God has led you to your current expressions of ministry. Along the way, have any persons (male or female) tried to hold you back or limit what you can do? If so, how have you been able to maintain such an upbeat, can-do attitude?

I remember a ministry director who so thoroughly and systematically demeaned both my person as a woman and the work of my hands that I was completely devastated. As my friend prayed with me later, I cried out to the Lord in my pain and confusion: "I don't understand! I *like* being a woman. And *you* like the fact that I'm a woman, because that's the way you made me. You called me into existence as a woman, and I bless the work of your hands. Father, how is it that this man can say these things? I don't understand!"

Over the years God has worked into my life some basic attitudes that shape how I choose to respond to such situations. First, I realize that I can't please all the people all the time, either by what I do or by who I am. I wish this were not so, because I like to be warmly accepted as much as anyone. However, from my earliest years as a Christian, God's provision for me has been demonstrated in a growing awareness of his unconditional love for me. And then, about ten years ago, I had a profound, life-changing encounter with my heavenly Father in which he revealed his heart of love for me personally. Because I know in the depths of my being that I am accepted by the most important Person in my life, I can work through the pain of rejection by others.

Second, when offense occurs, I know that my responsibility is to extend forgiveness and to pray for God's blessing on the person who has hurt me. If I have opportunity to speak the truth about the situation, I am willing to do so, and I will work for mutual understanding. But I do not need that person's apology in order to move ahead with my life.

Third, I feel the need to concentrate on what God has called me to do in ministry, the work my leadership is blessing me to do. In the great majority of cases my leadership has encouraged me to go well beyond my comfort zone into new areas of ministry. But I have indeed been in church situations in which certain ministry options were not available to me specifically because of my gender. My response was to look at the situation and say, "Fine. I accept that. Now what *can* I do?" It helps that God has blessed me with the gifts of being both creative and pragmatic. If one door is closed, then I will start looking for other doors, even though I may continue to ask the Lord to open the first one.

Chapter Six

REFLECTIONS ON COMPLEMENTARIAN ESSAYS

by the Editors

REFLECTIONS ON COMPLEMENTARIAN ESSAYS

by the Editors

Unlike the chapters by Craig Keener and Linda Belleville in the first half of this book, the two chapters by Thomas Schreiner and Ann Bowman are quite different in form and contents. This was neither demanded nor precluded by the instructions we gave our contributors. In fact, we were a little surprised by how much overlap there was between Keener's and Belleville's essays and by how little overlap there was between Schreiner's and Bowman's contributions. At any rate, just as it was natural to intertwine our comments on Keener and Belleville at the end of part 1 due to the interrelatedness of their essays, it is equally appropriate to comment here on Schreiner and Bowman largely one after the other.

As we noted in our reflections in chapter 3 (see page 166), egalitarians often begin with Galatians 3:28 ("there is neither Jew nor Greek, slave nor free, male nor female, for you are all one in Christ Jesus") and interpret the other problematic texts in Paul through a grid of their understanding of that seemingly more programmatic verse. Schreiner anticipates this and begins his essay by arguing for a view that takes all the relevant texts into account rather than assuming that certain more foundational or clearer texts take priority over other more peripheral or opaque passages. Interestingly, we suspect that our two egalitarian contributors would agree on this method. Moreover, as it turns out, all four of our essayists precede their discussions of the most controversial texts with surveys of numerous positive points Scripture teaches and various exemplary biblical models of women in ministry. We will comment more on this in our conclusion, but it is significant that almost all major parties in the current scholarly debate do go out of their way to stress the many important biblical roles women can fill, even if some draw lines with respect to other roles they think they cannot fill.[1]

One might, however, push the methodological question about the most determinative texts even further than any of our authors has. While some would begin with Genesis 1–2 because of its priority in the canonical sequence, and others would privilege broad New Testament principles like Galatians 3:28, one could argue that the texts that *most specifically* address the issue of gender roles in ministerial leadership should be privileged. After all, Ben Witherington has demonstrated that various Jewish and Greco-Roman parallels to Galatians 3:28 abound, even within writings that proceed to make more chauvinistic restrictions on women in religious leadership than anything found in the New Testament or in any of the major interpretations today![2] So what an ancient writer thought about a very specific question like "Can women hold the highest religious offices, or are certain ones prohibited to them?" must almost certainly be determined by attending to passages that address this actual question rather than examining broader, abstract generalizations. At the same time, and still following Witherington, we believe that Schreiner is right to emphasize that there is a social application to Galatians 3:28. The unity and equality implied by that verse go beyond an invisible spiritual dimension. And in addition to the way Paul interprets this social dimension elsewhere, we would add that the immediate context of Galatians 3:27 offers perhaps the most relevant example of this dimension—the ceremony of baptism. We often forget in our modern world that, with baptism replacing circumcision as the initiation rite of God's people into covenant with him, a ceremony reserved for men was replaced with one that visibly declared to the watching congregation the

---

[1]This is quite different from even a mere decade ago. It is encouraging that one looks mostly in vain for close scholarly equivalents today to either the substance or tone of works like the chapter by Robert Culver, "A Traditional View: Let Your Women Keep Silence," in *Women in Ministry: Four Views* , eds. Bonnidell Clouse and Robert G. Clouse (Downers Grove, Ill.: InterVarsity Press, 1989), 25–52, that substantially restricted the roles for women in church, home, and society.

[2]Ben Witherington III, "Rite and Rights for Women—Galatians 3.28," *New Testament Studies* 27 (1981): 593–604.

equality of men and women before God.[3] At the same time, none of this settles the exegetical questions surrounding the meaning and significance of 1 Timothy 2:11–15. It is probably correct, with all our essayists, to see the latter passage in many ways as most determinative of specific applications of the most debated issues in gender-role discussions.[4]

Schreiner also helpfully points out early on that the debate is not first of all about the ordination of women or about "calling" to ministry, notwithstanding the fact that it regularly gets couched in terms of one or both of these issues. As we noted earlier, the Bible teaches very little that can be explicitly demonstrated to relate to ordination, and evangelicals have consistently overestimated how much and what exactly is taught about "calling."[5] It would be extremely difficult to justify from Scripture that all people are given a specific vocational calling, although some clearly are. If a man were to declare, "I know that God has called me to be an associate pastor of worship on a church staff," even though no church of the numerous ones to which he had applied ever offered him even an interview, most of us would probably entertain the possibility that he had misheard God's call or made it overly specific. But it is far more controversial and volatile to suggest to a woman who declares, "God has called me to be a senior pastor on a church staff," that perhaps she has misconstrued God's will. Irrespective of which side of the egalitarian-hierarchicalist debate one comes down on, we suspect that at least Paul and Peter would have told both hypothetical individuals that their first responsibility is to determine their spiritual gifts and exercise them as faithfully as they can in whatever settings in life they find themselves, whether or not that exercise ever leads to a formal church office or paid staff

---

[3]See also Ben Witherington III, *Grace in Galatia* (Grand Rapids: Eerdmans, 1998), 270–81.

[4]For an important recent overview of scholarship on this passage, too new to have been used by any of our contributors, see I. Howard Marshall, *A Critical and Exegetical Commentary on the Pastoral Epistles* (Edinburgh: T&T Clark, 1999), 261–98. Marshall ultimately adopts an egalitarian perspective. For a hierarchicalist counterpart even more recent than Marshall, see William D. Mounce, *Pastoral Epistles*, Word Biblical Commentary (Nashville: Nelson, 2000), 94–149.

[5]See the work of our colleague, William W. Klein, "Paul's Use of *Kalein*: A Proposal," *Journal of the Evangelical Theological Society* 27 (1984): 53–64; Klein, *The New Chosen People* (Grand Rapids: Zondervan, 1990), 199–209.

position. And all parties to the debate agree that the gifts of the Spirit, including apostle, pastor, teacher, and prophet, are given as the Spirit determines, irrespective of gender.[6]

Because Schreiner addresses 1 Corinthians 11:5 (women praying or prophesying with appropriate head coverings) in more detail than any other contributor, a few comments about that passage are in order. Schreiner seems correct in distinguishing prophecy from ordinary sermon preparation, but scholars don't entirely agree that only direct "charismatic" revelations must be in view. David Hill, for example, whom Schreiner includes in his footnote supporting the above claim, actually allows for a broad spectrum of early Christian proclamation to come under the heading of prophecy. What all manifestations of this gift have in common is the speaker's sense that they have a "word from the Lord," but a preacher who has meditated on a text or theme long enough to have had such an experience may well then qualify as one prophesying when he or she speaks to a Christian gathering or congregation.[7] It does not follow, therefore, even for the hierarchicalist, that a restriction on a woman occupying the office of elder/overseer necessarily rules out her preaching a sermon, under the authority of the elders or overseers of a given congregation. Increasingly, evangelical churches that are still not egalitarian are nevertheless recognizing this distinction.[8]

On the other hand, Schreiner has made a plausible case for seeing the role of a New Testament prophet as less authoritative than the regular, ongoing offices of priest in the Old Testament

---

[6]Excellent theological treatments of the spiritual gifts appear in Kenneth Hemphill, *Spiritual Gifts: Empowering the New Testament Church* (Nashville: Broadman, 1988); and Siegfried Schatzmann, *A Pauline Theology of Charismata* (Peabody, Mass.: Hendrickson, 1987). For more practical questions, see Clyde B. McDowell, *How to Discover Your Spiritual Gifts* (Elgin, Ill.: David C. Cook, 1988); and Don and Katie Fortune, *Discover Your God-Given Gifts* (Old Tappan, N.J.: Revell, 1987).

[7]David Hill (*New Testament Prophecy* [London: Marshall, Morgan, & Scott, 1979], 213) defines Christian prophets as "those who have grasped the meaning of Scripture, perceived its powerful relevance to the life of the individual, the Church and society, and declare that message fearlessly."

[8]See already the approaches of John R. W. Stott, *Issues Facing Christians Today* (Basingstoke, UK: Marshall, Morgan, and Scott, 1984), 252–53; and James I. Packer, "Postscript: I Believe in Women's Ministry," in *Why Not? Priesthood and the Ministry of Women*, eds. M. Bruce and G. E. Duffield (Abingdon, UK: Marcham Manor, 1976), 164–74.

and elder/overseer in the New Testament. In his recent, defini-tive study of "the progress of prophecy" through both Testa-ments, Ben Witherington demonstrates the following:

> In the Jewish prophetic tradition, prophets were not rulers; at most they were the consultants to rulers. They were not leaders in the sense of those who controlled the structures or sacred traditions of Israel. One should not have expected them to do so with the Jesus tradition either, which largely bears a non-prophetic shape. Indeed, to judge from a figure like Agabus, Christian prophets filled the role prophets had always fulfilled for God's people—they offered, from time to time, a late word from God. They did not lead unless they were also apostolic figures or elders, nor should we conflate them with the teachers or Christian sages or the historians such as Luke, who were the likely bearers, with the apostles, of the Jesus tradition.[9]

And Schreiner seems correct in stressing that egalitarians have often squeezed far more out of Acts 18:26 than can be clearly demonstrated. That Priscilla, with her husband, Aquila, took Apollos aside privately "and explained to him the way of God more adequately" hardly leads to the sweeping claims of many egalitarians about her publicly ministering in an ongoing teaching and leadership role in the church.[10] She *may* have exer-cised such a ministry, but we are simply not given enough data in Scripture to be at all confident of that claim.

Somewhat more complicated is the issue of women apos-tles. Again, Schreiner seems correct to distinguish between the "Twelve" described so often in the Gospels and Acts and the broader category of "apostle" in Paul's writings. Paul calls not only himself and Junia apostles but also refers to Titus (2 Cor. 8:23), Epaphroditus (Phil. 2:25), James, the Lord's brother (Gal. 1:19), and Andronicus (Rom. 16:7) by that same title. Obviously he is using *apostolos* in its common and etymological sense in the

---

[9]Ben Witherington III, *Jesus the Seer: The Progress of Prophecy* (Peabody, Mass.: Hendrickson, 1999), 327.

[10]It is a historical curiosity that of all the women in the New Testament, Priscilla is the one who has been chosen periodically in modern biblical scholarship as the possible author of Hebrews, on the (relatively weak) argument that the anonymity of this letter was due to its having been written by a woman.

Greek language, influenced also by the Hebrew *šāliaḥ* or "sent one," to mean someone sent out on a mission. In a Christian context, this regularly becomes a "missionary" or "church planter."[11] What is harder to determine is if one can separate the authority of such an individual from (or subordinate it to) the authority of settled church leadership, even granted the observations that male and female missionaries alike may at times have overstepped their bounds and that their role is to turn over a local church to indigenous leadership as soon as it is ready for it. The disparity between what women are actually encouraged to do on the mission field by very conservative churches and parachurch groups, and what they are allowed to do in their (usually Western) countries of origin often remains an embarrassing double standard that undermines some of the credibility of the hierarchicalist position.[12]

Another strength of Schreiner's essay is to show how the hierarchicalist's case depends on far more than just one or two disputed texts in Paul's writings, or even on the five main texts (cited by the Council on Biblical Manhood and Womanhood) that Belleville treats. Schreiner's rather thorough treatment of Genesis 1–2 is important, especially since none of the other essayists goes into as much detail on these chapters. Refreshing, too, is his candor that not all of his arguments from these chapters carry the same amount of weight; in debates like this one it's easy for representatives of any given position to speak with the same high degree of confidence (and volume) on *every* text or issue! Particularly helpful are Schreiner's discussions of three issues that egalitarians commonly stress and that hierarchicalists often leave unanswered: (1) the argument from order of creation when applied to Genesis 1 rather than just to Genesis 2, (2) the comparison of "naming formulas" in Genesis 2 and 3, and (3) the use of the Hebrew term *'ēzer* ("helper") for the woman. Hierarchicalists traditionally have not claimed that the principle of "first created implies leadership" applies beyond the creation of like members of the same species; whatever animal-rights activists or

---

[11]See D. A. Carson, *Showing the Spirit: A Theological Exposition of 1 Corinthians 12–14* (Grand Rapids: Baker, 1987), 88–91.

[12]See Ruth A. Tucker and Walter L. Liefeld, *Daughters of the Church: Women and Ministry from New Testament Times to the Present* (Grand Rapids: Zondervan, 1987), 291–327.

people today concerned with "speciesism" may think, no one in the biblical world would ever have dreamed of elevating animals above humanity. The naming of "woman" in the immediate context of the naming of the animals does seem to suggest some outworking of the mandate given to Adam to exercise dominion, if we are going to argue that the naming of the animals has anything to do with this aspect of Adam's creation in God's image. And the fact that God is often described as a "helper" elsewhere in Scripture does not overrule the fact that people in subordinate positions also regularly offer "help," so that the immediate context of each use of *ʿēzer* must prove the most determinative of its meaning *in that passage*.[13]

On the other hand, it is not clear that hierarchicalists have grappled adequately with the fact that both man and woman, as jointly created in God's image and called *ʾādām*, are commanded to "fill the earth and subdue it" and to "rule over the fish of the sea and the birds of the air and over every living creature that moves on the ground" (Gen. 1:28). One might thus argue that, despite the other similarities between Adam's naming the animals and naming the woman, human dominion is exercised only in the former instance, because both Adam and Eve are created equally to exercise *joint* dominion over the rest of creation.[14] At the same time Schreiner is surely right to stress that modern American understandings of equality are heavily influenced by secular, post-Enlightenment thought. E. Earle Ellis offers helpful corroborating comments:

> The mind-set that places "equality and subordination" in opposition and that views distinctions of class and rank as evil per se is largely a modern phenomenon. It may reflect a justifiable resentment toward attitudes of disdain and elitism that often (and in a sinful society always) flow from such distinctions, but it seems to be

---

[13]For details of the context of Genesis 2:18, see Raymond C. Ortlund Jr., "Male-Female Equality and Male Headship: Genesis 1–3," in *Recovering Biblical Manhood and Womanhood*, eds. John Piper and Wayne Grudem (Wheaton, Ill.: Crossway, 1991), 101–103. For an egalitarian treatment of *ʿēzer*, see M. de Merode, "'A Helper Fit for Him': Genesis 2:18–24," *Theology Digest* 27 (1979): 117–19.

[14]It is important to recognize that *ʾādām* in Genesis 1:27 is not yet the proper name Adam, but refers generically to male and female alike. See especially Richard S. Hess, "Splitting the Adam: The Usage of *Adam* in Genesis I-V," in *Studies in the Pentateuch*, ed. J. A. Emerton (Leiden: Brill, 1989), 1–15.

less aware of the egoistic and antisocial evils inherent in egalitarianism itself and sometimes expressed in programs for economic or social conformity in a libertarian rejection of authority, and in a despisal of servanthood as a "demeaning" role.

In any case Paul, like the New Testament generally, holds together quite harmoniously an equality of value and diversity of rank and resolves the problems of diversity in a manner entirely different from modern egalitarianism.[15]

Still, one wonders if a hypothetical "first-time" reader of Genesis 1–3, even in the ancient Jewish world, would have picked up any of the six indications of female subordination that Schreiner discusses. It is virtually impossible for the Christian reader, so much more familiar with the New Testament, to read these chapters from Genesis without reading in understandings derived from 1 Corinthians 11:8–9, 1 Corinthians 14:34, and 1 Timothy 2:13–14. Of course, the evangelical Christian is bound by Scripture's principles, whichever Testament they come from, even when New Testament passages use the Old Testament in ways that do not seem to involve straightforward exegesis of their original intention.[16] But then we are driven back to Keener's questions about what kind of use of the Old Testament we have in these New Testament texts and whether it is one that does in fact lead to a binding, timeless "creation ordinance."

It is also worth raising the question of whether in a passage like 1 Corinthians 11:2–16 (even if verses 8–9 articulate a creation ordinance of wifely submission to husbands) verses 11–12 may suggest that the new creation in Christ goes beyond God's original creation. Clearly it will in the world to come, where God's people will no longer have the option of sinning as Adam and Eve initially had, even before the Fall. More difficult is the debate over whether in the present interim age—the time between the

---

[15]E. Earle Ellis, *Pauline Theology: Ministry and Society* (Grand Rapids: Eerdmans, 1989), 57–58.

[16]One recalls the vigorous debate in the 1970s that surrounded Paul K. Jewett's claims that 1 Corinthians 14:33–38 appealed to the Law in the (inappropriate) style of Jewish *midrash* and thus the passage was not binding on modern-day Christians (*Man as Male and Female: A Study of Sexual Relationships from a Theological Point of View* [Grand Rapids: Eerdmans, 1975], especially 111–19).

"already" and "not yet" of God's kingdom—submission is to be understood as one of the creation ordinances we should work to transcend. At this juncture, Schreiner rightfully calls attention to the parallels often cited throughout church history between the relationships of man and woman (or husband and wife) and the members of the Trinity among themselves. It is generally agreed that during the time Jesus was on earth, he was functionally subordinate to the Father. There is less agreement on the issue of whether or not he was (and is) eternally subordinate. Most egalitarians resoundingly declare that he is not, while hierarchicalists see the irreversibility of such patterns of interaction as God commanding and sending the Son (before the incarnation) and Christ turning all things over to the Father (at the end of time) as implying that he is.[17] But as Schreiner points out, Keener's recent study demonstrates that the two issues need not be dealt with in the same way at all.

Schreiner also does more with the issue of gender roles in the family than any of our other contributors (though the issue isn't always felt to be parallel to the debate on gender roles in ministry). He correctly identifies the meaning and function of Ephesians 5:21 ("Submit to one another out of reverence for Christ") as both *concluding* the thought begun in 5:18, and thus supplying one more sign of being filled with the Spirit, and *introducing* the tripartite "domestic code" of commands to wives and husbands, children and parents, slaves and masters. English translations, in their punctuation and paragraphing, will inevitably give one of these two functions priority over the other. But trying to preserve the dual role of this verse is what lands exegetes in a minefield. On the one hand, Belleville is right to stress the consistent function of the reciprocal pronoun *allēlois* (here in the dative case) as meaning "(to) one another." As a command to all church members, mutual submission makes good sense. On the other hand, Schreiner is correct to point out that nothing in Ephesians 5:22–6:9 justifies the claim that husbands

---

[17]On this theme in the history of theology, see John F. Jensen, "1 Corinthians 15:24–28 and the Future of Jesus Christ," *Scottish Journal of Theology* 40 (1987): 543–70. One observation emerges clearly: Neither side in this debate is alone orthodox (with the other side being heretical, as is sometimes charged). The potential risk of drawing analogies between the economy of the Trinity and the relationship styles of humans may rest in blurring the distinction between a central, core Christian doctrine (the Trinity) and a much more peripheral doctrinal conviction (gender in ministry).

submit to wives, parents to children, or masters to slaves. So how is one simultaneously and adequately to teach that all Christians have a responsibility to submit to one another while yet preserving the distinctive roles articulated for individuals in paired relationships of authority and subordination?[18]

Schreiner also steers a sane middle course in the vexed debate over the meaning of *kephalē* ("head"). Against those who argue that it never means "source" or (almost) never means "authority,"[19] Schreiner agrees with Belleville that both meanings, though rare, are found and that the immediate context of Paul's use must be ultimately decisive. And he advances the discussion considerably by adopting a perspective that sees in Ephesians 5 or 1 Corinthians 11 a "both/and" approach as perhaps best. Curiously, Stephen Bedale's pioneering study in the 1950s on *kephalē* as "source" is regularly cited by egalitarians without any admission that Bedale himself argued for both "source" and "authority" as the meaning of *kephalē* in the disputed Pauline texts.[20] Even the radical Christian feminist, Elizabeth Schüssler Fiorenza, agrees that this is what Paul meant, although she rejects this strand of hierarchicalism as normative for contemporary believers.[21] At the same time, it is interesting that the command to "obey" appears explicitly in Paul's instructions to children and slaves (Eph. 6:1, 5) but not in his commands to

---

[18]A similar quandary faces translators of Philippians 2:4, which in the Greek literally reads, "Not for the things of yourselves each of you looking out but for the things of others." But if one absolutizes this, person A always puts person B's interests above his or her own and B does the same with A. But all this does is lead to a reversal of roles and does nothing in breaking an impasse in decision making between A and B. Hence, translations like the NIV interpolate by translating as follows: "Each of you should look *not only* to your own interests, *but also* to the interests of others."

[19]See, for example, respectively, Wayne Grudem, "The Meaning of *Kephalē* ('Head'): A Response to Recent Studies," in *Recovering Biblical Manhood and Womanhood*, 425–68; and Berkeley Mickelsen and Alvera Mickelsen, "What Does *Kephalē* Mean in the New Testament," in *Women, Authority and the Bible*, ed. Alvera Mickelsen (Downers Grove, Ill.: InterVarsity Press, 1986), 97–110.

[20]Stephen Bedale, "The Meaning of *Kephalē* in the Pauline Epistles," *Journal of Theological Studies* n.s. 5 (1954): 211–15. On page 214 Bedale writes, "That is to say, the male is *kephalē* in the sense of *archē* [beginning] relative to the female; and, in St. Paul's view, the female in consequence is 'subordinate' [cf. Eph. 5:23]."

[21]Elizabeth Schüssler Fiorenza, *In Memory of Her: A Feminist Theological Reconstruction of Christian Origins* (New York: Crossroad, 1983), 229.

women. Given that *hypotassō* ("submit") may at times have the subdued sense of "defer to,"[22] it is not entirely obvious that "submit" as Paul uses it must include the concept of "obey." It certainly can, as with Peter's reference to Sarah (1 Peter 3:6), but that it must is open to question. And even in 1 Peter, Peter cannot be claiming that submission always entails obedience, since these Christian women had almost certainly already defied orders to convert to or retain their husbands' non-Christian religious commitments.[23]

We now turn to Ann Bowman's essay. Perhaps the most significant contributions of this chapter revolve around her autobiographical remarks of how God has guided and blessed her throughout her ministry within predominantly hierarchicalist circles; she shares the important lessons she has learned from Scripture and applied to her ministry—lessons that prove relevant for *all* authentically biblical ministry. In our twenty-first-century American culture, Christians need to be reminded that we cannot be fundamentally driven by the perennial quest in our society for the exercise of people's "inalienable rights" involving "life, liberty, and the pursuit of happiness." However deeply embedded in our national psyche these fundamental slogans may be, the Christian must first of all be motivated by the surrender of his or her rights and quest for happiness in favor of the ethics of the gospel and the service of Christ.[24]

Therefore, men and women alike who find themselves in Christian circles where certain doors may be closed to them should concentrate first of all on the numerous opportunities that are already available to them. As Bowman has discovered, even for women in more traditional settings there are numerous ministries and roles that allow for the exercise of virtually every conceivable mix of the spiritual gifts with which God has endowed them. More controversial is the question of whether an important secondary role is for Christians to lobby, as winsomely as possible, for greater freedoms and opportunities for those who

---

[22]J. Ramsey Michaels, *1 Peter*, Word Biblical Commentary (Dallas: Word, 1988), 156–57.

[23]I. Howard Marshall, *1 Peter*, IVP New Testament Commentary Series (Downers Grove, Ill.: InterVarsity Press, 1991), 98.

[24]For excellent reflections on "servant leadership" in ministry, see James A. Means, *Leadership in Christian Ministry* (Grand Rapids: Baker, 1989).

are, in their opinion, inappropriately marginalized. Clearly this is a major theme in Scripture—from the Mosaic laws about not discriminating against the poor and oppressed, through the prophetic denunciations of injustice, to Jesus' and James's concern for the impoverished and persecuted of their days.[25] But one looks in vain for commended biblical models of people fighting for their *own* rights. Thus, the more men or women in the church—those who do feel surrounded by unjust marginalization of other women from ministry—seek to create greater opportunities for those individuals rather than for themselves, the more likely the spirit of the biblical ethic will be practiced.[26]

This spirit of putting others' interests above one's own summarizes a large part of what is involved in the process of sanctification, a topic on which Bowman helpfully focuses in some detail. So, too, the classic spiritual disciplines should help Christians maintain a positive attitude, even in situations that may prove more restrictive than they might like. The topic of forgiveness proves crucial in this context; in a volatile debate such as this one, Christians will inevitably offend others, both consciously and unconsciously, with their positions and attitudes. If the gender-roles debate is not to become (or, in some circles, remain) the most divisive issue in the Western evangelical church today, we must all embrace a ready willingness to forgive those who hurt us by their views and actions. Although the parable of the unforgiving servant (Matt. 18:23–35) is literally about financial debt, its central thrust applies to every context

---

[25]For detailed documentation in the area of economic marginalization (often the plight of widows or single adult women in the biblical cultures), see Craig L. Blomberg, *Neither Poverty nor Riches: A Theology of Possessions* (Leicester: InterVarsity Press, 1999).

[26]Even Paul, who several times used his Roman citizenship to his advantage, did so only at those times that were most strategic for the broader interests of the gospel, and not when they would have most benefited him. For example, in Acts 16:19–40, he could have used his rights to avoid imprisonment altogether in Philippi, and he could have agreed simply to slip out of town quietly the next morning when offered his freedom by the authorities. Instead he announced his citizenship and demanded a public release at the time and in the way that would clearly maximize the benefits for the fledgling church in Philippi (Acts 16:37). The Roman authorities thus set a public precedent that should have forestalled further government-sponsored persecution of the Christians who remained in town even as Paul moved on in his itinerant ministry.

in which a Christian is wronged. If we cannot find in God's empowerment the ability somehow to forgive even the deepest hurts against us, the very existence of authentic Christian faith in us is called into question.[27] On the other hand, forgiveness can quickly slide over into an unbiblical "enabling," by which victims of abuse of various kinds think it is their responsibility not to intervene with the kinds of confrontations that will require victimizers to change their behavior. It is not coincidental that immediately preceding this parable in Matthew—and Peter's question that triggered the parable (18:21)—is the famous passage on church discipline for those who remain unrepentant (18:15–20). Forgiveness is not the same as "business as usual" or acting as though no wrong had ever occurred.[28]

Bowman proceeds to highlight the importance of spiritual gifts and their similarities and dissimilarities to natural abilities and personality traits. Surely these are more foundational issues for any would-be professional in ministry than aspirations to a specific office.[29] The same is true of her emphasis on healthy interpersonal relationships. A substantial majority of people fired from Christian ministries are dismissed primarily because of their inability to get along well with their coworkers. It does little good if one "wins the battle" for one's particular view of gender roles in ministry but leaves a wake of divisiveness or devastation among those whom one has trampled on in achieving the "victory."

When Bowman does come to key New Testament texts on women in ministry, she covers much of the same ground we've traversed with our other three essayists. Unlike Schreiner, she draws the line for women so as to exclude only the office of senior pastor. This is one way of identifying in a contemporary

---

[27]The most straightforward reading of the parable would suggest that even the forgiveness acquired from God can be forfeited. But the text can also be read in a manner consistent with a Calvinist understanding of the "perseverance of the saints." See Craig L. Blomberg, *Matthew,* New American Commentary (Nashville: Broadman, 1992), 282–85.

[28]A sobering but helpful anthology of essays that confront this issue, especially as it relates to women, is Catherine C. Kroeger and James R. Beck, eds., *Women, Abuse, and the Bible* (Grand Rapids: Baker, 1996).

[29]For a useful integration of Jesus' teaching with a modern personality inventory, see James R. Beck, *Jesus and Personality Theory* (Downers Grove, Ill. : InterVarsity Press, 1999).

multiple-staff congregation the functional equivalent of the New Testament elder/overseer. And in a way similar to viewing the distinction between the office of overseer/elder and the function of preaching (or the gift of prophecy), conservative evangelical congregations are increasingly coming to the conclusion that having a male senior pastor may in fact free them up to have women serve in subordinate pastoral-staff roles. Not a few hierarchicalist churches and denominations that formally adopt the position of Schreiner—no women pastors at all—nevertheless allow and even encourage women to hold full-time paid staff positions that give them the opportunity to exercise fully their spiritual gifts. At times, the job descriptions of these positions are indistinguishable from those of ordained pastors who have held the same positions.[30] The only difference is that the women are not ordained and not called pastors. One wonders, however, if the more consistent approach would be to admit that the theology implied in the permission for ministry outweighs the formal restrictions on titles and ordination, and thus to bring the two more closely into line with each other.

Bowman's section on "Practical Factors That Shape Ministry" introduces several issues that need more consistent application to the gender-roles debate as well. Frequently individual differences in ministry style or performance are held up as indicators of why women can or should not lead men in various contexts. Understanding cultural differences proves equally crucial to a sensitive application of one's position, whether hierarchicalist or egalitarian. To the extent that all interpreters agree on *some* cultural elements behind the biblical teaching, most notably a strong patriarchal culture in the ancient Near East and Mediterranean worlds, when one finds oneself in a secular society that values quite opposite (and egalitarian) gender roles, questions of how to apply the biblical principles so as to best replicate their intended effects must be raised. For the hierarchicalist, this may mean being open to implementing his or her convictions in as "minimalist" or least intrusive way possible. Conversely, when the Westerner carries out ministry abroad in very traditional non-Christian cultures (or at home in distinctive ethnic or religious

---

[30]Notable examples appear in congregations within the two American denominations in which the editors of this book hold membership—the Conservative Baptist Association and the Baptist General Conference.

subcultures), egalitarians may find themselves having to accommodate themselves to restrictions they would prefer were not present, simply for the sake of being able to effectively promote the more fundamental tenets of the faith.

We must likewise again recognize the effects of life circumstances. Not a few men and women have ultimately come to their opinion on whether a woman can or should serve in senior roles of ministry leadership based on the negative or positive examples they have observed in women filling those roles. Yet in any other theological context, these same people would be quick to privilege Scripture above personal experience. Finally, Bowman reminds us how crucially the issue of spiritual warfare comes into play. Satan loves to divide believers, pitting them against one another. We must all recommit to speaking what we understand to be the truth, with all the love we can muster (Eph. 4:15), and ban all the rhetoric from either side that would elevate one's position on gender roles to a fundamental of the faith that must be fought for at all costs. The Bible simply does not speak as unambiguously to this topic as some claim, or as we might wish, and we must learn to agree to disagree in love, recognizing that each of us could be wrong. But this leads into our concluding remarks, to which we turn next.

CONCLUSION

James R. Beck and Craig L. Blomberg

The four essays in this volume constitute an overview of the current debate among evangelicals regarding the role of women in ministry. The authors have described for us two well-articulated positions, one advocating an elimination of all restrictions in Christian ministry related to gender and one arguing for the retention of at least one gender-based qualification for leadership. Both positions are comprehensive in that they deal with material throughout the vast range of biblical revelation, and both positions are a mix of strong and less strong arguments on the various subpoints of the debate. Both egalitarian and hierarchicalist advocates can delineate a position that accounts for all related biblical teaching in a consistent manner. The authors of these essays have shown that they are acquainted with the writings of persons on the other side of the issue, that they have not only considered their arguments but conceded on some points and been unpersuaded on the balance. Both positions are linked to personal experience, and interpreters of both stripes are rooted in culture and history, although admittedly in different segments of each. Neither position is an exact representation of New Testament practice, although each position argues that it is the best expression of the New Testament principles underlying first-century practice. As Thomas Schreiner points out, many features of church life were quite fluid at the end of the New Testament era, a fluidity that also applied to terms used for roles and offices. Nonetheless, Schreiner and other hierarchicalists, as well as our other essayists, sense a strong core of principled values underlying the practice of the early church, a set of values regarding gender that can still be detected and implemented in the modern church.

Readers may find each individual essay quite convincing, only to discover by reading the next one that the issues are complex and multifaceted. For those who already have a preferred position on the subject of gender in ministry, reading these essays will have provided a better understanding of the favored position, as well as a greater appreciation of the other side of the debate. Increased respect for one's opponents in a debate is always helpful and civilizing. Other readers have yet to decide for themselves, hence our decision not only to provide high quality expositions of both sides of the debate but also to provide reflections on these essays from both perspectives in our jointly written commentary.[1] We recognize that many people prefer simply to be told by a respected leader what they should believe and that many leaders prefer simply to tell people "the truth." The combination of these approaches is not, however, a responsible one for Christian education in general or for specific issues on which equally godly evangelicals have found themselves so polarized.

We are convinced that evangelicals can deal with the topic of gender in ministry in either an emphatically unhealthy manner or in a God-honoring constructive manner. Bitter fighting that results in divisive attitudes and policies surely violates the New Testament principles that are to govern how we deal with church disputes.[2] On the one hand, leaders can dictate changes in policies and practice regarding women without engaging concerned parties in a rigorous and thorough examination of the topic. Or, on the other hand, denominations can convene balanced study groups that honestly seek the mind of God regarding how the matter should be handled within a given group of

---

[1]This approach has deep roots at the institution where we both teach. Denver Seminary senior professor Gordon R. Lewis is the author of *Decide for Yourself: A Theological Workbook* (Downers Grove, Ill.: InterVarsity Press, 1970), a useful volume that has seen numerous reprintings. The book touched on many theological issues and provided evangelicals with a profitable guide for exploring issues on which disagreement exists.

[2]The vice lists of the New Testament (especially the one in Gal. 5:19–21) describe acts of the old, sinful nature that can continue to characterize the believer's life if not swiftly dealt with. Believers must "put away" discord, dissensions, and factions—each of which can wreak havoc in congregational and denominational life.

God's people. A workable consensus obtained in such a manner is surely to be preferred over formal pronouncements or fiats, or negotiations behind closed doors.

To revisit some of the issues raised in our introduction, we can now say with even more certainty that both of the major positions regarding women in ministry agree that the Old and New Testaments, along with the example of Jesus during his earthly ministry, all support a wide range of ministry opportunities for women. The Bible teaches, and both sides in this debate agree, that all spiritual gifts are to be used for God's glory, that they are given without distinction of gender, and that their implementation is crucial to the success of God's work on earth. All of our contributors would probably also agree that we have yet to fully utilize all the gifts God has given to his people and that we are spiritually poorer because of it. Both the hierarchicalist and egalitarian sides of the discussion also affirm the dignity and worth of both genders and remind us that both women and men bear in themselves the image of God.

More than that, our authors argue that many, if not most, of the roles and offices of the church are open to gifted women and men. The experience of Ann Bowman, one of our essayists, illustrates this point well. She is a New Testament professor, a leader of prayer seminars all across North America, and a sought-after speaker around the world. And she carries out all this ministry within a hierarchicalist framework.

The reality is that very few churches or denominations have fully utilized this freedom to engage women in a wide variety of roles, functions, and offices. We sometimes tolerate male predominance just because "we've always done it that way" rather than because we are convinced that the Bible requires us to conduct ourselves in such a manner. Perhaps it's time for all parties to diligently and creatively incorporate women more fully into the leadership of the church, since both sides of the debate so clearly feel that the Bible encourages us so to act. We encourage all Christians and Christian leaders, no matter what view they ultimately adopt, to recognize that even if we apply standard hierarchicalist interpretations, the biblical texts offered women unprecedented opportunities and affirmation in their worlds. Can we do less? Or to put it another way: Once a given church or denomination decides where to draw the lines on women's roles, if at all, could a visitor nevertheless quickly perceive that this particular church or denomination was doing all it could to proactively affirm and encourage women to participate actively in the life and leadership of the church within their agreed-upon parameters?

We mentioned above that all interpreters, including those in this volume, are grounded in experience, history, and culture. Students of the science and art of hermeneutics will be familiar with this assertion, whereas other readers may be surprised by it. Some naively think that a plain reading of Scripture, accompanied by a commitment to let the Bible speak for itself, will surely solve all interpretive difficulties. Besides, they may reason, if we are committed to using only the finest of logic and reasoning strategies, the plain meaning of the text will be obvious. Such is not the case, however, especially when tackling a difficult subject such as the role of women in ministry.[3]

Given that we are all rooted to some extent in our own history and culture, it is vitally important that we remind ourselves of the dominance of patriarchal structures prior to the twentieth century. The twentieth century is the first epoch in human history when a major segment of the philosophical climate was arguing that women were equal to men in all ways and that they were just as capable of exercising leadership as men. Prior to this, interpreters generally had been exposed only to patriarchal thought-forms and thus weren't challenged to look at the inspired truths of Scripture through different lenses; this reality could provide a reason for the time-tested view in the church that males were created to lead in both home and church. While this observation doesn't resolve the debate, it does help to explain why egalitarian understandings have emerged only recently. Not a few men feel threatened by the twentieth-century feminist movement, and not a few women are deeply suspicious of the patriarchy that held sway for the first nineteen centuries of church life and thought. But the fact that women and men may be threatened by philosophical movements should always take second place to the larger issue: What does the Bible teach, and how can we faithfully interpret problematic texts in spite of our

---

[3]Study of both pre-critical and post-critical Christian reading strategies for the Bible shows a reliance on numerous factors other than clear logic and reason, tools probably most stressed in the partly non-Christian modernism period that developed after the Enlightenment.

inclination toward or our repulsion against either patriarchy or feminism?

The evangelical branch of Protestantism in North America has yet to reach consensus in this debate regarding gender in ministry. Neither side has been convincingly declared heretical; we believe neither side *is* heretical. The discussion to date has been profitable, both at the academic level and in the pew. In fact, we are convinced that the ongoing discussion will continue to yield valuable information and approaches that will serve the church well.

We need the very best scholarship executed by the finest of trained men and women to pursue this subject. Even though the issue is fairly well circumscribed, the peripheral biblical and doctrinal issues are numerous, and material from many subdisciplines must be brought to bear on the discussion. The new material offered in this volume by our essayists is further proof that the discussion is not over and that important new material is out there waiting to be discovered. The results of this new material may bring us closer to resolution. Notwithstanding Schreiner's answer to our questions about the future, it *does* seem that the gap is narrowing and that idiosyncratic approaches on both sides are diminishing. Maybe scholarship really can help the church at times!

In preparing for this volume we couldn't help but notice the continuing disparity between trained men and trained women who are participating actively in this debate, the latter of course being a far smaller number. While true of both sides in the debate, the shortage of women scholars advancing the discussion is most acute on the hierarchicalist side. Could it be that hierarchicalists have not been successful in encouraging women to pursue careers in scholarship, despite the fact that scholarship is not in any way organically linked to any of the New Testament offices or roles they believe are closed to women?[4]

One reason the gender-in-ministry debate causes considerable frustration for all parties concerned is that it is well nigh unto

---

[4]Of course, another explanation might be in order: Perhaps women begin their scholarly training with the goal of advancing the hierarchicalist position only to alter their viewpoint toward egalitarian understandings at some point along the way. We are unaware of any data that would help determine which explanation is the more accurate one.

impossible to implement both positions at once in the same church. By way of contrast, it is possible to allow families to decide if they wish to baptize or to dedicate their newborn, to welcome persons into church membership by either immersion or by sprinkling, and to allow persons of both premillennial and amillennial persuasions to lead Bible studies at the same church. But it is not possible to allow women into the pastoral office and at the same time to ban them from it. The positions are quite exclusive. Individual churches must make a choice between the two.[5]

Craig Keener's essay briefly raised an issue that Ann Bowman's essay explicitly developed. Does a third position, in fact, exist in this debate on gender and ministry, a position that makes a full egalitarian argument with one exception—the senior pastor role is reserved for males only? The reason this position may merit a category to itself revolves around the fact that its advocates could be considered essentially egalitarians who argue for only one rather well-defined and narrow restriction. One can argue that they actually have more in common with irenic egalitarian viewpoints than with classic hierarchicalist ones. We leave unsettled the question of whether these "senior pastor only" people represent a third identifiable position in the gender debate. Should this position begin to receive wider circulation and discussion, it could pave the way for a compromise of sorts between the egalitarian and hierarchicalist sides. For example, the "senior pastor only" advocates could agree that when a church has a single leader, the leader (or senior pastor) must be male. But when the church leadership consists of a team rather than a single person, both men and women can equally participate. The appendix by Dr. Blomberg further develops precisely such a "modified hierarchicalism." It stands as the only part of the volume without commentary largely because it was added very late in the process. We'll let our readers decide for themselves both how persuasive it is and whether or not it offers a viable middle ground within the debate.

What about the immediate future? As we said in our introduction, we cannot predict the outcome of the current discussion.

---

[5]Most denominations also conclude that they must select between the two options as the way it must be for all their churches, although those denominations that allow for a certain level of congregational autonomy can contain some egalitarian churches and some hierarchicalist congregations.

However, we are convinced that an irenic spirit on the part of all involved will continue to be a great need. In 1 Corinthians 14:33a, just before a portion of Scripture frequently discussed in this volume, Paul writes, "For God is not a God of disorder but of peace." Immediately after this reminder to his readers, he launches headlong into issues of gender in the church in Corinth—issues that were a matter of great concern to him. Perhaps Paul was all too aware that matters of worship (1 Cor. 14:26–32) and of gender in the church (1 Cor. 14:33b–40) are both subjects that have great potential for inflaming passions and triggering disorder. But God's intent is for peace in the church, in spite of stressful problems that confront God's people. God's very nature demands it. Our hope is that this volume models the same calm and peaceable spirit. Advocates can feel strongly regarding their gender convictions, but they can also display respect and charitableness toward others. And advocates of either side can voice their commitments clearly, while at the same time avoiding inflammatory language and unnecessary bombastic rhetoric.

Regarding the eschatological future, we can have more certainty. Gender appears to be of little concern to the apostle John as he records the Revelation given him by God. Evil is at times gendered as male (as with the beast in Rev. 13) and at other times as female (as with Jezebel in Rev. 2:20). Goodness appears in the character of one like a son of man (Rev. 1:13) walking among the lampstands and in the character of the woman who bears a child (Rev. 12). Descriptions of heaven do not detail God's will for gender in leadership there, as *all* leadership is focused on the Lamb and on the eternal, enthroned God who rules over all. The thorny matter of gender in ministry will have completely passed away,[6] along with the other travails of life, when we join together, women and men alike, to praise our King and Savior for eternity. Maranatha!

---

[6]Although some persons will no doubt relish the opportunity to ask Paul in glory exactly what he meant in some of these disputed gender texts!

APPENDIX

NEITHER HIERARCHICALIST NOR EGALITARIAN: GENDER ROLES IN PAUL

Craig L. Blomberg

Debates about the Bible's teaching on gender roles seem to continue endlessly. The literature that one must master to say anything credible grows in intimidating quantity: general works on men and women in antiquity; specific studies of the classical world, the Hellenistic period, the Old Testament and subsequent Jewish tradition, and the New Testament and constituent parts of Scripture; analyses of specific biblical texts, broader liberationist or feminist approaches, theologies of the Bible, of one Testament, or of one specific part of one Testament; commentaries; histories of Jewish and/or Christian interpretation of texts; church histories more generally; modern ecclesiastical debates; and contemporary social-scientific analysis![1] At the same time, it does appear that

---

[1] I have read widely in each of these areas for almost twenty-five years and published preliminary, partial findings in four different contexts: "Not Beyond What Is Written: A Review of Aída Spencer's *Beyond the Curse: Women Called to Ministry*," *Criswell Theological Review* 2 (1988): 403–21; *1 Corinthians*, The NIV Application Commentary Series (Grand Rapids: Zondervan, 1994), 207–26, 277–92; article on "woman," *Evangelical Dictionary of Biblical Theology*, Walter A. Elwell, ed. (Grand Rapids: Baker, 1996), 824–28; and my editorial reflections elsewhere in this book. My footnotes in this appendix focus almost exclusively on the most recent and/or important works, lest the footnotes overwhelm the text of the essay itself! The most comprehensive bibliography I know of is Mayer I. Gruber, *A Study Guide: Women in the World of Hebrew Scripture*, Volume 1 of *Women in the Biblical World*, ATLA bibliography series no. 38 (Lanham, Md.: Scarecrow, 1995). It would seem that a second volume related to the New Testament was conceived but has not yet appeared.

scholarship is making progress, both in ruling out certain extreme or idiosyncratic perspectives and in gaining greater insight into the probable meanings of disputed terms and syntax in key texts. And a surprisingly small percentage of the last twenty years of study focuses solely on Paul and, at the same time, on all of his writings.[2] So it is appropriate here to take stock of the progress that has been made on this topic and to chart out a plausible synthesis in the midst of the plethora of competing opinions.[3]

My thesis is that Paul was neither a classic hierarchicalist nor a full-fledged egalitarian,[4] despite numerous contemporary attempts to place him squarely in one or the other camp. Both attempts inevitably skew some of the data. Instead, Paul dis-

---

[2]After a flurry of such studies in the 1970s, the literature has tailed off substantially. The most important contributions of the last twenty years include James G. Sigountos and Myron Shank, "Public Roles for Women in the Pauline Church: A Reappraisal of the Evidence," *Journal of the Evangelical Theological Society* 26 (1983): 283–95; John T. Bristow, *What Paul Really Said about Women* (San Francisco: Harper & Row, 1988); Norbert Baumert, *Antifeminismus bei Paulus?* (Würzburg: Echter, 1992); Craig S. Keener, *Paul, Women and Wives: Marriage and Women's Ministry in the Letters of Paul* (Peabody, Mass.: Hendrickson, 1992); Wendy Cotter, "Women's Authority Roles in Paul's Churches: Countercultural or Conventional?" *Novum Testamentum* 36 (1994): 350–72; Judith M. Gundry-Volf, "Paul on Women and Gender: A Comparison with Early Jewish Views," in *The Road from Damascus*, ed. Richard N. Longenecker (Grand Rapids: Eerdmans, 1997), 184–212; and Andrew C. Perriman, *Speaking of Women: Interpreting Paul* (Leicester: Apollos, 1998).

[3]Anthony Thacker ("Was Paul a Sexist?" *Epworth Review* 23 [1996]: 85–94) identifies seven discrete perspectives, which he labels "misogynist," "confused oppressor and liberator," "male supremacist," "hierarchical authority," "dialectically egalitarian and supremacist," "partially implicit egalitarian," and "pragmatic egalitarian." Thacker himself determines Paul to be a "moderate feminist."

[4]I use the word *hierarchicalist* here to refer to the view that Paul actively promoted the cultural and scriptural practices, which he inherited, of barring numerous roles to women in the domestic and religious arenas and intended those restrictions to be normative for all Christians throughout time. I use *egalitarian* to refer to the perspective that Paul did not promote any timeless role differentiation among men and women. I avoid using *complementarian* and *feminist* as exact synonyms for these two terms, respectively. *Complementarian* does not in and of itself suggest any role restrictions and therefore can mislead. *Feminist* in and of itself suggests a priority to things female, which is by no means the perspective of those who identify themselves as *evangelical* or *biblical feminists*. Of course, all terms create problems: *Hierarchicalist* can suggest someone who promotes an elaborate hierarchy with authoritarian leaders, while *egalitarian* can suggest someone who blurs all distinctions between men and women to promote androgyny. I do not imply either of these notions by my use of the terms.

cerned no tension between preserving certain elements of his patriarchal culture and adopting countercultural, liberationist strands of thought within that larger framework. Careful exegesis discloses that Paul remains both coherent and consistent in articulating this middle ground throughout his apostolic career.

HISTORICAL BACKGROUND

As with most other Jews and early Christians, the Hebrew Scriptures would have formed the most important background literature for Paul. Space precludes consideration of the huge debates that rage over the correct interpretation of Genesis 1–3, but it is interesting to note agreement among a cross section of conservative, centrist, and liberal commentators that, if these opening chapters of the Bible do not demonstrably promote a hierarchy of authority of the man over the woman, they at least leave the door open for such an interpretation.[5] More pertinently, there is no evidence from ancient Jewish exegesis that Paul could have inherited an egalitarian interpretation of the beginnings of Genesis from his Jewish upbringing.[6] Nor does a completely egalitarian interpretation of Paul appear in the writings of any ancient Christian commentator, suggesting that if Paul did articulate such a perspective, he was uniformly misunderstood in the extant sources.[7]

---

[5]See Thomas R. Schreiner, "An Interpretation of 1 Timothy 2:9–15: A Dialogue with Scholarship," in *Women in the Church: A Fresh Analysis of 1 Timothy 2:9–15*, eds. Andreas J. Köstenberger, Thomas R. Schreiner, and H. Scott Baldwin (Grand Rapids: Baker, 1995), 134–40; Francis Watson, "Strategies of Recovery and Resistance: Hermeneutical Reflections on Genesis 1–3 and Its Pauline Reception," *Journal for the Study of the New Testament* 45 (1992): 79–103; David J.A. Clines, "What Does Eve Do to Help? and Other Irredeemably Androcentric Orientations in Genesis 1–3," in *What Does Eve Do to Help? and Other Readerly Questions in the Old Testament*, ed. David J.A. Clines (Sheffield: Sheffield Academic Press, 1990), 25–48. Over against Max Küchler (*Schweigen, Schmuck und Schleier* [Göttingen: Vandenhoeck & Ruprecht, 1986]), who argues that Paul's use of the Old Testament in 1 Corinthians 11 and 14 and 1 Timothy 2 cannot be derived from legitimate exegesis, but comes from a tendentious, *frauenfeindlich* Jewish interpretive tradition.

[6]For a survey, see Paul Morris, "Exiled from Eden: Jewish Interpretations of Genesis," in *A Walk in the Garden: Biblical, Iconographical, and Literary Images of Eden*, ed. Deborah Sawyer (Sheffield: Sheffield Academic Press, 1992), 117–66.

[7]See Gregory A. Robbins, ed., *Genesis 1–3 in the History of Exegesis* (Lewiston, N.Y.: Mellen, 1988).

The rest of the Old Testament includes numerous positive, countercultural leadership roles for women,[8] but every one of them remains the exception rather than the norm, and the Torah made it clear that one leadership role—the Israelite priesthood—was exclusively reserved for men (Ex. 28; Lev. 9). Diversity in the extent of patriarchy seems to have existed within the various periods covered by the Old Testament, Second Temple Judaism, and the rabbinic literature,[9] but again one looks in vain for anything resembling modern egalitarian perspectives. Many Christian scholars, especially those who embrace a more conservative feminism,[10] have so exaggerated the allegedly favorable contrasts between Christian and Jewish positions on gender roles that more liberal Christian feminist[11] and Jewish scholars are now rightly protesting that justice has not been done to the positive, pro-women strands within the relevant subgroups of ancient Judaism.[12] Jewish and Christian scholars alike usually agree that the post–A.D. 70 rabbinic literature imposed restrictions on Jewish women that earlier periods did not always require.[13] But at times it would appear that the scholarly pendulum has swung too far in the opposite direction; in an age of commendable ecumenicity, some are reluctant to acknowledge

---

[8]For helpful surveys, see Karen Engelken, *Fraue im Alten Israel* (Stuttgart: Kohlhammer, 1990); Athalya Brenner, *The Israelite Woman: Social Role and Literary Type in Biblical Narrative*, The Biblical Seminar 2 (Sheffield: Sheffield Academic Press, 1994).

[9]See Carol L. Meyers, *Discovering Eve: Ancient Israelite Women in Context* (New York: Oxford Univ. Press, 1988); Léonie J. Archer, *Her Price Is Beyond Rubies: The Jewish Woman in Graeco-Roman Palestine*, Journal for the Study of the Old Testament: Supplement Series 60 (Sheffield: Sheffield Academic Press, 1990); Shulamit Valler, *Women and Womanhood in the Talmud* (Atlanta: Scholars Press, 1999); Jacob Neusner, *How the Rabbis Liberated Women* (Atlanta: Scholars Press, 1998).

[10]Those who accept the historic Christian canon as a binding authority for theology and ethics but think that it promotes egalitarianism pervasively.

[11]Those who do not accept the majority strand of biblical teaching, believing it to promote patriarchy, and focus instead on a minority strand of liberationist teaching—a *de facto* canon within the canon.

[12]A recurring theme throughout Ross S. Kraemer and Mary R. D'Angelo, eds., *Women and Christian Origins* (New York: Oxford Univ. Press, 1999).

[13]Some (for example, Meir Bar-Ilan, *Some Jewish Women in Antiquity* [Atlanta: Scholars Press, 1998]) see a linear deterioration of freedoms for women from the Old Testament to the intertestamental period to the rabbinic era, while others (for example, Leonard Swidler, *Biblical Affirmations of Woman* [Philadelphia: Westminster, 1979], 75–159) think the intertestamental period offered greater freedoms than those available in the eras before and after it.

the genuine differences that did exist between ancient Judaism and emerging Christianity.[14] At any rate, it is difficult to imagine Paul inheriting terribly positive attitudes toward women from a culture that would shortly produce rabbinic debates as to whether women were even persons or merely chattel.[15] And for all of the possible inferences about women in synagogue leadership that Bernadette Brooten has catalogued, there remains a complete absence in both her survey and in the encyclopedic Jewish literature of the Tannaim of women as formal religious teachers or rabbis.[16]

If Paul could not have learned egalitarianism from any extant Jewish source, what about from the Greco-Roman world of his day? Again, there is diversity among the documents. Greek philosophy developed a much more idealized view of the equal personhood of men and women from the minority legacy of the teachings of Socrates and Plato than from the dominant Aristotelian tradition.[17] Roman laws combined significant restrictions with equally important freedoms for women.[18] In some respects, first-century Roman women had greater social opportunities than their Greek counterparts; in other respects, particularly in the domestic arena, Roman women were more oppressed, especially due to the *patria potestas* ("power of a

---

[14]One senses this with several of the chapters in Amy-Jill Levine, ed., *Women Like This: New Perspectives on Jewish Women in the Greco-Roman World* (Atlanta: Scholars Press, 1991); and in Levine, "Second Temple Judaism, Jesus, and Women: Yeast of Eden," *Biblical Interpretation* 2 (1994): 8–33. Contrast this with Tal Ilan's conclusion (*Jewish Women in Greco-Roman Palestine* [Peabody, Mass.: Hendrickson, 1996], 226): "All sources describe the same ideal picture of society: women provide what is asked of them, be it producing legal heirs, doing housework, remaining faithful to their husbands, avoiding contact with other men unrelated to them, or using their beauty to make their husbands' lives more pleasant. Women who deviate from this perfect behavior are described by all the sources as wicked."

[15]See Judith R. Wegner, *Chattel or Person? The Status of Women in the Mishnah* (Oxford: Oxford Univ. Press, 1988).

[16]Bernadette J. Brooten, *Women Leaders in the Ancient Synagogue: Inscriptional Evidence and Background Issues* (Chico, Calif.: Scholars Press, 1982). A random sampling of any portion of the Mishnah or other early rabbinic sources confirms this observation.

[17]Prudence Allen, *The Concept of Woman: The Aristotelian Revolution, 750 B.C.–A.D. 1250* (Grand Rapids: Eerdmans, 1997); Eva Cantarella, *Pandora's Daughters: The Role and Status of Women in Greek and Roman Antiquity* (Baltimore: Johns Hopkins Univ. Press, 1987).

[18]Jane F. Gardner, *Women in Roman Law and Society* (Bloomington, Ind.: Indiana Univ. Press, 1986).

father") that gave husbands almost unlimited authority as heads of their households.[19]

Local variations in practices must also be taken into account. It is interesting, for example, that all of Paul's directives, and even the more positive models of what women in his churches did, occur in particularly Romanized cities in the Hellenistic world.[20] Quite recently, Bruce Winter has begun to call attention to the sexually liberated (that is, promiscuous!) "new Roman women" of more well-to-do first-century Hellenistic circles who possibly formed the backdrop to some of the problems in the Pauline churches that the apostle had to address.[21] And across all of the cultures of antiquity, wealth almost always gave women freedoms that the vast majority of the poorer members of society lacked.[22] Still, once again, no statements about the complete interchangeability of men's and women's roles in either public or private spheres emerge in any of the relevant literature.

Sooner or later, of course, influential teachers break free entirely from their surrounding cultures. Paul was not bound to repeat the social conventions of his era. While many dispute the extent to which he was aware of the life and teachings of Jesus, a credible case can be mounted for Paul's substantial familiarity and continuity with Jesus by the time he began writing his epistles.[23] Perhaps he learned egalitarianism from this countercultural teacher from Nazareth; Jesus has, after all, frequently been viewed as a "proto-feminist."[24] On the other hand, scholarship is increas-

---

[19]Deborah F. Sawyer, *Women and Religion in the First Christian Centuries* (New York: Routledge, 1996); Sarah B. Pomeroy, *Goddesses, Whores, Wives, and Slaves: Women in Classical Antiquity* (New York: Schocken, 1975).

[20]Cotter, "Women's Authority Roles in Paul's Churches," 350–72.

[21]Bruce W. Winter, *New Roman Women and the Pauline Churches* (in preparation); see Winter's article "The 'New' Roman Wife and 1 Timothy 2:9–15: The Search for a *Sitz im Leben*," *Tyndale Bulletin* 51 (2000): 285–94.

[22]For a helpful collection of primary texts illustrating these and other patterns in ancient Greece and Rome, see Mary R. Lefkowitz and Maureen B. Fant, *Women's Life in Greece and Rome: A Source Book in Translation* (Baltimore: Johns Hopkins Univ. Press, 1982).

[23]See David Wenham, *Paul: Follower of Jesus or Founder of Christianity?* (Grand Rapids: Eerdmans, 1995). Cf. Ben Witherington III, *Women in the Ministry of Jesus* (Cambridge: Cambridge Univ. Press, 1984), 128–30.

[24]See especially Elisabeth Schüssler Fiorenza, *Jesus: Miriam's Child, Sophia's Prophet* (New York: Continuum, 1994); Luise Schottroff (*Let the Oppressed Go Free: Feminist Perspectives on the New Testament* [Louisville, Ky.: Westminster John Knox, 1993] and *Lydia's Impatient Sisters: A Feminist Social History of Early Christianity*

ingly reflecting a more restrained assessment of both the historical Jesus and the Gospels' portrait of Jesus. After centuries of playing down the genuinely liberating strands embedded in the Gospels, and after initial liberationist and feminist euphoria about the potential for reconstructing egalitarianism from those same sources,[25] a third, more mediating position is frequently emerging. As Grant Osborne explains, "Jesus did not abrogate the basic 'patriarchal' views of his surrounding culture. He chose twelve men to form an inner core of disciples. Women's place in the home is presented as honorable and part of the divine economy."[26]

To be sure, programmatic countercultural values were discernible as Jesus let Mary of Bethany learn in the manner male disciples would study with their rabbis (Luke 10:38–42) and as he permitted other women to travel with and even financially support his itinerant troupe (Luke 8:1–3). Throughout Jesus' ministry (in his ministries of healing, in his compassion for outcasts, in his teaching on marriage and divorce, in his pairing of male and female illustrations in his teaching, and in his offers of forgiveness of sins), he affirmed the personhood of women and their equal value before God with their male peers. But as Helga Melzer-Keller's careful and detailed study of all three Synoptic evangelists, the Q Source, and the historical Jesus concludes, in every stratum of the Gospel traditions Jesus stopped short of ever making any explicit pronouncements about the equality of men and women (even to the extent Paul does in Galatians 3:28), to say nothing of attempting to overthrow sociocultural conventions on gender roles. Melzer-Keller recognizes that Jesus cannot fairly be co-opted for modern liberationist or egalitarian agendas.[27]

[Louisville, Ky.: Westminster John Knox, 1995]) represents a common feminist trend to see a successive deterioration in pro-women attitudes from the Jesus of the Gospels to the undisputed Pauline Epistles, to Ephesians and Colossians, to the Pastoral Epistles, and finally to the post–New Testament church.

[25]As in Elisabeth Moltmann-Wendell, *The Women Around Jesus* (New York: Crossroad, 1982). Cf. the recent anthology of Ingrid R. Kitzberger, ed., *Transformative Encounters: Jesus and Women Re-viewed* (Leiden: Brill, 2000).

[26]Grant R. Osborne, "Women in Jesus' Ministry," *Westminster Theological Journal* 51 (1989): 259–91.

[27]Helga Melzer-Keller, *Jesus und die Frauen* (Freiburg: Herder, 1997). The same is increasingly proving true of feminist studies of Luke, the evangelist long viewed as most favorable to women. Contrast, for example, Jane Kopas ("Jesus and Women: Luke's Gospel," *Theology Today* 43 [1986]: 192–202) with Mary R. D'Angelo ("Women in Luke–Acts," *Journal of Biblical Literature* 109 [1990]: 441–61).

The final area of historical background that requires brief mention brings us closest to the ministry of Paul himself, namely, the experiences of earliest Christianity to the extent that they can be reconstructed from the book of Acts.[28] Once again there are important countercultural models: the Spirit (and thus his gifts) being poured out equally on all disciples from Pentecost onward (Acts 2:17–21); Sapphira being judged independently of her husband (5:1–11); the ministry and resurrection of Tabitha (9:36–42); Lydia, the first European convert, and her role as head of the (presumably maleless) household (16:11–15); the exorcism of the girl with the Pythian spirit (16:16–18); the well-to-do Thessalonian women who joined Paul's ministry (17:4); the joint ministry of Priscilla and Aquila (18:18–26); and the prophesying by Philip's unmarried daughters (21:9). Yet again, the most recent detailed study of women in Acts concludes that Luke's portrait remains androcentric even while introducing with varying degrees of emphasis important liberating motifs.[29] No text in Acts suggests that all roles in home and church are now open to men and women alike; prophecy was clearly distinguished in the ancient world from teaching,[30] and we actually know precious little about what Priscilla did, except for one occasion in which she joined with her husband in instructing Apollos in a context that suggests an informal, private encounter ("they invited him to their home," with no indication of anyone else being present, 18:26).[31]

There is increasing agreement, therefore, that neither the Gospels nor the book of Acts can prove decisive in answering the question of whether the first generation of Christians in general

---

[28]The substantial historicity of Acts has now been rehabilitated in the massive study by Colin J. Hemer (*The Book of Acts in the Setting of Hellenistic History*, ed. Conrad H. Gempf [Tübingen: Mohr, 1989]) and supported in the five-volume series edited by Bruce W. Winter and Andrew D. Clarke (*The Book of Acts in Its First Century Setting* [Grand Rapids: Eerdmans, 1993–96]). For a balanced treatment that desires to point out both the continuities and discontinuities between Luke's portrait of the apostle and the picture that emerges from his epistles, with a special focus on the speeches of Paul in Acts, see Stanley E. Porter, *The Paul of Acts* (Tübingen: Mohr, 1999).

[29]Ivoni R. Reimer, *Women in the Acts of the Apostles: A Feminist Liberation Perspective* (Minneapolis: Fortress, 1995).

[30]See especially Sigountos and Shank, "Public Roles for Women," 283–95.

[31]See Wendell Willis, "Priscilla and Aquila—Co-Workers in Christ," in *Essays on Women in Earliest Christianity*, ed. Carroll D. Osburn (Joplin, Mo.: College Press, 1993–95), 2:261–76.

or Paul in particular reserved any leadership roles for men. For that one must turn to Paul's writings themselves. It is possible that Paul became the first in his world to articulate a thoroughgoing egalitarianism, but if he did it will have to have been presented very clearly and unambiguously for it to have been recognized in a combination of cultures that were all far more traditional.[32]

DATA FROM PAUL'S EPISTLES

Descriptive Material

Methodologically, one should not treat Paul's didactic passages on gender roles in isolation from merely descriptive material. What did women actually do in the Pauline mission—actions for which Paul was grateful? Andreas Köstenberger has recently analyzed every reference to a named woman in the Pauline Epistles and comes to well-balanced conclusions.[33] In fact, he reflects a growing consensus across the theological divide with respect to the nature of Paul's coworkers. The references to Phoebe in Romans 16:1–2 suggest that she was a deacon (*diakonos*) and a patron (*prostatis*). We know that the office of deaconess existed for the first several centuries of church history (even before the separate feminine noun was utilized in the Greek language),[34] and Paul's calling her a deacon "of the church which is in Cenchreae"[35] suggests a fairly formal role. That *prostatis* means neither simply a "helper" nor anything as formal as a "church leader," but rather one who financially supported Paul's mission also now finds widespread acceptance.[36]

---

[32]Similarly Ernest Best (*A Critical and Exegetical Commentary on Ephesians* [Edinburgh: T&T Clark, 1998], 535), with respect to Ephesians 5:21–33.

[33]Andreas Köstenberger, "Women in the Pauline Mission," in *The Gospel to the Nations: Perspectives on Paul's Mission*, eds. Peter G. Bolt and Mark Thompson (Downers Grove, Ill.: InterVarsity Press, 2000), 221–47.

[34]See Anne Jensen, *God's Self-Confident Daughters: Early Christianity and the Liberation of Women* (Louisville, Ky.: Westminster John Knox, 1996), 59–73; Stephen Clark, *Man and Woman in Christ* (Ann Arbor, Mich.: Servant, 1980), 117–23.

[35]Unless otherwise indicated, all translations of Scripture are my own.

[36]On both points, see Caroline F. Whelan, "*Amica Pauli*: The Role of Phoebe in the Early Church," *Journal for the Study of the New Testament* 49 (1993): 67–85; Bruce W. Winter, *After Paul Left Corinth* (Grand Rapids: Eerdmans, 2001), 199–203. Over against Kazimierz Romaniuk, "Was Phoebe in Romans 16:1 a Deaconess?" *Zeitschrift für die neutestamentliche Wissenschaft* 81 (1990): 132–34.

The evidence is even more overwhelming that the person paired with Andronicus in Romans 16:7 is a woman—Junia— who is quite possibly his wife, and that both are considered to be apostles. On the other hand, this is clearly one of Paul's uses of "apostle" more akin to the gift listed among the charismata of 1 Corinthians 12:28 or Ephesians 4:11 than to the apostolate of the Twelve. In short, it refers to missionary service, in keeping with the primary Greek meaning of *apostolos* as "someone sent on a mission."[37] Apart from Phoebe and Junia, however, no other women are mentioned in Paul's letters with terminology that naturally suggests any leadership roles. One reads only of *synergois* ("coworkers," Rom. 16:3; Phil. 4:3; a term Paul can use of himself, Timothy, and God [1 Cor. 3:9; 1 Thess. 3:2], the three of whom are obviously not of identical status) and of others who labored very hard in Christian activity (Rom. 16:6, 12) or who hosted churches in their homes (1 Cor. 16:19; Col. 4:15; Philem. 2). It is certainly significant that out of the thirty-five people named in Romans 16, Paul alludes to no less than eleven women. But attempts to link female names besides Phoebe and Junia in Paul's letters with identifiable leadership roles simply outrun the data considerably.

What emerges from this brief survey proves strikingly parallel to Brooten's catalogue of occasional references to female synagogue leaders—exceptional women playing significant roles who still remain in a small minority (19 out of 107 names in the letters attributed to Paul)[38]—but no examples of women in the position of the ongoing authoritative teaching of God's word. When one adds unnamed women into one's purview, one must note that 1 Timothy 5:2 addresses *presbyteras*, which could theoretically be translated "women elders." But in the context Paul is contrasting the responsibilities of Timothy toward older and younger men and older and younger women. A partially parallel passage in Titus 2:3 uses the unambiguous term *presbytidas* for "older women," at which point the case for women elders in 1 Timothy evaporates altogether.

---

[37]See John Thorley, "Junia, A Woman Apostle?" *Novum Testamentum* 38 (1996): 18–21; Richard S. Cervin, "A Note Regarding the Name 'Junia(s)' in Romans 16.7" *New Testament Studies* 40 (1994): 464–70.

[38]Köstenberger, "Women in the Pauline Mission," 224.

Foundational Theological Principles

It is also appropriate to observe the larger theological framework into which Paul's extended teaching passages on gender roles fit. Clearly freedom in Christ is a major theme (see especially 1 Cor. 8:1–11:1), as is the newness (new creation) that Christian conversion brings (see especially 2 Cor. 5:11–21). In 1 Corinthians 12:11 Paul stresses that God's Spirit gives believers gifts as he determines, and there is no indication that any of the charismata are gender-specific (in light of Acts 2:17–21 quite the opposite is almost certainly the case). Thus, room must be made for Christian women to exercise such spiritual gifts as apostleship, prophesying, teaching, pastoring, and so on. But none of these necessarily requires a formal leadership office for its use, and conspicuously absent from all of Paul's lists of gifts is anything corresponding to the elder/overseer. Chapter 7 of Paul's first letter to the Corinthians includes a series of statements that make it clear Paul treats husbands and wives equally with respect to their rights to marry (7:2, 28, 33–34), to engage in sexual intercourse within marriage (7:3–5), and to divorce or stay married (7:10–13, 15–16). But nothing in this chapter answers the question of whether Paul envisioned distinct roles for husbands and wives within marriage at any point.

Pride of place in setting the broader theological framework for Paul's teaching on gender roles must, however, be given to Galatians 3:28: "There is neither Jew nor Greek, there is neither slave nor free, there is no male and female. For you all are one in Christ Jesus."[39] Perhaps nowhere else in Scripture does it become as clear as it does here how regularly commentators line up according to theological predispositions without truly exegeting the text!

On the one hand, as Ben Witherington stressed almost two decades ago, the baptismal context (Gal. 3:27) suggests considerably more than the simple equality of all persons in God's eyes with respect to access to salvation (on which all parties today agree). In their emphasis on baptism as an initiatory rite replacing circumcision, Christians were making a public, socially inclusive statement that contrasted sharply with their Jewish

---

[39]With appropriate nuancing, see Stanley J. Grenz with Denise M. Kjesbo, *Women in the Church: A Biblical Theology of Women in Ministry* (Downers Grove, Ill.: InterVarsity Press, 1995), 99–107.

forebears.[40] To the extent that baptism no longer automatically communicates that contrast in contemporary cultures, believers seeking to emulate Paul should find other important, regular, visible, and public forms of affirming the full ontological equality of men and women in Christ, a point missed by almost all of the contemporary hierarchicalist literature.

On the other hand, nothing in Galatians 3:28 demonstrates that Paul was thinking in terms of abolishing all role differentiation among men and women. The word *eis* ("one") does not obviously mean "equal in all respects" in any of its 344 other New Testament usages; "equal" is not even a definition found in the standard lexicons.[41] Equality may be suggested by certain contexts, but at this point another of Witherington's largely neglected observations comes into play. Later rabbinic sources could articulate propositions strikingly parallel to Galatians 3:28 (see especially *Seder Eliyahu Rabbah 7; Yalkut Lech Leka 76*) in the midst of literature that was far more chauvinistic than anything in the New Testament, even by typical hierarchicalist interpretations.[42] So the only way to determine Paul's views on specific questions like gender roles in home and church is to turn to passages that explicitly address them. They cannot be inferred one way or the other from Galatians 3:28.[43]

---

[40]Ben Witherington III, "Rite and Rights for Women—Galatians 3.28," *New Testament Studies* 27 (1981): 601. Cf. Wilhelm Egger, *Galaterbrief, Philipperbrief, Philemonbrief* (Würzburg: Echter, 1985), 29.

[41]Richard W. Hove, *Equality in Christ? Galatians 3:28 and the Gender Dispute* (Wheaton, Ill.: Crossway, 1999), 69–76, 107–21.

[42]Witherington, "Right and Rites for Women," *New Testament Studies* 27 (1981): 593–94.

[43]An interesting sidelight of Galatians 3:28 is the terminology "no male and female"—almost certainly an allusion to the Septuagint's wording of Genesis 1:27 on God creating humanity "male and female." This has led some expositors to propose that Paul (or some other wing of early Christianity that he cites) was promoting androgyny. See Dennis R. MacDonald, *There Is No Male and Female* (Philadelphia: Fortress, 1987). For a succinct refutation of this proposal, see E. Earle Ellis, *Pauline Theology: Ministry and Society* (Grand Rapids: Eerdmans, 1989), 82–85. More probable is the suggestion of J. Louis Martyn (*Galatians* [New York: Doubleday, 1997], 381), who thinks Paul is declaring that the answer to loneliness is no longer marriage but the "new-creational community" in Christ. See also Ben Witherington III (*Women in the Earliest Churches* [Cambridge: Cambridge Univ. Press, 1988], 125): "Galatians 3.28 was probably a dictum serving the same function for women in Paul's audience as Matthew 19.10–12 did for Jesus, i.e., allowing women to remain single for the Lord, a condition Paul clearly prefers (1 Cor. 7). As such it opened the possibility of women being involved in roles other than the traditional ones of wife and mother."

Didactic Material on Gender Roles
1 Corinthians 11:2–16

Chronologically, the first of Paul's more specifically didactic passages on gender roles appears in his first letter to the church in Corinth. The utter lack of manuscript support for any missing or dislocated verses in this passage renders the interpolation hypothesis a counsel of despair.[44] Only slightly less improbable is the view that 1 Corinthians 11:3–7 (or 3–10) articulate a Corinthian slogan, which verses 11–16 rebut.[45] There is nothing slogan-like about these unwieldy statements, and verses 13–16 further support the position of verses 3–10.[46] It is also widely agreed that, as with all of 11:2–14:40, Paul is referring to a Christian worship setting.[47]

Beyond a general consensus on these three points, almost every clause in the passage is debated. Antoinette Wire's reconstruction of the situation that generated Paul's correctives has, however, gained a fair measure of acceptance and remains plausible. Some Christian women (and maybe some men!) were interpreting their freedom in Christ to mean that they could flout social convention concerning public appearance with no adverse effects on the community.[48] Paul thus praises the Corinthians for

---

[44]As defended by a handful of exegetes; see especially William O. Walker Jr., "The Vocabulary of 1 Corinthians 11.3–16: Pauline or Non-Pauline," *Journal for the Study of the New Testament* 35 (1989): 75–88. Even more idiosyncratic is the suggestion of Hans-Friedemann Richter ("Anstössige Freiheit in Korinth: Zur Literarkritik der Korintherbriefe [1 Kor 8,1–13 und 11,2–16]," in *The Corinthian Correspondence,* ed. R. Bieringer [Leuven: Leuven Univ. Press, 1996], 561–75) that 1 Corinthians 11:2–22, 27–34 forms one of ten separate letters Paul wrote to the Corinthians!

[45]See Thomas P. Shoemaker, "Unveiling of Equality: 1 Corinthians 11:2–16," *Biblical Theology Bulletin* 17 (1987): 60–63.

[46]Over against the improbable interpretation of Thomas Schirrmacher (*Paulus im Kampf gegen den Schleier* [Bonn: Verlag für Kultur und Wissenschaft, 1993]) that 1 Corinthians 11:14–15 together should be punctuated as an ironic exclamation: "Not even nature itself teaches ...!"

[47]Over against Harold R. Holmyard III, "Does 1 Corinthians 11:2–16 Refer to Women Praying and Prophesying in Church?" *Bibliotheca Sacra* 154 (1997): 461–72.

[48]Antoinette Wire, *The Corinthian Women Prophets* (Minneapolis: Fortress, 1990). On the men, see David W. J. Gill, "The Importance of Roman Portraiture for Head Coverings in 1 Corinthians 11:2–16," *Tyndale Bulletin* 41 (1990): 245–60. August Strobel (*Der erste Brief an die Korinther* [Zurich: Theologischer, 1989], 165), however, thinks that 1 Corinthians 11:4–5 was not necessarily provoked by any specific situation in Corinth, much less a crisis in the church, but represented an issue Paul would have frequently encountered.

recognizing the essentially liberating message of the gospel—part of his Christian traditions that he passed on to them (1 Cor. 11:2)—but he cannot continue to allow their current behavior during worship.[49]

The specific problem is what men and women are or are not wearing on their heads (1 Cor. 11:4–5). So to introduce his instruction further, Paul articulates a foundational principle about metaphorical headship: "Now I want you to know that Christ is the head of every man but the man is a head of a woman and God is head over Christ" (11:3). Here one becomes entangled in the controversy over the meaning of *kephalē* ("head"). After earlier allegations that the word virtually never meant "authority" or absolutely never meant "source,"[50] it is increasingly agreed that both usages do occur in the relevant cognate Greek literature, but both are rare.[51] What has not been demonstrated, however, is that the singular *kephalē* (as opposed to the plural that can mean the source[s] of a river) ever means "source" or "origin" without simultaneously implying some dimension of authority.[52] So the statements about men's and women's origins in verses 8–9 and 11–12 in no way preclude a sense of authority residing in this word for "head." Egalitarians have frequently misrepresented Stephen Bedale's influential article by selective quotation as if he argued for "source"

[49]Gail P. Corrington, "The 'Headless Woman': Paul and the Language of the Body in 1 Corinthians 11:2–16," *Perspectives in Religious Studies* 18 (1991): 223–31. The further assumption, as in L. Ann Jervis ("'But I Want You to Know . . . .': Paul's Midrashic Intertextual Response to the Corinthian Worshipers [1 Corinthians 11:2–16]," *Journal of Biblical Literature* 112 [1993]: 231–46), that the women were promoting genderlessness is too specific to demonstrate, given the current state of the evidence.

[50]See, respectively, Wayne Grudem, "Does *Kephalē* ('Head') Mean 'Source' or 'Authority Over' in Greek Literature? A Survey of 2,336 Examples," *Trinity Journal* 6 (1985): 38–59; Berkeley Mickelsen and Alvera Mickelsen, "What Does *Kephalē* Mean in the New Testament?" in *Women, Authority and the Bible*, ed. Alvera Mickelsen (Downers Grove, Ill.: InterVarsity Press, 1986), 97–110.

[51]Authors defending "authority" draw especially on the Septuagint, Philo, and Plutarch; those favoring "source" draw on Philo (again), Herodotus, Artemidorus, the Orphic literature, and the Life of Adam. See Andrianjatovo Rakotoharintsifa, *Conflits à Corinthe* (Genève: Labor et Fides, 1997), 208.

[52]See the more nuanced discussion in Wayne Grudem, "The Meaning of *Kephalē* ('Head'): A Response to Recent Studies," in *Recovering Biblical Manhood and Womanhood*, eds. John Piper and Wayne Grudem (Wheaton, Ill.: Crossway, 1991), 425–68. See also Joseph A. Fitzmyer, "Another Look at *kephalē* in 1 Corinthians 11.3," *New Testament Studies* 35 (1989): 503–11; and Fitzmyer, "*Kephalē* in 1 Corinthians 11.3," *Interpretation* 47 (1993): 52–59.

apart from "authority"; in his conclusion he explains that "the male is *kephalē* in the sense of *archē* (beginning) relative to the female; and, in St. Paul's view, the female in consequence is 'subordinate' (cf. Eph. v. 23)."[53] It is also clearly appropriate to speak of Christ as an authority over men and of God as an authority over Christ (1 Cor. 15:28),[54] though again "source" fits in each of these instances too (as long as one does not lapse into Arianism, whereby God is viewed as the source of a Son who at one time did not exist).

Several recent writers have proposed intermediate solutions that translate *kephalē* as "preeminent" or "prominent"—and perhaps therefore "representative,"[55] but it is unclear if an entity can be most or even more prominent without implying some functional superiority, at least in a context in which the terms are used of God's and Christ's headships.[56] As for the unusual order of pairings, thought by some egalitarians to weigh against a hierarchicalist interpretation of the verse, it is more probable that Paul begins with the "head of the man" followed by the "head of the woman" because it is men's and women's misbehavior that triggers his teaching in the first place. This then allows his statement about the "head of Christ" to appear in the climactic final position of the verse. It is also worth noting that it is possible to take *anēr* and *gynē* in verse 3 as "husband" and "wife" (as in the

---

[53]Stephen Bedale, "The Meaning of *Kephalē* in the Pauline Epistles," *Journal of Theological Studies* 5 (1954): 214. See also Elisabeth Schüssler Fiorenza (*In Memory of Her: A Feminist Theological Reconstruction of Christian Origins* [New York: Crossroad, 1983], 229), who explains Paul's perspective as "a descending hierarchy, God—Christ—Man—Woman, in which each preceding member as 'head' or 'source,' stands above the other 'in the sense that he established the other's being.'"

[54]A passage that has not been adequately explained by those who want to deny functional subordination of Christ to the Father throughout all eternity, as Victor Hasler ("Die Gleichstellung der Gatlin: Situationskritische Reflexionen zu 1 Kor 11, 2–16," *Theologische Zeitschrift* 50 [1994]: 189–200) also points out, rightly stressing *kephalē* as "authority" in a context here, and throughout Paul's writings, of honor and status.

[55]Walter L. Liefeld, "Women, Submission and Ministry in 1 Corinthians," in *Women, Authority and the Bible*, 134–54; Andrew C. Perriman, "The Head of a Woman: The Meaning of *Kephalē* in 1 Corinthians 11:3," *Journal of Theological Studies* 45 (1994): 602–22; Richard S. Cervin, "Does *Kephalē* Mean 'Source' or 'Authority Over' in Greek Literature? A Rebuttal," *Trinity Journal* 10 (1989): 85–112. W. Bauer, F. W. Danker, W. F. Arndt, and F. W. Gingrich, *A Greek English Lexicon of the New Testament and Other Early Christian Literature*, 3d ed., s.v. "*kephalē*," suggests "a being of high status."

[56]As Perriman ("The Head of a Woman," 616) himself concedes is true "in many instances."

NRSV),[57] an ambiguity that will recur in 1 Corinthians 14 and 1 Timothy 2 as well.

Paul proceeds to mandate that these men and women in church should use their literal heads properly to honor their metaphorical heads (1 Cor. 11:4–6). The debate continues as to whether Paul has long and short hair in view, as he does unequivocally in verses 13–16, or if he is referring to the presence and absence of an external covering. Several recent studies, however, offer increasing support to the otherwise minority position that favors hair as in view throughout the whole passage (as in the NIV text note), an approach that gives Paul's argument tighter coherence.[58] Numerous contexts in both the Jewish and Greco-Roman worlds vie as explanations for why such coverings, whether external or intrinsic, would have mattered, but all share one common feature: The Christian worshipers would have been sending misleading signals suggesting sexual or religious infidelity.[59]

In the midst of these primary concerns, the additional implications of 1 Corinthians 11:5 dare not be missed: Paul assumes women will continue to pray and prophesy. And despite several attempts to limit prophecy in early Christian circles (or in the ancient Mediterranean world more generally) to spontaneous "inspired" utterances,[60] it seems clear that the term

---

[57]Especially since no one bothered with the head coverings or hairstyles of unmarried girls. See Jason D. BeDuhn ("'Because of the Angels': Unveiling Paul's Anthropology in 1 Corinthians 11," *Journal of Biblical Literature* 118 [1999]: 300–301), who thinks Paul then begins to generalize to all men and women in 1 Corinthians 11:7–9.

[58]See Marlis Gielen, "Beten und Prophezien mit unverhülltem Kopf?" *Zeitschrift für die neutestamentliche Wissenschaft* 90 (1999): 220–49; David E. Blattenberger, *Rethinking 1 Corinthians 11:2–16 through Archaeological and Moral-Rhetorical Analysis* (Lewiston, N.Y.: Mellen, 1997); Alan Padgett, "The Significance of *anti* in 1 Corinthians 11:15," *Tyndale Bulletin* 45 (1994): 181–87.

[59]See my commentary (*1 Corinthians*, 210–11, 215) for the various options and representative advocates. More recently, see the collection of primary quotations in Raymond S. Collins, *First Corinthians* (Collegeville, Minn.: Liturgical Press, 1999), 397–401. Curiously, Bruce Winter (*After Paul Left Corinth*, 121–41) opts for a veil without even discussing the alternatives, despite the fact that the Greek word for "veil" (*kalymma*) appears nowhere in the text (except in a few very late manuscripts in 1 Cor. 11:10).

[60]See David E. Aune, *Prophecy in Early Christianity and the Ancient Mediterranean World* (Grand Rapids: Eerdmans, 1983), 338; Christopher Forbes, *Prophecy and Inspired Speech in Early Christianity and Its Hellenistic Environment* (Tübingen: Mohr, 1995), 218–21; Ben Witherington III, *Jesus the Seer: The Progress of Prophecy* (Peabody, Mass.: Hendrickson, 1999), 321.

was used for a whole range of messages believed to be from God, including those into which previous thought and preparation had been given.[61] Paul is therefore tacitly granting women permission to preach God's word, so long as they do so under proper male authority. One must distinguish between the gift of prophecy, which could be exercised in the delivery of a sermon, and the ongoing office or more established role of overseer/elder (see also below, under 1 Timothy 2:8–15).

With its lack of symmetry between the two halves of the verse, 1 Corinthians 11:7 supports the interpretation that Paul is setting up a hierarchy of authority: Only man is the glory of God, while woman is the glory of man. The other asymmetrical feature (man is called "the image of God," but woman is not "the image of man") remains precisely to guard against the assumption of some interpreters that Paul thought women were not equally created in God's image.[62] Paul clearly knew Genesis (1:26–28) better than that!

Paul then goes on to ground his injunction in what have come to be called creation ordinances (1 Cor. 11:8–9).[63] He makes two observations that are asymmetrical: The woman was created out of the man, not vice versa, and the woman was created for the man, not vice versa. It is important to note carefully just what this theology of creation is supporting—not the presence or absence of head coverings, but the relationships of honor and glory described in verse 7, the immediate antecedent to verses 8–9. It is difficult to escape the conclusion that Paul is promoting some timeless relationship of authority and subordination here.

In 1 Corinthians 11:10 Paul further grounds his commands in the fact that angels are present. Despite the great consternation

---

[61]See David Hill, *New Testament Prophecy* (London: Marshall, Morgan & Scott, 1979), 213; Thomas W. Gillespie, *The First Theologians: A Study in Early Christian Prophecy* (Grand Rapids: Eerdmans, 1994), 23–28; Anthony C. Thiselton, *The First Epistle to the Corinthians* (Grand Rapids: Eerdmans, 2000), 960–61.

[62]As, for example, Jouette M. Bassler ("1 Corinthians," in *The Women's Bible Commentary*, eds. Carol A. Newsom and Sharon H. Ringe [Louisville, Ky.: Westminster John Knox, 1992], 326–27) alleges. Rakotoharintsifa (*Conflits à Corinthe*, 219–20) stresses that the notion that the man is not fully honored without the woman's glory also guards against the view that does not ascribe equal dignity to the woman.

[63]On Paul's specific uses of Genesis 1 and 2 here, see Jervis ("But I Want You to Know . . . ," 231–46), even though her egalitarian conclusions differ from those defended here.

this verse has caused commentators, as well as the numerous suggestions that have been proposed, it is hard to improve on Joseph Fitzmyer's treatment in the wake of the Qumran discoveries a half century ago. In much of ancient Jewish thought, angels watch over creation and protect the worship of God's people, and thus they would have a vested interest in seeing Christian services conducted with decorum.[64]

More relevant to the gender-roles debate is the meaning of *exousian echein epi* in 1 Corinthians 11:10. On the one hand, the NIV gratuitously adds "sign of" to the "authority" that the woman should have on her head. On the other hand, ever since Morna Hooker's influential article in the 1960s, many have assumed that Paul was here explicitly granting authority to the woman to pray and prophesy, when appropriately covered.[65] But every other use of this three-word expression in the New Testament means "to have authority (or control) over" (Matt. 9:6 [parallels in Mark 2:10; Luke 5:24]; Rev. 11:6; 14:18; 16:9; 20:6), as do similar constructions with synonyms for *epi* (Luke 19:17; 1 Cor. 7:37) or without forms of the verb "to have" (Luke 9:1; Rev. 2:26; 6:8; 13:7). This suggests a translation more along the lines of "For this reason . . . a woman should exercise control over her head [that is, keep the appropriate covering on it]."[66]

In 1 Corinthians 11:11–12, Paul introduces an important qualification to his theological argument from creation found in verses 8–9. In Christ—in the sphere of God's redemptive activity—men and women are mutually interdependent. But as in Galatians 3:28, Paul stops short of saying anything that can fairly be construed as excluding all role differentiation. What's

[64]Joseph A. Fitzmyer, "A Feature of Qumran: Angelology and the Angels of 1 Corinthians xi.10," *New Testament Studies* 4 (1957): 48–58. BeDuhn ("Because of the Angels," 308) has recently given this approach an interesting twist, suggesting that Paul is responding to a gnostic-like view that angels caused the original separation of man and woman. Winter (*After Paul Left Corinth*, 136–38) resurrects the idea of the *angeloi* as human "messengers"—that is, as potential informants to the Roman authorities.

[65]Morna D. Hooker, "Authority on Her Head: An Examination of 1 Corinthians xi.10," *New Testament Studies* 10 (1966): 410–16.

[66]Similarly Jerome Murphy-O'Connor, "1 Corinthians 11:2–16 Once Again," *Catholic Biblical Quarterly* 50 (1988): 271; Collins, *First Corinthians*, 411; BeDuhn, "Because of the Angels," 302–303. Over against Linda L. Belleville, *Women Leaders and the Church: Three Crucial Questions* (Grand Rapids: Baker, 2000), 130; 196, note 3.

more, verses 8–9 would be pointless if verses 11–12 entirely canceled them out, as many egalitarians imply.[67] Rather, Paul can appeal "to creation to support instructions which presume a hierarchicalist relationship of man and woman as well as undergird their new social equality in Christ without denying their difference."[68]

Finally, Paul returns in 1 Corinthians 11:13 to the specific topic of head coverings, this time unambiguously referring to long and short hair, but now using three specific culture-bound arguments: what is fitting (*prepon*) in verse 13, the ordering of how things are (*physis*) in verse 14,[69] and current universal Christian custom (*synētheia*) in verse 16. There is little disagreement that the key words in verses 13 and 16 suggest less than a once-for-all-time mandate. *Physis*, on the other hand, in every one of its nine other Pauline usages, probably means "the way God created things" or "that which inheres in the essence of an entity." Still, the word in Hellenistic Greek often meant simply "the regular or established order of things."[70] Its other three New Testament uses are quite different (James 3:7 [2x]; 2 Peter 1:4), and Paul would have known of Jewish Nazirites, Pentateuchal legislation against cutting one's hair (Lev. 19:22), and Spartans whose long hair was their glory. Moreover, the "natural" thing for hair to do is to grow long if it is not cut![71] So it seems best to acknowledge that Paul is using "nature" here in a different sense than he does elsewhere. In sum, he does not require the presence or absence of head coverings as a timeless mandate, but he does see male headship, at least within marriage and perhaps more broadly, as defining a timeless authority structure that the Corinthians' current practices in their culture called into question.[72]

---

[67]See C. H. Talbert, *Reading Corinthians* (New York: Crossroad, 1987), 70.

[68]Judith Gundry-Volf, "Gender and Creation in 1 Corinthians 11:2–16: A Study in Paul's Theological Method," in *Evangelium, Schriftauslegung, Kirche*, eds. J. Ådna, S. J. Hafemann, and O. Hofius (Göttingen: Vandenhoeck & Ruprecht, 1997), 152— quoted in Thiselton, *The First Epistle to the Corinthians*, 811.

[69]Thiselton, *The First Epistle to the Corinthians*, 844–46.

[70]Bauer, Danker, Arndt, and Gingrich (*A Greek English Lexicon*, s.v. "*physis*") include 1 Corinthians 11:14 under this definition.

[71]Yeo Khiok-Khng, "Differentiation and Mutuality of Male-Female Relations in 1 Corinthians 11:2–16," *Biblical Research* 43 (1998): 20.

[72]See my commentary *1 Corinthians*, 207–26.

1 Corinthians 14:33b–38

Three chapters later in the same epistle Paul again addresses gender roles in the Corinthian church. Because of the sequence of the two passages, Paul's meaning in 1 Corinthians 11:2–16 should influence interpretation here, not vice versa. Whatever Paul means in silencing the women cannot be a timeless absolute for all kinds of speech in church, since he has already permitted them to pray and preach.[73] As in the previous passage some interpreters suggest a non-Pauline interpolation to account for the seemingly contrary nature of this text.[74] In this instance, there is at least manuscript evidence of textual displacement, primarily in the Western family of texts (see D F G it[ar, b, d, f, g] vg[ms] Ambrosiaster Sedulius-Scotus), in which 1 Corinthians 14:34–35 are placed after verse 40. This ordering is not likely to be original, since verses 34–35 seem intrusive in their conventional location, interrupting a discussion of tongues and prophecy in verses 26–33 and verses 39–40. But the claim has been advanced that if Paul's autograph lacked these verses altogether, this could also explain their insertion into two different places in 1 Corinthians 14.

Philip B. Payne has thus argued that the sixth-century Latin Codex Fuldensis furnishes evidence for a textual tradition lacking 1 Corinthians 14:34–35 because, in addition to containing them in their normal sequence, it reproduces verses 36–40 in smaller handwriting in the bottom margin of the text and uses a "bar-umlaut" in the left-hand margin at the beginning of verse 34. Payne suggests that bar-umlauts consistently indicate textual variants of addition or omission in Codex Vaticanus (B) and therefore that the scribe creating Fuldensis was indicating that he knew of a version of 1 Corinthians that lacked verses 34–35 altogether.[75] Curt Niccum, however, has pointed out that the short horizontal bar and the umlaut that appear in the left-hand

---

[73]Over against those who see the two passages as flatly contradictory and thus dismiss one or more as secondary; see, for example, Wolfgang Schrage, *Der erste Brief an die Korinther* (Zürich: Benziger; Neukirchen-Vluyn: Neukirchener, 1991-95), 3:479–92.

[74]See Gordon D. Fee, *The First Epistle to the Corinthians* (Grand Rapids: Eerdmans, 1987), 699–708; Winsome Munro, "Women, Text and the Canon: The Strange Case of 1 Corinthians 14:33–35," *Biblical Theology Bulletin* 18 (1988): 26–31.

[75]Philip B. Payne, "Fuldensis, Sigla for Variants in Vaticanus, and 1 Corinthians 14.34-5," *New Testament Studies* 41 (1995): 240–62.

margins of Fuldensis before verse 34 are separate, unrelated sigla. The bars continue in the sixteenth-century additions to Vaticanus and merely indicate paragraph divisions. Only umlauts indicate textual variants, of all kinds, with the result that it is far more probable that Fuldensis was merely showing that it knew of the less common order—namely, verses 1–33, 36–40, 34–35.[76]

Undaunted, Payne subsequently turned to the twelfth-century Greek minuscule 88, which follows the less common sequence and also contains a "double slash" in the manuscript before and after 1 Corinthians 14:36–40. Payne again proposes that this indicates that the scribe knew of a textual tradition that lacked verses 34–35, even while conceding that in principle the double slashes could just as easily mean the scribe simply knew of the traditional sequence of all the verses.[77] In the absence of any single manuscript actually lacking these verses, this latter explanation becomes far more probable. It seems difficult to avoid the conclusion that some scholars are so committed to finding proof for their theories that they will twist the evidence in whatever direction is necessary to generate apparent support!

As with 1 Corinthians 11:2–16, some scholars have suggested that 1 Corinthians 14:34–35 reflect a Corinthian slogan, a theory that Paul rebuts in verses 36–37. After a flurry of support for this proposal in the 1980s, it largely and properly fell into disuse.[78] Again, such a theory would require this particular slogan to be far more lengthy and cumbersome than any others known from either 1 Corinthians or cognate literature. It would require the proponents of the slogan to be from a conservative, law-abiding wing of the church (for which we have no other solid evidence) rather than from the licentious faction that accounts for every other slogan. And it would demand taking $\bar{e}$ in verse 36 as a complete negation—an otherwise entirely unparalleled meaning of the word.[79]

---

[76]Curt Niccum, "The Voice of the Manuscripts on the Silence of Women: The External Evidence for 1 Corinthians 14.34–5," *New Testament Studies* 43 (1997): 242–55.

[77]Philip B. Payne, "MS. 88 as Evidence for a Text without 1 Corinthians 14.34–5," *New Testament Studies* 44 (1988): 152–58.

[78]Two recent exceptions are Collins, *First Corinthians*, 514–17; and J. M. Holmes, *Text in a Whirlwind: A Critique of Four Exegetical Devices at 1 Timothy 2.9–15* (Sheffield: Sheffield Academic Press, 2000), 229–38.

[79]See my commentary *1 Corinthians*, 280.

The two most probable explanations of 1 Corinthians 14:34–35, therefore, both acknowledge verses 34 and 35 as an integral part of what Paul himself both wrote and supported. Among hierarchicalists, the most popular of these two approaches is to see the "speaking" that Paul prohibits as limited to the evaluation of prophecy.[80] Verses 26–33a discuss tongues and their interpretation, as well as prophecy and its evaluation, in that order. But the first three of these forms of speech reflect spiritual gifts given irrespective of gender. The evaluation of prophecy, on the other hand (to be distinguished from the gift of discerning spirits),[81] is at one level the responsibility of the entire congregation (verse 29), but in instances of disagreement it would have devolved to the leaders of the congregation, that is, to the elders or overseers, who were most likely men.[82] Given that the verb *laleō* ("to speak") in twenty of its twenty-one other occurrences in this chapter refers to one of these more limited forms of charismatic speech or its evaluation, this approach gains a particular plausibility.

The other common option, particularly among egalitarians, is to understand the largely uneducated women in the Corinthian church as asking disruptive questions, probably because they required so much or such basic foundational instruction that the flow of teaching and worship would be destroyed.[83] There is evidence from the practice of Greco-Roman philosophers for students to be encouraged to interrupt with questions (see Plutarch, *On Lectures*), so such a reconstruction

---

[80]See, for example, Simon J. Kistemaker, *Exposition of the First Epistle to the Corinthians* (Grand Rapids: Baker, 1993), 511–15; D. A. Carson, "'Silent in the Churches': On the Role of Women in 1 Corinthians 14:33b–36," in *Recovering Biblical Manhood and Womanhood*, 140–53. Holmes (*Text in a Whirlwind*, 221) perceives that this is the most common interpretation among those who reject the interpolation theory.

[81]Wayne A. Grudem, *The Gift of Prophecy in 1 Corinthians* (Lanham, Md.: University Press of America, 1982), 58–67.

[82]Based on a combination of the evidence of Acts 14:23 that Paul and Barnabas appointed elders wherever they planted churches with Paul's greeting in Philippians 1:1 that points to overseers and deacons as to the two leadership offices in those churches, as well as with the observations made above about no mention of women elders and overseers in the Pauline churches. Chapters 2 and 3 of 1 Timothy reinforce this supposition.

[83]See, in various forms, Keener, *Paul, Women and Wives*, 80–88; Belleville, *Women Leaders and the Church*, 152–62; L. Ann Jervis, "1 Corinthians 14.34–35: A Reconsideration of Paul's Limitation of the Free Speech of Some Corinthian Women," *Journal for the Study of the New Testament* 58 (1995): 51–74.

seems credible. What is incredible, on this supposition, is Paul's response. Since there would also have been a large number of uneducated men and at least a few well-trained women, it seems "unbearably sexist" for Paul to have silenced all of the women and none of the men in this setting.[84] Anthony Thiselton, however, proposes a credible combination of these last two explanations—namely, that the women were asking disruptive questions as part of the evaluation of prophecy.[85] Not least because this could have led to wives contradicting their husbands, including husbands' prophecies, Paul must instruct them to refrain from this one specific kind of speech.[86]

Paul's point again, therefore, is to insist on proper roles of authority and subordination between men and women, or at least between wives and husbands (1 Cor. 14:34b).[87] The reference to *ho nomos* ("the law") does not likely point to church law or Greco-Roman law[88] or to Jewish tradition.[89] Paul nowhere else uses this term without qualification in either of these ways, and there are no contextual considerations that suggest such usage. Rather, he is likely appealing to "Torah" as Scripture as a whole and thinking of some combination of God's created order plus Old Testament regulations in general.[90] Verses 36–38 then provide further tripartite support for obeying Paul: The Corinthians have no unique dispensation from God (verse 36) to contradict the universal practice of the Pauline churches (verse 33b); those who do think they are particularly spiritual must all the more recognize Paul's instruction as a commandment from the Lord (verse 37), and those who ignore this warning will themselves be ignored (by God?—verse 38). The application of

---

[84]Carson, "Silent in the Churches," 147.

[85]Thiselton, *The First Epistle to the Corinthians*, 1150–61.

[86]James D. G. Dunn, *The Theology of Paul the Apostle* (Grand Rapids: Eerdmans, 1998), 592.

[87]See E. Earle Ellis, "The Silenced Wives of Corinth (1 Cor. 14:34–5)," in *New Testament Textual Criticism*, eds. Eldon J. Epp and Gordon D. Fee (Oxford: Clarendon, 1981), 213–20.

[88]Over against Belleville, *Women Leaders and the Church*, 158–59.

[89]Over against Holmes's interpretation in *Text in a Whirlwind*, 267–98.

[90]See Thiselton, *The First Epistle to the Corinthians*, 1153–55. This point is recognized also by Liefeld, "Women, Submission and Ministry in 1 Corinthians," 149–50. It is not likely that Genesis 3:16 is in view, since Paul elsewhere does not ground his ethics in the Fall (on 1 Tim. 2:14, see below, page 365). Over against, for example, Hans-Josef Klauck, *1. Korintherbrief* (Würzburg: Echter, 1987), 105.

Paul's injunction will look quite different from one time and place to another throughout church history, not least because of so much diversity in belief and practice over what constitutes prophecy and how it is evaluated, but whatever mechanisms are developed must respect the authority of male leadership in at least the highest level of a given ecclesiastical context.[91]

For many scholars, this study might come to an end at this point, because all of the remaining texts on gender roles in letters attributed to Paul appear in those epistles often labeled "deutero-Pauline." But, in fact, good cases can be marshaled for their authenticity,[92] and if there is even a slight possibility that Paul wrote them (or oversaw their writing by amanuenses with varying degrees of stylistic or literary freedom), one dare not exclude them from consideration in a study of this nature.

Colossians 3:18–19

This passage introduces a Christian *Haustafel* (literally, "house slate" or "household code") that spans Colossians 3:18–4:1. Without interacting in detail with the sizable quantity of literature on domestic codes, whether Christian, Jewish, Greek, or Roman, suffice it to say that what stands out about the New Testament codes is the reciprocal responsibilities they give to leadership figures in relationships of authority and submission.[93] The one unambiguously Christian feature in the otherwise succinct set of instructions for husbands and wives in Colossians is that the wives must submit "as is fitting in the Lord." As James Dunn explains, "only that degree of subjection to the husband which is 'fitting in the Lord' is to be countenanced."[94] A Christian

---

[91]See my commentary 1 *Corinthians*, 279–82, 286–87, 290–92.

[92]For judicious discussions, see the relevant introductory sections of James D. G. Dunn, *The Epistles to the Colossians and to Philemon* (Grand Rapids: Eerdmans, 1996); Peter T. O'Brien, *The Letter to the Ephesians* (Grand Rapids: Eerdmans, 1999); and William D. Mounce, *Pastoral Epistles,* Word Biblical Commentary (Nashville: Nelson, 2000).

[93]Observed by Joachim Gnilka (*Der Kolosserbrief* [Freiburg: Herder, 1980], 205–16) in an excellent excursus on *Haustafeln* in Paul's world. Andrew T. Lincoln (*Ephesians,* Word Biblical Commentary [Dallas: Word, 1990], 374) notes that commands to husbands to love their wives are infrequent outside the New Testament (citing only the Jewish sources *Pseudo-Phocylides* 195–97 and *Babylonian Talmud Yevamot* 62b), and that *agapē* ("love") is never used in Greco-Roman household codes as a husband's duty.

[94]Dunn, *The Epistles to the Colossians and to Philemon,* 247–48. See also Josef Pfammatter, *Epheserbrief/Kolosserbrief* (Würzburg: Echter, 1990), 80.

woman married to a non-Christian husband would already have been violating social convention by not maintaining (or converting to) the religion of her spouse. As with scriptural teaching on civil disobedience more generally (Ex. 2:1–10; Dan. 3, 6; Acts 4:19–20; 5:29–32), Paul[95] likewise would not have tolerated any behavior that violated the principles of the gospel, even on the grounds that the wife was simply obeying her spouse. When Ephesians 5:24 calls upon the wife to submit to her husband *en panti*, then, it must be referring to something like "in every area of life," not literally in every single request.[96]

The larger context of this Colossians text also gives the lie to the notion that there is a unique tension between the (supposedly egalitarian) teaching of Galatians 3:28 and the (more hierarchicalist) New Testament *Haustafeln*. For Colossians 3:11 contains the closest New Testament parallel to Galatians 3:28, but with clauses about "circumcised or uncircumcised" and "barbarian or Scythian" rather than "male or female." The author of Colossians, even if not Paul, obviously did not feel the same kind of tension between programmatic mandates about oneness in Christ and subsequent role differentiation that modern egalitarians do. What is more, this supposed tension is found even *within* the Colossian *Haustafel*, as it can declare that in God's economy "there is no favoritism"—right in the very paragraph that enjoins slaves to obey their masters (Col. 3:25).[97] More likely, the perceived contradiction is one of more recent invention.

The paralleling of injunctions concerning marriage, parenting, and slavery also invites comparison and contrast. On the one hand, Willard Swartley has documented in detail the parallels in argumentation concerning the abolition of slavery and the liberation of women throughout the history of Christian discussion of these topics.[98] On the other hand, other *Haustafeln* from antiquity, even in Christian circles, by no means necessarily group together institutions that they deem to be

---

[95]Without foreclosing the authorship debate, for convenience's sake we will continue to refer to the writer(s) of Colossians, Ephesians, and the Pastorals as Paul.

[96]O'Brien, *The Letter to the Ephesians*, 417.

[97]On both of these points, see Stephen Motyer, "The Relationship Between Paul's Gospel of 'All One in Christ Jesus' (Gal. 3:28) and the 'Household Codes,'" *Vox Evangelica* 19 (1989): 37, 44.

[98]Willard Swartley, *Slavery, Sabbath, War and Women* (Scottdale, Pa.: Herald, 1983).

entirely parallel.[99] Moreover, strictly speaking, the parallels to the abolition of slavery in the Colossian *Haustafel* would be the abolition of marriage and of parenthood, causes that do not form the objectives of most egalitarians![100]

Ephesians 5:21–33

The author of Ephesians utilizes a *Haustafel* discussing the same three pairs of relationships: wives and husbands, children and parents, and slaves and masters (Eph. 5:22–6:9). Here, however, the instructions, particularly to wives and husbands, are greatly elaborated. The domestic code is introduced by verse 21— "submitting yourselves to one another in the fear of Christ"—a clause that has been the subject of endless controversy. Again, mutually exclusive options have been debated. One side argues that Paul is using *allēlois* in its weakened, less than fully reciprocal sense to mean "some ... to others," so that verse 21 merely epitomizes the three relationships of submission to leadership about to be enunciated.[101] Interestingly, Luke 7:32 and Acts 19:37 both reflect this weakened sense where, in context, all people are not doing the same thing to all other people.[102] The other side replies that fully mutual submission must be in view, in keeping with the much more common meaning of the reciprocal pronoun, so that Paul's subsequent commands cannot set up one-directional lines of submission to authority.[103] In fact, a "both ... and" solution to this debate again seems by far the most probable.

Ephesians 5:21 is a hinge verse, serving to complete the series of participles that help define being "filled with the Spirit" (verse 18); in that context verse 21 means that there will be many situations in which every Christian will have to submit to many other Christians, irrespective of gender, status, and the like. But

---

[99]See, for example, *1 Clement* 21:6–9; Ignatius, *To Polycarp* 4:1–5:2; Polycarp, *To the Philippians* 4:2–3.1

[100]For a full analysis of similarities and differences (and bringing the vexed issue of homosexual behavior into purview as well), see William J. Webb, *Slaves, Women and Homosexuals* (Downers Grove, Ill.: InterVarsity Press, 2001).

[101]See James B. Hurley, *Man and Woman in Biblical Perspective* (Grand Rapids: Zondervan, 1981), 139–41; O'Brien, *The Letter to the Ephesians*, 418.

[102]On Luke 7:32 and its parallel in Matthew 11:16–17, see my *Interpreting the Parables* (Downers Grove, Ill.: InterVarsity Press, 1990), 208–10.

[103]For example, Keener, *Paul, Women and Wives*, 168–72; Belleville, *Women Leaders and the Church*, 120–21.

verse 21 also introduces the Ephesian domestic code, in which lines of submission are not described as reversible.[104] First Peter 5:5 affords the closest scriptural parallel to this dual function: Younger men must "submit" (*hypotagēte*) to the church's elders— a one-directional command—but all the believers must clothe themselves with humility toward "one another" (*allēlois*)—a functional equivalent to mutual submission.[105]

Although attempts have been made to define *hypotassō* (Eph. 5:21–24) so that no subjection to authority is implied at all,[106] none of the thirty-eight other occurrences of this verb in the New Testament suggests so weakened a usage.[107] And the combination of *hypotassō* with *kephalē* ("head") makes it doubly difficult to erase all implications of authority and subordination.[108] On the other hand, *hypotassesthe* as an imperative spoken directly to the wives is much more likely to be a middle than a passive voice, thus underlining that what Paul is enjoining is for them to voluntarily "submit themselves" to their husbands, not to forcibly "be subjected" by their spouses.[109] When one realizes that the same verb recurs, even in the passive voice, in the context of Christ's subjection to God (1 Cor. 15:28), one should acknowledge that the concept is entirely positive! And the absence of any command to the wives to "obey" (*hypakouō*) their husbands can scarcely be coincidental (contrast Eph. 6:1 and 6:5). One may respectfully submit to an authority (see Eph. 5:33) without necessarily setting up chains of command.[110]

---

[104]Similarly Michel Bouttier, *L'Épître de saint Paul aux Éphésiens* (Genève: Labor et Fides, 1991), 236–37. See also Hans Hübner, *An Philemon, An die Kolosser, An die Epheser* (Tübingen: Mohr, 1997), 242.

[105]Similarly, Lincoln, *Ephesians*, 366; George W. Knight III, "Husbands and Wives as Analogues of Christ and the Church: Ephesians 5:21–33 and Colossians 3:18–19," in *Recovering Biblical Manhood and Womanhood*, 167.

[106]J. Ramsey Michaels (*1 Peter*, Word Biblical Commentary [Dallas: Word, 1988], 154) translates the word *hypotassō* simply as "defer."

[107]Bauer, Danker, Arndt, and Gingrich, *A Greek-English Lexicon*, s.v. "*hypotassō*": "to cause to be in a submissive relationship, to subject, to subordinate (or subject oneself, . . . to obey)."

[108]O'Brien, *The Letter to the Ephesians*, 411.

[109]Best, *Ephesians*, 535. Just as in the extrabiblical literature, in Ephesians and Colossians *kephalē* can stress more the sense of "authority" (Eph. 1:22; Col. 1:18, 2:10) or more the idea of "source" (Eph. 4:15; Col. 2:19), but one does not find "source" without any sense of "authority" at all.

[110]See Klyne Snodgrass, *Ephesians*, The NIV Application Commentary Series (Grand Rapids: Zondervan, 1996), 285–318.

By the time Paul turns to his commands to the husbands, he has already radically redefined patriarchy. The asymmetrical relationship of "submission" (Eph. 5:23–24) and "love" (5:25–30) is likened to the relationship between the church and Christ. Without question Jesus is the authoritative head of the church, and he does not submit to believers in the way that believers must submit to him. On the other hand, there is no greater example of love than his self-giving, sacrificial death for humankind. A husband who seriously attempts to model such sacrifice will lead by seeking what is in his wife's best interests; he will put her concerns above his own.[111]

Once again, this *Haustafel* must be read in light of the entire epistle in which it is embedded, noting particularly the emphasis throughout Ephesians on unity in diversity as a manifestation of love.[112] Husbands and wives who consistently implement this radically redefined patriarchy need not fear the abuse and dysfunction so often associated with hierarchicalist marriages.[113]

Yet even more clearly than in the Corinthian passages, Paul puts forward these commands not merely as a vestige of creation and the old order of things, against which Christians should at times fight, but as a reflection of redemption—Christ's relationship with his people (Eph. 5:25–33). Abandonment of these lines of authority and submission in marriage, however well-intentioned, would appear to contravene the very foundation of *new* life in Christ.[114] Not surprisingly, there is a fair consensus among recent

---

[111]See Jean-Noël Aletti, *Saint Paul Épître aux Colossiens* (Paris: Gabalda, 1993), 251–52; Rudolf Schnackenburg, *Ephesians: A Commentary* (Edinburgh: T&T Clark, 1991), 245–46.

[112]On which, see Gregory W. Dawes, *The Body in Question: Metaphor and Meaning in the Interpretation of Ephesians 5:21–33* (Leiden: Brill, 1998). Over against Karl-Heinz Fleckenstein (*Ordnet euch einander unter in der Furcht Christi* [Würzburg: Echter, 1994]), who seems to collapse all of Ephesians' teaching into an utterly reciprocal love-command.

[113]On which, see James R. Beck and Catherine C. Kroeger, eds., *Women, Abuse and the Bible* (Grand Rapids: Baker, 1996).

[114]A point made convincingly throughout Stephen F. Miletic, *"One Flesh": Ephesians 5.22–24, 5.31: Marriage and the New Creation* (Rome: Biblical Institute Press, 1988). Andreas Lindemann (*Der Epheserbrief* [Zürich: Theologischer, 1985], 101) isolates three levels of rationale for the commands of submission and love: an anthropological-social level in the experience of loving one's spouse as oneself, a Christological-ecclesiological level of Christ as the loving head of the church, and a soteriological level of Christ as the Savior of the body.

specialized studies of this passage that it does not abolish patriarchy, even as it substantially refashions it into what has often been called "love-patriarchalism."[115] No longer does the husband have unique privileges, but rather unique responsibilities.[116] This Ephesians text thus demonstrates even more clearly than the Corinthian passages that, at least in the domestic realm, Paul preserves an irreversible hierarchy between husbands and wives. But also more clearly than in 1 Corinthians, it becomes apparent how marvelously re-created and wonderfully loving this hierarchy is to become. Given that Ephesians in these respects seems clearer than 1 Corinthians, it is not surprising that a few scholars think Paul held to hierarchy in the domestic realm while abolishing it in ecclesial circles.[117] But given the early church's predominant use of private homes for congregational gatherings, it is much more likely that relationships in church would be modeled on Christian teaching about domestic relationships than the reverse.[118]

1 Timothy 2:8–15

It is sometimes implied that the hierarchicalist's argument all boils down to 1 Timothy 2. This is patently not the case; this study could end here and the conclusions would be reasonably

---

[115]Thus, most recently, Turid K. Seim, "A Superior Minority? The Problem of Men's Headship in Ephesians 5," *Studia Theologica* 49 (1995): 167–81. See also, with varying emphases, David M. Park, "The Structure of Authority in Marriage: An Examination of *Hypotassō* and *Kephalē* in Ephesians 5:21–33," *Evangelical Quarterly* 59 (1987): 117–24; Robert W. Wall, "Wifely Submission in the Context of Ephesians," *Christian Scholars' Review* 17 (1988): 272–85; Andreas J. Köstenberger, "The Mystery of Christ and the Church: Head and Body, 'One Flesh,'" *Trinity Journal* 12 (1991): 79–94; Russ Dudrey, "'Submit Yourselves to One Another': A Socio-Historical Look at the Household Code of Ephesians 5:15–6:9," *Restoration Quarterly* 41 (1999): 27–44.

[116]See Jostin Ådna, "Die eheliche Liebesbeziehung als Analogie zu Christi Beziehung zur Kirche: Eine traditionsgeschichtliche Studie zu Epheser 5.21–33," *Zeitschrift für Theologie und Kirche* 92 (1995): 434–65.

[117]See, for example, Richard M. Davidson ("Headship, Submission, and Equality in Scripture," in *Women in Ministry: Biblical and Historical Perspectives,* ed. Nancy Vyhmeister [Berrien Springs, Ind.: Andrews Univ. Press, 1998], 259–95), who also cites Donald Bloesch, Ben Witherington III, and Sharon Gritz.

[118]Rightly Andreas Lindemann (*Der Kolosserbrief* [Zurich: Theologischer, 1983], 64), who notes similar logic in Aristotle on the relationship between the family and larger social institutions more generally. Over against Else Kähler (*Die Frau in den Paulinischen Briefen* [Zürich: Gotthelf, 1960], 140), who argues for the reverse.

secure. If anything, this passage complicates matters because the exegetical questions are so complex. On the other hand, some of the difficulties have been overestimated, and progress in interpretation has been made. The easiest way out, of course, is to declare the Pastorals non-Pauline and therefore not binding on Christians, but this move requires not merely rejecting Pauline authorship but also canonical authority.[119] The claim that the Pastorals reflect a late, institutionalized form of Christianity incompatible with first-generation Pauline theology ignores the indications of church organization alongside charismatic activity from the very beginning of the Christian movement,[120] as well as the evidence from throughout the Pastorals that places them much closer to Paul in time and character, even if pseudonymous, than to the end of the first century or into the second century, as has often been alleged.[121]

There is no question that false teaching prompted Paul to write 1 Timothy (1:3–7; 4:1–8; 6:3–5, 20–21).[122] The most elaborate recent reconstruction of the heresy in Ephesus is Catherine and Richard Kroeger's highly touted work that centers around hints of an Artemis cult and gnostic heresies that were putting women forward as superior to men and promoting the myth that Eve was even a creatrix of men.[123] This hypothesis then enables egalitarians to argue that 1 Timothy 2:13–14 does not provide reasons for Paul's silencing women in verses 11–12, but for refutations of the pagan claims that have infiltrated the church. Careful study of the ancient sources has demonstrated,

---

[119]See, for example, Joanna Dewey, "1 Timothy," in *The Women's Bible Commentary*, 355–56. See also Otto Knoch, *1. und 2. Timotheusbrief, Titusbrief* (Würzburg: Echter, 1990²), 26.

[120]For a wide-ranging discussion, see Ronald Y. K. Fung, "Ministry, Community and Spiritual Gifts," *Evangelical Quarterly* 56 (1984): 3–20; Fung, "Function or Office: A Survey of the New Testament Evidence," *Evangelical Review of Theology* 8 (1984): 16–39. Given that much of the argument for an early noninstitutionalized church comes from the Corinthian epistles, Andrew Clarke's study of the structure and leadership of the Corinthian church (*Serve the Community of the Church: Christians as Leaders and Ministers* [Grand Rapids: Eerdmans, 2000]) now proves highly significant.

[121]I. Howard Marshall (*A Critical and Exegetical Commentary on the Pastoral Epistles* [Edinburgh: T&T Clark, 1999]) prefers to coin the term *allonymity* rather than use the term *pseudonymity*, which connotes intent to deceive.

[122]Over against Holmes, *Text in a Whirlwind*, 117–39.

[123]Richard Clark Kroeger and Catherine Clark Kroeger, *I Suffer Not a Woman: Rethinking 1 Timothy 2:11–15 in Light of Ancient Evidence* (Grand Rapids: Baker, 1992).

however, that the Kroegers have culled information from numerous unrelated documents spanning a period of several centuries before to several centuries after the time of Paul and that they have made numerous unwarranted inferences from very slender data.[124] The relevant gnostic literature is no earlier than the third century A.D., and the pre-Christian information on the Artemis cult does not allow one to relativize 1 Timothy 2:13–14 as responding to specific mythological claims.[125] And a careful study of the Pastoral Epistles discloses that, while women were being victimized by the false teaching in Ephesus, whatever it was (1 Tim. 5:15; 2 Tim. 3:6–9), no passage ever suggests that they were numbered among the false teachers themselves.[126] Again, as in 1 Corinthians 14, if all Paul were prohibiting were some kind of improper teaching, it would be horribly prejudicial for him to ban all women and no men. Obviously, plenty of men *were* caught up in the heresy; that much we know for sure! So no genuine evidence emerges from either the historical or literary contexts of 1 Timothy 2:8–15 to predispose one to treat its teaching as merely culture-bound or situation-specific.

Paul begins here in 1 Timothy 2:8 with a call to men "to pray in every place, lifting up holy hands without wrath or wranglings." "Place" here probably means "place of worship," just as *topos* without qualification in Judaism often referred to the temple (and see 1 Tim. 3:15).[127] The typical Jewish posture of prayer is presupposed; the actual mandate is to be *holy* in one's prayers, which is clearly a transcultural principle. If the men were the primary church leaders and were quarreling in some way with each other, one can understand why Paul would single

---

[124]See Steven M. Baugh, "A Foreign World: Ephesus in the First Century," in *Women in the Church: A Fresh Analysis*, 13–52. This is being increasingly recognized even by egalitarians. See, for example, Kevin Giles, "A Critique of the 'Novel' Contemporary Interpretation of 1 Timothy 2:9–15 Given in the Book *Women in the Church*," *Evangelical Quarterly* 72 (2000): 213.

[125]See conclusions drawn by Sharon Gritz, *Paul, Women Teachers, and the Mother Goddess at Ephesus: A Study of 1 Timothy 2:9–15 in Light of the Religious and Cultural Milieu of the First Century* (Lanham, Md.: University Press of America, 1991), 157–58, conclusions that are almost always overlooked by egalitarians who cite her.

[126]As the egalitarian Walter Liefeld ("Response," in *Women, Authority and the Bible*, 220) concedes.

[127]Everett Ferguson, "*Topos* in 1 Timothy 2:8," *Restoration Quarterly* 33 (1991): 65–73.

them out for this rebuke. Next, he commands the women to dress modestly and to be adorned with good works rather than with ostentatious clothing and hairstyle (1 Tim. 2:9–10). The NIV and the NRSV both mistranslate an important conjunction in verse 9; Paul does not object to braided hair per se, but to "braided hair and (*kai*) gold or (*ē*) pearls or (*ē*) costly clothing," referring to lavish hairdos with precious gems interwoven.[128] With a few exceptions, such adornment would be limited to the tiny but influential minority of wealthy women in town.[129] Such fashion at best flaunted one's external beauty and at worst imitated the practice of a courtesan, or "available woman," neither of which was acceptable for Christians.[130] Thus the inappropriateness of the behavior proscribed in verses 9 and 10 remains as timeless as that in verse 8. Nothing in these first three verses, any more than the historical or literary contexts, suggests that we are dealing with merely situation-specific issues.[131]

Paul proceeds in 1 Timothy 2:11–15 to elaborate on the roles of the women in the Ephesian church. Verse 11 instructs them to learn with a quiet demeanor in proper subjection (presumably to those who are teaching—that is, certain men). *Hēsychia*, like its cognate *hēsychios*, refers to orderly behavior that causes no disturbance;[132] in none of their four other New Testament uses do these words suggest total silence (Acts 22:2; 2 Thess. 3:12; 1 Tim. 2:2; 1 Peter 3:4). The 1 Timothy 2:2 reference is particularly significant, appearing as it does earlier in this same chapter and speaking of the "quiet" lives believers should live in general—hardly an injunction to silence at all! As in 1 Corinthians 14, Colossians 3, and Ephesians 4, the women must also submit to their male leaders. But the countercultural force of the command to let the women learn, namely, the teachings of the Christian faith, must not be missed. Like Jesus with Mary of Bethany, Paul is cutting sharply against the grain of the vast majority of

---

[128]Thus Hurley, *Man and Woman in Biblical Perspective*, 199.

[129]Alan Padgett, "Wealthy Women at Ephesus: 1 Timothy 2:8–15 in Social Context," *Interpretation* 41 (1987): 19–31.

[130]George W. Knight III, *The Pastoral Epistles*, The New International Greek Testament Commentary (Grand Rapids: Eerdmans, 1992), 135–36; Holmes, *Text in a Whirlwind*, 62–63.

[131]Over against, for example, Steve Motyer, "Expounding 1 Timothy 2:8–15," *Vox Evangelica* 24 (1994): 91–102.

[132]See Bauer, Danker, Arndt, and Gingrich, *A Greek-English Lexicon*, s.v. "*hēsychia*."

contemporary Jews and a sizable majority of Greeks and Romans.[133]

Enormous controversy surrounds 1 Timothy 2:12 and especially the meaning of *authentein*. Attempts to relativize Paul's injunctions here on the basis of diction or grammar consistently misunderstand both Hellenistic Greek and basic hermeneutics. Paul's "I" does not relativize his teaching; he regularly believes his instructions come directly from the Lord (even 1 Cor. 7:12 must be balanced by 7:40, understood as gentle irony).[134] The word "permit" (*epitrepō*) does not relativize Paul's instruction, because it is negated. The negation of "I sometimes allow" is "I never allow," not "I sometimes do not allow" (which in fact is synonymous with, rather than the opposite of, the first of these three statements). Barring contextual qualifications, "I do *not* permit" is an absolute prohibition! The present tense does not suggest Paul is making only a temporary ban; it is regularly used in a gnomic or timeless sense for proverbial instruction.[135] In fact, the verbal aspect of the present tense *epitrepō*, bolstered by the present tense nonindicative mood verbs *didaskein* and *authentein*, suggests continuous action: "I *continually* do not permit."[136]

But what is Paul proscribing? Traditionally translations have answered with "to teach or to have authority over men." *Didaskein* ("to teach") is not difficult; without qualification it will refer to positive, Christian instruction (1 Tim. 4:11; 6:2; 2 Tim. 2:2; while in Titus 1:11 the context clarifies that the teaching is negative—"what they shouldn't").[137]

---

[133]Rightly, Aída B. Spencer, *Beyond the Curse: Women Called to Ministry* (Nashville: Nelson, 1985), 74, though her translation "they must learn" may be too strong for this third-person imperative.

[134]See my commentary *1 Corinthians*, 134–35, 153–54.

[135]Rightly, Marshall, *The Pastoral Epistles*, 454–55.

[136]See Holmes, *Text in a Whirlwind*, 82; F. Blass, A. Debrunner, and R. Funk, *Grammar of the New Testament and Other Early Christian Literature*, sec. 318.

[137]Andreas J. Köstenberger ("A Complex Sentence Structure in 1 Timothy 2:12," in *Women in the Church: A Fresh Analysis*, 103) notes that Paul would have in all likelihood used *heterodidaskalein* or some other contextual qualifier if the teaching were viewed negatively. Marshall's objection (*The Pastoral Epistles*, 458, note 157) that if the writer had used *heterodidaskalein* he would have been implying "but I do allow men to give false teaching" does not carry force because the prohibition still could have been clearly framed to avoid this conclusion (for example, "I do not permit the women to continue their false teaching").

Authentein (usually rendered "to have authority over"), a hapax legomenon in the New Testament, proves far more difficult. The more common Greek verb for exercising authority is *exousiazō*. Egalitarians often argue that if Paul meant the positive (or even neutral) function of simple authoritative leadership, he would have used this verb and therefore, since he didn't, one must look for some specialized (usually negative) meaning in *authenteō*.[138] But interestingly, *exousiazō* appears only four times in the New Testament, twice as the neutral or positive use of authority (1 Cor. 7:4 [2x]) and twice as very domineering authority—"mastering" improper behavior in 1 Corinthians 6:12 and parallel to "lording it over" in Luke 22:25. So if it were determined that *authenteō* was commonly used positively, one might actually argue that Paul chose it to *avoid* the more ambiguous *exousiazō*!

As it turns out, *authenteō* is ambiguous as well. Leland Wilshire's survey of all the 329 occurrences of the word and its cognate *authentēs* in the TLG database showed that prior to the first century, this root often had negative overtones of "domineer" or even "murder." After the first century, especially in Christian circles, it was frequently used positively for the appropriate exercise of authority.[139] At the conclusion of his study, Wilshire understandably seemed to favor the more positive sense of authority for the interpretation of 1 Timothy 2:12. After all, what would have led to this change of meaning, particularly for Christian writers of Greek, unless someone very influential (like Paul) had begun to use it differently?[140] Wilshire subsequently denied that this was what he meant and opted for a more negative definition.[141]

Scott Baldwin observed that the most negative meanings occurred with the adjective *authentēs* and argued that *authenteō*

---

[138]See, for example, Walter L. Liefeld, *1 and 2 Timothy, Titus*, The NIV Application Commentary Series (Grand Rapids: Zondervan, 1999), 99.

[139]Leland E. Wilshire, "The TLG Computer and Further Reference to *authenteō* in 1 Timothy 2.12," *New Testament Studies* 34 (1988): 131.

[140]Wilshire, "The TLG Computer and Further Reference," 131. This perception was confirmed by Paul W. Barnett, "Wives and Women's Ministry (1 Timothy 2:11–15)," *Evangelical Quarterly* 61 (1989): 225–37.

[141]Leland E. Wilshire ("1 Timothy 2:12 Revisited: A Reply to Paul W. Barnett and Timothy J. Harris," *Evangelical Quarterly* 65 [1993]: 52) opted for "to initiate violence," a not terribly likely meaning in this context.

should be treated separately. His list of possible meanings in this context is "to control, to dominate," "to compel," "to influence someone," "to assume authority over," and "to flout the authority of."[142] Decisively supporting the more positive sense of assuming appropriate authority is Andreas Köstenberger's study of pairs of infinitives in "neither . . . nor" constructions both throughout the New Testament and in a wide-ranging swath of extrabiblical Greek literature. Without exception, these constructions pair either two positive or two negative activities. So if the "teaching" in view in 1 Timothy 2:12 is not false teaching but proper Christian instruction, then *authentein* must be taken as appropriate authority as well.[143] The upshot of the discussion is that the most probable meanings of the individual words in this verse yield the translation, "I do not permit a woman to teach or have authority over a man."

The next question, however, involves the relationship of the two infinitives (*didaskein* and *authentein*). Do they represent two separate activities or one? Much ink has been spilled over whether to treat this as a formal hendiadys or not.[144] But largely overlooked is Paul's more informal pattern throughout 1 Timothy 2 of using pairs of partly synonymous words or expressions to make his main points. Verse 1 speaks of "petitions," "prayers," "intercessions," and "thanksgivings"; verse 2a, of "kings and all those who are in authority"; verse 2b, of "peaceful and quiet" lives and of "godliness and holiness"; verse 3, of "good and acceptable" behavior; verse 4, of being "saved" and coming "to a knowledge of the truth"; verse 5, of our "God and Savior"; verse 7a, of a "herald and apostle"; verse 7b, of Paul's assertion, "I speak truth; I do not lie"; verse 8, of "wrath and wranglings"; verse 9a, of "decency and propriety"; and verse 9b, of "gold and silver."[145]

---

[142]H. Scott Baldwin, "A Difficult Word: *authenteō* in 1 Timothy 2:12," in *Women in the Church: A Fresh Analysis*, 79–80.

[143]See Köstenberger, "A Complex Sentence Structure." Belleville (*Women Leaders and the Church*, 176–77) notes other ways that the paired elements in "neither . . . nor" constructions are related to each other in the New Testament when one looks at parts of speech beyond just the infinitive.

[144]At this point, Belleville's study does prove helpful, because she shows the diversity of relationships among paired items in similar constructions; one cannot simply assume the two terms are mutually defining because of the grammar.

[145]See my article "Not Beyond What Is Written," 412, note 29.

The point here is not that the two terms in each case refer to identical entities, but that in every instance they are closely related and together help to define one single concept.[146] This makes it overwhelmingly likely that in 1 Timothy 2:12 Paul is referring to one specific kind of authoritative teaching rather than two independent activities.[147] Given that 1 Timothy 3:2 (in the very next pericope in this letter) requires an overseer to be able to teach (his most distinctive function as compared to a deacon), that 1 Timothy 5:17 speaks of elders as teaching and exercising authority,[148] and that Titus 1:5–7 equates elders and overseers, it seems highly likely that Paul is restricting women in one (and in only one) way: They must not occupy the office of elder/overseer.[149] This meshes with the fact that women are mentioned among the deacons in 1 Timothy 3:8–13 (see verse 11), but not among the overseers in verses 1–7.[150]

---

[146]A point not grasped by Holmes, *Text in a Whirlwind*, 89, note 56. How she can argue that my language betrayed my own "lingering doubts" is beyond me!

[147]Similarly Philip B. Payne, "*Oude* in 1 Timothy 2:12" (unpublished paper—Atlanta: Evangelical Theological Society, 1986).

[148]It is sometimes argued, especially in Presbyterian circles, that 1 Timothy 5:17 distinguishes between ruling and teaching elders. But see T. C. Skeat, "'Especially the Parchments': A Note on 2 Timothy IV.13," *Journal of Theological Studies* 30 (1979): 173–77. In the Pastoral Epistles, *malista* consistently means "namely" or "that is," not "especially."

[149]See my article "Not Beyond What Is Written," 418. Robert Saucy ("Women's Prohibition to Teach Men: An Investigation into Its Meaning and Contemporary Application," *Journal of the Evangelical Theological Society* 37 [1994]: 91) doesn't think one can limit Paul's meaning to a specific office, but in his conclusion he determines that the passage reserves merely "ultimate leadership of the Church" for men (page 97). William Mounce (*Pastoral Epistles*, 124) misses my distinction between office and function by attributing to me the same general conclusion as his, namely, that "women may not, therefore, authoritatively teach the men in authority." Holmes (*Text in a Whirlwind*, 90–95) is on the right track with her discussion of verbal aspect, but she doesn't observe how naturally this leads to a restriction solely on the office of elder. Andrew C. Perriman ("What Eve Did, What Women Shouldn't Do: The Meaning of *authenteō* in 1 Timothy 2:12," *Tyndale Bulletin* 44 [1993]: 129–42) comes close with his argument that Eve took initiative or acted authoritatively in causing Adam to sin, that is, taking on an authority she didn't have (page 141), although he goes on to claim, without offering any evidence, that Paul's prohibition is merely a specialized local reference. Victor Hasler (*Die Briefe an Timotheus und Titus* [Zürich: Theologischer, 1978], 25) recognizes that only a teaching office is in view, but strangely puts both elders and deacons into this category.

[150]There is increasing agreement that these are women deacons and not deacons' wives. See Jennifer H. Stiefel, "Women Deacons in 1 Timothy: A Linguistic and Literary Look at 'Women Likewise ...' (1 Tim. 3.11)," *New Testament Studies* 41 (1995): 442–57.

In 1 Timothy 2:13 Paul gives the reason for the prohibition he declares in verse 12. Attempts to account for this clause as anything other than causal prove singularly unconvincing.[151] The vast majority of the *gar* clauses in ancient Greek are causal; the twelve other examples in 1 Timothy alone are unambiguously so (2:5; 3:13; 4:5, 8, 10, 16; 5:4, 11, 15, 18; 6:7, 10).[152] Paul is thus explaining that the reason he excludes women from the office of elder/overseer is because Adam was created first. Odd as the argument sounds to modern ears, it would have made perfect sense in a Jewish milieu that recognized the firstborn son as receiving a double portion of the inheritance.[153] That the Old Testament knows several celebrated exceptions to this principle (for example, Ishmael, Esau, Reuben) is significant precisely because they are exceptions and not the rule. Those who lampoon the hierarchicalist position by arguing that Paul was not inferring leadership of animals over humans when they were created first (Gen. 1) miss the point altogether. Paul is not arguing that "first created" always leads to privilege; merely that it does in the case of the creation of Adam and Eve (Gen. 2). Attempts to relativize 1 Timothy 2:13 by appealing to the motive clauses in Titus 2:5, 8, and 10 that ground authority and submission in the need to make the gospel attractive to a patriarchal world that no longer exists miss the fact that Titus equally frequently describes his commands simply as "what is good" in and of itself (Titus 2:3, 7, 14).[154]

Perhaps the hardest verse to understand in all of Paul's teaching on gender roles is 1 Timothy 2:14. Virtually all perspectives today have rejected the common Jewish and Christian belief throughout history that women are actually ontologically

---

[151]The approach favored by the Kroegers has already been discussed. Even more tortuous is the suggestion of Holmes (*Text in a Whirlwind*, 267–98) that 1 Timothy 2:13–15 constitutes a pre-Pauline Jewish saying quoted verbatim and identified as the faithful saying of 3:1a, thus making the *gar* at the beginning of verse 13 part of the quote and not a causal connective with what goes before.

[152]Douglas J. Moo ("The Interpretation of 1 Timothy 2:11–15: A Rejoinder," *Trinity Journal* 2 [1981]: 202–204) expands the study to all of the Pastorals and comes to the same conclusion.

[153]Knight, *The Pastoral Epistles*, 143. Lorenz Oberlinner (*Die Pastoralbriefe* [Freiburg: Herder, 1994], 1:106–107) agrees that the text is arguing from recognized Jewish and Hellenistic models of patriarchy.

[154]Rightly Knight, *The Pastoral Epistles*, 316–18. Against Padgett, "Wealthy Women at Ephesus," 19–31.

inferior to men.[155] Attempts, however sophisticated, to defend the view that women are inherently more gullible fly in the face of all contemporary social-scientific analysis and do not fit the context of 1 Timothy, even if we assume a culture that did believe in the inherently greater defectibility of women.[156] For then it would surely be wrong for women to teach anyone, especially their own male children who will become the leaders of the next generation. An exegesis that sees Paul merely as claiming that Adam sinned without having been deceived in the manner Eve was deceived may be true to the Genesis 3 account,[157] but it again leaves Paul in the paradoxical position of favoring Adam because he sinned with his eyes wide open—a presumably less excusable situation and thus a greater character flaw than with Eve, who was tricked!

The view that carries "first" over from 1 Timothy 2:13, making Paul's point to be that Eve was deceived first, carries a certain grammatical plausibility.[158] But there are no well-known principles from antiquity, like the Old Testament laws of primogeniture, that would make the order in which one was deceived in any way significant. The claim that "Eve was deceived by the serpent in the Garden (Genesis 3:13) precisely in taking the initiative over the man"[159] founders on the fact that

---

[155]A point Kevin Giles ("A Critique of the 'Novel' Contemporary Interpretation") exploits to argue that even Köstenberger, Schreiner, and Baldwin (*Women in the Church: A Fresh Analysis*) reflect a "novel" interpretation with respect to the entire sweep of church history.

[156]After a thorough and helpful survey of approaches to this passage, Schreiner ("An Interpretation of 1 Timothy 2:9–15," 145) concludes, with no exegetical or psychological support provided, that "women are less prone than men to see the importance of doctrinal formulations, especially when it comes to the issue of identifying heresy and making a stand for truth." Marshall (*The Pastoral Epistles*, 466) rightly responds: "However one may evaluate this judgment, there is no evidence that such a thought was in the author's mind, and therefore it must be pronounced totally irrelevant to the exegesis of the passage."

[157]Hurley (*Man and Woman in Biblical Perspective*, 214–16) argues that only the man was given the power of religious discernment, even if it could be used for evil as well as for good. But this is scarcely a straightforward reading of the text, and it is probably susceptible to the same critique as Schreiner's view presented in the previous note.

[158]See Barnett, "Wives and Women's Ministry," 234.

[159]Douglas Moo, "What Does It Mean Not to Teach or Have Authority Over Men? 1 Timothy 2:11–15," in *Recovering Biblical Manhood and Womanhood*, 190.

she was tricked by Satan and sinned by eating the forbidden fruit *before* turning to Adam and thus only afterwards played a role in helping him to fall.

I therefore stand by my suggestion, offered more than a decade ago, which has received almost no scholarly response, that perhaps 1 Timothy 2:14 is not meant to provide a second rationale for Paul's proscription at all.[160] The *gar* is not repeated, verses 13–14 are linked to each other solely with a *kai*, while verses 14–15 are in a mildly adversative relationship to one another, as supported also by the postpositive *de* at the beginning of verse 15. Having alluded to Genesis 2, it would have been natural for Paul's thoughts to move to Genesis 3 and the fall of Adam and Eve, along with God's subsequent punishment of the first couple. If the heresy in Ephesus was promoting celibacy as a Christian ideal (probably implied by 1 Timothy 4:3), Paul would have felt the need to stress the appropriateness of the traditional motherly roles of childbearing (and, by synecdoche, child rearing)—thus verse 15.[161]

William Mounce objects on three counts: (1) First Timothy 2:12–13 does not raise any "concern for Eve's salvation," (2) "the structural similarities" between verses 13 and 14 are ignored, and (3) the "emphatic negation of Adam's deception" at the beginning of verse 14 is unexplained.[162] By way of reply, I would observe that (1) both the Genesis story and the heresy's proscription of marriage would have made Paul think of the issue of women's (and men's) salvation, (2) there are at least as many differences as similarities in the structure of verses 13 and 14, and (3) there is nothing emphatic about Adam's role in verse 14.

We do not have to solve all the vexed problems surrounding 1 Timothy 2:15 in order to grasp Paul's main points. The verse literally reads, "But she shall be saved through the childbearing, if they continue in faith and love and sanctification with sobriety." The "she" is probably generic, referring to the female gender as a whole. "Saved" will then refer to eschatological salvation, that is, the culmination of the process of restoring the cosmos to God's intended ideals (cf. the use of *sōzō* in 1 Tim. 4:16 and 2 Tim. 4:18). But not all women can or should bear children;

---

[160]See my article "Not Beyond What Is Written," 414.

[161]Moo, "What Does It Mean Not to Teach or Have Authority Over Men?" 192.

[162]Mounce, *Pastoral Epistles*, 142.

the distributive plural "they" introduces the second clause, which *does* explain how every individual woman is restored to a right relationship with God.[163] As I wrote previously, one might paraphrase the flow of thought from 1 Timothy 2:12–15 as follows:

> Women are not to hold the authoritative teaching position in the church because that is not a role for which they were created. Moreover, things subsequently deteriorated for the woman, after creation, when she fell, through the deception of the serpent. But there is a bright side.... Women, collectively, will be preserved/restored as they exercise in a godly fashion their distinctive role of rearing children.[164]

In light of the case that can be made for limiting Paul's instructions to husbands and wives in 1 Corinthians 11 and 14, and in light of the obvious limitations of the *Haustafeln* of Colossians 3 and Ephesians 5 to married men and women, it is tempting to argue that 1 Timothy 2 envisions similar semantic restrictions on *anēr* and *gynē*. Given the more general injunctions of verses 8–10, most commentators think this to be unlikely here. Still, Sharon Gritz believes that the shift from the plural in verses 8–10 to the singular in verses 11–15a justifies narrowing the meaning of *gynē* in the latter verses (see also NRSV text note).[165] Jerome Quinn and William Wacker appeal to the use of *gynē* in Titus 1:6 and translate 1 Timothy 2:11 as "Let a married woman learn . . ." and verse 12 as "Moreover, I do not allow a wife to teach in the public worship . . . and to boss her husband."[166] It is

---

[163]See my article "Not Beyond What Is Written," 415. This approach combines the strengths of M. D. Roberts ("'Women Shall Be Saved': A Closer Look at 1 Timothy 2:15," *Theological Students Fellowship Bulletin* 5.2 [1981]: 4–7), on the shift from singular to plural, and those of Andreas Köstenberger ("Ascertaining Women's God-Ordained Roles: An Interpretation of 1 Timothy 2:15," *Bulletin for Biblical Research* 7 [1997]: 107–44). It is also close to the position of Stanley E. Porter ("What Does It Mean to Be 'Saved by Childbirth' [1 Timothy 2.15]?" *Journal for the Study of the New Testament* 49 [1993]: 87–102), but with a more nuanced understanding of *sōzō*. Mounce's perspective (*Pastoral Epistles*, 146–47) is even more similar.

[164]See my article "Not Beyond What Is Written," 414, 416.

[165]Gritz (*Paul, Women Teachers, and the Mother Goddess*) argues that the singular in the Pastorals *always* refers to a "wife." This is probably true but is due to the context of each of the other occurrences and not necessarily to the number of the noun.

[166]Jerome D. Quinn and William C. Wacker, *The First and Second Letters to Timothy* (Grand Rapids: Eerdmans, 1999), 199–200. See also Gordon P. Hugenberger, "Women in Church Office: Hermeneutics or Exegesis? A Survey of Approaches to 1 Timothy 2:8–15," *Journal of the Evangelical Theological Society* 35 (1992): 341–60.

possible that a "both . . . and" approach again fits best. As Paul Barnett explains:

> Paul's negative response is not in terms of a woman's inability to occupy the office of *episkopos* . . . *didaktikos* (bishop . . . teacher) but rather what effect this incumbency would have on marriages within the church and indeed on the value of the mothering role. Paul's concern is not superficially cultural but profoundly creational.[167]

One might suggest, in settings where these broader concerns do not come into play, that faithful application of Paul's principles would require merely that a wife not be an overseer over her husband in the same congregation. Unmarried women would then have no restrictions placed on them, and Paul could not be accused at any point of setting up a system that forever barred half of the human race from a particular role.[168] Marriage is entered into voluntarily; those not prepared to accept its restrictions "need not apply." And even within marriage, a called and gifted woman could exercise every level of leadership, save the highest office in whatever congregation in which her husband participated.

If, on the other hand, Paul's commands *are* intended for all men and women, it is still necessary to ask what the contemporary functional equivalent is to the New Testament office of elder/overseer. Except in the pure Plymouth Brethren model of a team of elders identically sharing in authoritative teaching responsibilities, contemporary congregationally organized churches would presumably identify their senior pastor (or in single-staff churches the sole pastor) as this functional equivalent of the elder/overseer. Women could then hold any other subordinate pastoral role.[169] In presbyterian and episcopal forms of church government, one could argue that the equivalent is the

---

[167]Barnett, "Wives and Women's Ministry," 236–37. Timothy J. Harris's subsequent critique of Barnett's approach to 1 Timothy 2:14 ("Why Did Paul Mention Eve's Deception? A Critique of P. Barnett's Interpretation of 1 Timothy 2," *Evangelical Quarterly* 62 [1990]: 335–52) does not invalidate this particular conclusion.

[168]A point stressed frequently by Rebecca M. Groothuis. See especially her *Women Caught in the Conflict: The Culture War Between Traditionalism and Feminism* (Grand Rapids: Baker, 1994) and *Good News for Women: A Biblical Picture of Gender Equality* (Grand Rapids: Baker, 1997).

[169]See Ann L. Bowman, "Women in Ministry: An Exegetical Study of 1 Timothy 2:11–15," *Bibliotheca Sacra* 149 (1992): 193–213.

person at the head of larger denominational structures.[170] But before straying too far into contemporary application, this study must be brought to a close.

CONCLUSIONS

It is difficult to improve on the conclusions of Judith Gundry-Volf in her comparative study of Paul, Philo, ben Sira, and Joseph and Aseneth:

> In sum, Paul seems to affirm *both* equality of status and roles of women and men in Christ *and* women's subordinate or secondary place. He appears to think that sometimes the difference between male and female is to be expressed in patriarchal conventions and that sometimes these conventions should be transcended or laid aside.[171]

Earle Ellis, Ben Witherington, Klyne Snodgrass, and Donald Bloesch have all come to similar conclusions.[172] We have discovered no evidence that the Paul of the undisputed epistles was a full-fledged egalitarian whose liberating emphases were increasingly lost in the deutero-Paulines—first in Colossians and Ephesians and then even more so in the Pastoral Epistles—as is so often alleged. The tensions between patriarchy and equality appear at every stage of the early church's development.[173] There is in fact increasing agreement among both liberal feminist and hierarchicalist authors that neither Paul nor any other New Testament writer or character can be fairly labeled egalitarian.[174]

For non-Christian interpreters or for liberal Christians

---

[170]The expositor convinced on scriptural grounds of congregational government might then choose to protest these alternate forms of church structure before addressing the issue of gender roles.

[171]Gundry-Volf, "Paul on Women and Gender," 186.

[172]E. Earle Ellis, *Pauline Theology: Ministry and Society* (Grand Rapids: Eerdmans, 1989), 53–86; Witherington, *Women in the Ministry of Jesus*; Witherington, *Women in the Earliest Churches*; Klyne R. Snodgrass: "Galatians 3:28—Conundrum or Solution?" in *Women, Authority and the Bible*, 161–81; Donald G. Bloesch, *Is the Bible Sexist? Beyond Feminism and Patriarchalism* (Westchester, Ill.: Crossway, 1982).

[173]Witherington, *Women in the Earliest Churches*, 212. Marshall (*The Pastoral Epistles*, 438) generalizes, observing that "strongly feminist interpreters have tended to adopt the same understanding of [these passages] as the traditionalist."

[174]A trend presaged already by Clark H. Pinnock ("Biblical Authority and the Issues in Question," in *Women, Authority and the Bible*, 55): "The radical feminists and

whose doctrine of Scripture does not bind them to the entire historic canon, this observation almost inevitably leads to a rejection of the authority of what they perceive to be the nonliberating portions of the Bible, usually including most or all of the passages in 1 Corinthians, Colossians, Ephesians, and 1 Timothy discussed here.[175]

Hierarchicalists, who do not find Paul's restrictions objectionable, simply seek to implement his teachings according to their understanding of their contemporary significance. Egalitarians who do accept the authority of all of the New Testament (including evangelical or biblical feminists) have vacillated between two different exegetical approaches. The most common recent one has been to redefine key words in the relevant texts or to propose specific historical backgrounds that relativize Paul's apparently more sweeping charges and allow him to be viewed as an egalitarian. This option now seems to be the least convincing of all.

More promising is the second approach, which agrees that Paul was no egalitarian, and that he viewed his strictures as universally applicable in his day, but which argues that the world has changed sufficiently today to warrant a different approach that still fulfills the underlying intent of Paul's original commands.[176]

the traditionalists both argue that such texts are not feminist in content, and I suspect that their view, agreeing as it does with the 'plain sense' reading so widely held, will prevail and not be successfully refuted by biblical feminists. Of course, the biblical feminist interpretation is possible; the problem is that it does not strike many people, either scholarly or untutored, as plausible."

[175]See, for example, Caroline Vander Stichele, "Is Silence Golden? Paul and Women's Speech in Corinth," *Louvain Studies* 20 (1995): 241–53; Jürgen Roloff, *Der Erste Brief an Timotheus* (Zürich: Benzinger; Neukirchen-Vluyn: Neukirchener, 1988), 125–47.

[176]Giles, "A Critique of the 'Novel' Contemporary Interpretation," 213. Cf. the particularly transparent comments of Andrew T. Lincoln (*Truth on Trial: The Lawsuit Motif in the Fourth Gospel* [Peabody, Mass.: Hendrickson, 2000], 479–80): "A recognition is also required that the attitude of needing to have the Bible on one's side at all costs may well be detrimental to faithful witness. Instead of attempting a revisionist exegesis, it seems far better to admit, on some occasions, that John or Paul, for example, said one thing but now contemporary advocates need to say something different in different circumstances, with different questions to address, as they strive to be faithful to the same gospel to which John or Paul bore witness—whether on obvious ethical issues such as the role of women, slavery, or homosexuality, or on Jew-Gentile concerns, or on soteriological formulations—and that they need to be open to debate whether and in what ways they are being faithful to the same gospel." A hybrid of both views often appears, too. See, for example, Royce G. Gruenler, "The Mission-Lifestyle Setting of 1 Timothy 2:8–15," *Journal of the Evangelical Theological Society* 41 (1998): 215–38.

Yet even this variation runs aground on Paul's appeals both to original creation and to re-creation in Christ as motives for his mandates. It may be time to admit that full-fledged egalitarianism is simply not the most likely synthesis of the biblical data within a historic Christian hermeneutic.

At the same time, Paul comes tantalizingly close to egalitarianism at numerous junctures. Most current hierarchicalists (or traditionalists or complementarians, depending on your terminology preference) have not recognized just how much Paul (and the rest of the New Testament) permits to women. Only the single office of elder/overseer (or its functional equivalent) is excluded. Countless other contexts remain for women to exercise any spiritual gift to the full, and many other leadership offices or roles in hierarchicalist settings are not populated by women nearly as much as they could be. Many hierarchicalists seem to be more preoccupied with keeping men in positions of authority than in nurturing women to become all that God wants them to be in the spirit of Paul's radically redefined patriarchy and consistent with biblical *servant* leadership more generally. It is worth reminding those who remain dubious that Paul would exclude women from *only* one leadership role that this is precisely the pattern we see in both the Old Testament (only the priesthood is excluded) and the Gospels (only the apostles are all male). In short, we may have to coin a new term for Paul altogether. What seems certain is that he is neither hierarchicalist nor egalitarian, in the classic sense of either term.[177]

---

[177]Interestingly, this conclusion concurs with the findings of Thomas Schmeller (*Hierarchie und Egalität* [Stuttgart: Katholische Bibelwerk, 1995]) on Paul and his churches more generally.

SUBJECT INDEX

SCRIPTURE INDEX

More Counterpoints:

Find Counterpoints *at your favorite Christian bookstore*

ZondervanPublishingHouse
Grand Rapids, Michigan 49530
http://www.zondervan.com

A Division of HarperCollins*Publishers*